Translating Slavery

TRANSLATION STUDIES
Albrecht Neubert, Gert Jäger, and Gregory M. Shreve, Editors

Translation Studies is the successor of the German language series *Übersetzungswissenschaftliche Beiträge*, published since 1978 in Leipzig, Germany.

Translating Slavery

Gender and Race in French Women's Writing, 1783–1823

Edited by Doris Y. Kadish

&

Françoise Massardier-Kenney

The Kent State University Press
KENT, OHIO, AND LONDON, ENGLAND

© 1994 by The Kent State University Press, Kent, Ohio 44242

ALL RIGHTS RESERVED

Library of Congress Catalog Card Number 93-34207

ISBN 0-87338-498-9

Manufactured in the United States of America

Library of Congress Cataloging-in-Publication Data

Translating Slavery : gender and sex in French women's writing,
1783–1823 / edited by Doris Y. Kadish and Françoise Massardier-
Kenney.

    p. cm. — (Translation studies : 2)

Includes bibliographical references and index.

ISBN 0-87338-498-9 ∞

   1. French literature—Women authors—History and criticism.

2. French literature—19th century—History and criticism.

3. French literature—18th century—History and criticism. 4. Women
and literature—France—History. 5. Slavery and slaves in
literature. 6. Sex role in literature. 7. Sex in literature.

I. Kadish, Doris Y. II. Massardier-Kenney, Françoise. III. Series.

PQ288.T73 1994

840.9'9287'09033—DC20   93-34207

                                      CIP

BRITISH LIBRARY CATALOGING-IN-PUBLICATION DATA ARE AVAILABLE.

Contents

"A House of Many Rooms"
The Range of Translation Studies

Albrecht Neubert and Gregory M. Shreve

The monograph series *Translation Studies* is the successor of the German language series *Übersetzungswissenschaftliche Beiträge*, published since 1978 in Leipzig, Germany. For twelve years the *Beiträge* was the voice of an approach to translation studies known as the "Leipzig School." In the pages of the series, Otto Kade, Gert Jäger, Albrecht Neubert, Heide Schmidt, and others explored the various possibilities of a translation studies that integrated linguistics, pragmatics, sociolinguistics, text linguistics, and the traditional concerns of philology in a new and dynamic discipline. Now with a new publisher and a broader scope, *Translation Studies* continues the tradition of the *Beiträge*. Transcending the primarily linguistic orientation of the original series, its purpose is to explore the boundaries of translation scholarship and to present in the scope of a single monograph series the breadth of scholarly concern with translation.

The first volume of the series, *Translation as Text*, interprets translation studies as an empirical discipline, based in the study of translation practice and viewing the translation process as a valid object of scientific study. This conception of translation evolved from a German milieu. Like the broad German approach to translation of which it is a part (*Übersetzungswissenschaft*), this text-based translation science goes beyond linguistics proper. It emphasizes the systemic and objective character of translation, not just as a recoding of sign sequences, but as a recreation of worlds of discourse. Further, this form of translation studies is part of a historical attempt to lay the disciplinary foundations for university-level training in language mediation in a multilingual Europe and world.

The processes and results of translation are described in terms of an empirical approach to the concept of "text." Translation reality is seen as "text-induced text production," capable of description and, by implication, of being taught to translation students in academic and professional programs. The scientific frame of reference for this approach is the concept of *textuality*, which permeates the complex processes and products of bilingually mediated communication. The empirical bases of the textual approach, the analytical tools it employs, and the results it achieves, are certainly much more comprehensive and pertinent to translation practice than the more restricted hardcore "linguistic" translation theory of thirty years ago. But the old linguistic and the new textual approaches are not the only methodologies translation studies has to offer.

Volume 2, *Translating Slavery: Gender and Race in French Women's Writing 1783–1823*, presents another quite different conception of translation. We have selected this volume, in some respects at the other end of the spectrum of scholarly thought on translation, as a means to frame the expanse of translation studies. Where volume 1 presents a textual approach to translation studies and seeks to integrate linguistics with new movements in discourse analysis and the social and behavioral sciences, volume 2 presents a primarily critical and humanistic conception of translation which seeks to integrate into translation studies critical and ideological concerns, such as those of race and gender. This approach to translation has evolved from an American milieu. Like the various European academic approaches to translation, and, in particular, the German *Übersetzungswissenschaft*, it is a product of its own unique evolution and demands.

In a country mostly devoid of translation schools, without a tradition of translation training, and where translation practice is, for the most part, alienated from translation studies, American academic interest in translation derives primarily from the literary, critical, and humanistic concerns of individual scholars in the humanities—scattered throughout American university English, German, French, and Spanish departments. These humanistic concerns are, to be sure, not purely an American interest, but are shared with other like-minded scholars in Europe and around the world. In the solitary wake of Eugene Nida, scholars like William Frawley, Gregory Rabassa, Joseph Graham, Lawrence Venuti, Jill Levine, Carol Maier, Marilyn Gaddis-Rose, Douglas Robinson, and the founders and members of the American Literary Translators Association, have undertaken to define a new kind of humanistic "American translation studies."

It is true that Eugene Nida is still the best-known American translation scholar on the international scene. His writings have strongly influenced European thought on the subject. But it should be noted

that his original linguistic orientation, as well as the pedagogical moti-
vation of the theory of Bible translation, established a kinship with
those European scholars who had been looking for suitable models
for a pedagogy of translation—a pedagogy demanded by the rapidly
expanding number of translation students at specialized schools and
universities in Europe. But Nida is not the only American voice in
the translation choir.

Before we proceed to describe some of the characteristics of the
humanistic branch of American translation studies, we should make
it clear that American translation practitioners have long understood
that it is important to study their own practice. The American Translators Association and its monograph series have for many years provided a forum for reflection on the practice of translation. The
professional association has had to take the lead in this regard, since,
with only a few exceptions, most American university language departments have evinced only a limited interest in translation outside
of its literary aspects. In fact, the leading practice-oriented translator
and interpreter training program in the United States is not universi-
ty-affiliated. The ATA series, however, has not until recently claimed
to be a forum for the development of a general disciplinary perspective on translation, and its volumes have not yet cohered into a corpus
defining an American translation studies. Perhaps Mildred Lawson's
Theory and Practice, Tension and Interdependence, the fifth volume of the
American Translators Association Scholarly Monograph Series, is the
best and most recent effort to bridge the gulf between the academic
discourses on translation in the United States and Europe (Lawson's
Meaning-based Translation: A Guide to Cross-language Equivalence is also
of interest in this regard).

On the whole, however, there appear to be historically distinct
American and European approaches to translation studies. Of course,
the European approach is anything but unified. There are are a host
of "regional traditions" in the various countries. But interestingly
enough, translation theorists and practitioners in the various European countries and Canada have participated in creating a remarkably
varied, but nevertheless comprehensive, effort to turn translation
studies into a unique academic discipline. For almost half a century
they have developed a flourishing tradition of academic discourse
which has, often in spite of philological limitations and traditions,
inaugurated a broadly international conception of the discipline of
translation studies.

There are, of course, differences of opinion within this international collegium. There are many points of divergence: just consider

the anti-theoretical, entirely practice-oriented approach of Newmark; the interculturality of Holmes; the descriptivist methods of Lambert and van den Brook; the Göttingen team's concern with the impact of translation on target language literature; the philological and text-typological translation described by Reiß; the textual approaches of Neubert, Hatim, and Mason; and the empiricism of Gideon Toury. These rough labels illustrate the variety of scholarly approaches and emphasize their points of difference. However, even though Wills and Vermeer of Germany, Kommisarov and Svejcer of Russia, Snell-Hornby and Bühler of Austria, and Harris and Séguinot of Canada all have their points of agreement and disagreement—sometimes quite serious ones, sometimes just a matter of different terminologies—they have all actively engaged in a common theoretical discourse.

There has been a multi-lateral and long-standing participation in academic conversation at international conferences and in the literature—there are a multitude of books and several journals that have created the discourse that establishes what we call European or international translation studies. This continuing academic discourse has flourished in spite of some very real arguments. There is a major theoretical distance, for instance, between adherents of the so-called *skopos* theory, which asserts the primacy of the purpose of the target text, and those scholars who emphasize the centrality of communicative equivalence between original and translation.

Have the Americans, with the exception, perhaps, of Nida, Lawson, and a few others, been a part of this discourse? For the most part, the answer is negative. This is not an indictment, but an observation. The international approach to translation studies has evolved primarily from a linguistic tradition and from a context of translation as a profession. From this heritage an academic discipline dealing with interlinguistic practice in an intercultural setting came into existence. Like other university disciplines, international translation studies has been trying to define its status as a "systematic" and teachable body of knowledge. Whatever the differences among those who profess the discipline, this search for "system" persists as a central concept. Perhaps the most apt reflection of this trend is the recent term *translatology*, which has come to express the scientific/systemic aspirations of scholars whose aim it is to form and educate (not just to train) prospective translators and interpreters in academic settings.

Translatologists may focus on different aspects of the systematics of translation—on the purpose like Vermeer, on the message and the commission like Holz-Mänttäri, on syntactic, lexical, and stylistic strategies like Newmark—but they all basically assume that translation, as a specific form of intercultural and interlinguistic interaction, is a rule-governed, empirical phenomenon capable of some kind of systematic description. This is perhaps because the field of translation studies in Europe has left its philological roots behind and, usually as a part of applied linguistics, is oriented toward professional as well as academic goals.

The Americans, on the other hand, are almost all products of a quite different, more literary and humanistic tradition. Douglas Robinson, in *The Translator's Turn*, speaks for a generation of American translation scholars when he says, "I come to the field from literary theory where the normative moralizing so typical of translation theory was largely eradicated in the thirties and forties by the New Critics" (1991, 177). Robinson's term "normative moralizing" is, in fact, an indictment of the systemic view of translation. While Robinson is quite vocal in his dismissal of the modern international approach (and it is not our intent here to argue this point), he does underscore a major difference between the Americans and the Europeans: the replacement of an objective systematics rooted in linguistics with a more subjective approach (is it a systematics?) deriving from a variety of critical and philosophical approaches of the last several decades—phenomenology, existentialism, deconstruction, Marxism, and feminism. This view of translation is concerned less with the study of the objective relations between linguistic system, cultural system, translation process, and text, and more with the translated text as a carrier of social and ideological messages and the translation process as a tool for shaping those messages. Thus, the authors of the current volume reflect in their conception of translation studies less involvement with the literature of international translation studies and more concern with modern ideological and critical issues—particularly those of race and gender.

Is this approach also "translation studies?" It is not in the mainstream of the international tradition as we have defined it—although, to be sure, Venuti's resistive translation (Venuti 1991) and Reiß's description of philological translation share the common goal of highlighting the semantic and pragmatic uniqueness of the original text. This is one, we expect, of many points of intersection the reader will discover in the text which follows. Although this new American tradition is, for the most part, the product of a different intellectual discourse on translation—Chamberlain, Godard, Levine, Lotbinière-Harwood, Niranjana, and Spivak are cited in the text—it nevertheless falls within the broad domain of translation studies, whether it is itself aware of this or not. In fact, the bibliographies of the writings of the proponents of the "American humanistic school," including this volume, are ample proof of the divergence of the American humanistic and European academic traditions. In this volume only Basnett-McGuire, Lefevere, and Newmark make an entrance. But it is our firm conviction that translation is a "house of many rooms," and that these different rooms are often simply different discourses and perspectives on a common object of interest—translation.

In the first volume of the series we addressed the question of unity and difference in the discourse of translation studies. We defined translation studies as a discipline where many different research interests might be accommodated as long as the research aims of the particular inquiry were defined. We offered a set of possible research parameters, including emphases on criticism and on translation as a vehicle for mediating value systems. From the different permutations of research interests a set of models of translation was derived. Without claiming to encompass the whole range of possible perspectives on translation, we singled out and defined seven models, and, of these, the current work seems to fit best into the critical model. The critical model is concerned with the critical appraisal of the target text as a translation (Neubert and Shreve 1991, 17). In our description of the critical model we called for the development of a methodology to expand the scope of the model, claiming that

> translation criticism should always be comparative, maintaining the source and target texts as a pair. A full development of the critical model would have to develop a research methodology which is essentially contrastive. It would have to merge translation values, translation results, and source and target language values.

Translating Slavery seems to be a major first step in defining a broader scope for translation criticism. In chapter 11, "*Ourika's* Three Versions: A Comparison," Doris Kadish fulfills our call for a comparative and contrastive method. The authors, however, expand our original definition of the model, demonstrating that the translation itself can be a critical tool. The translations, as Massardier-Kenney claims, "provide critical readings" and become a tool for presenting alternative views of the source text, for "reconstituting traditions which have been ignored," for "reconstituting forgotten voices," or for participating in the constitution of culture. This notion of the translation as a critical and ideological tool is a significant one; it doubles the power of the critical model. The translation is a critical reading of the source text—in another language—but it may also, then, itself be subject to a critical reading—focusing on what the translation says, or does not say, about the original text, its author, and the issues of race, gender, or class that may be present there. The authors use this device success-fully throughout the volume, providing new translations of the key texts and then giving extensive commentary on the translations. This self-reflective and self-critical commentary is not usual in translation. The authors go so far as to provide an interesting peek into the critical translator's thought processes by providing a transcript of an in-sightful dialogue between two of the translators in chapter 8 "Black on White: Translation, Race, Class, and Power."

The language of this critical model diverges from that common in the academic models of the European translatologists. We cannot, therefore, expect a close terminological match between them: witness Massardier-Kenney's critique of what she calls the "unfortunately loaded terms of 'source' and 'target' language curently in use," be-cause "they represent a notion of language that has been discred-ited." Of course, these terms have not been discredited in all of the many discourses of translation, but only in the one from which this volume derives.

The model developed in this volume is not only critical, but in-volves itself in translation practice. In a remarkably reflected and reflecting way, the authors explore the interaction of practical transla-tion decision-making with the critical position taken by the translator and evidenced in the translation. The dialogue in chapter 8 is specifi-cally concerned with the motivations for certain kinds of decisions and, as such, is an example of the "first-order descriptive level of translation process and procedure" where translators and translation users reflect on textual results and on the conscious manifestations of the translation process (Neubert and Shreve 1992, 51). In fact, while our original concept of the critical model presupposed a finished translation, the current work addresses some of the issues at work in the translator's mind when critical translation is done. Thus, an active, process-oriented element is added to the critical model. This active translation criticism is best conducted by the translator, who, of all readers, may have the best access to both the source and target texts.

The authors claim that "translation theory inevitably emerges out of a specific practice." Their volume describes a particular kind of translation practice—ideologically motivated, critically directed, and focused on the act of translation itself. In the first volume of this series, *Translation as Text*, we made the claim that there is no single translation process, that there are many forms of translation, defined by a specific intersection of interests, motivations, competences, and texts. The critical translations of Massardier-Kenney, DeJulio, Molta, Bell, Kadish, and Sallardene define a new mode of translation proceeding from the critical model, but adding new dimensions to it.

The discourse of this text is not the usual discourse of the international translation studies we described earlier. But it is a discourse that we need to hear; it informs us that regardless of our academic backgrounds and diverging interests and terminologies, we recognize some common problems and opportunities in the act of translation. We have a common object of interest. It is clear, for instance, that Neubert and Massardier-Kenney held the same thought when she described translation as "gendered production, as the labor of childbirth, of bringing forth a text out of another text," and when he claimed that translation was "text-induced text production." The mission of the series *Translation Studies* is to explore the staggering range of thought about translation. It is not our purpose to focus on or support just one tradition, region, or school, but to bring together in one forum the variety of thinking about translation. Each volume will argue a different position—and each foreword will look for the unity in our diversity. In this way we can explore our differences and exploit our agreements to pursue a more inclusive and more global conception of translation studies.

References

Lawson, M. 1984. *Meaning-based Translation: A Guide to Cross-language Equivalence*. Lanham, Md: University of America Press.

———. 1991. *Theory and Practice, Tension and Interdependence*. ATA Scholarly Monograph Series Volume V. Binghamton, N.Y.: SUNY Binghamton.

Neubert, A., and G. M. Shreve. 1992. *Translation as Text*. Translation Studies 1. Kent, Ohio: Kent State University Press.

Reiß, K. 1990. Das Mißverständnis vom "eigentlichen" Übersetzen. In *Übersetzungswissenschaft: Ergebnisse und Perspektiven. Festschrift für Wolfram Wilss zum 65.Geburtstag*, ed. R. Arntz and G. Thome, 40–54. Tübingen: Narr.

Robinson, D. 1991. *The Translator's Turn*. Baltimore and London: Johns Hopkins University Press.

Venuti, L. 1991. "Translation as a Social Practice; or, The Violence of Translation." Paper presented at conference, Humanistic Dilemmas: Translation in the Humanities and Social Sciences, 26–28 September, at the State University of New York, Binghamton, New York.

Acknowledgments

This volume results from the unstinting efforts of a team of writers and translators who were involved in all stages of its production, from early discussion of basic ideas to final proofreading and editing. Special acknowledgment needs to be made of those participants who contributed the most actively: Professors Sharon Bell, Maryann De Julio, and Marie-Pierre Le Hir. Several graduate students at Kent State University also made meaningful contributions to the project, either as translators (Sylvie Molta and Claire Salardenne) or as clerical assistants (Susan Brown, Michelle Foss, and Pamela Waldschmidt). Their gracious assistance with this project is most appreciated. We also wish to acknowledge the advice and editing provided by our Kent State colleagues, Carol Maier and Gregory Shreve, as well as the invaluable suggestions for improvement made by our outside readers, Professor Carrol Coates and Lawrence Venuti. M. Amadou Gay, cultural attaché at the Embassy of Senegal in Washington, graciously provided his expertise for a translation into Wolof. We also wish to thank the Office of Research and Graduate Studies at Kent State University and the Kent State University Press for their support of this project. Finally, we extend our most sincere thanks to William Kenney and Raymond Woller for the intellectual, moral, and technical support they provided, at so many times and in so many ways.

Introduction

Doris Y. Kadish

Translation, gender, and race, the main topics of this volume, have often been relegated to a marginal status. In recent years, however, they have begun to receive the serious attention they deserve. Each of these topics stands at the frontier of much of the most challenging theoretical, linguistic, and historical activity occurring in the humanities and social sciences today.[1] However, the important ties among these three topics have been insufficiently explored, leaving a gap in the treatment of the complex interrelationships that exist among them. *Translating Slavery* attempts to fill that gap by focusing on the French revolutionary period in the late eighteenth and early nineteenth centuries in France, from 1783 to 1823, a paradigmatic period in which a number of French women spoke out against the oppression of slaves and women.

Antislavery writings by French women have tended to be overshadowed by the far more negative, repressive works produced by French men writing in the second half of the nineteenth century. Those works functioned to crystalize and legitimize a fictive Africanist discourse that served, as Christopher Miller has shown, like Orientalism to generate a set of mythic concepts and categories which stood as a screen between European subjects and the reality of the Other.[2] Although it is true that antislavery works by women in the late eighteenth and early nineteenth centuries contributed to the creation of that discourse, it is also true that those works by women contributed significantly to a tradition of resistance against that discourse. Admittedly it is a mistake, as David Brion Davis points out, to glorify early antislavery writers, to overestimate their contribution, or to fail to acknowledge that their writings were motivated by a variety of economic, religious, humanitarian, and other considerations, not all of which were noble and disinterested.[3] But it is also a mistake, as Raymond Williams states, to overlook the importance of works and ideas which, while clearly affected by hegemonic limits and pressures, are at least in part significant breaks beyond them, which may again in part be neutralized, reduced, or incorporated, but which in their most active elements nevertheless come through as independent and original.[4]

This volume discovers in French women's writings of the revolutionary period evidence of those significant breaks and independent, original elements.

The period in French history from 1783 to 1823 highlighted for consideration in this volume can be divided into two phases with respect to issues regarding slavery. The first, covering the years immediately before, during, and after the French Revolution, from 1783 to 1799, is marked by French support for abolition, which was actually decreed in 1794. The second, from 1800 to 1823, spanning the years of Napoleon's Consulate and Empire as well as the Restoration under Louis XVIII from 1814 to 1823, is characterized, in contrast, by a general retreat from the earlier support for abolition. During this phase the more overt abolitionist activities that occurred during the revolutionary period are replaced by various, more indirect forms of opposition to the proslavery policies that prevailed following Napoleon's revocation of abolition in 1802. For the purposes of this volume, 1783 and 1823 have been chosen as convenient and representative boundaries not only because they mark the dates when the principal works translated in this volume were written or published,[5] but also because they delineate an especially active period in which French women resisted the joint oppression of slaves and women. However, for more than a century before 1783, and for decades after 1823— even after 1848, when slavery was officially abolished once and for all in France and the French colonies—the interrelationships of gender and race continued to run through the fabric of French culture.

This volume focuses on translation, with specific emphasis on gender and race. In addition to the marginalization that they typically undergo in literary and historical studies, translation, gender, and race all entail the same kind of mediating process. Looking closely at what happens when translators translate and when writers treat gender and race, we can see that literature is not an objective expression of universal values, as has been traditionally assumed, but an ideological expression of local values. "Ideology" is defined broadly here as the process by which particular groups produce meanings, beliefs, and values that are central to the social and political order of their time.[6] When translators translate works and women writers write works about the highly charged issues of gender and race, the processes of mediation and ideology that occur need to be made visible to critical scrutiny through analysis.

A crucial component of telling the story of translating gender and race entails looking at what happens when persons of color write about the subject of slavery or translate works about that subject. Unfortunately, little on this topic has been unearthed or explored in depth. The voice of the racial Other is not yet as readily available in French during the period highlighted in this volume as is the voice of the feminine Other. However, various ways of trying to hear that voice from the past that has been largely silenced have been adopted in this volume. Whenever possible, there will be mention of specific persons of color who have spoken about this period and who may have thus perhaps given a voice to those who remain silent: for example, the political leader, Toussaint L'Ouverture; the critic and historian, C. L. R. James; the modern writers Caryl Phillips and Patrick Chamoiseau; the eighteenth-century writer and translator, Phillis Wheatley; the model for the nineteenth-century writer Claire de Duras's character Ourika; and other victims of the institution of slavery. Special attention will be given to the voice that may have been heard by those women writers—notably Aphra Behn and Claire de Duras—who lived in the colonies and responded favorably to African women in their literary works. Lastly, as translators and critics, the group that has produced this volume has attempted to sustain a dialogue that shows at least the willingness to listen in order to produce echoes today of that distant, muted voice. The dialogue that appears in chapter 8 and that tries to bring into the open some of the ways in which translators' racial and cultural backgrounds affect their translations is the result of just such an attempt.

This volume argues, then, that the processes of mediation and ideology are essential for understanding translation and, accordingly, that translation should not be taken as rising above or standing outside of those processes. For translators in the twentieth century, as for writers or translators of an earlier time, ideological factors inevitably affect the treatment of issues of gender and race. The purpose of the analyses of translation provided in this volume is to identify some of those factors and to provide an occasion for reflecting upon the way they affect translators, critics, or readers of literary and historical works. Rather than allowing silence to surround the problems encountered in producing translations of gender and race, this volume seeks instead to identify such problems and thereby increase our awareness of the constraints of ideology. Rooted in the choices that translators make regarding gender and race, it is a method that scrutinizes works of literary translation textually, linguistically, and ideologically.

The numerous literary and expository texts dealing with slaves and slavery that women produced, especially those works by French women in the late eighteenth and early nineteenth centuries singled out for close consideration here, deserve to be better known. By making them better known, this volume foregrounds the existence of a French tradition of women's antislavery writing—Moira Ferguson similarly identifies "a gynocentrically-oriented discourse on slaves" that existed in England from the seventeenth through the nineteenth centuries—that plays a significant but often overlooked role in French literature and history.[7] This volume provides as well a selection of modern translations that will make some of the works in that feminine tradition available to English-speaking readers interested in issues of translation, gender, and race. This volume attempts to highlight key issues in the theory and practice of translation by providing both the original works and their translations, as well as essays on the theoretical and practical issues involved in translating gender and race. Since those issues include both the gender and the cultural background of translators, it is significant to note that the translations provided here have been produced collaboratively by a group of women, of French, American, and African American origin. This group of women has attempted to make accessible the work of women writers of the past and thereby to maintain in some measure the tradition of women's resistance to those hegemonic cultural and social practices that have adversely affected women and persons of color.

Chapter 1 presents a theoretical framework for the issues of translating slavery that are raised in this volume. Drawing on the contributions of a number of recent translation theorists, this chapter articulates an approach that has among its goals to textualize and contextualize translation, to produce a collaborative patchwork of textual components, to de-essentialize race and gender, and to practice a "creole translation" that distances itself from claims of universality and monolinguism. It is also an approach that attempts to be self-reflective and to address openly the ideological and linguistic limitations of its own theory and practice. In addition, chapter 1 dwells on some of the strategies adopted in order to maintain or restore the resistant elements of the works translated in this volume. Further discussion of those strategies and of specific problems encountered in translating particular authors occurs in later chapters.

Chapter 2 establishes the kind of broad historical context that is necessary for dealing adequately with the specific topic of translating gender and race in the revolutionary period highlighted in this volume. In order to set the stage, the chapter begins by moving back before 1783 and taking up an example that illustrates especially well how the processes of mediation and ideology at work in translation affected a work about slavery. That example is the translation into French by a French male writer, Pierre Antoine de La Place, of what is commonly acknowledged as the seminal novel about slavery, *Oroonoko*, by the English woman writer Aphra Behn.[8] Although Behn's novel dates from the late seventeenth century and La Place's translation from the mid-eighteenth century, the issues surrounding the translation of *Oroonoko* provide a highly relevant context for discussing those issues about gender and race that resurface in producing translations of works from the period examined in this volume. After the discussion of *Oroonoko*, the second chapter then takes up the period from 1783 to 1823 in order to provide the historical and literary context necessary to understand more fully the significance of the works by women writers translated and analyzed later in the volume. The second chapter comes to a close with careful consideration of a second example which again stands outside of the specific period of interest in this volume but which, like the first example, is part of the broad context necessary for understanding the intricate ties among translation, gender, and race in the revolutionary period. This second example consists of the translation into French by the Irish writer Louise Belloc, in collaboration with Adélaïde de Montgolfier, of what is undoubtedly the most well known work about slavery, Harriet Beecher Stowe's *Uncle Tom's Cabin*. By contrasting that translation by a woman, which Stowe singled out for praise, claiming that "I am convinced that a feminine mind can more easily mould itself to my own,"[9] with the translation of the novel by a man, Emile de la Bédollière, further light is shed on the complex interaction historically among translation, gender, and race.

Parts 2, 3, and 4 focus on three women writers. The first, Olympe de Gouges, wrote about the subject of slavery directly before and during the early years of the revolution at a time when overtly abolitionist sentiment was prevalent. The second, Germaine de Staël, wrote about that subject at the same time as Gouges as well as at the end of the Napoleonic period, when pressure from England to end the slave trade internationally was being exerted. The third, Claire de Duras, wrote her novel depicting an African heroine during the 1820s, when a moderate resurgence in antislavery occurred. In addition to their different historical contexts, these women differ from one another with respect to social class, political views, and attitudes toward women's issues. The introductory essays in parts 2, 3, and 4 provide a context for understanding the particular nature of these women's contributions and for understanding the differences among them. Produced by members of a collaborative team who have different backgrounds and who were dealing with authors having a greater or lesser degree of direct connection to translation per se, these introductory essays sketch different kinds of contexts: in some cases focusing more on literary history; in others, more on biography and translation practice. Parts 2, 3, and 4 then go on to provide representative translations, the orginal texts of which appear at the end of the volume.[10] Each translation is followed by a translation analysis that looks at the issues of gender and race that those translations bring to the fore. Like the introductory essays, these analyses adopt very different approaches, according to the disparate backgrounds and interests of their authors. In the case of Gouges, the translator comments on her intentions and the decisions that she made. In the case of Staël, two of the translators engage in a dialogue aimed at identifying, however tentatively and preliminarily, the ways in which the existence of different cultural and linguistic backgrounds affects translation, especially for the highly sensitive and ideologically charged issue of race. In the case of Duras, where other published translations of *Ourika* exist, a comparative analysis of those translations is provided alongside the one presented in this volume. The purpose of these three very different kinds of analysis is to provide examples of ways to address the ideological issues that inevitably arise in translation. Each of these analyses, like the translations themselves and other textual components included here, has its limitations. The process of reflection upon those limitations, begun by the contributors to this collaborative project within the pages of this volume, needs to be continued by its readers.

   This volume is intended for a variety of readers, both bilingual and monolingual. It is hoped that bilingual readers will want to go back to the original texts presented here after reading the translations and that their own reading will be informed by the translators' theory and practice. It is hoped that bilingual readers will scrutinize those texts for the interventions of the translators and assess what was done or could have been done. It is further hoped that, as a result of the kind of scrutiny practiced by the translators here, monolingual readers will be more aware in reading translations that translation has occurred, and that they will be reminded that translation is a kind of cultural mediation which we need to explore and examine, all the more so since we live and write under conditions of cultural protectionism that act to exclude languages and values other than our own.

This volume is also intended to serve a variety of academic purposes. Some readers may wish to focus on the translations as applications of the theoretical principles that this volume develops, especially in chapter 1 and the translation analyses. Other readers may wish to focus on the women whose work as writers and translators is highlighted in this volume, especially in chapter 2 and the introductory sections of each part. Still other readers interested primarily in literature may wish to focus on the literary texts, which are difficult to obtain either in French or in translation. The authors of this volume hope, of course, that most readers will want to read the book in its entirety and that a comprehensive reading will make the important point that translation, literature, and history are all most clearly illuminated when their inextricable links are acknowledged and understood.

PART ONE
Theory, Practice, and History

Translation Theory and Practice

Françoise Massardier-Kenney

As the title indicates, *Translating Slavery: Gender and Race in French Women's Writing, 1783–1823* inextricably links theory and practice. The collaborators of this volume are not speaking of literary and cultural translation in general, nor are they essentializing race and gender. Translating "gender and race" suggests that race and gender are already textualized. "Translating" race and gender already implies a transitive operation which is necessarily contextualized. The translators who worked on the pieces by Olympe de Gouges, Germaine de Staël, and Claire de Duras have doubled these authors' common discourse, a discourse that iterates that race, class, gender, and culture are figures of difference that are essentialized as causes of differences rather than as effects of a specific power imbalance. The texts presented here include analyses of the contribution of three French women authors of a specific period, women who wrote about people of color at a time when race was starting to be defined in essentializing terms[1] and who have not been part of the canon of French literature; translations of the French texts; comments on the translations by the translators themselves or by translators of other pieces; and the original French texts. This collaborative patchwork of texts, comments, original, and translated texts (to avoid the unfortunately loaded terms of "source" and "target" language currently in use)[2] deliberately fuses/ diffuses the differences between text and translation, between translating and writing, between reading and critiquing. The consequence of this attempt to present translations and departure texts, theory and practice, gender and race, as inextricably linked in a kind of hybrid text is that this presentation will inevitably require a discourse that cannot, that will not neatly separate these strands, that will only leave gender to come back to it via a discussion of race, that will describe cultural difference only to question it in the practice of translation.

This displacement of writing and translation implied in the patchwork created by the translators of Gouges, Staël, and Duras reproduces these authors' own practices and awareness of the importance of translation for the representation of race and gender. As the following chapter and the introductions to the translations will make clear, each of these three authors was directly involved in translation. Olympe de Gouges wrote in French, not her native language, so that for her the very act of writing was a translation. It is therefore not surprising that her writing-in-translation produced results which pushed the limits of the genre of French theater. Germaine de Staël's involvement with translation was more mediated but no less central. She was a practitioner of translation, a theorist of translation, and her story *Mirza,* presented here, fuses the three key elements of translation, race, and gender. Similarly, Claire de Duras practiced translation, criticized it, and created a powerful Senegalese heroine who represents the colonized subject as a "translated being,"[3] as someone who is seen, and sees herself through the lens of the colonizing dominant culture.

In *Siting Translation* Tejaswini Niranjana has said about translators' prefaces that "[t]he work from which they seem to exclude themselves (i.e., the translation) is constituted by the traces of their historicity, and the gesture of exclusion they perform makes possible the presentation of the text as a unified and transparent whole."[4] Here the collaborators of this volume wish to come out into the open, to move, so to speak, from the preface, to the surface, to face, and perhaps "deface" these texts in a movement which acknowledges that translation practice is always a practice of a "theory" or a working out of an ideological position, but also that translation theory inevitably emerges out of a specific practice.

This attempt at a self-reflecting translating practice follows in the steps of the most recent and interesting theoretical discussions of translation that have appeared in English. These discussions emphasize the ideological position implied by translation practices, the inevitable "refraction," to use André Lefevere's term, which occurs when a foreign text enters another culture.[5] One of these positions, as Lori Chamberlain has demonstrated,[6] involves the traditional representation of translation in gendered terms. This representation implies a hierarchical relation (translation is like woman, i.e., secondary) which Chamberlain proposes to challenge by advocating a translating practice that asserts the role of the translator as that of an active textual producer. Barbara Godard is also struggling against the ancillary, feminine conception of translation when she advocates a conception of translation within the context of the theory of feminist discourse as "production not reproduction," and within "a logic of disruptive excess in which nothing is ever posited that is not also reversed."[7]

Rather than accept the opposition that Godard retains between production and reproduction, an opposition which goes back to the notion of origin, authority, and superiority of the one who produces, translators could perhaps reclaim "reproduction" for translation as that operation which produces, through labor, something issued of something else, of an Other something. Thus reproduction as gendered production, as the labor of childbirth, of bringing forth a text out of another text, is a metaphor rich in implications for our understanding of translation as a linguistic mediation rather than as a linear "source/target" movement which reinscribes the notion of writing as origin.[8]

Of course, since translation is also a legitimizing process for a writer—a writer takes on the authority implied in being an author in so far as he or she becomes translated—a translator can become an active textual producer in the very process of choosing who will be translated, a choice which does not have to be left to the editors of commercial publishing houses or even to the academic establishment. Translation may not be a form of discourse encouraged by the cultural hegemonic powers in this country, but its very obscurity gives its practitioners a certain amount of freedom.[9]

It is because of this awareness that translation is a way to bring a certain authority to texts, a way to alter specific cultural power structures that the collaborators of this volume have chosen works by authors who stand in some cases in the margins of French literature, and whose texts are often hard to obtain in English, if not in their native language. These European women attempt to make us hear colonized voices at a time when such voices were barely audible. Translating these authors—Gouges, Staël, and Duras—means that their attempt at revoicing the colonized will be heard again. Significantly, their voices, as each introduction will make clear, are part of a tradition of political opposition which expressed itself, among other things, as an opposition to the politics of slavery and racism. Our choice of authors, which points to the intersection of gender, race, and translation at the level of practice, reflects the increasing number of translations of non-canonical or older texts made by women translators and editors.

That the work of translation can be the process of creating meaning and restoring literary reputation is clear within the context of these writers: Gouges's work in French has been dismissed as "bad" as

Marie-Pierre Le Hir shows in chapter 3, Staël's *Mirza* dismissed as "awkward," her essay on translation ignored, and Duras's *Ourika* forgotten. The translations of the works presented in this volume, by pushing on the texts' resistant features, provide critical readings which follow the hidden threads of female agency and contribute to show that women authors of this period were, perhaps because of their cultural position, sensitive to the plight of Africans and opposed slavery textually in ways that their male counterparts (canonical writers such as Hugo or Merimée) did not or could not.[10]

The practice of translation can be conceived of as a kind of "archeology of knowledge": translation can reconstitute traditions that have been ignored because of their radicalness, or of their difference, or it can show how isolated voices could be seen as constituting traditions. By translating, one participates in the constitution of culture, and the very gesture of translating can create pockets of resistance in the cultural hegemony. Translation does not necessarily have to be market driven and geared to producing easily digested versions of compliant texts which mirror American cultural values, which is how Lawrence Venuti defines the major output of translations into American English.

However, translating a text is more complex than just choosing a text, since it puts into play not only gender and race, but the issues of social class and nationality as well; and it is the very complexity of translation that the translators and critics of this volume foreground here. These issues directly confront the translator as woman who has to mediate between her desire to be visible in all it implies in terms of her own ideological investment, and between the necessarily different ideological positions of the text she translates. Any attempt to bring into another language or another culture the racial or cultural "other"—women or persons of color—inevitably implicates the translator-mediator in the exploitative conditions which link otherness to a specific power structure. Because of the specific historical and social circumstances in which Gouges, Staël, and Duras wrote, their texts present characteristics which the modern reader is likely to view as compliant with the dominant culture rather than as "radical," in spite of the fact that these authors were generally progressive (Staël for example) or revolutionary (in the case of Gouges). For instance, Staël writes to urge the abolition of the slave trade, not the abolition of slavery itself and in *Mirza*, uses a male narrator who stereotypes "African blacks" in what may be offensive terms to present-day readers. At the same time, Staël's story valorizes her Jolof heroine and gives her access to language in a movement that was certainly resistant at the time.[11] What can the translator do to make this resistant gesture apparent? Is it sufficient to acknowledge this resistance in the "margins" of the translation, in the preface, or can this gesture be included in the translation itself? Since the goal of the collaborators of this volume is to reconstitute a tradition of women writing in a specific historical context, any intervention of the translator for the benefit of the modern reader could scramble the very voices the translator sought to bring back. Instead of stemming from an attention to the French author's particularity, adapting the radical gesture of the text could very well be another way of making the text "culturally fluent," of making it fit our own contemporary expectations of what constitutes "resistant" writing. Making Staël "politically correct" could be far more compliant than producing a text whose mixture of radical and compliant elements makes us see the struggle involved against the dominant patriarchal discourse of the time and the inevitable limits that ideology places upon any writing, our own included—if not always acknowledged. As Gayatri Spivak has observed about the translation of Indian works into English, the translator "must be able to confront the idea that what seems resistant in the space of English may be reactionary in the space of the original language"[12] and we may add that the reverse is true: what may appear compliant in English might have been resistant in the original language, and the translator-reader needs to decide how to handle the discrepancy between the two cultures.

This choice (unconscious as well as conscious) of whether to radicalize the text or not is scarcely gender free. A question one might ask about some of the translation practices discussed in chapter 2, "The Historical Context," is whether they are the result of a historical shift in translation theory (after the 1800s, the concept of translation as something "faithful" displaced the concept of translation as adaptation),[13] or whether the kinds and the number of liberties translators take with their texts may also have to do with gender. For instance, Louise Belloc, who translated Harriet Beecher Stowe's *Uncle Tom's Cabin* in 1853, produced a translation which was very close to the American text and contained very few added or deleted elements, while Emile de la Bédollière, in his translation of that same text in 1852, produced a "freer" adaptation. We must notice that Belloc, a woman translating another woman, very carefully listened to the voice of her text, whereas the male translator La Bédollière felt free to rewrite Stowe's work to fit the expectations of his audience or his own expectations of what male and female characters could say. These examples may or may not be representative, but they bring out the question of whether the range of the translator's textual intervention is linked to gender positions.

The global strategies used by the different translators—all women—who worked on the texts presented here seem to follow parallel patterns. While the translators all refrain from adapting the French authors' politically and racially radical positions to the new Anglo-American context, and thus seem to produce linguistically conservative versions, they nonetheless do what Godard describes as "feminist discourse as translation." For Godard, "translation is one among many ways of rewriting within literary systems, pushing them in a certain direction through canonization."[14]

First, the translators have attended to the specific linguistic experiments, to the stylistic difference of the authors they were translating; in that, the translators were furthering their agenda of reconstituting forgotten voices, looking toward their French texts rather than their audience. Maryann De Julio's translation of Olympe de Gouges, for instance, emphasizes the polemical, rhetorical tone of the author, a tone which contributed to create a new kind of ideologically engagé (i.e., politically committed) theater which has been largely ignored. The translator emphasized the legal aspect of Gouges's writing by adding expressions from the language of contracts.

Staël's pieces, in turn, are translated with an attention to word choice which stresses the male/female opposition and valorizes the female in an effort to emphasize Staël's position as a woman writer, in conformity with the view that "[t]he task of the feminist translator is to consider language as a clue to the workings of gendered agency."[15] Similarly, the translation of *Ourika* by Claire Salardenne and Françoise Massardier-Kenney purposefully heightens the eloquence of the black female character in an effort to make heard a female voice that reaches the modern reader muted, already in translation (since Ourika does not know her "mother-tongue," does not know the tongue of her mother). Here Ourika's fluency is not a way to satisfy the demands of the intended reader, but a strategy that emphasizes the strength of a voice formed and perhaps deformed by the colonizing culture. It satisfies the demands of the translators as readers. It should be added that the two collaborators, working on different pieces of *Ourika*, both purposefully effaced what sometimes appeared to them as the whining undertones of the character Ourika. This decision was made because of their common intention to produce a text that presents an oppressed but dignified woman of color. Specific lexical choices were thus made on the basis of the impression the translators wanted the whole text to make. Our project of presenting these authors as exemplary presences who gave voice to forgotten subjects (women and blacks) made the translators aware of the patronizing implications of presenting a woman and a colonized subject strictly as a victim.

The collaborators' own desire as women translators to empower the female characters dictated a number of their choices. In this regard, as the feminist translator Susanne de Lotbinière-Harwood points out about feminist translation in general, they recognize that "context determines translation strategies"[16] and that this particular context (women authors, women translators, a university press, and a sympathetic audience) made it possible for us to make the feminine visible in the text and valorize it.

Translation, as a self-reflective activity which contributes to the construction of a specific gender position, does not necessarily need to work on texts already, transparently, "feminist." As the examples presented here show, the translator can bring to the surface elements which specific historical and cultural modes of discourse bury. The translator can bring out in specific parts of the text the hidden or implied gender identification of the text as a whole. They can bring it out or "subvert" it in the case of sexist male writers, in the sense of bringing out a version of the text which is there only implicitly, as Susan Jill Levine argued about her own translation of Latin American works.[17]

However, unlike Lotbinière-Harwood, because of the very nature of our project, we refused to consider gender as a factor overriding all others, gender as a unified "context" which determines all translation strategies. The translators attempted to attend to the interrelationship of all the factors—gender, race, or class—that were present in the texts. The translators of this volume reacted to the texts in ways that suggested that race, gender, and class were equally important ideological issues. For instance, Sharon Bell's translation of Staël's essays "Appel aux souverains" and "Préface pour la traduction d'un ouvrage de M. Wilberforce" was the result of conflicting responses to the texts. On the one hand, in her position as a woman translator, Bell reported her appreciation for Staël's tactful use of logic to convince her audience. She was drawn to Staël's conciliatory tone and her effortless passage from logic to feelings, a quality she attributed to her being a "woman." As a result, Bell's translation reflects an author-centered strategy, a strategy which expresses the translator's respect for the author's achievement. On the other hand, Bell is also African American and Staël's use of words like "primitive" or her mention of slavery as an African practice offended her. Because of these "details" in the text, she experienced a racial, a historical, and a class distance from Staël. To handle that distance in her translation, she stayed very close to the French text, a "closeness" here which paradoxically expressed her alienation, her lack of intimacy with Staël. Thus, the same strategy of translating very close to the French text, of not attempting to make it "transparent," resulted from both respect and repulsion, reactions which fell along specific ideological identifications.

Bell's strong reactions to specific words that had to do with the description of race helped the other European American translators to become more sensitive to the translation of these terms, helped them to attend to race as much as to gender issues in the texts. The sensitivity thus acquired is apparent, for example, in Maryann De Julio's discussion of her reasons for not translating "primitif" as "primitive" in Gouges's play *L'esclavage des noirs*. For specific words like "noir" and "nègre," the translators' work was collaborative.

A major working decision for the translators' handling of race was to find out what kinds of connotations these words had when they were used at the time. By consulting dictionaries of the times, we found that "nègre" often tended to be synonymous with slave, and that "noir" became associated with abolitionist politics. As William Cohen claims, "It was no accident that, at its founding in 1788, the abolitionist society took on the title Société des amis des noirs."[18] It must be added that a modern French dictionary like the Larousse gives "nègre" as synonymous of "slave," but also defines "nègre" as "a person of black race," a revealing definition since the concept of "black *race*" has been discredited as having little scientific validity.[19] But even dictionaries of the period hide the complexity of this semantic issue, a complexity linked to specific historical changes, as Serge Daget shows in his statistical study of the use of the words "esclave," "nègre" and "Noir" in French abolitionist literature from 1770 to 1845.[20] Although there was no strict consensus on usage, an analysis of abolitionist writings shows that until 1791 the term "esclave" tended to be avoided (the disappearance of the term being linked to a push for the disappearance of slavery), while "nègre" was still used, but since some of its uses were pejorative, "Noir" came to be the preferred term. Daget argues that since in seventeenth-century literature, "Noir" was rarely used with capitalization, using it capitalized was a significant innovation (as in the Société des Amis des Noirs). This use stemmed from a desire to give a moral lesson to proponents of the slave trade. The use of "Noir" with capitalization led to strong violent reactions, which proved that changing the word was indeed perceived as a way to work for abolition. However, even Claivière, the president of the abolitionist Société des Amis des Noirs, used traditional vocabulary (i.e., "esclave" or "nègre") as well as "Noir" to "convince everyone and not only people already devoted to the abolitionist cause."[21] Furthermore, specific historical events triggered changes in usage. For instance, the word "nègre" was widely used during the rebellion in Santo Domingo in 1791, while, paradoxically enough, the 1792 suppression of subventions to the slave trade led to the disappearance of the word "Noir" as free people of color "categorically rejected nègre or Noir."[22] But after the 1794 decree abolishing slavery, "Noir" regained favor in France. With the restoration of slavery by Napoleon in 1802, "Noir" lost ground to "nègre," which became again the preferred term. After Napoleon's fall in 1814, the term "Noir" came back into favor. Daget's study shows that translating terms connected with race is complex and that even typographical markers like a capital letter are significant. Whether an author uses "nègre" instead of "noir" is thus linked to specific times and to the kinds of audience the author had in mind.

The dictionary equivalent for "nègre" is "negro," but its use in our translations was debatable since today it is rejected by African Americans. Geneva Smitherman's description of the changing use of the word "Negro" shows the complexity of its use, a complexity which parallels that of French usage. According to Smitherman, in Colonial America, whites used "negroes," "slaves," and "niggers" to designate African Americans. "Negro" and "nigger" were used interchangeably, and "[i]t was not until the twentieth century that whites began to semantically distinguish "negro" and "nigger," with the latter becoming a racial epithet."[23] At that time "negro" was not capitalized, as in the original Spanish form it was an adjective. However, in Colonial America, blacks used the term "African," which was abandoned in the nineteenth century. At that time, some blacks began to use the white man's term "negro" as well as "colored." In the 1920s black leaders advocated the capitalization of "Negro," and a number of blacks adopted it. Although "Negro" was never totally acceptable nor universally used by blacks themselves,[24] it was widely used in its capitalized form until the 1960s.[25]

Since our translations are sited as historical texts and since "Negro" was used until the 1960s by blacks themselves, we chose to keep the term. Bell's knowledge of the current vocabulary of race sensitized the native French translators to the many connotations that terms describing "race" have in the United States and helped us make our decision, not because of any "intuition" based on race, but because of her familiarity with several types of "black culture" in the United States. The collaboration of several translators working from different cultural backgrounds helped us balance our specific ideological interest. The mixture of black, white, American, and French translators produced what we hope are translations in which all the factors of race, gender, or nationality intersect.

A specific challenge was presented by the translation of *Ourika* since this is the only case where there exist other translations. To emphasize translation as process, and as ideological mediation, we did not consult the existing translations; we wanted to be able to verify whether our attempt to work self-consciously could produce a translation different from the two others, which we assumed had been written without the kind of attentiveness to racial or gender context that we had. The analysis by Doris Kadish of the three translations allows the reader to see how this situation of translation consciousness has worked out. Normally, a final version of a new translation of any work would only come after the translators consulted the existing versions and modified their own version to include particularly felicitous items from the others, or to clarify in their text what the other versions do effectively. However, here the translators skip this final step because they want to use the translation of *Ourika* as a kind of "control" that indicates whether their experiment with race and gender can produce a different kind of translation. The translators also acknowledge that one of the translations is by the British writer John Fowles and that one of the best ways not to be swayed by the language of the canonical writer is to not read or hear her/him.

That translation is a powerful cultural activity for the construction of race as well as gender has recently been argued in its most negative consequences, most pointedly by Niranjana. She argues about the translation of Indi texts into English (and this specific context will be particularly important) that translation, by presenting specific versions of the colonized subject in coherent and transparent texts, contributes to the repression of difference and is part of the process of colonial domination. Niranjana's argument that translation practices are overdetermined by religious, racial, sexual, and economic discourses, in other words, that they are a significant component of cultural hegemony, to use Gramsci's[26] terms, is both a criticism and a reminder of the power of translation, since translation not only legitimizes specific authors, but also gives a seal of authority to certain versions of entire cultures or races. Although Niranjana's examples deal specifically with the way British translation is implicated in the

construction of the colonized Indian, her observations pertain generally to translations of culturally and racially different texts. Race can
therefore be seen as a key issue in translation. The implications of
Niranjana's work for our project are many and force us to ponder the
following questions: Is her description of the translation process when
it involves a first world culture and a third world culture applicable
to the translating situation when the power balance seems to be even,
such as when two Western first world languages such as French and
English are involved? Is translation's constitutive power over the colonial subject the same kind of power as for the colonizing (i.e., French)
subject? Next, how can Niranjana's call for a need to "translate, that
is (disturb or displace) history," be applied to texts which present
beings already in translation, i.e., African voices available only
through the French colonizer's language?[27]

Although the texts by Gouges, Staël, and Duras are "coherent,"
and certainly "transparent" texts which represent characters of color
and do minimize differences between cultures and races, their representation of race and difference is embedded in a specific historical
situation which produces an opposite effect to that described in general terms by Niranjana. These authors do construct images of women
and people of color, but they do not necessarily "repress" difference;
instead, they de-essentialize it, they displace it: they present people
who are different not because of an essential, inherent Otherness, but
because of specific historical conditions. For example, the violence of
Gouges's black hero Zamor is not shown as being a trait of his race,
but as the only resource available to a slave who has to protect his
honor and his life.[28] Moreover, Gouges does not naively indulge in a
romantic view of the "Other." She also represents another "Other," a
Native American, a cruel man who is opposed to the lofty Zamor.

Similarly Staël's *Mirza* contrasts the situation of the white male
narrator to that of her three West African characters, but she carefully
distinguishes between them. These characters belong to different
tribes who are at war (here Staël expresses her distance from the
myth of "the" African), and these characters are individualized. For
example, the women characters react very differently to authority:
Ourika is presented as a beautiful and dutiful wife while Mirza is a
solitary thinker. Gouges and Staël do, in some instances, minimize
difference by suggesting that blacks and whites are not essentially
different. What is different is their specific circumstances and their
relation to power. In these instances Gouges and Staël are writing
against their own culture, which stakes its political, economical, and
moral superiority on the belief that people of color are essentially

different, i.e., so unlike oneself that one does not have to treat them like oneself. In this context, if the translator were to affirm difference, a practice that Niranjana recommends as "enlightened," it would be a racist strategy. The lesson for us is that any theory of translation must be embedded in a specific practice. It must be theoretical, but it must not be universalizing. In this, we could argue that translation is like creoleness as it is defined by Bernabé et al. in "In Praise of Creoleness"; "Creoleness is an annihilation of false universality, of monolinguism, and of purity."[29]

In *Ourika* Duras takes the de-essentializing of difference a step further since she recounts the excruciating experience of difference by a character who is precisely like the members of the hegemonic culture. *Ourika* exposes a situation described by Fanon, and more recently, by Caribbean writers Bernabé, Chamoiseau, and Confiant, as "a terrible condition to perceive one's interior architecture, one's world, the instants of one's days, one's values with the eye of the other."[30] For Duras, racism, which makes an outcast of the Senegalese Ourika in French culture, is precisely that which insists on essential differences. So while the presentation of characters can seem to "repress" difference, it can as well be seen as an effort to deconstruct the notion that a different shade of complexion is essential, rather than a detail used by a powerful group to facilitate the repression of a less powerful group. This holding at bay of difference, of color which acknowledges its existence, is a central paradox of translation. Translation is a linguistic mediation conducive to creoleness. By setting up all the factors of race, gender, class, and culture for a kind of "creole translation practice," translators can produce a text that claims its hybridity,[31] that distances itself from the claims of universality, monolinguism, and purity.

Significantly, the French texts presented here heighten the problematic link between difference and translation. They represent race (i.e., exemplary difference) in a language that negates that difference: literally, all the West African characters speak and think in French (and English in the translations). So translation starts from a desire to give voice to the other but can only do so under erasure, as it were. Staël's characters are West Africans but their representation is monolingual; and some readers may be too. These characters come to us already in translation, a translation which inscribes a specific power balance: a French version of the West African colonized for a French reader. Although Staël's goal of promoting antislavery sentiments is anti-hegemonic, the text replays the historical and cultural imbalance, and so will the translation in English, unless some gesture is made to restore that balance in the direction of the absent language.

It is at this moment perhaps that the radicalization of the text that we discussed earlier can be done: not in the direction of the English speaking reader, but in the direction of the language that was never there, in the direction of multilinguism, of an intersection of several languages, and this gesture would not be a fluent, compliant strategy. A localized linguistic intervention can defamiliarize the text and make the readers experience directly the absent otherness in its disquieting foreignness. For instance, the West African characters in *Mirza* reach us already in translation, a fact hidden by the white narrator whose "guide" is really an interpreter who makes it possible for him, and for us as readers, to communicate with the Senegalese characters. Perhaps then, the translator can present a version of the missing voice and emphasize that all the French author has given the reader is a translation of a translation. The translator can recover Ourika's speech in Wolof and make clear that the interpreter's version in French is a sign of the narrator's and the reader's linguistic weakness.[32] By translating from French into Wolof, rather than from French into English in strategic parts of the text, the translator can momentarily "withhold translation"[33] to make the translation apparent, to restore multilinguism. The strategic use of Wolof could also be paired with "code mixing," i.e., the regular interspacing of words of one language in sentences from another language spoken in a multicultural environment. Although such code mixing is considered an "interference," for example in an interpreting situation, the translator could rather claim it as an "intersection," where languages can meet.

Since code mixing is most often used in speech, using it in a written text would also have the advantage of emphasizing the "orality" of the translated text, an orality which is an important component of the texts by Gouges, Staël, and Duras, as the analyses provided in the following chapters will make clear. Moreover, orality is an especially important component for the cultural survival of the people of color who were enslaved in a number of West African countries as well as the West Indies.[34] Attending to the orality of the texts we present here is thus a necessity; as Bernabé, Chamoiseau, and Confiant convincingly argue, the "nonintegration of oral tradition was one of the forms and one of the dimensions of our alienation."[35]

Orality is situated at the intersection of gender and race, and, as translators, editors, and critics, we needed to attend to it. Although the strategy of code mixing was very appealing, our lack of familiarity with the specifics of code mixing in French and Wolof made us refrain from using it. However, if code mixing was not possible within the translation of *Mirza*, its use was still possible in the comments following the translation. Thus, the critical essay which was supposed to follow *Mirza*'s translation became a dialogue between two translators of Germaine de Staël. The code mixing became a text mixing between the language of writing and that of speaking, between translating and analyzing.

The momentary withholding of translation in the English version of *Mirza*, however, is not possible for the translation of *Ourika* because the very issue presented in the novel is that there is nothing to translate back to. The Senegalese character's only language is French, the language of the slave traders who took her away from her family and that of the man who brought her back to France to save her from slavery. Duras presents an extremely pessimistic view of cultural translation as that which presents the cultural other as deprived of her own language. Duras presents an indictment of translation conceived as monolinguism, as the presence of the discourse of the master. Translating a text which so deeply points to the repressive aspect of cultural translation can be daunting; but if we remember that what is condemned is translation as erasure of the language of departure, the producer of the English version can ensure that, at least, traces of that language be left in the text. In this case, since the translators of *Mirza* were both French, moving from their mother-tongue into the foreign language, their translation is inevitably marked by Gallicisms, which are not signs of linguistic weakness, but a reminder to the reader that *Ourika* is a translation of a French text, which far from being absent, is but a few pages away. The fact that a French text is translated into English by French natives contributes to providing a shift in the balance of cultural power since their version of *Ourika* is then partially dependent on their identification with the culture of departure rather than with the dominant values of American culture.[36]

Similarly texts strongly marked by race and gender would probably need to be translated by people who are concerned by these issues. That is not to say that only a woman can translate a woman author, or that only a person of color can translate an author of the same color, but that a translator aware of issues of the construction of gender and race will be better equipped to pick up in the texts the strands that are significant in terms of gender, or of race, as is the case with the translation of Gouges, Staël, and Duras.

Obviously, the conscious valorization of gender or race can better be done by translators who have a stake in it, and who can read the intertexts present in the text they translate, as Lotbinière-Harwood has demonstrated about feminist works.[37] Since this is the case, the ideological investment of the translator determines the kinds of practice the translator engages in, although ideally (or perhaps utopically) this investment should not lead to the absence of questioning of the very notions he or she seeks to promote. Thus, while the collaborators of this volume want to investigate the interrelations of gender, race, and translation, they also recognize that it is important to problematize these very notions of "gender" and "race," or at least avoid forgetting to be sensitive to other issues such as social class and nationality.

The very authors we present here lead us to include many such issues since their texts bring together all of these ideological formations—race, gender, social class, nationality—and de-essentialize them. Their female characters at times act in ways conventionally defined as manly; the authors often seem to identify with their black characters; the rigid class structure they represent is frequently questioned; they iconoclastically blur differences between French and Senegalese. In brief, their representations of race, class, gender, and nationality suggest that these are figures of difference that are essentialized as causes of differences to mask the real gap; that is a power gap. It is this gap that the translator straddles. Because of its very nature as language mediation, translation can only exist in a situation of difference, but the work of translation consists precisely in de-essentializing and recontextualizing this difference. That some translation practices attempt to erase difference, be it linguistic or cultural difference, is but an extreme example of the process of translation as the necessary inclusion of both sameness and difference. The translations presented in this volume, the critical comments, and the inclusion of the French texts are an attempt to practice translation as a coexistence of sameness and difference, as a kind of situation of "créolité" which privileges a discourse on race and gender.

Translation in Context

Doris Y. Kadish

TRANSLATING OROONOKO

The importance of translation and women's antislavery writing during the period from 1783 to 1823 needs to be situated within a broad historical context. To achieve the necessary breadth, this chapter begins and ends by stretching the boundaries of that period, at the beginning, with the example of Pierre Antoine de La Place's 1745 translation of Aphra Behn's 1696 *Oroonoko;* and, at the end, with the example of Louise Belloc's 1853 translation of Harriet Beecher Stowe's 1852 *Uncle Tom's Cabin.* Those two examples provide detailed illustrations of the ideological nature of translation, of the importance of women writers' relation to antislavery, and of the inextricable links among translation, gender, and race.

To record the trajectory from *Oroonoko* to *Uncle Tom's Cabin,* and from La Place to Belloc, is also to record a significant shift that occurred in translation theory and practice in the eighteenth and nineteenth centuries.[1] Although that shift in no way eliminates or even lessens the ideological nature of translation, it is an integral component in the historical context of the period and works under consideration in this volume. Unlike Germany, where a tradition of "faithfulness" in translation existed, other countries, especially France, adhered to the neoclassical notion of translation as a "belle infidèle" (a lovely but unfaithful woman). In the French tradition it was the accepted standard for translators to change the original substantially in order to "improve" it and enhance its beauty.[2] Indeed, changes were necessary in order to achieve the chief goals of pleasing and, concomitantly, not offending, a French audience. Adaptations, modifications, corrections, and additions for a variety of reasons were considered acceptable. When Voltaire translated the celebrated monologue from *Hamlet* in 1734 he added a denunciation of the hypocrisy of the clergy ("nos prêtres menteurs") on moral and political grounds; and when Helen Maria Williams translated Bernardin de Saint Pierre's *Paul et Virginie* in 1789 she added eight sonnets, presumably to enhance the novel's lyrical and pastoral tone, and eliminated many philosophical dialogues, on the grounds that they would be uninteresting to English readers.[3]

By the time in the middle of the nineteenth century of Belloc's very close and careful translation of *Uncle Tom's Cabin,* containing no major adaptations or modifications, a shift in thinking about translation had occurred. Fundamental to that shift was a newly developed belief, which the various women writers, translators, and abolitionists discussed in this chapter played a significant role in developing and implementing, that national and racial particularities needed to be acknowledged through translation and other forms of cultural mediation. Acknowledging those particularities required shifting the focus of translation to the source-language text and culture and away from the earlier, more exclusive focus on the conventions and expectations of the target-language society. As this chapter attempts to show, women writers and translators played a role in implementing that shift and even in articulating its principal bases, as is clear in Staël's 1816 essay "The Spirit of Translations," discussed and translated later in this volume.

A number of lessons about the workings of translation can be learned from looking closely now at La Place's translation of Behn's *Oroonoko.* To begin with, the substantial changes that La Place made help to put the concept of "fidelity" into an instructive historical perspective, reminding us that standards for what constitutes a legitimate translation vary over time. As noted above, in La Place's time, it was the accepted standard for translators to change the original substantially. Summing up the attitude of his time, La Place states in the preface to *Oroonoko* (spelled *Oronoko* in his translation),

> My intention was not to produce a literal translation, nor to adhere scrupulously to my author's text. *Oronoko* was popular in London dressed in English clothes. To be popular in Paris, I believed that it needed French attire. This way of translating works of pure entertainment may well be the best.

La Place explains that many changes were necessary to preserve "good taste," and he expresses his wish that the enjoyment thus procured for his refined readers will compensate for "what may be lacking in terms of precision."[4] Although readers today may be tempted to think of the French *Oronoko* more as an adaptation than a translation, eighteenth-century readers accepted it as a translation, La Place's substantial additions and deletions notwithstanding.[5]

Oroonoko and La Place's translation also provide a useful lesson about the need to give serious attention to literary translation and women's writing, both of which have been frequently marginalized in French literary and historical studies. Such marginalization is especially surprising in the case of *Oroonoko,* whose importance in France has been recognized by a few literary historians. Stressing the central role in French eighteenth-century literature and thought played by the seven immensely popular editions of *Oroonoko* in translation, Seeber explains that

> in this early English novel we can find the substance and technique of much of the *littérature négrophile* of the eighteenth century, a period when the Negro emerges from his despised condition and takes on heroic qualities and possibilities. . . . [T]his English story, of which the purpose might well have been didactic, written by "the first literary abolitionist . . . on record in the history of fiction," as Swinburne called Mrs. Behn, was to have far-reaching consequences in French humanitarian thought. . . . Thus did a strong current of English abolitionist thought pass into France three years before Montesquieu published in his *Esprit des lois* the first formal and concise arraignment of slavery in the French language.

Seeber goes on to observe that *Oroonoko* was among the most widely read English novels in France in the middle of the eighteenth century, exceeded in popularity only by Richardson's and Fielding's novels; and that its popularity even exceeded that of most celebrated French novels of the time.[6] Citing Seeber, Philippe Van Tieghem even claims that this book was "largely the cause of the suppression of slavery in 1794,"[7] a claim that forms a curious echo of similar claims often made about *Uncle Tom's Cabin.* One is surprised to note, then, that French literary historians often fail to acknowledge fully Behn's role, focusing instead on male writers—Jean-François Saint-Lambert, Victor Hugo, Prosper Mérimée[8]—who extended the vogue of stories about African slaves that she launched.[9] And although Behn's work unquestionably contains strong ambivalences and ambiguities regarding slavery, as Ferguson has demonstrated,[10] it also contains a select but significant number of abolitionist and resistent elements which are typically not found in the works of those male writers. Readers are thus often left with the impression that most writing about slavery by Europeans was negative, if not altogether racist. This volume attempts to correct that impression by showing, starting with Behn, the existence of a more positive and emancipatory intertextual tradition of women writing about slaves.

Further marginalization and devalorization of this tradition of women's writing and of important works in translation such as La Place's occurs among critics who, failing to adequately relativize or contextualize their aesthetic judgments about works of literature, often relegate translations and works about gender and race to an inferior position. Thus, for example, Jürgen von Stackelberg fails to come to grips with the abolitionist thrust of either Behn's or La Place's texts by essentially dismissing Behn's achievement altogether. He describes *Oroonoko* derisively at one point as "an English text that generates disorder on all sides, that is constructed without rules or taste, and that notwithstanding the existence of certain narrative elements is overwhelmed by exoticism," and he speaks dismissively of the "legend of the revolutionary importance attributed to this novel."[11] Along similar lines, William B. Cohen asserts that, "[w]hile not often depicted in the first-rate literature of the nineteenth century, the black man and the African continent were more wont to be the subject of second-and even rather third-rate literature," which he further characterizes as "often mediocre works by unoriginal writers."[12] Although Cohen acknowledges that these works have historical importance, he still indirectly affirms the existence and superiority of certain presumably fixed, universal aesthetic criteria. The application of those criteria often has the deleterious effect of placing works about gender and race, works by women, and literary translations outside of the mainstream of literary history. The criteria for what constitutes "first-rate" literature need to be reexamined to include not only narrowly aesthetic standards but broadly cultural, historical, and political criteria as well.

Further lessons to be learned from *Oroonoko* and La Place's translation concern the ideological aspect of translation and the close connection between gender and race to which translators need to pay special attention. Because La Place's translation mediates so visibly the treatment of gender and race in Behn's novel, his translation serves to illustrate, writ large as it were, the profoundly ideological nature of translation, as a brief summary of the plot and the major differences between Behn's and La Place's texts can serve now to illustrate.

The major difference in the first half of the novel is that when Oroonoko, an African prince and the favored grandson of his country's autocratic ruler, is trained to be a brave warrior and enlightened gentleman, the general who trains him is African in Behn's work whereas he is European in La Place's. Since Oroonoko's love for the daughter of that general, Imoinda, provides the dominant romantic element in both Behn's and La Place's texts, it is clearly significant that Imoinda is a black woman in Behn's novel whereas La Place never addresses the issue of her racial identity explicitly. The second half of the novel contains numerous, substantial modifications. In both Behn's and La Place's texts, Oroonoko and Imoinda are sold into slavery, having been renamed Caesar and Clemene, and transported to the colony of Surinam. Purchased by a kindly owner, Trefry, they are reunited and, despite Trefry's willingness to liberate them, they are unable to obtain their freedom from the absent Governor, who alone has the power to authorize the emancipation of slaves. Oroonoko's desire for freedom, the dominant plot line in Behn's novel, competes in La Place's translation with romantic subplots introduced through page-long digressions concerning other contenders for Imoinda's affections. In those digressions La Place departs from the abolitionist logic of Behn's novel to create scenes of jealousy, confession, and outraged honor in the French seventeenth-century style of Corneille or Mme de La Fayette. The most substantial differences occur at the end. In Behn's text, as the time approaches for Imoinda to give birth to a child, Oroonoko becomes desperate that he has failed to obtain his freedom and chooses to kill his beloved wife rather than see her and their child continue to live in slavery. This violent and relatively precipitous conclusion to Behn's novel is changed to a happy and very long, drawn out concatenation of events in La Place's translation, the result of which is that both slaves and their child eventually return to their African homeland, where Oroonoko assumes his rightful place as king. (An American translation of *Paul et Virginie* in 1824 similarly gave that novel a happy, and in that case an abolitionist ending as well, by inventing a black slave, the son of a king, who saves Virginie and then gains his freedom by this proof of heroism.)[13] A major part of the ending in La Place's text consists of some twenty-five pages in which Imoinda recounts her version of the concluding drama.

These substantial differences between Behn's and La Place's texts can be accounted for, up to a point, in terms of literary and linguistic conventions, as a number of translation critics have demonstrated,[14] but without emphasizing the important extent to which those conventions feed into and become inextricably linked with ideology. At issue specifically in the case of Behn's and La Place's texts is the systematic application of French neoclassical conventions, which resulted in La Place's edulcorating an English work that a French eighteenth-century audience would have found excessively direct, descriptive, and violent. Consider for example the opening lines of the address made by Oroonoko (aka Caesar) to his fellow slaves:

> Caesar, having singled out these men from the women and children, made an harangue to them, of the miseries and ignominies of slavery; counting up all their toils and sufferings, under such loads, burdens and drudgeries, as were fitter for beasts than men; senseless brutes, than human souls. He told them, it was not for days, months or years, but for eternity; there was no end to be of their misfortunes. . . .

La Place provides the following translation of this passage:

> César, ayant trouvé le moyen de tirer les hommes à l'écart, tandis que les femmes et les enfants continuaient à se réjouir, leur fit un discours touchant, sur la misère, et l'ignorance de leur condition. Il leur repré-senta, avec les couleurs les plus vives, les travaux attachés à l'esclavage: Espèce de travaux, ajouta-t-il, plus convenables à des bêtes, qu'à des hommes! Encore, criait-il avec feu, si c'était pour quelques jours, pour quelques mois, pour quelques années mêmes? . . . Mais c'est pour toujours![15]

To mention just a few of the ways in which La Place softens and attenuates the abolitionist thrust of Behn's text, as he does consistently throughout his translation, he translates "harangue" as "discours tou-chant," a less political and more sentimental choice of expressions; and he renders with the single, ideologically neutral term of "les travaux" (work) what in the original appears as the highly charged repetition of such terms as "toils, sufferings, loads, burdens, and drudgeries." Structural or stylistic features of translation thus assume ideological content in their application.

It must also be pointed out that the rest of Oroonoko's address to the slaves is left out altogether. In the section that is omitted, Oroonoko reproaches the slaves for putting up with their condition,

> like dogs, that loved the whip and bell, and fawned the more they were beaten . . . and were become insensible asses, fit only to bear: nay, worse; an ass, or dog, or horse, having done his duty, could lie down in retreat, and rise to work again, and while he did his duty, endured no stripes; but men, villanous, senseless men, such as they, toiled on all the tedious week . . . and then, whether they were faulty or meriting, they, promis-cuously, the innocent with the guilty, suffered the infamous whip, the sordid stripes, from their fellow-slaves, 'till their blood trickled from all parts of their body; blood, whose every drop ought to be revenged with a life of some of those tyrants that impose it. (B, 190–91)

This passage that La Place omits is characterized by a number of features of Behn's work that neoclassical style eschewed: highly concrete language (whip and bell, dogs, asses, horses) as well as violent and indelicate expressions (stripes, blood trickled from all parts of their body). Style functions ideologically in translation here. With respect to political content too, La Place unquestionably weakens the abolitionism of the original by omitting some of the accusations leveled against slave owners in this passage and, most notably, the cry for revenge at the end.

A similar ideological process involving both style and content applies to La Place's far less direct or concrete treatment of African women, one of the ways in which the translation differs most markedly from the original. As noted earlier, Imoinda is changed from a black woman in Behn's novel to a woman of indeterminate race in La Place's translation; and to a certain extent this change may reflect a characteristically neoclassical unwillingness to deal openly with issues of race. Accordingly, as Léon-François Hoffman has perceptively observed, the translation fails to translate the reference to color in such descriptions of Imoinda in the original as "the beautiful black Venus" and "the most charming black" (B, 137, 171) by omitting those passages altogether. In other instances, such passages are translated but modified so that color is not an issue. Thus the phrase "he was infinitely surprized at the beauty of this fair queen of night" (B, 137) is translated as "il fut vivement frappé de sa beauté" (LP, 1, 22). La Place also omits the kind of detailed physical descriptions of Africans generally and Imoinda as an African woman especially that are so unique in Behn's work. On one occasion, for example, Behn describes Imoinda's body as "being carved in fine flowers and birds"; and she goes on to explain:

> I had forgot to tell you, that those who are nobly born of that country, are so delicately cut and raised all over the fore-part of the trunk of their bodies, that it looks as if it were japanned, the works being raised like high point round the edges of the flowers. (B, 174)

That a European woman writer chose to dwell, albeit imaginatively, on the physical beauty of an African woman in this truly amazing description, for which there are few if any precedents, suggests a sympathetic response between women that is an important ingredient in the abolitionist meaning of Behn's novel. *Oroonoko* can even be imagined as a translation of a text by a black woman in the sense of an attempt on Behn's part to give voice to a feminine presence that was silenced at that historical moment. A similar kind of translation can be imagined with Duras's *Ourika*, a work written by a woman like Behn who, having lived in the colonies, was perhaps especially attuned to hearing the Other's voice.

The profoundly ideological aspect of translating *Oroonoko* observed above leads to a number of conclusions that will have significance throughout the pages of this volume. The first is that it is necessary to judge literary works and literary translation from the past according to the criteria of their time, not only our own. Hoffman rightly observes that La Place's changes reflect the slower development of abolitionism in France than in England; and he concludes that if La Place diminished the abolitionist force of the original, "we should undoubtedly not blame him for it, for he was obliged to submit to the taste of his time." In a similar vein, Laura Brown observes that "even though Behn can see colonialism only in the mirror of her own culture, that occluded vision has a critical dimension,"[16] as of course does La Place's translation, which captures the critical image of Behn's work in the mirror of eighteenth-century French culture. In contrast with Hoffman and Brown, however, Stackelberg downplays the abolitionism of both Behn and La Place by judging them according to twentieth-century standards. It is true, as Stackelberg points out, that Behn views Oroonoko's color as detracting from his otherwise uniformly beautiful European appearance; and that by describing his willingness to trade slaves for his release she points the finger at African complicity in the European slave trade.[17] What Stackelberg fails to appreciate fully, however, is that Behn's adherence to the ideological values of her time, even ones that to us today may seem offensively Eurocentric, does not obviate her abolitionism according to seventeenth- or eighteenth-century standards. Brown rightly explains that,

> The obvious mystification involved in Behn's depiction of Oroonoko as a European aristocrat in blackface does not necessarily damage the novella's emancipationist reputation: precisely this kind of sentimental identification was in fact the staple component of antislavery narratives for the next century and a half, in England and America.[18]

To fail to acknowledge the emancipationist significance of *Oroonoko*, in the original and in translation, is tantamount to blurring the distinction between pro and antislavery writers and to diminishing the literary and historical significance of contributions made by women writers and by literary translators to the antislavery movement.

A second conclusion is that it is essential that translators, and of course critics and general readers as well, not lose sight of the vital connections between gender and race. Brown indicates a number of bases of this connection, claiming, indeed, that "*Oroonoko* can serve as a theoretical test case for the necessary connection of race and gender"; and she goes on to explain that the two are connected in *Oroonoko* among other ways through Behn's treatment of race according to the generic conventions of French heroic romance, conventions developed by seventeenth-century women writers such as Mlle de Scudéry and produced largely for a feminine aristocratic audience.

> Behn's novellas, like other English prose works of the Restoration and early eighteenth century, draw extensively upon this French material, and the foregrounding of female authorship in *Oroonoko* through the explicit interventions of the female narrator signals the prevalent feminization of the genre.[19]

Significantly, in a recently published novel, Caryl Phillips's *Cambridge,* about nineteenth-century slavery in the English West Indies, the black author chooses to tap into the strongly feminine tradition that marks *Oroonoko* and other abolitionist novels of the past by creating two narrative voices, one that of a European woman and the other that of a male slave.[20] Such an understanding of the close connection in literary history between gender and race is similarly reflected in La Place's addition of Imoinda's story at the end of his translation. Like the authors of *Oroonoko* and *Cambridge,* La Place used the non-dominant voice of a woman to double and reinforce the similarly non-dominant voice of a slave. The fact that such close connections between gender and race have existed historically is clearly not understood by Stackelberg, who draws only negative conclusions about La Place's choice to tap into the intertextual tradition of the French heroic romance. Thus, he is dismayed that "the translator integrates the English text into the narrative tradition of his country and makes Mrs. Behn into a Mlle de Scudéry!"; and he blames La Place for having "pushed gallantry to the limit" by elevating the status of women in the novel, letting Imoinda speak far more in his translation than she does in the original text.[21]

Gender and race in *Oroonoko* are connected in other ways that translators and translation critics need to appreciate. Admitting that "the treatment of slavery in *Oroonoko* is neither coherent nor fully critical," although still distinctly emancipationist for its time, Brown explains that Behn's novel operated both within the feminized aristocratic code of heroic romance and within the similarly feminized bourgeois code of imperialism, in which women were imagined to be the chief beneficiaries of colonial commerce: "Dressed in the products of imperialist accumulation, women are, by metonymy identified . . . with the whole fascinating enterprise of trade itself."[22] It is not enough simply to point out, as does Stackelberg, that aristocratic allegiances are evident in Behn's novel. Dismayed that "this novel by a Tory sympathizer displays a thoroughly aristocratic plot,"[23] Stackelberg adduces such traces of aristocracy as further evidence against Behn's abolitionism. Brown provides a far more nuanced and illuminating explanation of the relevance of class for *Oroonoko*. She enables us to see that because Behn's class allegiances are complex and subject to conflict, and because they intersect with her emancipatory attitudes toward gender and race, *Oroonoko* creates a site—a perspective and a conceptual framework—from which the author can call colonialism into question and resist the forces of opposition. Brown explains the creation of that site in terms of the special role that Behn grants to women:

> But though they have no independent place to stand in, in their media-tory role between heroic romance and mercantile imperialism, they anchor the interaction of these two otherwise incompatible discourses. They make possible the superimposition of aristocratic and bourgeois systems—the ideological contradiction that dominates the novella. And in that contradiction we can locate . . . a point of critique and sympathy produced by the radical contemporaneity of issues of gender with those of romance and race.[24]

It is clearly not only possible, but absolutely essential, to develop an approach to translation that strives to integrate the multifarious forces of gender, race, and class as well as the broad range of linguistic, literary, and historical determinants that come into play in works such as Behn's and La Place's. It is also essential in both the analysis and the translation of the antislavery literature produced by women to explore the numerous links connecting women and slaves. As Brown observes in her concluding remarks, it is enlightening to juxtapose "the figure of the woman—ideological implement of a colonialist cul-ture—with the figure of the slave—economic implement of the same system." She adds, "Though Behn never clearly sees herself in the place of the African slave, the mediation of the figure of the woman between the two contradictory paradigms upon which her narrative depends uncovers a mutuality beyond her conscious control."[25] A cen-tury after *Oroonoko*, French women will see themselves very clearly "in the place of the African slave" and will push the mutuality between women and slaves to new emancipatory lengths.

TRANSLATING ANTISLAVERY, 1783–1823

The survey of the period from 1783 to 1823 provided in this section is intended to supply the historical background necessary for under-standing the specific topics and allusions that will be encountered later in the translations and analyses of the writings of Olympe de Gouges, Germaine de Staël, and Claire de Duras. In addition, this historical survey situates translation as one kind of mediation within a broad spectrum of mediating linguistic and political activities, the purpose of which is to bring about communication or compromise between disparate social groups. This period from 1783 to 1823, during which linguistic and political mediation played such a noteworthy role, can be divided into two abolitionist phases and illustrated through the activities of the women writers translated in this volume. During the first phase, from 1783 to 1799, abolitionist activities were visible and direct, as can be seen by looking generally at the wide variety of political and literary activities that occurred at that time, including the diverse endeavors that Gouges undertook in the political and literary arenas. During the second phase, from 1800 to 1823, abolitionist activities were more limited and sporadic, as examples from that period illustrate, including pertinent writings by Staël and Duras. During both phases, however, women writers typically joined with other liberal writers and thinkers in adopting what we would today consider a moderate, reformist position that failed to call into question the economic infrastructure underlying the system of slavery. They argued, instead, that the amelioration of the slaves' lot was compatible with the preservation of European commercial interests, and they avoided addressing the issue of eventual emancipation. Acts of linguistic and political mediation functioned during both phases to affirm and advance that moderate position.

In order to appreciate fully women writers' activities as linguistic and political mediators during the first phase, it is important to take note of the exceptionally important role played at that time by the type of mediation that is of most concern to us in this volume, translation. Translation's significance at the time represents the culmination of several decades during which French Enlightenment works that denounced the abuses of slavery were translated into English to further abolitionist causes in Britain and America. This period coincides with the shift in translation practice noted earlier whereby national and racial particularities began to be taken seriously, and translators refrained, especially in political and philosophical works, from the kinds of modifications that occurred in *Oronoko* and other neoclassical literary translations in the eighteenth century. Early French works that had a decisive impact when translated into English include the Baron de Montesquieu's 1748 *L'esprit des lois*, translated into English as *The Spirit of the Laws* in 1751, and the Abbé Raynal's *Histoire des deux Indes* [*History of the Two Indies*], which was first published in 1770 and then subsequently reprinted in thirty-eight French and eighteen English editions during the following decades.[26] These and other works from the French Enlightenment attacked the cruelty and injustice of slavery, warned of such dangers as desertion [*marronage*] or revolt by slaves, and pleaded for more enlightened colonial policies and enforcement of the *Code noir,* instituted in 1685 under Louis XIV to assure humane treatment of slaves but never strictly observed. Although Raynal's work does on occasion address the need for the eventual abolition of slavery and even, in later editions, calls for violent revolt led by a black leader, for the most part his and other works of this period take the moderate, reformist position adhered to by Gouges, Staël, Duras, and other liberal writers whereby an amelioration of the slaves' lot and preservation of European commercial interests were viewed as feasible and compatible goals. Translation from French into English and from English into French of works that adopted this position contributed substantially to setting the tone and the objectives of eighteenth- and nineteenth-century abolitionism in France, England, and the United States.

The importance of translation for the abolitionist cause continued to be acknowledged during the revolutionary period itself. Translations of works that would further the agenda of antislavery, widely acknowledged among abolitionists to be an international cause that transcended narrow national interests, were actively sponsored by abolitionist societies in Paris, London, Philadelphia, and elsewhere, including the French Société des Amis des Noirs, which was founded in 1788 by Brissot de Warville and whose other leaders included the Marquis de Condorcet and the Abbé Grégoire. The Amis des Noirs were responsible for obtaining translations of key works by such English abolitionists as Thomas Clarkson, whose *Essay on the Slavery and Commerce of the Human Species,* published in England in 1786, was translated by Gramagnac and published in French in 1789.[27] Seeber records that "[i]mmediately after the organizing of the Amis des Noirs, Brissot wrote to James Philips, a Quaker and an original member of the English abolition society, to inform him, among other things, that the new French society had decided to translate and publish English anti-slavery works"; and Seeber also provides the list of the more than thirty-five such works supplied by the Amis des Noirs.[28] To understand the importance that Staël will later attribute to translation one needs to remember that her parents, Jacques and Suzanne Necker, were members of the Amis des Noirs and that Necker's publication in 1784 of *De l'administration des finances de la France,* which expressed outrage over the fact that twenty thousand Africans were being carried away from their homeland each year and subjected to inhumane treatment during the transatlantic passage and subsequently under slavery, was one of the works that was translated into English; it appeared in England in 1787 as *Treatise on the Administration of the Finances of France*.[29] Staël's interest in translation and her concerns about slavery expressed in *Mirza*, written in 1786 and published in 1795, like the related interests and concerns of Gouges around the same time, need to be understood in the context of the importance that Staël's parents and French society of the time attributed to the wide range of related political and linguistic mediations to which translation belongs.

The importance of translation during the first phase from 1783 to 1799 is not limited to political or theoretical works such as those written by Montesquieu, Raynal, Clarkson, and Necker, however. Literary works that would further the agenda of antislavery were also of interest to abolitionists, as Seeber records: "Brissot's correspondence makes clear also the early determination of the Amis des Noirs to disseminate anti-slavery thought through literature."[30] Nor is the importance of translation during the revolutionary period limited to works produced by men. An interesting case involving a black woman translator concerns the publication in 1789 of Joseph La Vallée's novel *Le nègre comme il y a peu de blancs*, in which the enslaved Senegalese hero Itanoko epitomizes all of the virtues that eighteenth-century Europeans imagined Africans to possess. The fact that La Vallée's work, which bears many resemblances to the literary works presented in this volume, was translated by the celebrated emancipated slave Phillis Wheatley—her translation, *The Negro Equalled by Few Europeans*, appeared first in England in 1790 and in the United States in 1791, followed by other editions—indicates the importance of women as active participants in achieving abolitionist goals, including the production of literary translations. It also indicates the importance that white abolitionists and persons of color working for abolition attributed to literature, especially to the kind of literary works translated in this volume.

Olympe de Gouges provides an especially salient illustration of women's role as linguistic, cultural, and political mediator during the French Revolution. Although not a translator per se, Gouges embodies the mediating position between two cultural and linguistic groups that the translator occupies. She herself constantly had to mediate between the official use of the French language and her own regional use of Occitan. The fact that her works were typically dictated rather than written, suggests a curious parallel between Gouges and

Toussaint L'Ouverture, the black military and political leader of Santo Domingo, who also dictated speeches and statements that were rewritten and revised in standard French by secretaries.[31] To some extent, then, a comparison can be drawn between the disempowerment of the persons of color about whom she wrote and Gouges's own linguistic disempowerment as a speaker of Occitan. (The matter of Gouges's relation to language is considered more fully in the introductory essay in chapter 3.) As Vèvè Clark observes: "When the ruling French elite succeeded in diminishing the importance of a provincial language such as the *langue d'oc*, and, moreover, standardized correct speech through the offices of academies and dictionaries, they subjected the lower classes to a form of internal colonization."[32] Standing as she does between regional and official languages as well as between the language of the cultural elite and the language of the masses or the downtrodden, Gouges dramatizes what Clark identifies as the problem of "the bilingual landscape of the Revolution and the history of communication between colonials and African slaves beginning in the seventeenth century."[33] It is against the background of that bilingual landscape that Gouges's writing and thinking about gender and race need to be understood.

Gouges's literary and political activities, which will also be discussed in greater detail in chapter 3, provide a number of further indications of her role as a mediator. In literature she straddled the high culture of theater as practiced at the Comédie-Française on the one hand, a cultural domain from which women writers were typically excluded, and the popular culture of pamphlets, speeches, and melodrama on the other hand, whose intended audience included members of the lower classes and the downtrodden. (Curious parallels exist also between Gouges and Behn, who were among the few female dramatists of their times and were similarly imprisoned at some time. Both complained that their authority as writers was insufficiently recognized and that they were considered suspect with respect to their paternal origins and to the authenticity of their writings.) In addition to straddling these two disparate cultural domains, Gouges sought to mediate between them. While persisting in attempts to gain acceptance by those in positions of power at the Comédie-Française, a bastion of conservatism, Gouges also advocated the mediating structure of an alternative national theater that would perform works by women. More generally, as Joan Wallach Scott has explained, Gouges stands at the juncture of two conflicting cultural positions: "De Gouges at once stressed her identity with the universal human individual and her difference."[34] Gouges's literary works consistently bespeak the desire to reconcile high and low, conservative and radical, masculine and feminine, universal and particular.

Gouges sought the same kind of reconciliation, compromise, and mediation in the political realm as in the linguistic and literary arenas. She was an ardent abolitionist. Not surprisingly, then, she was the only woman among the seventy French writers and political figures that Grégoire named in his 1808 *De la littérature des nègres,* translated in 1810 as *An Enquiry concerning the Intellectual and Moral Faculties and Literature of Negroes,* which he dedicated to "all the courageous men who have pleaded the cause of the unfortunate blacks."[35] She was not, however, a political extremist. On the contrary, her moderate Girondin politics, which she shared with Brissot and the other Amis des Noirs, placed her between the right-wing proponents of the ancien régime and colonialism who gathered at the Club Massiac and the left-wing, Jacobin proponents of radical change and republican government. Those on the far right viewed her as one of the rabble-rousers responsible for the violent events in Santo Domingo in 1791 when rebellious slaves took the lives and destroyed the property of white planters. Members of the Club Massiac denounced and attacked her, unconvinced by her protestations that her writings about slavery were intended, as she states in the preface to *L'esclavage des noirs,* to preserve for the colonists "their properties and their most cherished interests." The fact that the hero of her play is a black man who kills a white man and is ultimately exonerated for his crime surely did not sit well with her critics on the right. Those on the far left found her politics equally offensive, however, because of her unwavering monarchism, which she retained until the end, when she was guillotined as a counterrevolutionary in 1793. It must be remembered, however, that her monarchism was shared not only by the Third Estate generally but also by Toussaint L'Ouverture and his black followers in Santo Domingo at that time.[36] For Gouges, monarchism and antislavery were compatible, as is evident in her signing her letter to the actors at the Comédie-Française, "the most committed royalist and mortal enemy of slavery."[37] (That she similarly saw monarchism and feminism as compatible is evident in her dedicating her celebrated *Déclaration des droits de la femme* to the queen.) Unlike members of the far left, moreover, she rejected and denounced violence in all its forms, whether in France under the Terror or in Santo Domingo during the slave revolts. Above all, she differed profoundly from Marat or from Robespierre and other Jacobins who contributed to widening the rifts among the various factions on the left and who failed to adhere unanimously or consistently to an antislavery position. Her great dream, in contrast, was reconciliation of difference, compromise, and mediation, a dream in which the end to the oppression of slaves was a primary and recurrent component.

Politically there is much common ground between Gouges's *L'esclavage des noirs* and Staël's *Mirza*. In these works both authors seek to resolve the problem of slavery by proposing compromise solutions, which they saw as successfully mediating the differences between the colonizers and the colonized, but which today seem fraught with contradictions. Both women writers deplore the abuses of slavery, and both seek to discover nonviolent solutions to improve the lot of slaves, while cautiously refraining from calling for any radical measures that would jeopardize the economic interests of planters in the immediate future. Gouges offers such moderate, reformist proposals as providing instruction for slaves; promoting kindness and generosity on the part of colonists; and relying on faith, hope, and love. Staël is more concrete in favoring a proposal developed by Dupont de Nemours and others, and articulated by literary figures such as Bernardin de Saint-Pierre, La Vallée, and Saint-Lambert, whereby the use of slaves in the West Indies would be gradually rendered unnecessary by teaching Africans to cultivate sugar and engage in free trade themselves.[38] To us today it, of course, seems contradictory to wish to empower blacks economically while at the same time wishing to preserve the planters' economic interests, but moderates at the time believed that such apparent contradictions would disappear with time. (Numerous contradictions can also be discovered in Staël's life: in 1791 her guests included such members of the Amis des Noirs as Condorcet and Brissot as well as such spokesmen for the Club Massiac as Barnave and the Lameth brothers, whom she helped save in 1792, she also helped save her lover Narbonne, whose fortune derived from his wife's sugar plantations in the West Indies;[39] and she herself was given a slave, baptized as Robert Jean Marie Chaumont.)[40] Further contradictions in Gouges's and Staël's works derive from the authors' firm belief in the benevolent influence and mediating function of the patriarchal figures of fathers, governors, and above all the king. Although Gouges's and Staël's belief in the necessity for patriarchal authority may seem to us today to contradict their belief in the necessity for racial or sexual equality, both sets of beliefs tended to prevail among French abolitionists until the execution of Louis XVI in 1793 and the dramatic events that occurred subsequently during the Terror and the Directory, when abolitionism as an active movement virtually disappeared. Clearly the moderate, mediating solutions envisioned by

Gouges, Staël, and others early in the revolutionary period were inadequate, ineffectual, and probably premature; it is not clear that they had any real effect on the eventual abolition of the slave trade or slavery. The same is true, however, of the more radical solution, the abolition of slavery, which occurred in 1794 but was revoked by Napoleon in 1802. Neither moderate nor radical solutions were adequate to resolving the problem of slavery, which would only be resolved many decades later in the nineteenth century.

To look now at the second phase of our history—from 1800 to 1823—is to look at a period that held far fewer opportunities for the kinds of mediation that flourished during the revolutionary period. Although antislavery opinion continued to exist, it was largely silenced under repressive, proslavery governments. Quoting Chateaubriand's famous statement in *Le génie du christianisme*—"who would still dare to plead the cause of blacks after the crimes they have committed?"[41]—Seeber reminds us that this statement

> by no means belies his sympathy for the negro so clearly expressed in this work and in *Les Natchez*. It is symptomatic, rather, of the decline of overt opposition to slavery during the decade and a half following 1802, when slavery was reinstated by Bonaparte as a supposedly necessary adjunct to his vigorous colonial program. . . . Neither does the citation from *Le Génie du christianisme* reflect a general condemnation of the excesses committed by the revolted Santo Domingan slaves. On the contrary, the rebel leader Toussaint Louverture was regarded as a sort of glamorous hero, the incarnation of the numerous literary progeny of Oroonoko. . . .[42]

Authors were reluctant to plead "the cause of blacks" overtly. But many enlightened individuals continued to believe in the necessity of doing away with the slave trade and eventually slavery itself. That Staël sustained that belief to the end is evident in her *Considérations sur la révolution française,* written in 1816 and published posthumously in 1818, in which she evokes her heartfelt commitment to freedom for slaves in the closing paragraph. In that work she responds to Chateaubriand by comparing the black slaves in Santo Domingo to the French people during the Terror, stating that if the former "committed more atrocities, it was because they had been oppressed more."[43]

Although frequently only covert or sporadic, the work of mediating the competing interests of antislavery and proslavery factions did continue during the period from 1799 to 1823, however, and translation, both from French into English and vice versa, continued to constitute an important component of that work. Its chief impetus was what David Turley has called "internationalizing the argument,"[44] that is, using the arguments or achievements of one country to further the abolitionist goals of another. The most notable achievement, which was emphasized by the few French abolitionists such as Grégoire and Staël who spoke out publicly during the Napoleonic era, was the abolition of the slave trade in England in 1806 and in the United States the following year. In his 1808 *De la littérature des nègres*, Grégoire deplores France's failure to follow the English and American example and draws his French audience's attention to some of the noteworthy antislavery arguments that had been set forth by abolitionists in England. His role, then, resembles that of the translator, who similarly transposes ideas originating in one culture and makes them available to readers in another culture. The translation of Grégoire's work into English further extends the same process whereby abolitionists in England and especially America drew upon and disseminated the arguments developed in France and other countries. As the preface to the American translation in 1810 makes clear, the translator's intention is to use the compelling case that Grégoire makes to demonstrate the intelligence and intellectual achievement of Negroes in order to move beyond the abolition of the slave trade in England and to achieve the goals of "universal emancipation."[45]

Internationalizing the antislavery argument necessitated various kinds of mediations, as can be seen in the translations in this volume of the two short works written by Staël in 1814. In those works she strives to mediate between France and England, and between what was perceived as more radical French liberal thought and more moderate English abolitionism, urging broad general support among the French for the English example. The key figure in her mediating efforts was Wilberforce, whom she described as "the most beloved and respected man in all of England" and to whom she wrote that "no purer glory has ever been given to any man."[46] Such elevated praise needs to be understood in the context of the opinion voiced by Chateaubriand and undoubtedly held by Staël and others during the historical phase from 1800 to 1823 that France possessed no leader who, like Wilberforce, was free of association with the radical, Jacobin politics of the 1790s, an association that for most of the French marred the earlier abolitionist activities of the Amis des Noirs. Chateaubriand wrote that "the principal defender of abolition among us is a regicide," presumably referring to Grégoire's failure to oppose the execution of Louis XVI in 1793 by absenting himself at the time of the vote.[47]

Staël's efforts at mediating between France and England, and between French and English attitudes toward abolition, is apparent in the "Préface pour la traduction d'un ouvrage de M. Wiberforce sur la traite des nègres." In this short work Staël presents to the French public Wilberforce's 1807 *A Letter on the Abolition of the Slave Trade, addressed to the freeholders and other inhabitants of Yorkshire,* a work which "consolidated and summarised all the arguments that the Abolitionists had been using since they began their crusade."[48] In her preface she calls attention to such other prominent English legislators as William Pitt and Charles Fox who, like Wilberforce, were instrumental in achieving the abolition of the slave trade in England, as well as to the writings and efforts of such other major English abolitionists as Clarkson and Thomas Macaulay. She also counters the argument that the English motive in pushing for international abolition of the slave trade is to weaken France and enhance England's own economic position. Staël views England as "the richest and most fortunate nation in the universe," a country where "enlightenment is so widespread, and the circulation of ideas so free" that the pursuit of truth and justice regarding slavery can be wholly disinterested. And if it is true that most historians today would view such anglophile views as excessive and would accept David Brion Davis's argument that both economic and humanitarian factors motivated the British in seeking to obtain the abolition of the slave trade by the French and other European countries,[49] it is also true that many enlightened French thinkers in Staël's time shared her view of England as a model that could serve to help develop an acceptable compromise between the opposing pro-slavery and antislavery factions in France.

Staël's mediating efforts in the two short works from 1814 also have a certain number of specific goals. One is to influence the newly restored king Louis XVIII—"a monarch enlightened by religion"—and convince him to abandon the negrophobic policies of Napoleon, whom she calls "the oppressor who lay like a pall over the human race." Another goal, as indicated in the title "Appel aux souverains réunis à Paris pour en obtenir l'abolition de la traite des nègres," is to influence other European leaders to join with France in following England's example of abolishing the slave trade. Her other goals were to influence public opinion and to enlist Talleyrand's and Wellington's support for getting a measure to abolish the slave trade internationally passed at the Congress of Vienna.[50] Other efforts to influence political leaders and French opinion about slavery were widespread in England at the time. As Davis explains, "In 1814 the country was alive with public meetings; hundreds of petitions demanded the universal abolition of the slave trade. Reformers appealed to the humanitarian sentiments of the pope, the czar of Russia, and of the treaty-making dignitaries of Europe."[51] These efforts in England, which were taking place already during Staël's stay in London in 1813 when she encountered Wilberforce, met with mixed success. Ironically, it was Napoleon who, after his downfall, abolished the slave trade during his hundred days in 1815 in an attempt to gain British support. Although that abolition was maintained by the restored Bourbon monarchy following the Congress of Vienna in 1815, no provisions for enforcement were made, and it was only effectively eliminated in France after 1830.

There were other important arenas for Staël's activities as a political, cultural, and linguistic mediator. As her descendant Mme de Pange writes in 1934, Staël's contributions to abolition in France were intricately related to her opposition to Napoleon in general and to his negrophobic policies in particular. Pange writes: "In 1803 . . . she emerged definitively as Bonaparte's adversary. Under the Consulate her salon soon became the center of the liberal opposition and of overt war against the First Consul."[52] Pange thus underlines one of the chief vehicles for mediation in Staël's time, the salon. As historians have observed, the salon enabled women to mediate between the public and private spheres, between diverse social classes, and between men and women. Although not engaged directly themselves in policy-making activities, women often influenced and helped form those activities in the salon. By today's standards influential women like Staël may seem to stand on the sidelines of history; but their effect on society generally and the history of antislavery specifically should not be underestimated. Consider the case mentioned earlier of Abbé Raynal's call for a black leader in the highly influential *Histoire des deux Indes,* which, according to James, had a direct impact on the course of history when "it came into the hands of the slave most fitted to make use of it, Toussaint L'Ouverture."[53] Regarding women's role in relation to antislavery, it is enlightening to learn that Raynal's work is considered to have been composed collectively in the salon, where women, writers, and philosophers joined together to exchange ideas, letters, manuscripts, and a variety of other intellectual and political materials; and to learn, moreover, that "he wrote his book in the Necker salon, according to those he spoke to at the time."[54]

In addition to the salon, the family served an important mediating function in relation to abolitionism. As Turley explains, antislavery was "a cultural response to change," not just a series of written documents or legislative actions.[55] It was a cultural response created together by men and women, especially within Protestant families and social circles, over several generations. Staël's family provides a striking example. As noted earlier, her father Jacques Necker and her mother Suzanne Curchod Necker were members of the Amis des Noirs. Moreover, Necker spoke out publicly against the abuses of slavery and addressed those abuses in his published works beginning in 1784, before Wilberforce's antislavery campaign in England; and, indeed, in his first speech to the British Parliament Wilberforce invoked Necker's testimony.[56] Staël's own efforts were later followed by those of her son and the members of her immediate circle. Hugh Honour contends that

> there can be little doubt that she influenced if she did not form the abolitionist sentiments of her son-in-law the duc de Broglie, her onetime lover Benjamin Constant, and her admirer Sismondi as well as her son Auguste who was similarly a spokesman for the Société de la Morale Chrétienne.[57]

Auguste de Staël worked actively with that Société, which was founded in 1821 to militate for the suppression of the slave trade. Up until the moment of his untimely death in 1827, he also conducted an extensive letter writing campaign, travelled, published pamphlets, gave lectures, brought to the attention of the public instruments of torture used by slave traders, and even spoke directly to the king regarding the inhumane treatment of slaves. Pange reports that, writing to his sister, he states that the issue of slavery "preoccupies me entirely. I write, I get others to write in every direction and I express my indignation to so many people that it will perhaps finally have an effect."[58] In the decades following his death, the tradition of antislavery in the Staël family was vigorously pursued in the legislative arena by Victor de Broglie, the husband of Staël's daughter Albertine, who, in turn, played her part by translating one of Wilberforce's short works on the slave trade in 1814.[59]

Ultimately, however, none of Staël's diverse activities as a political, cultural, and linguistic mediator overshadows those activities pertaining to her overriding interest in literature and literary translation, as several of the translations provided in this volume illustrate. Her treatment in *Mirza* of noble, sensitive, even poetically inspired African men and women in their native African land contributed to establishing an intertextual tradition tapped by writers during the Restoration, as is clear from Duras's adoption of the name of one of Staël's heroines, Ourika, for the protagonist of her novel. Edith Lucas even goes so far as to maintain that Staël's return to Paris in 1815 actually brought about a rebirth of negrophile literature during the Restoration.[60] Staël also made a major contribution to bridging the gap between diverse national, cultural, and political groups by promoting the study of comparative literature, most notably in her celebrated *De l'Allemagne* in 1813. The goal of the numerous translations that she provides in that work was to introduce new elements that would enrich French culture, a goal that she and her followers at Coppet pursued actively, in her case, for example, by translating Italian poems by Minzoni and Filicaja and German works by Goethe and Schiller into French.[61]

Special mention needs to made of "De l'esprit des traductions" which, as noted earlier, crystalizes many of the newer ideas about translation theory and practice developed during the course of the nineteenth century. The Italian translation by Pietro Giordani, published in January 1816 in the *Biblioteca italiana,* provoked both lively debate and hostility among Italians, some of whom were insulted by Staël's exhortation to them, as to the French in *De l'Allemagne,* to enrich their culture through translation of works from other cultures.[62] Among the important ideas expressed in "De l'esprit des traductions" is the notion that "one should not follow the French who give their own color to everything they translate," a very clear and, for the time, a very modern rejection of the kind of translation practiced by La Place and others in the eighteenth century. Staël also rejects a narrow notion of literal translation, which she claims is inadequate to producing literary meaning in anything but the most mechanical and prosaic of ways; or, in her words, "translating a poet is not like taking a compass and measuring the dimensions of a building. It is making a different instrument vibrate with the same breath of life as the one we normally hear." Indeed, to practice literal, mechanical translation is tantamount to treating language as a slave, as is clear from the recurrence in her essay of words pertaining to translation such as conquest, submission, imprisonment, and liberation. It is also clear from her repeated use of a vocabulary of commerce, profit, wealth, and value that Staël conceives of translation as an active social and economic process, as well as an active process that rejuvenates and enriches the foreign and translated literature. In numerous ways, then, translation represents for Staël the prototypical mediating activity, a paradigm of the social, economic, and cultural mediation that is central to her life and her published works.

To look at the example of Claire de Duras is to discover many of the same mediating patterns observed in the lives and works of Gouges and Staël, including translation, as will be seen later in chapter 9. She too was a moderate who upheld the monarchist, Girondin politics, for which, like Gouges, her father the Admiral de Kersaint went to the guillotine. At the same time, her life reveals many of the same kinds of contradictions found in the lives of Staël and her contemporaries: she derived her personal fortune from her mother's properties in Martinique, where Duras lived for several years and where her mother died following Kersaint's execution in 1793, Duras subsequently married a leading member of the right while continuing to adhere largely to her father's liberal politics. Similar contradictions mark Duras's literary works, although in the balance those works display largely liberal attitudes to race, gender, and class. To our eyes today *Ourika* may seem far from openly emancipationist and may, indeed, at times seem highly conservative, even reactionary, with respect to slavery—for example in the black heroine's unqualified denunciation of the revolt in Santo Domingo. Within its historical context, however, it needs to be seen as a work that sought to mediate between extreme positions on the left and right. That it was not viewed as conservative or reactionary in its time is evidenced by the fact that Duras was excoriated by the colonists, as Gouges had been in her efforts at mediation several decades earlier. *Ourika* was received very negatively in Martinique where, according to a French naval officer,

> the colonists see every newly arrived Frenchman as a negrophile, and the clever and generous author of *Ourika* is constantly accused of having succeeded in her detestable novel in making readers interested in a negress, who does not even have the advantage of being a creole negress.[63]

Such a strongly negative statement helps us to understand the historical context in which Duras attempted to mediate between proslavery and antislavery sentiments.

Duras fulfilled a further mediating function by serving as a focal point of moderate, liberal politics. Like Staël, whom she knew and admired, Duras respected and maintained the principles of her father, Kersaint, who resembled Staël's father Necker in actively promoting political reforms, denouncing social privileges, and supporting emancipatory, egalitarian principles. Duras also followed Staël's example in other ways. One was in attempting to mediate between French attitudes and the political and cultural attitudes of various other nationalities, especially the English, whom she knew well from having lived in London during the emigration. Another was in exerting her mediating influence from within the sphere of the salon, which served as an especially active center of political, social, and cultural activity during the 1820s. As G. Pailhès explains, her salon, the most influential and prestigious during the Restoration, was frequented by writers, artists, intellectuals, diplomats, nobles, and persons of all political positions.

> It was the meeting point where the old and the new France met and learned to know one another. . . . The nobility learned how to be more open there, to follow the lady of the house who, always faithful to the liberal traditions she inherited from her father as well as to the dogmas of the hereditary monarchy, set the example of how to be more conscious of the new times. . . . The duchesse of Duras's salon was naturally monarchist, but with strongly marked nuances of English constitutionalism and French liberalism. Thanks to the generous and highly literary mind of the woman who constituted its very soul, it formed a kind of neutral territory in many ways where great inequalities of fortune and opinion, of ranks and highly diverse talents, were brought together.[64]

Indeed, *Ourika* was conceived, circulated, and first exerted its mediating effect within the salon.

The chief arena for Duras's mediating activities was literature, however, and her most ambitious attempt at mediation was trying to bridge the gap between white and black in *Ourika,* which will be translated and discussed in detail in chapter 10. For now it will suffice to call attention to a number of features of this work that are especially helpful for placing it in an historical context. One is the strong and reciprocal feelings between Ourika and her benefactress, Mme de B. Rather than pitting white against black, Duras highlights the shared experiences between the two women and their concern for one another's welfare, a concern that goes counter to a number of the unfavorable practices and racial stereotypes of Duras's time. Servanne Woodward observes that Africans like Ourika were commonly acquired by aristocrats as "pets" and signs of prestige but were later unfeelingly placed in domestic service by their former benefactors.[65] It is perhaps against the backdrop of this practice that Duras chose to highlight Mme de B.'s enlightened and humanitarian behavior. It is also relevant in this context to highlight Ourika's feelings toward Mme de B. as going counter to a common stereotype of the time whereby former slaves were unreliable, ungrateful, and potentially dangerous. That stereotype was rooted in the notoriety surrounding Zamor, the "pet" belonging to Mme du Barry, the mistress of Louis XV. (Gouges's choice of Zamor as the name of her black hero may well have derived from this historical figure.) At the time of the Terror, Zamor denounced his former benefactress, and his denunciation led to her execution in 1793. He is reported to have said that "if the beautiful countess took him in and raised him, it was to make a toy out of him; she allowed him to be humiliated in her home, where he was incessantly subject to mockery and insults."[66] It is perhaps to counter the widely held racial stereotype occasioned by Zamor's behavior that Duras chose to emphasize Ourika's gratitude toward and understanding for Mme de B.

Another feature of *Ourika* that helps to place it in a historical context is Duras's sympathetic treatment of an African woman, which marks her novel as distinctly different from such other works about blacks by male authors published in the 1820s as Hugo's *Bug-Jargal* and Mérimée's *Tamango*. Whereas those works dwell consistently on stereotypically negative racial traits—violence, unrestrained or menacing sexuality, drunkenness, incompetence, willingness to sell each other into slavery—Duras's novel probes the mind and the feelings of its black heroine. Ferguson has recorded the example set by a woman writer as early as the middle of the seventeenth century of giving a voice to a black woman by projecting her reality through a white woman's text;[67] and it is this significant example of narrative and cultural mediation that Duras follows in *Ourika*. In doing so she continues but also goes beyond Gouges's and Staël's treatment of African heroines. Their African women are more abstractly idealized constructions than Ourika, inspired by an actual Senegalese girl who was raised in the lofty aristocratic home of the Maréchale de Beauvau. (Historical records even provide a trace of Ourika's own voice: Mme de Beauvau states in her memoirs that at the time of the girl's death a handwritten passage was found, bearing the words "my father and mother abandonned me, but the Lord took pity on me.")[68] By focusing on Ourika's voice and her intellectual accomplishments, Duras uses the novel to make much the same argument in the realm of fiction about the intelligence of black individuals that Grégoire made in essay form and that Wheatley made through poetry and personal testimony. And although, admittedly, Ourika is like other literary works of the eighteenth and nineteenth centuries which are, as Ferguson emphasizes, deeply embedded in Africanist discourse and values,[69] they constitute noteworthy activities by women writers that deserve to be acknowledged as part of the historical and literary record of abolitionism.

We can sum up by emphasizing that it is clearly a mistake to glorify writers such as Gouges, Staël, and Duras or to fail to acknowledge that as members of a European, privileged society their concern for slaves was inevitably fraught with contradiction, ambiguity, and ambivalence. It is also necessary to acknowledge that the abolitionist efforts which they directly or indirectly promoted may even have had negative effects. Winthrop Jordan notes that "[b]y concentrating on elimination of inhumane treatment, the humanitarian impulse helped make slavery more benevolent and paternal and hence more tolerable for the slaveowner and even for the abolitionist"; but at the same time he emphasizes that abolitionist efforts helped turn attention toward the slave trade. As Davis states, "[i]f there had been no abolitionists, the injustices of slavery, which mankind had tolerated for several millennia, would hardly have seemed a serious problem."[70] This volume will show that, in addition to those limited but significant forms of direct participation in abolitionist activities by French women writers of the revolutionary period noted above, these women used literature to call attention to that serious problem of the injustice of slavery.

TRANSLATING *UNCLE TOM'S CABIN*

The concluding example of Harriet Beecher Stowe's celebrated *Uncle Tom's Cabin*, published in March 1852, can help to reemphasize the main points developed in this chapter: that translation is profoundly ideological; that translation, gender, and race are inextricably linked in ways that translators and translation critics need to recognize; and that women writers maintained over time a special relation to anti-slavery. Specifically, this section will consider the reception and production of *Uncle Tom's Cabin* in relation to gender, a consideration which will set the stage for a comparative analysis of Louise Belloc's and Emile de La Bédollière's translations of that novel. The ideological limitations of Belloc's translation as well as the attempts made in it to resist oppression can help us as translators and translation critics to reflect upon the similar limitations and attempts that we grapple with in the present.

Literary history undoubtedly contains few more striking examples than *Uncle Tom's Cabin* of a major work that has been identified with women and that has continued to interest and inspire women critics and readers. Abraham Lincoln's celebrated remark on meeting Stowe—"So this is the little woman who made this big war"—draws attention to the feminine stamp that from her lifetime to the present time has marked the author and her work. (It also brings to mind the similarly strong claims about a woman writer's influence that have been made about Behn's novel.) Emphasizing Stowe's feminine status, John Lemoine wrote in the autumn of 1852 in the *Journal des débats* that *Uncle Tom's Cabin* "levels against the unholy institution of slavery perhaps the most severe blow it has ever received; and this blow has been struck by the hand of a woman."[71] Other accounts similarly show that at the time of its publication critics and general readers worldwide perceived the book as having special relevance or appeal to women:

> Women responded to Mrs. Stowe from all over the world—George Sand from France, Jenny Lind and Frederika Bremer from Sweden, Anna Leonowens on behalf of a Siamese court lady, impelled to free all her slaves. Queen Victoria's friend, the Duchess of Sutherland, Lady Byron, Mrs. Browning and a half million other women in Europe and the British Isles filled twenty-six folio volumes with their greetings and sig-natures—and protests against slavery—and forwarded this Affectionate and Christian Address to Mrs. Stowe.[72]

It is significant that Sand, a celebrated French woman writer and prominent humanitarian voice, not only chose to promote *Uncle Tom's Cabin* in her article about the novel that appeared in *La Presse* in December 1852, thereby contributing to its success in France, but also that she did so by emphasizing its feminine qualities. She states that "mothers, young people, children, and servants can read and under-stand" what she calls "an essentially domestic novel," going on to observe that even "superior men" will be touched by Stowe's unique descriptive and sentimental talents, which she compares to Walter Scott's and Honoré de Balzac's. Asserting the superiority of moral over aesthetic values, heart over mind, and female saints over male writers, she eulogizes her American fellow novelist by attributing to Stowe "the most maternal soul that has ever existed."[73]

Uncle Tom's Cabin stands as a striking example, furthermore, of the collaborative and overlapping efforts of women in the production, translation, and criticism of literature. Stowe's sister-in-law is credited with having urged her to write the book; and Mrs. Weston Chapman, an author and abolitionist, with assuring its translation into French by the Irish writer Louise Belloc in collaboration with Adélaïde de Montgolfier. Stowe, in praising that translation—which is distin-guished from most others in its willingness to grapple with the transla-tion of the black dialect used in the novel—called attention, as noted earlier, to the issue of feminine gender, stating: "I am convinced that a feminine mind can more easily mould itself to my own."[74] (Stowe's novel can itself be read as a translation inasmuch as it strives to trans-late black language and culture into an idiom that white readers of her time could appreciate and understand.) That women identify with Stowe's sympathetic treatment of racial and sexual others is evident from the attention that women critics have given to her work. Sand, as noted earlier, helped to assure Stowe's popularity in France, seeing in the American writer's social, humanitarian, and religious thought an echo of her own. Another especially noteworthy woman critic for our purposes here is Edith Lucas, whose *Littérature anti-esclavagiste au dix-neuvième siècle: étude sur Madame Beecher Stowe et son influence en France* provides a thorough analysis of translations of Stowe's novel. Other important critical works by women include Elizabeth Ammons "Heroines in *Uncle Tom's Cabin*," which dwells on the feminine, Christlike figures of Tom and Eva and highlights the resistant thrust of Stowe's advocacy of maternal over patriarchal values; and Jane Tompkins's "Sentimental Power: *Uncle Tom's Cabin* and the Politics of Literary History," which explores the crucial links between sentimental literature, religion, and the political empowerment of women in Stowe's novel and nineteenth-century American literature.[75]

The strong involvement or association of women with *Uncle Tom's Cabin* raises the thorny issue of the ideological implications that can be drawn from those women's attempts to deal with the issues of gender and race. Needless to say, those attempts do not always appear from a modern perspective to display sufficient sensitivity to racial issues or sufficient self-awareness of their ideological limitations.[76] Sand's essay on Stowe, for example, like many other similar nineteenth-century texts, could be accused of complacency, of allowing middle-class whites to congratulate themselves for their pity and compassion while failing to call into question the system that produced and sustained slavery. Sand wrote about Stowe in the early 1850s under Napoleon III's repressive imperial regime, which Sand chose not to oppose; and, indeed, Stowe's success in France, to which Sand contributed, can be attributed at least in part to the censorship of French works addressing social issues that existed at that time and the tolerance of discussion of such issues in foreign books.[77] Among the many objections that have been raised against *Uncle Tom's Cabin*, at least some have stemmed from a suspicion that complacency, complicity, or hypocrisy were common denominators among popular authors producing antislavery works, general readers avidly consuming those works, and figures of power in France encouraging discussion of social issues abroad yet censoring discussion of such issues at home.

The best known accusation against Stowe herself for lacking sufficient sensitivity to racial issues is undoubtedly to be found in James Baldwin's article "Everybody's Protest Novel," published in the *Partisan Review* in 1949. Baldwin is suspicious of Stowe's appeal to the emotions of her reading public. Accordingly, he states acrimoniously,

> *Uncle Tom's Cabin* is a very bad novel, having, in its self-righteous, virtuous sentimentality, much in common with *Little Women*. . . . the wet eyes

of the sentimentalist betray his aversion to experience, his fear of life, his arid heart; and it is always, therefore, the signal of secret and violent inhumanity, the mask of cruelty.[78]

Baldwin's article has the merit of challenging modern readers, critics, and translators to consider seriously the underlying complicity that Stowe and other antislavery writers may have had with those responsible for the cruelty practiced by whites against blacks during slavery. However, by labeling the sentimental literature that nineteenth- and twentieth-century women typically produced and read as categorically inferior, Baldwin repeats the kind of undervaluing of feminine genres and literary conventions noted earlier in this chapter with respect to Behn's intertextual ties to French women in the tradition of heroic romance. By addressing solely the issue of race, and by failing to see it in relation to gender, Baldwin ends up substituting, if not sexism, then gender insensitivity for racism, and he thereby ends up failing to perceive the complexity and multifariousness of resistance to oppression in nineteenth-century literature by women. Many elements of that resistance found in *Uncle Tom's Cabin* are precisely those that other antislavery writings by women also developed: emphasis on the sympathetic response between black and white women; on the voice of the other; on the mental, spiritual, or creative strengths of persons of color.

Gustave Flaubert provides another example of a male critic who applies aesthetic criteria that effectively function to dismiss the legitimacy of women's writing. In a letter to Louise Colet dated December 9, 1852, he states his negative reaction to Stowe's novel based on two closely related set of criteria. The first set, a combination of metaphysical and aesthetic considerations, serves to relegate women's writing to an inferior status because that writing is typically concerned with pragmatic concerns or domestic issues. Flaubert objects, for example, that *L'oncle Tom* is too narrow and too topical. Limited to the current situation of slavery, it fails to aspire to "eternal truth" and "pure beauty." His second set of criteria focuses on the abstract narrative principle of objectivity, a principle that, if adopted by women writers, would effectively function to silence their voices as women. Claiming to be "incessantly irritated" by Stowe's reflections about slavery, Flaubert asserts that the novel should "cancel out the author"; and he goes on to say that "the author in his work should be like God in the universe, present everywhere, and visible nowhere," and that the author should manifest "a hidden and infinite impassibility."[79] Ironically, Flaubert maintained close personal and artistic relationships with women writers such as Colet and Sand, and was writing to a woman to express these views that can be interpreted as excluding women's voices. Clearly there was a gender-based conflict between the kind of socially oriented literature that appealed to women writers and readers and his own more masculine "art for art's sake."

In turning now to an analysis of how gender and race function both as ideological limitations and as sites of resistance in translations of *Uncle Tom's Cabin,* it is important to point out the unusual facts surrounding the translation and publication of Stowe's novel in France. Due to its unprecedented popularity—in its first year alone, 120 editions and 300,000 copies in the United States; forty editions and an estimated million and a half copies in Great Britain—there was a tremendous rush to translate and publish *Uncle Tom's Cabin,* which, when it appeared, enjoyed an unprecedented success for a foreign book. Within ten months, eleven different French translations were published.[80] (A fictitious story published in the humorous periodical, *Charivari,* describes ten translators who arrive at Mrs. Stowe's hotel during her visit to Paris in 1853. Unable to speak any English, they resort to speaking to her in a black dialect of French. Puzzled and frightened, she calls the police and they end up in jail!)[81] The flurry of competing translations stirred debates over such issues as the relative merits of translating "Uncle Tom" as "l'oncle Tom" or "le père Tom," or of translating "cabin" as "case" or "cabane." Among the various translations, the one by Belloc, which, as noted earlier, was singled out for praise by Stowe herself, represents an attempt to reproduce the original text without major deletions or additions. It thus can stand as an example of the kind of translation envisioned by Staël and developed in the nineteenth century, which strives to respect national and racial particularities. An instructive contrast can be made with the first and perhaps the best known translation of *Uncle Tom's Cabin,* produced by La Bédollière and published in 1852. That translation, which dramatically shortens the novel and leaves out much of the descriptive detail in order to enhance its dramatic effect, is closer to the example examined at the beginning of this chapter of La Place's *Oronoko,* which focuses more on the translated-language text and culture than on the text and culture of the foreign language.[82]

It is a complex and difficult matter, however, to try to discover appropriate criteria for justifying the relative superiority of Belloc's full-length translation over La Bédollière's more abbreviated version, as one can see from Lucas's attempts to evaluate the various translations of Stowe's novel. Interestingly, she does not adopt the criterion of "faithfulness" as a way to justify the superiority of one translation over another. Lucas subscribes to the notion, which seems to have been shared by all of the translators, that Stowe's style could profit from stylistic corrections, and that the need for such correction would override the need to remain faithful to the original. Speaking of the translation by Alfred Michiels, Lucas states: "Mrs. Stowe's English is not even always correct. The French version is superior to the original text in distinctness and precision."[83] (The anecdote mentioned earlier also relates Stowe's having learned that her translators were coming to call and, not as yet questioning their competence in English, politely sending them a note acknowledging "that the French often improved upon the original style, and that they had a finer appreciation of the subtle shades of meaning than the English.")[84] Lucas, the translators, and in this anecdote even Stowe herself thus end up agreeing essentially with Flaubert, who complained that the success of *Uncle Tom's Cabin* was not attributable to its literary merit and who firmly adhered to the position that that there are objective criteria for judging artistic value. It is only a short step from that position to the related position that the translator should improve rather than faithfully render the original.

A countervailing position would consist of justifying the superiority of Belloc's full-length translation on the grounds that it respects and preserves distinctive features of women's writing, notably women's narrative voice and narrative traditions, rather than erasing those features in the name of such universalist aesthetic criteria as Flaubert's objectivity and narrative omniscience. And although it is true that neither Belloc nor such sympathetic women critics as Sand and Lucas articulated this position per se, it is implicit in their writings about Stowe and about translation. In her preface Belloc takes strong exception to the exclusively aesthetic criteria applied by Flaubert and others of his time, stating, "To judge this work from a purely literary point of view would in our opinion be sacrilegious" (B, viii). Belloc's conviction that women's writing such as Stowe's cannot be judged according to universalist aesthetic criteria is echoed by Sand, who demonstrates a highly modern awareness of the relativity of aesthetic values and the importance of the relativity in judging works by women writers. Sand states in this vein,

> If the best compliment that can be given to authors is liking them, the truest compliment that can be given to books is liking them for their defects. Those defects should not be shrouded in silence; discussion of them should not be avoided; and you should not be bothered when people tease you for crying naively over the fate of victims in stories about simple, true events.

Those defects only exist in relation to artistic conventions that have never been and will never be absolute. If critics who are enamored of what they call structure discover tedious passages, repetitions, awkwardness in this book, look carefully, in order to reassure yourself about your own judgment, and you will see that their eyes will not be perfectly dry when you read them a chapter taken at random.[85]

Although the issue of translation does not arise here specifically, these comments demonstrate the respect for differences based on gender that translators and translation critics need to possess. Sand's awareness that artistic conventions vary, and that women's writing does not always follow the same conventions as men's, constitutes the kind of understanding that translators and critics need to have in dealing with works like *Oroonoko* and *Uncle Tom's Cabin,* both of which have been seen to have profound ties with feminine intertextual narrative traditions. Lucas too seems to have sensed that Belloc, as a woman translator, was especially sensitive to preserving Stowe's feminine voice, echoing thus Stowe's own response. Although writing in the 1930s Lucas does not possess the awareness of ideological issues that one finds among critics today, her praise for Belloc's treatment of stylistic elements such as lively portraits, comic effects, descriptive detail, and clear style reveal her awareness of the special attention to Stowe's distinctive style and voice that characterizes Belloc's translation.

It is worth turning now to comparisons of a few passages from the original and from the translations by La Bédollière and Belloc to look at the ideological limitations as well as the resistant features of those texts. One of the most noteworthy differences involves the emphasis that both the original and Belloc's translation place on the feminine gender of the authorial voice. That emphasis begins with the author's preface, not included in La Bédollière's translation, which highlights feminine agency from the outset. Although Belloc transposes indications of gender and authorship from one paragraph to another according to the linguistic dictates of the French language, she creates an equivalent effect. In the original, for example, two successive paragraphs contain the phrases "Experience has shown *her . . .*" and "What personal knowledge *the author* has had, of the truth of incidents such as here are related, will appear in its time" (S, vi). In the translation, those two paragraphs contain the equivalent phrases *"l'auteur* le sait par expérience" and "Ce que *l'auteur* a vu et su par *elle-même* des événements racontés paraîtra en son temps" (B, xviii).

The concluding chapter, which like the author's preface places a strong emphasis on gender and authorial voice, is especially illustrative of the difference between the two translations. Belloc follows

Stowe in acknowledging the author's feminine gender, although specific linguistic markers of gender in French such as "elle" or "elle-même" do not appear in the opening paragraphs as they do in the original. La Bédollière, in contrast, chooses to erase both the presence of the author and her feminine gender by adopting the gender neutral pronoun "we" ("nous"). Consider the two translations of the following sentence from the original: "*The author* hopes *she* has done justice to that nobility, generosity, and humanity, which in many cases characterize individuals at the south" (S, 470). Belloc translates this sentence as "*Elle* espère avoir rendu justice à la noblesse, à la générosité, à l'humanité qui distinguent parfois les habitants du Sud" (B, 585), whereas La Bédollière's translation reads "*Nous* espérons avoir rendu hommage à la générosité, à la grandeur d'âme, à l'humanité, qui caractérisent un grand nombre d'habitants du Sud . . ." (LB, 319). He thereby fails to capture the feminine agency that is crucial not only to *Uncle Tom's Cabin* but to abolitionism and antislavery literature as well. He also overstates her claim that "in many cases" Southerners respond in ways that are noble, generous, and humane: whereas Belloc presents those responses as occurring "parfois" (sometimes), La Bédollière attributes them to "un grand nombre" (a great number) of people in the South.

With respect to race, matters are less clearcut, however. In some cases Belloc's greater respect for Stowe's voice results in a resistance to oppressive notions of both gender and race. In the author's preface, for example, Stowe feminizes Africa and thereby suggests the related oppression of women and slaves that, as noted earlier, was a recurrent theme in women's antislavery writing. She writes,

> In this general movement, unhappy *Africa* at last is remembered; *Africa,* who began the race of civilization and human progress in the dim, gray dawn of early time, but who, for centuries, has lain bound and bleeding at the foot of civilized and Christianized humanity, imploring compassion in vain.
>
> But the heart of the dominant race, who have been *her* conquerors, *her* hard masters, has at length been turned towards *her* in mercy. . . . (S, v)

The three occurrences of feminization in the original are not only preserved but greatly intensified in Belloc's translation, which reads,

> Dans ce mouvement général, on s'est enfin rappelé *la malheureuse Afrique, elle* qui, *la première,* ouvrit aux clartés douteuses et grisâtres du crépuscule la carrière de la civilisation et du progrès; *elle* qui, après des siècles entiers, *enchaînée* et *saignante* aux pieds de l'humanité chrétienne et civilisée, implore en vain la compassion.

> Mais la race dominatrice s'est laissé fléchir; le coeur des maîtres, des conquérants s'est amolli. . . . (B, xviii)

That there are eight occurrences of feminization in Belloc's translation, as opposed to three in Stowe's original, is attributable in part to the morphological properties of the French language, in which gender appears in articles and adjectival forms as well as pronouns and possessive adjectives. However, Belloc also appears to wish to accentuate the resistant thrust of relating gender and race in this passage about Africa; feminine gender appears in association with Africa six more times subsequently in her text whereas it does not reappear in the original. At times Belloc also uses footnotes to intensify the abolitionist thrust of the novel (e.g., 172, 572) and on occasion strengthens the abolitionist tone through translation itself, as for example her translation of a passage in which Stowe states that Africans have won from the Anglo-Saxon race "only misunderstanding and contempt" (S, v), which Belloc translates by writing that the African race, which "n'a pu se faire comprendre de ses oppresseurs, reste prosternée sous le poids de leur mépris" (B, xvii).

There are as many instances, however, in which Belloc actually intensifies the implicit racist overtones of the original. Whereas she strives to render what Stowe presents as black dialect in the original, Belloc at times makes that dialect more ungrammatical, as for example in her translation of "Ah, master trusted me, and I couldn't" (13) as "Oh! moi, pas pouvoir: maître s'être fié à Tom" (3). As this example illustrates, Belloc consistently employs unconjugated infinitives as the mark of black speech, with the result that the wide variety of grammatical and lexical features of that speech in Stowe's novel is narrowed and rendered more stereotypical in Belloc's text. Predictably, then, a phrase such as "How easy white folks al'us does things!" (S, 32) becomes "Comme petit blanc faire tout bien!" (B, 28). Belloc also introduces the seme of animality, in some cases by adding an element that is altogether absent in the original ("le malin singe," 52, "ces chiens de nèg," 259), and in other cases by translating a less racially charged expression with a more offensive one, as in the translation of "what a young un" (S, 14) by "voilà un curieux petit singe" (B, 5).

There are other times when Belloc's commitment to respecting the tone and voice of the original seem to backfire and to add a racist element that is missing in La Bédollière's more neutral and shorter version of the novel. Consider the following passage, in which the nominal and pronominal references to black children have been underlined:

"Now, Augustine, what upon earth is this for?" said Miss Ophelia. "Your house is so full of *these little plagues*, now, that a body can't set down their foot without treading on 'em. I get up in the morning, and find *one* asleep behind the door, and see *one black head* poking out from under the table, *one* lying on the door-mat,—and they are mopping and mowing and grinning between all the railings, and tumbling over the kitchen floor! What on earth did you want to bring this *one* for?" (S, 259)

Belloc's translation of this passage seems to revel in the multiplication and intensification of racial terms:

—Or ça, Augustin, qu'est-ce que cela signifie? dit miss Ophélia. La maison regorge déjà de *ces petites pestes:* on ne saurait marcher sans mettre le pied dessus. Ce matin, je me lève, *un négrillon* roule endormi de derrière ma porte; *une tête noire* se dresse de dessous la table; je heurte *un troisième moricaud* couché sur le paillasson. De tous côtés, sur les balcons, sur les balustrades, on voit grimacer *quelque face de suie;* partout *moricauds, moricaudes, négrillons, négrillonnes,* dorment, rient, pleurent, cabriolent, se roulent à terre, et fourmillent sur le plancher de la cuisine. Au nom du ciel, pourquoi nous embarrasser d'*une* de plus? (B, 313–14)

Not only does Belloc retain the reference to "plagues" ("pestes") and "black head" ("tête noire"). She adds a reference to a "face de suie" (a sooty face); three occurrences of the French terms for Negro children in the masculine and feminine ("négrillon," "négrillonne"); and three more occurrences of a pejorative term for persons of color, also in both the masculine and feminine forms ("moricaud," "moricaude"). In contrast, La Bédollière's translation, in striving less to capture the tone and detail of the original, appears less racially offensive.

—Augustin, dit miss Ophélia, qu'est-ce que cela signifie? votre maison est si remplie de *ces petites pestes,* qu'on ne peut faire un pas sans marcher dessus. Le matin, en me levant, je trouve *un négrillon* sur le paillasson; je vois *une tête noire* sortir de dessous la table. Au nom du ciel, pourquoi m'avoir amené *cette fille?* (LB, 173)

It is worth noting that Stowe's passage of ninety-four words is reduced to sixty-one in La Bédollière's translation whereas it is expanded to 108 in Belloc's. In this instance, as in many others, one can see that the kind of attention to descriptive detail and comic effect that Lucas praises in Belloc's translation and interprets unproblematically in stylistic terms has significant ideological effects.

In short, it is clear from Belloc's translation, as it was from La Place's and others referred to in this chapter, that ideological pitfalls surround translation at every turn. Whether translators shorten or expand, whether they correct the original or choose to remain faithful to it, whether they emphasize gender or race, they make choices that ultimately have profound effects on the meaning that they give to an original text that they present to another audience, often, as in the translations contained in this volume, at another, very different moment in time. To understand fully those original works in translation entails the complex interweaving of theoretical, practical, and historical considerations which this chapter has attempted to provide. Only within the interwoven fabric of those considerations can we as contemporary readers and translators discover ways to appreciate the literary contributions made by Olympe de Gouges, Germaine de Staël, and Claire de Duras and to reflect intelligently upon the ideological implications of their works.

PART TWO
Olympe de Gouges (1748–1793)

THREE

Feminism, Theater, Race

L'esclavage des noirs

Marie-Pierre Le Hir

Until recently, when Côté-femmes committed itself to reinscribing Olympe de Gouges's presence in theater history by publishing her plays, her drama had not received much critical attention.[1] On the one hand, her literary fate does not seem exceptional, for it is often expressed that if French revolutionary drama deserves some posthumous credit it is more for the impressive quantity of plays produced during those years than for their literary quality.[2] As a result, revolutionary drama has been studied more frequently by historians and theater historians than by literary critics. The latter have tended to neglect late eighteenth-century and early nineteenth-century drama, which they usually consider to be lacking the aesthetic qualities associated with good theater.[3] On the other hand, it is obvious that Gouges's drama has not been evaluated seriously simply because she was a woman and a militant feminist. In Gisela Thiele-Knobloch's words, "the reception of Olympe de Gouges' literary works is usually negative and characterized by an incredible misogyny."[4] It has even been suggested that she was illiterate, and that, as a result, she could not have written her plays herself, a notion convincingly rejected by Thiele-Knobloch as a "myth" imposed by "Michelet, Monselet and many others."[5] Referring to "the large number of Olympe de Gouges' autographs in National Archives and the archives of the Comédie-Française" as "proofs to the contrary," Thiele-Knobloch reminds us that women playwrights' claims to authorship were often ridiculed: it was "a commonplace expressed by Rousseau and so many others to think that, behind every woman writer, stood a man. . . . In the registers of the Comédie-Française women playwrights' names were after all followed by a man's name precisely for that reason."[6] Still, critics who do not dispute Gouges's claims to authorship do not necessarily approve of the quality of her work. Their objections to Gouges's melodramatic style and to the political nature of her plays have fed her reputation as a bad playwright.

Even the best intentioned critics usually dismiss her dramatic style as awkward and inappropriate for the stage. Benoîte Groult, for instance, attempts to excuse this weakness by suggesting that Gouges's cultural background—her roots in an oral meridional culture—was a handicap for her as a playwright.[7] But she is nonetheless clearly perturbed by the "constant digressions" and "inflated lyricism" characteristic of Gouges's drama.[8] Her style, she concludes, "was much more appropriate for her rousing patriotic pamphlets than for the plays she took into her head to write."[9] Gouges's reputation as a "bad playwright" also rests on the more general assumption that emphasis on content, and in particular on a political message, precludes literary quality. In spite of the general consensus on this issue, I would like to argue that to criticize Gouges on the basis of her style is to consider her work from the very aesthetic perspective she rejected. The purpose of this introduction is therefore to emphasize *L'esclavage des noirs'* originality as a powerful drama committed to a double agenda of sociopolitical and dramatic reform and, further, by studying the play's immediate impact in 1789, to dispel some misconceptions on which Gouges's reputation as a "bad" and "failed" playwright rests.

Because of its melodramatic style and political nature, Gouges's drama has been associated with the minor, popular stages, disregarded for their lack of literary tradition. The so-called popular stages, however, did not truly exist until January 1791 when the National Assembly abolished privileges formerly granted to Royal theaters by declaring that "any citizen was free to establish a public stage and have plays of any genre represented on it."[10] *L'esclavage des noirs* was performed in December 1789, before this ruling took effect, and on the most prestigious stage in Paris, the Comédie-Française—or Théâtre de la Nation as it was then called.[11] As Rodmell reminds us:

> [t]he strength of the position of the Comédie-Française lay in the fact that not only did it possess a monopoly of plays from the golden years of the seventeenth century but also in the fact that the overwhelming majority of playwrights in the eighteenth-century eagerly sought to gain the prestige which derived from having their plays included in the Comédie's repertory.[12]

Moreover, the politization of Parisian stages did not originate from the minor stages; the Théâtre de la Nation took the lead.[13] Marie-Joseph Chénier's *Charles IX*, performed on November 4, 1789, a month before *L'esclavage des noirs,* is considered a turning point in that regard. It is precisely because Chénier's play "was a political tragedy of a type hitherto unknown in French literature"; because "it introduced revolutionary propaganda into the tragic genre" that it was well-received at the Comédie.[14] Its success therefore illustrates that it was possible to be considered a "good" playwright and to write politically committed plays. How then, can we explain that following *Charles IX* Chénier became "the foremost poet of the French Revolution,"[15] while Gouges, with *L'esclavage des noirs,* allegedly only proved her "uncanny ability for writing unsuccessful plays on apparently foolproof subjects"?[16] Leaving misogyny aside, the contrast between these two critical appraisals might partially be explained by Chénier's choice of a "foolproof" genre, tragedy in verse, and by comparison, Gouges's choice of a more recent genre, drama in prose. It might also be explained, more strikingly, by the contrast between their respective treatments of their political subject matter and their divergent political views. Chénier used the St. Bartholomew Massacre to attack the monarchy, a "foolproof subject," since the topic was "used all during the eighteenth-century by the philosophes in their concerted attack on the fanaticism of the Catholic Church";[17] Gouges openly advocated monarchist views and vehemently denounced slavery, another controversial and politically touchy issue.

L'esclavage des noirs is a *drame,* and as such, it belongs to an ambitious project developed during the second half of the eighteenth century which aimed at reforming French theater and at imposing the new genre at the Comédie-Française. As the endless quarrels on rules of unity and *bienséances* exemplify, French classical tradition—as embodied in the works of Corneille or Racine—emphasized form and "good taste." Proponents of the *drame,* who rejected the aesthetics of classical theater and the premises on which it was based, had quite a different agenda. For Gouges and many contemporary playwrights drama was not a remote aesthetic domain, it was part of "nature," of life. This continuity of life was expressed in the conception of *drame* as a bridge over the division between comic and tragic genres and in the choice of a language accessible to all, prose, as opposed to poetry—which only selected audiences of *connaisseurs* could appreciate. With the *drame,* theater lost its primary aesthetic function to take on a new social role: to turn spectators into better men, women, and citizens.

Denis Diderot, Sébastien Mercier, and Gouges shared a perhaps naive assumption about the dynamics of drama performance: they thought that through the powerful emotional communion with their characters' sufferings, the spectators' true nature, their "humanity," would resurface, allowing them to shake prejudices and be better human beings. The proper way to convince was to reach the heart first, or, to quote Mercier, to make "cold, shrunken, souls" feel again. Without this emotional preparation, Mercier argued, spectators would not readily receive the grave lessons in "honesty and virtue" a playwright had to offer.[18] To that effect, sentimental and bourgeois drama resorted to various techniques. *Tableaux,* usually at the end of an act, presented characters in a state of emotional upheaval, with teary eyes to convey their heartfelt emotions. Melodramatic style, which combined both sentimental, flowery language and grandiloquent phrases, was used for the same purpose.

All of this, tableaux and melodramatic language, is found in *L'esclavage des noirs.* The redundant qualifiers ("scoundrel," "wretch," "barbarian"), exclamatory comments ("How we are to be pitied!", "How I pity him, this unhappy man!", "How their misfortune renders them interesting!"), lengthy monologues, and affected a-parte clearly belong to the melodramatic register. For Gouges, however, as for proponents of the *drame* in general, style no longer was the aesthetic cornerstone and sole measure of achievement. The play's lesson and the playwright's effectiveness in conveying it became the proper criteria by which to determine the value of a play. Gouges's own declarations concerning her lack of stylistic and literary talents have to be considered in that context. They have often been taken at face value, or at best, as indications of her feminine modesty—with a few critics rightly arguing that, judged by contemporary standards, her alleged "terrible" style was by no means any worse than her contemporaries'.[19] Both interpretations, however, fail to take into account the specific function of Gouges's emphasis on her alleged stylistic deficiencies: to stress them was her way to distance herself from the classical tradition and to direct the reader or spectator to what she considered the essential aspect of her drama, its content. As she insisted in the preface of *L'esclavage des noirs,* "talent might be wanting in this play, but not morals."[20]

Her choice of a melodramatic style as the appropriate means to convey this moral content was also no coincidence. Today, we often fail to appreciate how widely popular melodramatic style was in revolutionary France: melodrama was a dominant mode of expression which pervaded the entire public sphere, the stage, the political assemblies, and, as historian Sarah Maza has shown, the legal and political writings of the time.[21] To use melodramatic forms of expression was to speak the language of politics and thereby to assert theater's

place within the political sphere.[22] Relegating aesthetics to the background, Gouges opted for this highly politicized dramatic style and
thereby also asserted her filiation with *drame* theorists.

This filiation, however, is nowhere better exemplified than in her
choice of politically relevant topics. The plot of *L'esclavage des noirs*
can be summarized in a few sentences: two fugitive slaves, Zamor and
Mirza, are wanted for the murder of a slave-master who had tried to
seduce Mirza. On the desert island where Zamor and Mirza have
found refuge, they rescue from a shipwreck Valère and Sophie, a
young French couple in search of Sophie's father. But Zamor and
Mirza are captured and condemned to death. Only the governor of
the colony they have fled, who turns out to be Sophie's father, can
save them. Thanks to him, Valère and Sophie are able to save their
new friends' lives. At the end of the drama, the two slaves are freed
and married.

Thematically, *L'esclavage des noirs* is linked both to Diderot's *drame
bourgeois* and to Mercier's *drame civique*, but it goes further, insofar as
it represents an attempt to merge the two. In his theoretical writings
as well as in his plays, Diderot focused on the private sphere in an
attempt to redefine relationships within the family and to replace the
feudal family model, based on the absolute authority of the father, by
a bourgeois model, still patriarchal, but based on love and understanding. *Zamor et Mirza*—as *L'esclavage des noirs* was first called—
shares a common theme with Diderot's *Le fils naturel*, the recognition
by fathers of all of their children, even those born out of wedlock.
Sophie's recognition by her father illustrates Diderot's ideal of family
relations centered on love and equality among children. Politically,
both plays argue against *droit d'aînesse*—the Old Regime right of the
first-born son to be considered sole heir—since in both cases illegitimate children inherit from their fathers. Gouges, however, goes a step
further than Diderot since Sophie is not only illegitimate, but also
female. She thereby exemplifies her refusal to exclude women from
any redefinition of family relationships.

As frequently stated in her biographies, Gouges had a personal
interest in defending the cause of illegitimate children since she
claimed to be, and probably was, the illegitimate daughter of Lefranc
de Pompignan, himself a playwright. Yet, it is difficult to argue that
in defending the cause of illegitimate daughters, Gouges was only
pleading her own case, i.e., making a direct appeal for recognition to
her father: Lefranc de Pompignan had died before the play was written. This filiation was apparently of great importance to Gouges, but
more so in its symbolic than in its biological dimension. Her obstinate

efforts to have her first play performed where her father had been acclaimed, at the Comédie-Française, indicate that she was determined to be his literary daughter. In trying to establish this literary filiation, she took the burden of proof on herself: to show herself worthy of him, she had to succeed without his help and in spite of her mixed social status; like her friend Mme de Montanclos, she had to gain literary recognition thanks to her own merits. This symbolic filiation would then bring her what her illegitimacy had deprived her of, social status and financial rewards: to have a successful play performed at the Comédie meant both literary recognition and financial security. *Zamor et Mirza* therefore helps characterize Gouges's literary endeavors as feminist in two ways: her vindication of daughters' rights is doubly exemplified in her determination to be a successful playwright and in the arguments put forward in the play.

L'esclavage des noirs is not only related to the *drame bourgeois*, since, as the final title of the play indicates, its main focus is on the issue of slavery. This topic had earlier been suggested as worthy of a *drame* by Gouges's friend Mercier in *Du théâtre* (1773). Mercier did not write a play on slavery, but he listed "slave trade, this hateful public violation of natural rights" as an appropriate topic for a *drame*.[23] For Mercier as well as for Diderot, drama's function was didactic and political, but for Mercier, drama's primary vocation was to produce good citizens. His *drames* therefore focused not only on the family, but on the social and political sphere as well. Centered on both private and public life, *L'esclavage des noirs* illustrates Gouges's conviction that private life is part of a larger political context.

As a political narrative *L'esclavage des noirs'* importance lies in its examination and redefinition of gender and race relations in a radically new society, based on democratic principles. In the opening scene, the topos of the desert island signals the allegoric dimension of the play. Gouges proceeds the same way Marivaux had done in *L'île des esclaves* (1725): in both cases, the island serves to establish a sociopolitical context which greatly differs from contemporary society. But whereas Marivaux's island harbors a utopian society in which former slaves hold the political power, no organized society is found on Gouges's island: her desert island symbolizes nature at first. Stranded on a desert island, Zamor and Mirza are beings in and of nature. What does "nature" mean for Gouges? For her, nature exists at two levels: on the surface, it is complex, "bizarre et variée," but at another deeper level, it is also one. Late in the play, Zamor illustrates Gouges's conception of nature through the following remarks:

Nature seems to stand in contrast with herself in this spot. Formerly she smiled upon us: she has lost none of her attractions; but she shows us both the image of our past happiness and the horrible fate to which we shall be victim. (III, 2)

Nature, without changing, can be perceived differently according to circumstances. For Gouges, the same holds for human nature: human nature does not only exist at the level of perception, where it is *bizarre* and *variée*. Like others of her time, Gouges invokes "nature as the origin of both liberty and sexual difference,"[24] but for her liberty and sexual difference are not equally weighted: nature is invoked as the origin of liberty and equality first. According to her, human nature is first revealed in that which distinguishes men from animals, not men from women, blacks from whites, or masters from slaves: in the same blood which flows in human veins. This primary distinction between humans and animals is introduced in act I, scene 9 when Sophie rejects the opinion that blacks "were born to be savages" and should therefore be "tamed like animals" as the origin of racial prejudice ("What frightful prejudice!"). Failure to stress human commonality is at the origin of racial, but also sexual or class prejudices.

It is therefore important to view the desert island in *L'esclavage* not solely as a symbol of (primitive) nature, but also as a symbol of liberty: the island is the site of resistance to political oppression. Zamor, by murdering the governor's "confidential agent," has fled from and rejected the sociopolitical order of the colony. Mirza, as the indirect cause of the murder, exemplifies the potential danger woman represents for that existing order. For the two runaway slaves, the island clearly means freedom from slavery. But similarly, and as we will see shortly despite Gouges's support for the king, the island also represents freedom from the prevailing feudal order for Valère and Sophie. This idea is embodied in the metaphor of the shipwreck and directly expressed through a comparison: the parallel situations of the French people (Valère and Sophie) "groaning under despotism of Ministers and Courtiers" (I, 7) and of the black people (Mirza and Zamor) groaning under "the frightful despotism" of "barbaric masters" (I, 1). Unlike Marivaux, whose play can be read as advocating a reversal of master and slave relations, Gouges's ideal is to abolish this type of relations, to promote social equality. This notion is clearly expressed in the second act by Coraline who declares: "We lack but liberty; let them give it to us, and you will see that there will no longer be masters or slaves" (II, 2). It is already illustrated in the first act through the harmonious relations between the islands' four inhabitants. Gouges does not deny that differences exist in nature. On the contrary, her choice of characters stresses differences of race (black and white), of gender (man and woman) and of social class (slaves, bourgeois). In the touching scene where Mirza and Sophie study each other's beauty, they recognize each other as humans, and therefore as equal, and yet as different. Liberty and equality are therefore the first characteristics of Gouges's ideal society, the last one being solidarity. Better than "fraternity," solidarity expresses the main characters' natural propensity to want the best for fellow human beings: in Gouges's play this form of altruism is far from being restricted to "brothers," it further characterizes all humans, not only men. A woman, Mirza, is the first to express that it is "sweet . . . to soothe the misfortunes of others" (I, 2), a notion repeatedly expressed by other characters throughout the play. Empathy, compassion, the instinctual desire to recognize others as human and to help them, is for Gouges what constitutes Mirza, Zamor, Valère, and Sophie as human beings. This ideal of solidarity is expressed through the recurrent motive of "saving someone else's life" and illustrated through the characters' actions: Valère attempts to save Sophie from drowning; Mirza actually saves Valère's life; Zamor, Sophie's. It is because human nature transcends difference that equality and solidarity are possible: the desert island is for all of them, they share it in spite of their differences. "All men are born free and equal" therefore doesn't mean "all men as opposed to women," but "all human beings as opposed to animals." In summary, the island serves to establish a new ideal sociopolitical framework founded on the republican principles of liberty, equality, and solidarity.

In this context, it is particularly striking that Gouges's ideal society, as presented in act I, is elaborated in the absence of a male figure of authority. Unlike Diderot, who, in *Le père de famille*, centered on the father in his redefinition of private relations, and Marivaux, who, in *L'île des esclaves*, granted political power to a male slave in his reversal of social hierarchy, Gouges presents as ideal a society which is not founded on the authority of a father-king. In act I, the concept of sovereignty of the people, symbolized by the free association of the four equal young men and women, replaces that of patriarchal authority as the foundation of society. The father, however, is not altogether absent from the play. In act I already, Sophie, and to a certain extent Zamor, are "searching for him," and in acts II and III, he figures prominently as father and governor in the person of M. de Frémont. The important role granted to the father in acts II and III therefore seems to cancel the democratic ideal presented in act I and to indicate a return to the patriarchal order. This important issue calls for an examination of gender relations in the play.

Joan W. Scott rightly argues that for Gouges "[t]he union of man and woman replace[s] the single figure of the universal individual, in an attempt at resolving the difficulty of arguing about rights in univocal terms."[25] For Scott this notion of union is "ambiguous": "It could be read as an endorsement of functional complementarity based on sex, but also as an attempt to dissolve and transcend the categories of sexual difference."[26] But for Gouges, it is and can be both, complementarity and transcendence of the categories of sexual difference, because complementarity is not fixed: in the freely consented unions, unions based on love, complementary roles are not ascribed to a specific gender. There is no typical female character in *L'esclavage*, no typical couple, no typical relation between man and woman. In the relation between Zamor and Mirza, Mirza seems to accept the passive role, domesticity: when Zamor asks her to "go and gather some fruit," she obeys. Yet Zamor and Mirza's relationship is only one among other possible configurations. In other words, the division of labor is arbitrary; the roles of man and woman vary for every couple. Sophie, for instance plays a more "masculine" role than Mirza: she makes common cause with the slaves and is ready to die for the sake of her ideal. Since Mirza is a slave and Sophie a bourgeoise, the different roles they fulfill as women could be construed as resulting from their different social origins. But Gouges's careful selection of her two other couples shows this interpretation to be inaccurate. In act II, for instance, it is an educated slave woman, Coraline, who exposes Gouges's political views, while Azor, a male slave, listens; in the de Frémont couple, the wife not only has the economic power, she has also given her name to her husband. With regard to gender relations, Gouges's position is consistent with the position outlined in her general social framework: equality prevails in couples in spite of sexual difference, not in a fixed complementarity, which ascribes certain functions to a certain sex, but in a flexible complementarity. Unlike many women writers later on, Gouges does not subscribe to a kind of complementarity that would dictate gender specific roles in the couple, she does not advocate the myth of two separate spheres. Her conception of complementarity helps her sustain an egalitarian doctrine. Gender equality, however, seems curiously at odds with the prominent role granted to the father figure, M. de Frémont, in the play. By replacing the play in its historical and political context, however, we can account for this apparent contradiction.

L'esclavage des noirs was retitled to better serve the cause of abolition, but its original political scope was wider. As a political narrative, the play is a commentary on France's political options at the time of the

1789 revolution; it centers on Gouges's vision of the society to come. That Gouges herself considered the views expressed in the play and in the political pamphlet entitled *De l'Esclavage des noirs* as essential is illustrated by the fact that she referred specifically to them during her own trial in 1793. Accused of anti-republican sentiments, Gouges countered "that for a long while she had professed only republican sentiments, as the jurors would be able to convince themselves from her work entitled *De l'Esclavage des noirs*."[27] So far, my analysis seems to corroborate Gouges's claims.

As a dramatic theme, the "quest for the father" characterizes *L'esclavage* as a politically committed play: it allows the author to move from utopia (the ideal society) to reality, to the colony and by extension, contemporary France. If act I should be viewed as an illustration of Gouges's ability to conceive of a truly democratic society, acts II and III exemplify her rejection of this ideal model as utopian. As a political theme, the "quest for the father" has another function: it enables Gouges to articulate her political preference for a monarchy, but for a monarchy based on republican principles.

Gouges's political views have often been interpreted as inconsistent. Many critics find it difficult to reconcile her self-proclaimed republicanism and her monarchism. There is no question that *L'esclavage des noirs* advocates monarchy, and if there were questions we would still have to account for her vain but persistent efforts to defend the king and queen at their trials. What needs to be stressed, however, is that the binary opposition between "monarchy" and "republic" is not a particularly useful way to define Gouges's political stand. That her preference was for monarchy *and* a democratic ideal can only be appreciated from her historical vantage point: in 1789, France was still a monarchy, not a republic, the French were still trying to regenerate their monarchy, to rebuild it on democratic principles. *L'esclavage des noirs* provides not only evidence of the continuity in Gouges's political thought over a period of years—since the play was written in 1783 and represented in 1789—but also material of particular importance for understanding her political views and showing their consistency: it stands as an illustration of the general consensus which, in 1789, still made monarchy seem compatible with the democratic ideal proclaimed that same year in the *Déclaration des droits de l'homme*.

Acts II and III focus on this issue and, in particular, on what Gouges considers as the king's duty in transforming the old feudal monarchy into a republican monarchy. As the governor of the colony, M. de Frémont exemplifies the ideal of the citizen-king envisioned by the National Assembly, the father of the nation, dedicated to the freedom and happiness of all of his subjects. M. de Frémont loves and recognizes all of his children, daughters and slaves included. Rejecting tyranny and its "barbaric laws" which contradict his natural goodness and his sense of justice, he struggles and triumphs over institutions (justice, police) which oppress the slaves and serve the most powerful only (here, the colonists). In short, he shares the same ideal as Coraline, the woman slave who envisions a society based on freedom, education, and work, with no masters or slaves. Struck by the similarity between Coraline's republican views and M. de Frémont's, Azor exclaims: "You speak like a man! You sound like the governor!" (II, 2). As if good example was not enough, M. de Frémont directly appeals to Louis XVI to abolish all forms of oppression:

> Sovereigns render their Peoples happy: every Citizen is free under a good Master, and in this country of slavery one must be barbaric in spite of oneself. Hey! how can I help abandoning myself to these reflections, when the voice of humanity cries out from the bottom of my heart: "Be kind and sensitive to the cries of the wretched." I know that my opinion must displease you: Europe, however, takes care to justify it, and I dare hope that before long there will no longer be any slaves. O Louis! O adored Monarch! would that I could this very moment put under your eyes the innocence of these outlaws! (II, 6)

Even though M. de Frémont's speech comes as a response to proslavery arguments advanced by the judge, the address to the king indicates that the message has to be lifted out of this particular context: the king is being asked to abolish not only slavery, but all forms of political oppression. It is obvious Gouges's "opinion" would "displease" some people. The urgency of the message indicates its true nature: it is an ultimatum to the king, a plea to recognize popular sovereignty. The hope that "before long there will no longer be any slaves" expresses the new creed that "all men are born free and equal." The sovereign people calls on the father-king to chose between the old feudal order—tyranny symbolized in the play as the violent rule of weaponry—and the new egalitarian order based on freedom, nonviolence, and work. To live up to his new role, the king has to become a patriot-king, "the father of the French, the King of a free people."[28] Gouges's vision thus represents a radical departure from the old patriarchal order. The king's absolute political authority is being questioned and his role entirely redefined. This rather bold move, if we consider that the play was written in 1783, might explain why the play was not performed until 1789.

M. de Frémont's plea is also a direct appeal for the abolition of slavery. In that respect, however, Gouges's position might appear more timid. Even though the play advocates the education of its slaves, hints that slaves should be free to farm their own land, and openly promotes the abolition of slavery as a practice unworthy of the human race—"A commerce of men! o heaven! humanity is repulsive!" (II, 2)—M. de Frémont's speech clearly indicates that for Gouges the abolition of slavery depends upon the generosity of a "benevolent and enlightened government" (III, 13). Far from advocating political empowerment by slaves, Gouges seems to postpone the abolition of slavery to a not foreseeable future: Zamor refuses to defend his own cause and he later intervenes to end the slave rebellion he has indirectly caused: "never deliver yourselves into excess to escape slavery; fear breaking your irons with too much violence . . ." (III, 11). With hindsight, then, Gouges's demands might appear modest: the end to the slave trade, humane treatment of slaves. In fact, Gouges openly rejected the fears expressed by actors that *L'esclavage* would cause slaves' rebellions:

> But, sirs, we are in Paris; my drama won't be performed in front of Negroes and I insist that [if it were] it would incite them to submission; I maintain that everything in it breathes morality and obedience to the laws. How can this drama be considered dangerous today when you accepted to perform it eight years ago, and when, under a despotic government, censors approved of it?[29]

Both Gouges's moderation with regard to the slavery issue and her insistence on retaining the monarchy originate in her conception of freedom as socially binding. A great number of situations in the play make it clear that for Gouges the right of the individual should not be viewed independently from the collective good, which, in turn, implies preservation of some form of governing structure to legitimize the communities' claims. The notion that to free slaves would destroy the economy of the colony, that their individual freedom would be detrimental to the good of the colony, is rejected by Coraline in the play: "Let the Masters give liberty, no slave will leave the workshop. Imperceptibly, the rudest among us will instruct themselves, recognize the laws of humanity and justice . . ." (II, 2). This declaration is only conceivable to the extent that even slaves are seen as part of the community—independently from the fact that they are mistreated and poorly rewarded for their labor: they are not the other ("our enemies"); they play an important role in the community, they are "nos cultivateurs" (our farmers).[30] Even when men are free, it is in their best interest to contribute to the good of the community (the nation or the colony); even when they are free, it is their responsibility to live by society's rules, a notion clearly expressed by Zamor in his address to the rebelling slaves and to the colonists: "Slaves, colonists, listen to me: I have killed a man, I deserve to die; do not regret my punishment, it is necessary for the good of the Colony" (III, 11). In all instances, relinquishing individual rights for the good of society and making sacrifices for the benefit of others are presented as ideals: when Mme de Saint-Frémont encourages her husband to search for his daughter at the risk of finding his ex-wife; when Sophie throws herself in front of the firing squad to defend Zamor and Mirza; when slaves offer to eat less and work more in exchange for Zamor's and Mirza's lives, their generosity, which cuts across all differences of class, gender, or race, defines them as human beings.

Gouges has accordingly little to say about individual rights in the play. It is true that she grounds the right to be free in nature; Valère speaks of "rights under Natural law" (I, 7)—but this right can also "be lost in nature"; Zamor mentions "giv[ing] man back the rights he has lost in the very bosom of Nature" (I, 1). More to the point, Valère's prediction that the people will "resum[e] all rights" (I, 7) confirms Gouges's conception of the rights of individuals as derived from their belonging to the same collective entity, from their citizenship. In other words, in 1789 Gouges still took the *Déclaration des droits de l'homme et du citoyen* to apply to all citizens, including women and slaves. When she wrote the *Déclaration des droits de la femme et de la citoyenne*, two years later, her position had changed, she had come to understand that her interpretation of "man" would not prevail.

The importance Gouges attached to the father-figure of the king can be seen as representing a guarantee that the claims of the community at large would prevail against the claims of the individual: as the "father of all" the king symbolized all of his people. In *L'esclavage*, it is the king, through M. de Frémont, who sets the social tone for the nation, who advocates tolerance. It is also not by chance that M. and Mme de Frémont represent the most untraditional couple in *L'esclavage*. Through this unorthodox relationship, in which the husband takes his wife's name and accepts to share her fortune, Gouges further advances her political agenda: poised at the intersection of private and public spheres, the royal couple serves to articulate the political dimension of private relations and to point to new social configurations different from the traditional patriarchal order.

As evidenced in the happy ending of the play, Gouges was confident that the "republican monarchy" she had envisioned would prevail. When the play was performed in 1789, her original political
message had lost some of its topical interest since the new order she
had envisioned was being realized. Later, her desperate attempts to
save the king's and queen's lives show how consistent these efforts
were with the political creed professed in *L'esclavage des noirs*, deprived
of a royal couple's symbolic guidance, Gouges assumed, the revolutionaries would only meet her political agenda halfway. Leaving issues
of gender and race unaddressed, they would be unable to achieve
"perfect equality."[31]

If, according to Howarth, the degree of commitment of a playwright can be measured by his or her willingness to defend causes
that have not yet gained general approval, *L'esclavage* offers a perfect
example of a truly committed play.[32] In 1789, the abolition of slavery
was such a cause. Brissot and Mirabeau had just created the Société
des Amis des Noirs, and it is very likely that this abolitionist society
played a role in ensuring the representation of *L'esclavage* at the Théâtre de la Nation: even though Olympe de Gouges was not a member
of the Société,[33] she had had contacts with Mirabeau, who had read
the play.[34] The Société des Amis des Noirs relied on pamphlets and
newspaper articles to promote abolition, but as Daniel P. Resnick has
shown, because of its "narrow base of recruitment" and its failure to
provide an economic instead of a purely moral critique of slavery, it
was relatively powerless in countering the diplomatic maneuvres of
the proponents of slavery, who met at the Hôtel Massiac.[35] According
to Gabriel Debien, "Club Massiac's influence through other friendly-
minded clubs" was "a particularly noticeable activity . . . [f]rom December 1789 onward . . . , when the Club's main struggle against
Amis des Noirs and free people of color begins."[36] *L'esclavage des noirs*
was performed during this period of intense confrontation between
the pro- and antislavery camps.

From the colonists' perspective, the danger of Gouges's play was
not so much its content, but rather the fact that it brought attention
to and openly discussed the issue of slavery at a time when their
political strategy was to silence it. Indeed, by stressing France's vital
economic interests in the West Indies, the colonists were able to successfully prevent the issue of slavery from being directly raised at the
National Assembly, with the result that "[s]ubsidies to investors in the
slave trade were not halted until the fall of 1793."[37] This strategy
was also successfully applied to silence Gouges, when overrating the
didactic powers of her *drame*, she set out to convince an audience with

a vested interest in preserving the colonial system that slavery was both immoral and cruel. There is no question that the colonists had a strong interest in opposing the performance of *L'esclavage des noirs* and that they acted to prevent the Comédie-Française from performing it. As it turned out, the abolitionists won the first round: the play was performed in its entirety on December 26. Given this highly politicized context, it was very difficult, if not impossible, for Gouges to obtain a clear success on the stage.

The play's success in 1789 was largely determined by two factors: the affinities between its message and the political views of the audience and its reception in the press. Chénier, for instance, whose two previous plays had failed at the Comédie and who was determined to succeed with *Charles IX,* made sure he had strong, influential political supporters in the audience: "Several deputies of the National Assembly attended, headed by Mirabeau, who led the applause from his box. Danton, Desmoulins, and the future nucleus of the Cordelier Club were on hand as the play proceeded, right to the end, amid shouting, stamping of feet, bravos, and *without the slightest murmur of disapproval being heard.*"[38] Unlike Chénier, who preached to the converted only, Gouges's audience was, at best, divided along the lines of the slavery issue.

Accounts on whether *L'esclavage* failed or not diverge, however, with most critics arguing that it was a failure. Carlson, for instance, writes that "[d]espite the appropriateness of its subject matter to the sentiment of the times and superlative interpretations by Molé and Suin, the play was hissed from the stage."[39] Welschinger, who otherwise stresses the importance of *L'esclavage des noirs* as "one of the most important plays, together with the works of the *philosophes,* in the fight against slavery," also asserts that the play failed: "The famous Olympe de Gouges . . . could find no solace after *L'esclavage des Nègres* [*sic*] failed."[40] These assessments are problematic in several regards. First, they rely on reviews in the press without considering the partiality of the press on slavery.[41] Welschinger's comments on the play's reception are characteristic in that respect. His review is presented as an objective evaluation based on a study of the press ("according to newspapers"), when it is, in fact, just a quote—as the quotation marks indicate—taken from a single, unnamed newspaper:

> According to newspapers, "this play failed on the first night. We know of few performances as stormy as that one. Outcries from both parties have nearly ended it twenty times. People shouted, harangued, laughed, whispered, whistled. . . . Very poor style, patched-up plot, far-fetched

situations, trite, outdated dramaturgy.... Someone stood up and said the author was a woman, but this did not make the audience more indulgent."[42]

Defamation was a strategy frequently used by the Club Massiac to silence abolitionists,[43] and Gouges's reputation as "an eccentric old lady" or "half-mad" originates to a large extent in these biased accounts.[44] But as Gabriel Debien has stressed, many newspapers were partially financed or at the service of the colonists. In the *Gazette de Paris*, for instance, Rozoi, "who made himself useful to the club [Massiac] by directly attacking books, pamphlets and plays in favor of abolition" denounced, after the performance of *L'esclavage des noirs*, "the 'indirect link' between theater audience and National Assembly as a way of preparing public opinion to blame or confirm decisions of vital interest."[45] Second, critics have frequently evaluated the literary merits of the play on the basis of its alleged failure: the play failed, it was therefore a "bad" play. Summarizing Gouges's career as a playwright, Carlson clearly establishes a link between the two when he mentions her works to prove that "pièces de circonstance were not necessarily successful even in the receptive surroundings of Revolutionary Paris."[46] Last but not least, critics have largely ignored Gouges's own testimony: according to her the play was a success.[47] Pitting one opinion against another does not help, however. A more useful and neutral way to assess the success or failure of *L'esclavage des noirs* is to consider the following: according to the rules of the Comédie-Française, had the play failed to bring in at least 1500 *livres* on opening night, it would not have been performed a second time. Since *L'esclavage* was performed three times, there is no reason to question Gouges's testimony: the play succeeded on opening night.[48]

In *Les comédiens démasqués* Gouges accused the actors, Molé in particular, of having done all they could to ensure the failure of *L'esclavage*—she mentions for instance the actors' refusal to paint their faces black to play the roles of slaves. According to her, colonists had used their influence to warn that if the play succeeded, they would voice their protest by cancelling forty subscriptions for *loges* at the Comédie; they had also used their money to buy actors, she said: those who played poorly were financially rewarded.[49] These accusations have usually been treated with sarcasm by critics—Welschinger views them as yet another proof of Gouges's paranoia ("délire de la persécution")—as a proof of Gouges's inability to concede defeat and to admit simply that her play was "bad."[50] But since critics such as Carlson and Welschinger have wrongly argued that the play failed on opening night, serious consideration should be given to Gouges's account of the fate of her play in December 1789. Why, if the play succeeded at first, did it cease to be represented after January 1790?

According to Gouges, her efforts to defer the second performance of *L'esclavage* and to make proper revisions to her manuscript were rejected by Molé, who convinced her not to adjourn the second representation. She soon realized, however, that Molé's eagerness to go on with the performances of *L'esclavage* was meant to better ensure its failure.[51] Granted, this accusation sounds absurd at first: why would an actor insist on performing a play if he wanted it to fail? Gouges was far from raving, however. There was a good reason, alluded to in *Les Comédiens démasqués,* and later clearly exposed by Le Chapelier at the National Assembly in 1791, it was a question of literary property.[52] A Royal ruling for the Comédie, still enforced in 1789, stated that a play had to be performed twelve times during the winter months (or ten in the summer) and bring in 1500 *livres* per performance to remain the property of the author. If it did not, it "fell into the rules" and became the property of the Comédie.[53] When a play failed to bring in that amount twice, the author no longer could ask to have it performed; he or she also lost his or her property rights. This is precisely what happened to *L'esclavage.* Gouges lost her rights to her play because the second and third performance failed to bring in 1500 *livres.*[54]

The comédiens' practice of making a play fail in order to assume the rights was widespread and protested by all playwrights. Their outrage led to the measures which gave France her first "copyright" legislation, the *Le Chapelier* law of 1791. Summarizing playwrights' complaints, Le Chapelier justified the new law with the following arguments:

> But to crown it all, playwrights are told: if actors perform your play in a cowardly manner, on a day when other entertainments will attract audiences; if they choose to put on the program another play which keeps spectators away; all these *ifs* which foul play and interest make not only likely, but very common: you've lost your property.[55]

Gouges's complaints about the comédiens were identical:

> . . . they'll pick bad days, they'll perform my play three times in the same week and cut it crudely, they'll put the most outdated play the repertory has to offer on the program with it; they'll choose days when the audience is sure to be absent . . . : and as a result of these gentle precautions, my drama will fall into what the Comédie calls its rules; which is another way of saying that they will own it, simply because the takings will not have reached the fixed minimum.[56]

In her case, however, the comédiens truly won. They not only became the owners of the play, it is more than likely that they were paid for it. The Club Massiac was known for having offered or given money to political figures in exchange for their influence on similar occasions; it is probably no coincidence that, for some "unaccounted" reason, the treasury of the Club Massiac was empty in December 1789, precisely at the time of the first performance of *L'esclavage des noirs*. According to Debien "the account of the position on December 26 [1789] shows a deficit of [unknown] origin" but which "must be important,"[57] a statement confirmed by Lucien Leclerc: "It is doubtful that *all* revenues and expenditures appear on the books and registers located in the archives. We know, however, that in November 1789 expenditures were such that the treasurer had to remind club members of their obligation to pay their dues."[58]

Failure to take into account the historical circumstances under which *L'esclavage des noirs* was performed has led to Gouges's reputation as a failed and bad playwright. This reputation has actually little to do with the literary merits of her play; it proceeds more from the unpopular political views she defended. Gouges, however, was proud of her achievements as a playwright, and she had good reasons to be. Shortly before her death, she abandoned the modesty characteristic of earlier statements concerning her alleged lack of talent. In *Testament politique* she compared herself to Chénier, whom she had admired but bitterly envied, insinuating that political correctness, rather than literary talent, was the source of Chénier's success on the Parisian stages. To make it clear that she considered her achievements to rank at least as high as his, she wrote: "I bequeath . . . my creative genius to playwrights, they can use it [il ne leur sera pas inutile], and to the famous Chénier in particular, my know-how in drama [ma logique théâtrale]."[59] The comparison with Chénier is not out of place, for it is true that Gouges's willingness to experiment with dramatic forms and language certainly exceeded Chénier's. In that respect, her attempts to break new ground in drama are remarkable in themselves (her insistence that actors should "adopt negro color and clothing" to portray *L'esclavage*'s characters, for instance, was seen as such a radical suggestion that actors refused to comply with it).

Yet Gouges's emphasis on form (*logique théâtrale*) as the distinguishing factor between her and Chénier is of particular interest because it situates her work as a counter-discourse which opposes tragedy as expression of the revolutionary doxa. Through her own conception of *drame*, Gouges successfully challenges the authority of the revolutionary dominant discourse in order to allow the minority voice raised against it to be heard: on the woman question, which she embodies in her determination to be a successful playwright; on her vision of the ideal form of government for France; and also on the issue of slavery—however moderate her demands might seem today. Functioning as discourses of dissent, her plays, and *L'esclavage des noirs* in particular, articulate Gouges's opposition to the male, revolutionary consensus. They should therefore be viewed as politically committed drama.

FOUR

Translations of Gouges

REFLECTIONS ON NEGROES[1]
Translated by Sylvie Molta

I have always been interested in the deplorable fate of the Negro race. I was just beginning to develop an understanding of the world, at that age when children hardly think about anything, when I saw a Negress for the first time. Seeing her made me wonder and ask questions about her color.

People I asked did not satisfy my curiosity and my reason. They called those people brutes, cursed by Heaven. As I grew up, I clearly realized that it was force and prejudice that had condemned them to that horrible slavery, in which Nature plays no role, and for which the unjust and powerful interests of Whites are alone responsible.

Convinced for a long time of this truth and troubled by their dreadful situation, I dealt with their story in the very first work I wrote. Several men had taken an interest in them and worked to lighten their burden; but none of them had thought of presenting them on stage in their costume and their color as I would have tried, if the Comédie-Française had not been against it.

Mirza had kept her native language, nothing was more touching; it added a lot to the interest of the play. All the experts agreed, except for the actors at the Comédie-Française. But let us not talk about the reception of my play. Now I hand it over to the Public.

Let us go back to the dreadful lot of the Negroes. When will we turn our attention to changing it, or at least to easing it? I know nothing about the Politics of Governments; but they are fair. Now the Law of Nature was never more apparent in them. People are equal everywhere. Fair kings do not want any slaves; they know that they possess obedient subjects, and France will not abandon the wretched in their suffering, ever since greed and ambition have inhabited the most remote islands. Europeans, thirsting for blood and for this metal that greed calls gold, have made Nature change in these happy lands. Fathers have repudiated their children, sons have sacrificed their fathers, brothers have fought, and the defeated have been sold like cattle at the market. What am I saying? It has become a trade in the four corners of the world.

Trading people! Heavens! And Nature does not quake! If they are animals, are we not also like them? How are the Whites different from this race? It is in the color. . . . Why do blonds not claim superiority over brunettes who bear a resemblance to Mulattos? Why is the Mulatto not superior to the Negro? Like all the different types of animals, plants, and minerals that Nature has produced, people's color also varies. Why does not the day argue with the night, the sun with the moon, and the stars with the sky? Everything is different, and herein lies the beauty of Nature. Why then destroy its Work?

Is mankind not its most beautiful masterpiece? Ottomans exploit Whites in the same way we exploit Blacks. We do not accuse them of being barbarian or inhuman, and we are equally cruel to people whose only means of resistance is their submissiveness.

But when submissiveness once starts to flag, what results from the barbaric despotism of the Islanders and West-Indians? Revolts of all kinds, carnage increased with the troops' force, poisonings, and any atrocities people can commit once they revolt. Is it not monstrous of Europeans, who have acquired vast plantations by exploiting others, to have Blacks flogged from morning to night? These miserable souls would cultivate their fields no less if they were allotted more freedom and kindness.

Is their fate not among the most cruel, and their labor the hardest, without having Whites inflict the most horrible punishments on them, and for the smallest fault? Some speak about changing their condition, finding ways to ease it, without fearing that this race of men misuse a kind of freedom that remains subordinate.

I understand nothing about Politics. Some predict that widespread freedom would make the Negro race as essential as the White race, and that after they have been allowed to be masters of their lives, they will be masters of their will, and able to raise their children at their side. They will be more exact and diligent in their work. Intolerance will not torment them anymore, and the right to rise up like others will make them wiser and more human. Deadly conspiracies will no longer have to be feared. They will cultivate freely their own land like the farmers in Europe and will not leave their fields to go to foreign Nations.

Their freedom will lead some Negroes to desert their country, but much less than those who leave the French countryside. Young people hardly come of age with the requisite strength and courage, before they are on their way to Paris to take up the noble occupation of lackey or porter. There are a hundred servants for one position, whereas our fields lack farmers.

This freedom will produce a large number of idle, unhappy, and bad persons of any kind. May each nation set wise and salutary limits for its people; this is the art of Sovereigns and Republican States.

My instincts could help, but I will keep myself from presenting my opinion, for I should be more knowledgeable and enlightened about the Politics of Governments. As I have said, I do not know anything about Politics, and I freely give my observations either good or bad. I, more than anyone, must be interested in the fate of these unfortunate Negroes since it has been five years since I conceived a play based on their tragic History.

I have only one piece of advice to give to the actors of the Comédie-Française, and it is the only favor I will ask of them, that is to wear the color and costume of the Negro race. Never has the occasion been more opportune, and I hope that the Play will have an effect in favor of these victims of Whites' ambition.

The costume will contribute greatly to the interest of this Play, which will inspire the pens and the hearts of our best writers. My goal will thus be attained, my ambition satisfied, and the Comédie-Française will be honored rather than dishonored by the issue of color.

My happiness would be too immeasurable if I were to see my Play performed as I wish. This weak sketch would require a poignant group of scenes for it to serve posterity. Painters ambitious enough to paint the tableau would be considered Fathers of the wisest and most worthwhile Humanity, and I am convinced that they would favor the subject of this small Play over its dramatic expression.

So, Ladies and Gentlemen, act out my Play, it has waited long enough. As you have wanted, it is now published. I join every Nation in asking for its production, and I am convinced they will not disappoint me. This feeling that could be considered self-pride in others, results from the impact which the public outcry in favor of Negroes has had on me. Any reader who appreciates my work will be convinced of my sincerity.

Forgive me these last statements; they are painful to express, but therein lies my right to them. Farewell Ladies and Gentlemen, act my play as you see fit; I shall not attend the rehearsals. I turn over all rights to my son; may he make good use of them and protect himself from becoming a Writer for the Comédie-Française. If he believes me, he will never pick up a pen to write Literature.

BLACK SLAVERY,
OR THE HAPPY SHIPWRECK
Translated by Maryann DeJulio

Preface[2]

In the Dark Ages men made war; in the most Enlightened Age, they want to destroy themselves. Will there ever be a science, a regime, an epoch, or an age when men will live in peace? The Learned may dwell upon and lose themselves in these metaphysical observations. I, a woman, who have only studied the good principles of Nature, I no longer set forth man's nature; my rude learning has taught me to judge things only after my soul. My works, therefore, bear but the color of human nature.

Here, at last, is my Play, which avarice and ambition have pro-scribed, but which just men approve. What must my opinion be of these varying opinions? As an Author, I am permitted to approve this philanthropical work; but as an earwitness of the disastrous accounts of the troubles in America, I should abhor my Work, if an invisible hand had not performed this revolution in which I did not participate except to prophesy its occurrence. However, you blame me, you ac-cuse me without even having seen *Black Slavery,* accepted in 1783 by the Comédie-Française, printed in 1786, and performed in December 1789. The Colonists, whose cruel ambition was effortlessly satisfied, won over the Comedians, and you can be sure . . . that the inter-ception of my Play did not hurt their receipts; but it is neither the Comedians nor the Colonists whom I wish to put on trial, it is rather myself.

I denounce myself publicly; here I am under arrest: I am going to plead my own case before this august Tribunal, frivolous . . . but redoubtable. I deliver myself to a vote of conscience; I shall win or lose by a majority.

The author and friend of the truth who has no interest but to remind men of the charitable principles of Nature, who respects laws and social conventions no less, is still an estimable mortal, and if her writings do not produce all the good that she had hoped for, she is to be pitied more than blamed.

It is, therefore, important for me to convince the Public and the detractors of my Work, of the purity of my maxims. This work may lack talent but not morals. It is by means of these morals that public opinion must reconsider my case.

When the Public has read my Play, conceived in a time when it was to appear as a Novel drawn from an old Fairy tale play, it will recognize that it is the faithful tableau of the current situation in America. I give you, today, in the fourth year of the Republic, my Play such as it was approved under the despotism of the press. I offer my Play to the Public as an authentic document, which is necessary for my vindication. Is my work inflammatory? No. Is it insurgent? No. Does it have a moral? Yes, without doubt. What, then, do these Colonists want from me when they speak of me in such unsparing terms? But they are wretches; I pity them and shall respect their deplorable fate; I shall not even permit myself to remind them of their inhumanity: I shall permit myself only to mention all that I have written to preserve their properties and their most cherished interests: my Play is proof thereof.

I shall now address myself to you, slaves, men of color; perhaps I have an incontestable right to blame your ferocity: cruel, you justify tyrants when you imitate them. Most of your Masters were humane and charitable, and in your blind rage you do not distinguish between innocent victims and your persecutors. Men were not born in irons, and now you prove them necessary. If force majeure is on your side, why exercise all the fury of your fiery lands? Poison, irons, daggers, they say you invent the most barbarous and atrocious tortures with no effort. What cruelty! what inhumanity! Ah! How you make them moan, they who wanted to prepare you, by temperate means, a kinder fate, a fate more worthy of envy than all those illusory advantages whereby the authors of the calamities in France and America have misled you. Tyranny will follow you just as crime clings to depraved men. Nothing will reconcile you with yourselves. Fear my prediction, you know whether it be well-founded or not. My pronouncements are based on reason and divine justice. I retract nothing: I abhor your Tyrants, your cruelties horrify me.

Ah! If my counsel reaches you, if you recognize its worth, I dare believe that your untamed wits will be calmed and that my counsel will restore harmony, which is indispensable to the colonial commonweal and to your own interests. These interests consist only in social order, your rights within the wisdom of the Law; this Law recognizes that all men are brothers; this august Law that cupidity had plunged into chaos has been finally extricated from the dark. If the savage, a ferocious man, fails to recognize this Law, then he is made for irons, to be tamed like a brute.

Slaves, people of color, you who live closer to Nature than Europeans, than your Tyrants, recognize these gentle laws and show that an enlightened Nation was not mistaken to treat you like men and give you rights that you never had in America. To draw nearer to justice and humanity, remember, and never lose sight of this, your Fatherland condemns you to a frightful servitude and your own parents put you up for sale: men are hunted in your frightful climes like animals are hunted elsewhere. The true Philosophy of the enlightened man prompts him to snatch his fellow-man from the midst of a primitively horrible situation where men not only sold one another, but where they still ate each other. The true man has regards for all men. These are my principles, which differ greatly from those of these so-called defenders of Liberty, these fire-brands, these incendiary spirits who preach equality and liberty with all the authority and ferocity of Despots. America, France, and perhaps the Universe, will owe their fall to a few energumen that France has produced, the decadence of Empires and the loss of the arts and sciences. This is perhaps a fatal truth. Men have grown old, they seem to want to be born again, and according to the principles of Brissot, animal life suits man perfectly; I love Nature more than he, she has placed the laws of humanity and wise equality in my soul; but when I consider this Nature, I often see her in contradiction with her principles, and everything then seems subordinate. Animals have their Empires, Kings, Chiefs, and their reign is peaceable; an invisible and charitable hand seems to conduct their administration. I am not entirely an enemy of M. Brissot's principles, but I believe them impracticable among men: I have treated this matter before him. I dared, after the august Author of *The Social Contract,* provide *Man's Original Happiness,* published in 1789. I wrote a Novel, and never will men be pure enough, great enough, to recover this original happiness, which I found only in a blissful fiction. Ah! If it were possible for them to achieve this, the wise and humane laws that I establish in this social contract would make all men brothers, the Sun would be the true God that they would invoke; but always fickle, the *Social Contract, Original Happiness* and the august Work of M. Brissot will always be chimerae and not a useful instruction. Imitations of Jean-Jacques are defaced in this new regime, what, then, would those of Madame de Gouges and M. Brissot be? It is easy, even for the most ignorant, to make revolutions in paper notebooks; but, alas! every People's experience, and now the French experience, teaches me that the most learned and the most wise do not establish their doctrines without producing all kinds of troubles.

I stray from the aim of my Preface, and time does not permit me to give free reign to philosophical reasons. It was a question of justifying *Black Slavery,* which the odious Colonists had proscribed and presented as an incendiary work. Let the public judge and pronounce, I await its decree for my justification.

Dramatis Personae

Zamor, educated Indian
Mirza, young Indian, Zamor's lover
M. de Saint-Frémont, Governor of an island in the Indies
Mme de Saint-Frémont, his wife
Valère, French gentleman, Sophie's husband
Sophie, M. de Saint-Frémont's natural daughter
Betzi, Mme de Saint-Frémont's maid
Caroline, Slave[3]
Indian, M. de Saint-Frémont's slave steward
Azor, M. de Saint-Frémont's valet
M. de Belfort, Major from the garrison
Judge
M. de Saint-Frémont's **Man-Servant**
Old Indian
Several Indian Planters of both sexes, and Slaves
Grenadiers and French Soldiers

The scene in the first act is a deserted island; in the second, a large, neighboring city in the Indies, and in the third, a nearby Plantation.

BLACK SLAVERY, OR THE HAPPY SHIPWRECK

Act I

Shore of a deserted island, surrounded by steep cliffs, from which the high sea is visible in the distance. On one side in front is the open door of a hut surrounded by fruit trees from the region: the entrance to a seemingly impenetrable forest fills the other side. Just as the curtain rises, a storm agitates the waves: a ship has just broken to pieces on the rocks. The winds die down and the sea becomes calm.

SCENE I

Zamor, Mirza

ZAMOR: Dispel your fears, my dear Mirza; this vessel is not sent by our persecutors: as far as I can judge, it is French. Alas! it has just broken to pieces on these rocks, none of the crew has escaped.

MIRZA: Zamor, I fear only for you; punishment does not frighten me; I shall bless my fate if we end our days together.

ZAMOR: O my Mirza! How you move me!

MIRZA: Alas! What have you done? my love has rendered you guilty. Without the unhappy Mirza you would never have run away from the best of all Masters, and you would not have killed his confidential agent.

ZAMOR: The barbarian! he loved you, and that made him your tyrant. Love rendered him fierce. The tiger dared charge me with the chastisement that he inflicted upon you for not wanting to respond to his unbridled passion. The education that our governor had given me added to the sensibility of my rude manners and rendered the frightful despotism that commanded me to punish you even more intolerable.

MIRZA: You should have let me die; you would be beside our Governor who cherishes you like his child. I have caused your troubles and his.

ZAMOR: Me, let you perish! Ah! Gods! Hey! Why remind me of the virtues and kindnesses of this respectable Master? I have performed my duty to him: I have paid for his kindnesses, rather with the tenderness of a son, than the devotion of a slave. He believes me guilty, and that is what renders my torment more frightful. He does not know what a monster he had honored with his confidence. I have saved my fellow-men from his tyranny; but, my dear Mirza, let us destroy a memory too dear and too fatal: we no longer have any protectors save Nature. Benevolent Mother! You know our innocence. No, you will not abandon us, and this deserted spot will hide us from all eyes.

MIRZA: The little that I know, I owe to you, Zamor; but tell me why Europeans and Planters have such advantage over us, poor slaves? They are, however, made like us: we are men like them: why, then, such a great difference between their kind and ours?

ZAMOR: That difference is very small; it exists only in color; but the advantages that they have over us are huge. Art has placed them above Nature: instruction has made Gods of them, and we are only men. They use us in these climes as they use animals in theirs. They came to these regions, seized the lands, the fortunes of the Native Islanders, and these proud ravishers of the properties of a gentle and peaceable people in its home, shed all the blood of its noble victims, sharing amongst themselves its bloody spoils and made us slaves as a reward for the riches that they ravished, and that we preserve for them. These are their own fields that they reap, sown with the corpses of the Planters, and these crops are now watered with our sweat and our tears. Most of these barbaric masters treat us with a cruelty that makes Nature shudder. Our wretched species has grown accustomed to these chastisements. They take care not to instruct us. If by chance our eyes were to open, we would be horrified by the state to which they have reduced us, and we would shake off a yoke as cruel as it is shameful; but is it in our power to change our fate? The man vilified by slavery has lost all his energy, and the most brutalized among us are the least unhappy. I have always shown the same zeal to my master, but I have taken care not to make my way of thinking known to my comrades. God! Divert the presage that still menaces these climes, soften the hearts of our Tyrants, and give man back the rights that he has lost in the very bosom of Nature.

MIRZA: How we are to be pitied!

ZAMOR: Perhaps our fate will change before long. A gentle and consoling morality has unveiled European error. Enlightened men gaze compassionately upon us: we shall owe them the return of this precious liberty, man's primary treasure, of which cruel ravishers have deprived us for so long.

MIRZA: I would be happy to be as well instructed as you; but I only know how to love you.

ZAMOR: Your artlessness charms me; it is the imprint of Nature. I leave you for a moment. Go and gather some fruit. I am going to take a walk down to the shore to collect the debris from this shipwreck. But, what do I see? A woman who is struggling against the waves! Ah! Mirza, I fly to her rescue. Must excessive misfortune excuse us from being humane? *(He descends toward the rock)*

SCENE II

MIRZA: *(Alone)* Zamor is going to save this poor unfortunate soul! How can I not adore such a tender, compassionate heart? Now that I am unhappy, I am more conscious of how sweet it is to soothe the misfortunes of others. *(She exits toward the forest)*

SCENE III

Valère, alone, enters from the opposite side

VALÈRE: Nothing in sight on the agitated waves. O my wife! You are lost forever! Hey! Could I survive you? No: I must be reunited with you. I gathered my strength to save your life, and I have only escaped the fury of the waves. I breathe but with horror: separated from you, each instant redoubles my sorrow. I search for you in vain, in vain do I call out your name: Your voice resounds in my heart, but it does not strike my ear. I fly from you. *(He descends with difficulty and falls at the back of the Theatre propped up against a boulder)* A thick cloud covers my eyes, my strength abandons me! Almighty God, grant me strength that I may drag myself as far as the sea! I can no longer hold myself up. *(He remains immobile from exhaustion)*

SCENE IV

Valère, Mirza

Mirza, rushing up and catching sight of Valère

MIRZA: Ah! God! Who is this man? Suppose he were coming to lay hands on Zamor and separate me from him! Alas! What would become of me? But, no, perhaps he does not have so evil a scheme; he is not one of our persecutors. I am suffering. . . Despite my fears, I cannot help myself from coming to his aid. I cannot see him in this state much longer. He looks like a Frenchman. *(To Valère)* Monsieur, Frenchman. . . He does not respond. What to do! *(She calls out)* Zamor, Zamor. *(With reflection)* Let us climb upon the rock to see if he is coming. *(She runs up to it and immediately climbs down)* I do not see him. *(She returns to Valère)* Frenchman, Frenchman, answer me? He does not answer. What help can I give him? I have nothing; how unhappy I am! *(Taking Valère's arm and striking his hand)* Poor stranger, he is very ill, and

Zamor is not here: he has more strength than I; but let us search in our hut for something that will revive him. *(She exits)*

SCENE V

Valère, Zamor, Sophie

Zamor, entering from the side by the rock, and carrying Sophie who appears to have fainted in his arms, garbed in a white dressing-gown, belted, and with her hair disheveled

ZAMOR: Regain your strength, Madame; I am only an Indian slave, but I shall help you.

SOPHIE: *(In a dying voice)* Whoever you may be, leave me. Your pity is more cruel to me than the waves. I have lost what was most dear to me. Life is odious to me. O Valère! O my spouse! What has become of you?

VALÈRE: Whose voice is that I hear? Sophie!

SOPHIE: *(Noticing Valère)* What do I see. . . It is he!

VALÈRE: *(Getting up and falling at Sophie's feet)* Almighty God! You have returned my Sophie to me! O dear spouse! Object of my tears and my tenderness! I succumb to my suffering and to my joy.

SOPHIE: Divine Providence! you have saved me! Complete your work, and return my father to me.

SCENE VI

Valère, Zamor, Sophie, Mirza, bringing some fruit and water; she enters running, and surprised to see a woman, she stops

ZAMOR: Approach, Mirza, there is nothing to fear. These are two unfortunates like us; they have rights on our souls.

VALÈRE: Compassionate being to whom I owe my life and my spouse's life! You are not a Savage; you have neither the language nor the manners of one. Are you the master of this Island?

ZAMOR: No, but we have been living here alone for several days. You seem like a Frenchman to me. If the company of slaves does not seem contemptible to you, they will gladly share the possession of this Island with you, and if destiny wills it, we shall end our days together.

SOPHIE: *(To Valère)* How this language interests me! *(To the slaves)* Generous mortals, I would accept your offers, if I were not going farther to look for a father whom I shall perhaps never find again! We have been wandering the seas for two years, and we have found no trace of him.

VALÈRE: Well then! Let us remain in this spot: let us accept the hospitality of these Indians for awhile and be persuaded, my dear Sophie, that by dint of perseverance we shall find the author of your days on this Continent.

SOPHIE: Cruel destiny! We have lost everything; how can we continue our search?

VALÈRE: I share your sorrow. *(To the Indians)* Generous mortals, do not abandon us.

MIRZA: Us, abandon you! Never, no, never.

ZAMOR: Yes, my dear Mirza, let us console them in their misfortunes. *(To Valère and Sophie)* Rely upon me; I am going to examine the entire area by the cliff: if your lost goods are among the debris from the vessel, I promise to bring them to you. Enter our hut, unhappy Strangers; you need rest; I am going to try to calm your agitated spirits.

SOPHIE: Compassionate mortals, we must repay you for so much kindness! You have saved our lives, how shall I ever acquit myself toward you?

ZAMOR: You owe us nothing, in helping you I obey only the voice of my heart. *(He exits)*

SCENE VII

Mirza, Sophie, Valère

MIRZA: *(To Sophie)* I like you, though you are not a slave. Come, I shall care for you. Give me your arm. Ah! what a pretty hand, so different from mine! Let us sit here. *(Gaily)* How happy I am to be with you! You are as fair as our Governor's wife.

SOPHIE: Yes? You have a Governor on this Island?

VALÈRE: It seems to me that you told us that you live here alone?

MIRZA: *(With frankness)* Oh! It is quite true, and Zamor has not deceived you. I spoke to you of the Governor of the Colony, who does not live with us. *(Aside)* I must be careful of what I am going to say; for if he knew that Zamor has killed a white man, he would not want to remain with us.

SOPHIE: *(To Valère)* Her ingenuousness delights me, her countenance is sweet, and prejudices in her favor.

VALÈRE: I have not seen a prettier Negress.

MIRZA: You mock me; I am not for all that the prettiest; but, tell me, are all French women as fair as you? They must be so; for Frenchmen are all good, and you are not slaves.

VALÈRE: No, Frenchmen have a horror of slavery. One day more free they will see about tempering your fate.

MIRZA: *(With surprise)* More free one day, how so, are you not free?

VALÈRE: We are free in semblance, but our irons are only the heavier. For several centuries the French have been groaning under the despotism of Ministers and Courtiers. The power of a single Master is in the hands of a thousand Tyrants who trample the People underfoot. This People will one day break its irons and, resuming all its rights under Natural Law, it will teach these Tyrants what the union of a people too long oppressed and enlightened by a sound philosophy can do.

MIRZA: Oh! Dear God! There are then evil men everywhere!

SCENE VIII

Zamor, on the cliff, Sophie, Valère, Mirza

ZAMOR: The worst has happened, unhappy Strangers! You have no hope. A wave has just swallowed up the remains of the equipage along with all of your hopes.

SOPHIE: Alas! What shall become of us?

VALÈRE: A vessel can land on this Island.

ZAMOR: You do not know, unhappy Strangers, how dangerous this coast is. There are only unfortunates like Mirza and me, who have dared to approach it and overcome all perils to inhabit it. We are, however, only two leagues from one of the bigger towns in the Indies; a town that I shall never see again unless our tyrants come and tear us away from here to make us suffer the punishment to which we are condemned.

SOPHIE: Torture!

VALÈRE: What crime have you both committed? Ah! I see; you are too educated for a slave, and the person who gave you your instruction has paid a high price no doubt.

ZAMOR: Monsieur, do not hold your fellowmen's prejudices against me. I had a Master who was dear to me: I would have sacrificed my life to prolong his days, but his Steward was a monster whom I have purged from the land. He loved Mirza; but his love was scorned. He learned that she preferred me, and in his fury he had me suffer frightful treatment; but the most terrible was to demand that I become the instrument of his vengeance against my dear Mirza. I rejected such a commission with horror. Irritated by my disobedience, he came at me with his naked sword; I avoided the blow that he wanted to give me; I disarmed him and he fell dead at my feet. I had but the time to carry off Mirza and to flee with her in a longboat.

SOPHIE: How I pity him, this unhappy man! Though he has committed murder, this murder seems worthy of mercy to me.

VALÈRE: I am interested in their fate; they brought me back to life, they saved yours: I shall defend them at the cost of my days. I shall go myself to see his Governor: If he is a Frenchman, he must be humane and generous.

ZAMOR: Yes, Monsieur, he is a Frenchman and the best of men.

MIRZA: Ah! If all the Colonists were like him, we would be less unhappy.

ZAMOR: I have belonged to him since I was eight years old; he took pleasure in having me educated and loved me as if I had been his son; for he never had one, or perhaps he was deprived of one: he seems to regret something. Sometimes you hear him sighing; surely he strives to hide some great sorrow. I have often surprised him in tears: he adores his wife, and she him in kind. If it depended only upon him, I would be pardoned; but they need an example. There is no hope of a pardon for a slave who has raised a hand against his Commander.

SOPHIE: *(To Valère)* I do not know why this Governor interests me. The account of his sorrows lies heavy on my heart; he is generous, clement; he can pardon you. I shall go myself and throw myself at his feet. His name? If only we could leave this Island.

ZAMOR: His name is Monsieur de Saint-Frémont.

SOPHIE: Alas! This name is unknown to me; but no matter, he is a Frenchman: he will hear me, and I hope to move him to mercy. *(To Valère)* If with the longboat that saved them, we could guide ourselves into port, there is no peril that I would not brave to defend them.

VALÈRE: I admire you, my dear Sophie! I approve of your plan: we have only to make our way to their Governor. *(To the Slaves)* My friends, this step barely discharges us of our obligation to you. Happy if our entreaties and our tears move your generous Master! Let us leave, but what do I see? Here are some slaves who are examining us and who are hurrying toward us. They are carrying chains.

SOPHIE: Unhappy lovers, you are lost!

Zamor: *(Turns around and sees the Slaves)* Mirza, the worst has happened! They have found us.

SCENE IX

The Same, an Indian, *several slaves who are running down from the rock*
INDIAN: *(To Zamor)* Scoundrel! At last, I find you; you will not escape punishment.
MIRZA: May they put me to death before him!
ZAMOR: O my dear Mirza!
INDIAN: Put them in chains.
VALÈRE: Monsieur, listen to our entreaties! What are you going to do with these Slaves?
INDIAN: A terrible example.
SOPHIE: You are taking them away to put them to death? You will take away our lives before tearing them from our arms.
VALÈRE: What are you doing? My dear Sophie! We can place all our hope in the Governor's indulgence.
INDIAN: Do not flatter yourself. The Governor must set an example for the Colony. You do not know this cursed race; they would slit our throats without pity if the voice of humanity spoke in their favor. That is what you must always expect, even from Slaves who have received some instruction. They are born to be savages and tamed like animals.
SOPHIE: What frightful prejudice! Nature did not make them Slaves; they are men like you.
INDIAN: What language do you speak, Madame?
SOPHIE: The same which I would speak before your Governor. It is gratitude that interests me in these unfortunates, who know better than you the rights of pity; he whose position you uphold was no doubt a wicked man.
ZAMOR: Ah! Madame, cease your entreaties; his soul is hardened and does not know kindness. It is his daily task to make this rigor conspicuous. He believes that he would not be performing his duty if he did not push rigor to cruelty.
INDIAN: Wretch!
ZAMOR: I fear you no longer. I know my fate and shall submit to it.
SOPHIE: How their misfortune renders them interesting! What would I not do to save them!
VALÈRE: *(To the Indian)* Take us away with them, Monsieur. You will oblige us to withdraw from here. *(Aside)* I hope to move the Governor to mercy.

INDIAN: I consent with pleasure, especially as the danger leaving this Island is not the same as that risked to reach it.

VALÈRE: But Monsieur, how were you able to land here?

INDIAN: I risked everything for the good of the Colony. See if it is possible to pardon them. We are no longer the Masters of our Slaves. Our Governor's life is perhaps in danger, and order will be restored on the plantations once these two poor wretches are punished. *(To the Negroes)* Negroes, fire the cannon, and let the prearranged signal announce to the Fort that the criminals are taken.

ZAMOR: Let us go Mirza, we are going to die.

MIRZA: Ah! God! I am the cause of his death.

ZAMOR: Our good action in saving these Strangers will cast some charm on our last moments, and we shall taste at least the sweetness of dying together.

Zamor and Mirza are led away; the other characters follow them, and they are all about to embark. The next moment the ship carrying them goes past.

End of Act One.

Act II

A Company Drawing-room with Indian furnishings.

SCENE I

Betzi, Azor

BETZI: Well, Azor, what do they say about Mirza and Zamor? They are searching for them everywhere.

AZOR: There is talk of putting them to death on the rock by the plantation; I even believe that preparations for their punishment are being readied. I tremble that they may find them.

BETZI: But the Governor can pardon them. He is their master.

AZOR: That must be impossible; for he loves Zamor, and he says that he never had any complaint with him. The whole Colony is asking for their death; he cannot refuse it without compromising himself.

BETZI: Our Governor was not made to be a Tyrant.

AZOR: How good he is to us! All Frenchmen are the same; but the Natives of this country are much more cruel.

BETZI: I have been assured that we were not originally slaves.

AZOR: Everything leads us to believe that. There are still climes where Negroes are free.

BETZI: How fortunate they are!

AZOR: Ah! We are really to be pitied.

Betzi: And no one undertakes our defense! We are even forbidden to pray for our fellow men.

AZOR: Alas! the father and mother of the unfortunate Mirza will witness their daughter's punishment.

BETZI: Such ferociousness!

AZOR: That is how they treat us.

BETZI: But, tell me, Azor, why did Zamor kill the Steward?

AZOR: I was assured that it was from jealousy. You know quite well that Zamor was Mirza's lover.

BETZI: Yes, it was you who informed me of it.

AZOR: The Commander loved her too.

BETZI: But he ought not to kill him for that.

AZOR: That is true.

BETZI: There were other reasons.

AZOR: That may well be, but I am unaware of them.

BETZI: If we could let them escape, I am sure that Monsieur and Madame de St-Frémont would not be angry.

AZOR: I think that too, but those who would serve them would put themselves at great risk.

BETZI: No doubt, but there would not be a death penalty.

AZOR: Perhaps, I still know that I would not risk it.

BETZI: We should at least talk to their friends; they could win over the other slaves. They all love Zamor and Mirza.

AZOR: There is talk of arming the entire regiment.

BETZI: It is hopeless.

AZOR: On the contrary, we must urge them to obey for the good of our comrades.

BETZI: You are right; do it if you can, for I would never have the strength for it.

SCENE II

The Same, Coraline

CORALINE: *(Running)* O my dear comrades! What bad news I bring you! It is certain that cannon fire has been heard and that Zamor and Mirza are captured.

AZOR: Come, that is not possible, Coraline.

BETZI: Almighty God!

CORALINE: I was at the port when they announced this unfortunate news. Several Colonists were awaiting impatiently a ship that could be seen in the distance. It finally entered port, and all the planters surrounded it immediately. I ran away, trembling. Poor Mirza! unhappy Zamor! our tyrants will not pardon them.

AZOR: Oh! You may take my word for it; they will soon be dead.

BETZI: Without a hearing? Without a trial?

CORALINE: Trial! We are forbidden to be innocent and to justify ourselves.

AZOR: What generosity! And, in the bargain, they sell us like cattle at the market.

BETZI: A commerce of men! O Heaven! Humanity is repulsive.

AZOR: It is quite true, my father and I were bought on the Coast of Guinea.

CORALINE: There, there, my poor Azor, whatever our deplorable fate, I have a presentiment that we shall not always be in irons, and perhaps before long . . .

AZOR: Well then! What shall we see? Shall we be masters in our turn?

CORALINE: Perhaps; but no, we would be too wicked. Indeed, to be good, one must be neither master nor slave.

AZOR: Neither master, nor slave; Oh! Oh! And what do you want us to be? Do you know, Coraline, that you no longer know what you are saying, though our comrades assure us that you know more about this than we do?

CORALINE: There, there, my poor boy, if you knew what I know! I read in a certain Book that to be happy one need only be free and a good Farmer. We lack but liberty, let them give it to us, and you will see that there will no longer be masters or slaves.

AZOR: I do not understand you.

BETZI: Neither do I.

CORALINE: My God, how kind you both are! Tell me, was Zamor not free? And because of that, did he want to leave our kind Master?; we shall all do the same thing. Let the Masters give liberty; no Slave will leave the workshop. Imperceptibly, the rudest among us will instruct themselves, recognize the laws of humanity and justice, and our superiors will find in our attachment, in our zeal, the reward for this kindness.

AZOR: You speak like a man! You sound like the Governor . . . Oh! One must have wit to retain everything that others say. But, here is Madame.

BETZI: Here is Madame, let us be silent!

CORALINE: We must not tell Madame that we fear that Zamor has been captured. That would grieve her too much.

AZOR: Oh! Yes.

SCENE III

The Same, Mme de Saint-Frémont

MME DE SAINT-FRÉMONT: My children, I need to be alone. Leave me, and do not enter unless I call for you, or you have some news to announce. *(They exit)*

SCENE IV

MME DE SAINT-FRÉMONT: *(Alone)* My spouse has gone out on account of this unfortunate matter: he went to one of the plantations where his attendance was requested. Since this catastrophe revolt reigns in the minds of our slaves. All maintain that Zamor is innocent, and that he only killed the Commander because he saw himself forced to; but the Colonists have gathered to ask for the death of Mirza and Zamor, and Mirza and Zamor are being sought everywhere. My husband really wanted to pardon Zamor, though he pronounced his judgment, as well as that of poor Mirza, who is to perish with her lover. Alas! Expectation of their punishment throws me into a profound sadness. I am thus not born to be happy! In vain am I adored by my spouse: my love cannot conquer the melancholy that consumes him. He has been suffering for more than ten years, and I cannot divine the cause of his sorrow. It is the only one of his secrets which he has not entrusted to me. When he returns I must redouble my efforts to wrench it from him. But I hear him.

SCENE V

Mme de Saint-Frémont, M. de Saint-Frémont

MME DE SAINT-FRÉMONT: Well, then! My dear, did your presence dispel this unrest?

M. DE SAINT-FRÉMONT: All of my slaves have returned to their duties; but they ask me to pardon Zamor. This matter is quite delicate, (Aside) and as a crowning misfortune, I have just received heart-rending news from France.

MME DE SAINT-FRÉMONT: What are you saying, my dear, you seem to reproach yourself. Ah! If you are only guilty with regard to me, I forgive you so long as your heart is still mine. You look away; I see the tears in your eyes. Ah! My dear, I no longer have your trust; I am becoming tiresome to you; I am going to retire.

M. DE SAINT-FRÉMONT: You, become tiresome to me! Never, never. Ah! If I could have strayed from my duty, your sweetness alone would have brought me back to your feet, and your great virtues would render me still more in love with your charms.

MME DE SAINT-FRÉMONT: But you hide a secret worry from me. Confess it to me. Your stifled sighs make me suspect so. France was dear to you; she is your Country ... Perhaps an inclination ...

M. DE SAINT-FRÉMONT: Stop, stop, dear spouse, and do not reopen an old wound that had closed beside you. I fear distressing you.

MME DE SAINT-FRÉMONT: If I were dear to you, you must give me proof of it.

M. DE SAINT-FRÉMONT: What kind of proof do you demand?

MME DE SAINT-FRÉMONT: The kind that reveals the causes of your affliction to me.

M. DE SAINT-FRÉMONT: This is what you want?

MME DE SAINT-FRÉMONT: I demand it; be forgiven, by this complaisance, for this secret that you have kept from me for so long.

M. DE SAINT-FRÉMONT: I obey. I am from a Province where unjust and inhuman laws deprive younger children of the equal share that Nature gives to children born of the same father and mother. I was the youngest of seven; my parents sent me to the Court to ask for employment; but how could I have succeeded in a country where virtue is a chimera, and where nothing is obtained without intrigue and baseness. However, I made the acquaintance of a worthy Scottish Gentleman who had come in the same purpose. He was not rich, and had a daughter in a Convent: he took me there. This interview turned fatal for both of us. The father, after several months, left for the army: He enjoined me to go and see his daughter, and even said that she could be entrusted to me when she wanted to go out. This worthy friend, this good father, did not foresee the consequences occasioned by his imprudence. He was killed in battle. His daughter was all alone in the world, without family or friends. She saw only me, and appeared to desire only my presence. Love rendered me guilty: Spare me the rest: I swore an oath to be her spouse; there is my crime.

MME DE SAINT-FRÉMONT: But, my dear, did you determine by yourself to abandon her?

M. DE SAINT-FRÉMONT: Who, me? to have abandoned such a fine

woman? Ah! The longest absence would never have made me forget her. I could not marry her without the consent of my whole family. She became the mother of a daughter. Our liaison was discovered; I was banished. They procured me a commission as Captain in a regiment that was leaving for the Indies and made me embark in it. Not long after I received the false news that Clarisse was dead, and that only my daughter remained. I saw you every day; with time your presence weakened the impression that Clarisse's image still made on my heart. I requested your hand, you accepted my vows, and we were united; but by an over-refinement of barbarity, the cruel relation who had deceived me informed me that Clarisse was still living.

MME DE SAINT-FRÉMONT: Alas! At what fatal price have I the honor of being your spouse! My dear, you are more unhappy than guilty. Clarisse herself would forgive you, if she were witness to your remorse. We must conduct an intensive search, so that your property and mine may acquit us toward these unfortunates. I have no other relations but yours. I am making your daughter my heiress; but your heart is a treasure that it is not in my power to surrender to another.

M. DE SAINT-FRÉMONT: Ah! Worthy spouse, I admire your virtues. Alas! I see only Clarisse who was capable of imitating them. It is thus at opposite ends of the earth that I was destined to meet the fairest and the most virtuous of your sex!

MME DE SAINT-FRÉMONT: You deserve a companion worthy of yourself; but, my dear, consider that in marrying me you consented to take the name of my father, who, by giving you his name, had no other aim save yielding his position to you as to an adopted son. You must write your relations, especially your most faithful friends, that they renew the search, and give us prompt news of these unfortunates. I believe, my dear, that I shall have the strength to leave you in order to seek the daughter whom you fathered. I already feel a mother's compassion for her; but at the same time I shudder. O my dear, my dear! If I had to separate from you! If Clarisse tore you from my arms!. . . Her misfortunes, her virtues, her charms . . . Ah! Forgive, forgive my despair, forgive me, dear spouse, you are not capable of abandoning me and making two victims for one.

M. DE SAINT-FRÉMONT: Dear spouse! O half of myself! Cease breaking this heart which already grieves too much. No doubt Clarisse is no longer alive, as it has been two years now that all of the funds that I send to France for her and for my daughter are sent back to me. What has become of them is not even known. But someone is coming; we shall resume this conversation later.

SCENE VI

M. and Mme de Saint-Frémont
A Judge

JUDGE: Monsieur, I have come to inform you that the criminals are captured.

MME DE SAINT-FRÉMONT: What! So soon! Time would have erased their crime.

M. DE SAINT-FRÉMONT: *(Grieved)* What a frightful example I am obliged to give!

JUDGE: Remember, Monsieur, your father-in-law's disgrace in this instance. He was constrained to give up his position for having exercised it with too much kindness.

M. DE SAINT-FRÉMONT: *(Aside)* Unhappy Zamor, you are going to perish! I have thus raised you from childhood only to see you dragged off to be tortured. *(Aloud)* That my good offices should become fatal for him! If I had left him in his rude manners, perhaps he would not have committed this crime. He had no vicious inclinations in his soul. Honesty and virtue distinguished him in the bosom of slavery. Raised in a simple and hard life, despite the instruction that he had received, he never forgot his roots. How sweet it would be for me to be able to justify him! As a simple planter, I would perhaps be able to temper his arrest; but as Governor I am forced to deliver him to the full rigor of the law.

JUDGE: They must be put to death at once, more especially as two Europeans have incited a general revolt among the Slaves. They depicted your Commander as a monster. The Slaves listened avidly to these seditious speeches, and all have promised not to execute the orders that they were given.

M. DE SAINT-FRÉMONT: Who are these foreigners?

JUDGE: They are French citizens who were found on the coast where these criminals had taken refuge. They claim that Zamor saved their lives.

M. DE SAINT-FRÉMONT: Alas! These unfortunate French citizens were no doubt shipwrecked, and gratitude alone has produced this indiscreet zeal.

JUDGE: You see, Governor, sir, that there is no time to lose, if you want to avoid the total ruin of our plantations. There is hopeless disorder.

M. DE SAINT-FRÉMONT: I do not have the good fortune of having been born in your climes; but what sway the unfortunate hold over sensitive souls! It is not your fault if the manners of your country familiarized you with these harsh treatments that you exercise without remorse on men who have no other defense save their timidity, and whose work, so ill recompensed, increases our fortunes by increasing our authority over them. They have a thousand tyrants for one. Sovereigns render their People happy: every Citizen is free under a good Master, and in this country of slavery one must be barbaric in spite of oneself. Hey! How can I help abandoning myself to these reflections, when the voice of humanity cries out from the bottom of my heart: "Be kind and sensitive to the cries of the wretched." I know that my opinion must displease you: Europe, however, takes care to justify it, and I dare hope that before long there will no longer be any slaves. O Louis! O adored Monarch! Would that I could this very moment put under your eyes the innocence of these condemned souls! In granting their pardon, you would render freedom to those too long unrecognized; but no matter: you want an example, it shall be done, though the Blacks assure us that Zamor is innocent.

JUDGE: Can you believe them in this?

M. DE SAINT-FRÉMONT: They cannot deceive me, and I know more than they the virtues of Zamor. You want him to die without a hearing? I consent with regret; but you will not be able to reproach me for having betrayed the interests of the Colony.

JUDGE: You must do it, Governor, sir, in this matter in which you see that we are threatened with a general revolt. You must give the orders to arm the troops.

M. DE SAINT-FRÉMONT: Follow me; we shall see what decision should be made.

MME DE SAINT-FRÉMONT: My dear, I see you go in sorrow.

M. DE SAINT-FRÉMONT: My presence is necessary to restore order and discipline.

SCENE VII

MME DE SAINT-FRÉMONT: *(Alone)* How I pity these wretches! The worst has happened! They are going to die. What chagrin for my spouse; but a greater chagrin agitates me once more. All that bears the name of a French woman terrifies me! If it were Clarisse! Oh! Unhappy me, what would be my fate? I know the virtues of my spouse, but I am his wife. No, no! let us cease in our deception! Clarisse, in misfortune, has greater rights on his soul! Let us hide the trouble that agitates me.

Mme De Saint-Frémont, Betzi *rushing up*

MME DE SAINT-FRÉMONT: What news is there, Betzi?

BETZI: *(With exaltation)* The Governor is not here?

MME DE SAINT-FRÉMONT: No, he has just gone out, speak?

BETZI: Ah! Let me regain my senses . . . We were on the terrace; from time to time we glanced sadly at the plantation. We see Mirza's father arrive from afar with another Slave; amid them was a foreigner, her hair disheveled and sorrow coloring her face: her eyes stared at the ground, and though she walked quickly, she seemed very preoccupied. When she was near us, she asked for Mme de Saint-Frémont. She informed us that Zamor had saved her from the fury of the waves. She added: I shall die at the feet of the Governor if I do not obtain his pardon. She wants to implore your assistance. Here she is.

SCENE IX

The Same, Sophie, *followed by all the Slaves*

SOPHIE: *(Throwing herself at the knees of Mme de Saint-Frémont)* Madame, I embrace your knees. Have pity on an unhappy stranger who owes everything to Zamor and has no other hope but in your kind actions.

MME DE SAINT-FRÉMONT: *(Aside)* Ah! I breathe again. *(Aloud, while lifting Sophie to her feet)* Rise, Madame, I promise to do all that is within my power. *(Aside)* Her youth, her sensibility, touch my heart beyond words. *(To Sophie)* Interesting Stranger, I shall use every means to make my spouse grant the pardon that you demand. Believe that I share your sorrows. I sense how dear these unfortunates must be to you.

SOPHIE: Without Zamor's help, as intrepid as it was humane, I would have perished in the waves. I owe him the good fortune of seeing you. What he did for me earns him my heartfelt assurance of his natural rights; but these rights do not render me unjust, Madame, and the testimony that they render to your rare qualities shows well enough that Zamor and Mirza cannot be reproached with a premeditated crime. What humanity! What zeal in succoring us! The fate that pursues them was to inspire them with fear rather than pity; but, far from shunning peril, Zamor has dared all. Judge, Madame, if with these feelings of humanity, a mortal can be guilty; his crime was involuntary, and to acquit him as innocent is to treat him as he deserves.

MME DE SAINT-FRÉMONT: *(To the Slaves)* My children, we must unite with the Colonists and ask that Zamor and Mirza be pardoned. We have no time to lose: *(To Sophie)* and you, whom I am burning to know, you are a French woman, perhaps you could . . . but moments are dear to us. Go back beside these unfortunates; Slaves, accompany her.

SOPHIE: *(Transported)* Ah! Madame, so many kindnesses at once! Alas! I should like, as much as I desire it, to prove my gratitude to you. *(She kisses her hands)* Soon my spouse will come and acquit himself of his obligation to you. Dear Valère, what happy news I am going to tell you! *(She exits with the Slaves)*

SCENE X

Mme de Saint-Frémont, Betzi, Coraline

MME DE SAINT-FRÉMONT: *(Aside)* I find a resemblance in the features of this Stranger . . . What a chimera! . . . (Aloud) And you, Coraline, summon M. de Saint-Frémont's Secretary.

CORALINE: Ah! Madame, you are unaware of what is happening: he has just commanded your doors closed by order of the Governor. Everything is ablaze . . . Listen, Madame . . . There is the call to arms . . . and the sound of bells . . . *(The alarm must be heard in the distance)*

MME DE SAINT-FRÉMONT: *(Going with fright to the back of the theatre)* Wretched! What is to become of me? What does my husband do?

BETZI: I tremble for my comrades.

MME DE SAINT-FRÉMONT: *(Having given way to the greatest sorrow)* God, my Spouse is perhaps in danger! I fly to his aid . . .

CORALINE: Set your mind at rest, Madame, there is nothing to fear for the Governor. He is at the head of the regiment. But even if he were in the midst of the tumult, all the Slaves would respect his life. He is too cherished for anyone to want to harm him. The Slaves bear ill will only against some planters: they reproach them with the punishment of Zamor and Mirza; they are certain that

without these planters Zamor and Mirza would not have been
condemned.

MME DE SAINT-FRÉMONT: *(Agitated)* What! They are going to put
them to death.

CORALINE: Alas! Soon my poor comrades will be no longer.

MME DE SAINT-FRÉMONT: *(With alacrity)* No, my children, they
shall not perish: my husband will be moved by my tears, by this
Stranger's despair, who, perhaps better than I, will know how to
move him. His heart does not need to be incited to do good; but
he can take everything upon himself. *(Aside)* And if this French
woman were to give him news of his daughter! Almighty God! he
would owe everything to these victims who are being dragged off
to torture. *(Aloud)* Let us go, Betzi, we must join my husband, tell
him . . . But how to enter into an explanation just now? I must
see him myself. Where is he now?

CORALINE: I do not know precisely with which regiment he is: the
entire army is in rout. They say only that M. de Saint-Frémont
restores calm and order wherever he passes. It would be very
difficult to find him just now. We have but to return to the plantation, if we have not already been forestalled. But the roads are
broken up or cut off. It is hardly conceivable that they could have
done so much damage in so little time.

MME DE SAINT-FRÉMONT: No matter. I fear neither danger nor
weariness when the lives of two unfortunates are at stake.

End of Act II

Act III

A wild spot from which two pointed hills are visible, bordered by
clusters of shrubby trees for as far as the eye can see. On one side is
a steep cliff whose summit is a platform and whose base is perpendicu-
lar to the fore-stage. All of the characters come on stage from the
side of one of the hills so that the audience can see them enter. A few
Negro huts are scattered here and there.

SCENE I

Valère, Zamor, Mirza

VALÈRE: Free! Both of you are free! I hasten to your chief. It will
not be long before my wife reappears before our eyes. She will
no doubt have obtained your pardon from M. de Saint-Frémont.
I leave you for a moment but do not lose sight of you.

SCENE II

Zamor, Mirza

ZAMOR: O my dear Mirza, our fate is deplorable! It is becoming so frightful that I fear this Frenchman's zeal to save us will only harm him and his wife. What a devastating idea!

MIRZA: The same idea pursues me: but perhaps his worthy wife will have succeeded in moving our Governor to mercy; let us not grieve before her return.

ZAMOR: I bless my death since I die with you; but, how cruel it is to lose one's life a culprit! I have been judged such, our good master believes it; that is what makes me despair.

MIRZA: I want to see the Governor myself. This last wish must be granted me. I shall throw myself at his feet; I shall reveal everything to him.

ZAMOR: Alas! What could you say to him?

MIRZA: I shall make him know the cruelty of his Commander and of his ferocious love.

ZAMOR: Your tenderness for me blinds you: you want to accuse yourself to render me innocent! If you scorn life at this price, do you believe me miserly enough to want to preserve it at your expense? No, my dear Mirza, there is no happiness for me on earth if I do not share it with you.

MIRZA: It is the same for me; I could no longer live without seeing you.

ZAMOR: How sweet it would have been for us to prolong our days together! This spot reminds me of our first encounter. It is here that the tyrant received his death; it is here that they are going to end our lives. Nature seems to stand in contrast with herself in this spot. Formerly she smiled upon us: she has lost none of her attractions; but she shows us both the image of our past happiness and the horrible fate to which we shall be victim. Ah! Mirza, how cruel it is to die when one is in love.

MIRZA: How you move me! Do not distress me more. I feel that my courage abandons me; but this good Frenchman is returning to us; what shall we learn from him?

SCENE III

Zamor, Mirza, Valère

VALÈRE: O my benefactors! You must run away. Avail yourselves of these precious moments that your comrades procure for you. They are blocking off the roads; respond to their zeal and their courage. They risk themselves for you; flee to another clime. It is quite possible that my wife will not obtain your pardon. Several troops of soldiers can be seen approaching: you have time to escape by this hill. Go and live in the forests: your fellow men will receive you in their bosom.

MIRZA: This Frenchman is right. Come, follow me. He loves us; let us profit from his advice. Run away with me, dear Zamor; do not fear returning to live in the heart of the forest. You scarcely remember our laws, but soon your dear Mirza will recall their gentle impression for you.

ZAMOR: Well! I yield. It is but for you that I cherish life. (*He embraces Valère*) Farewell, most generous of men!

MIRZA: Alas! I must leave you, then, without the pleasure of throwing myself at your wife's feet!

VALÈRE: She will share your regrets, you can be sure; but flee this fatal spot.

SCENE IV

The Same, Sophie, Slaves

SOPHIE: (*Rushing into Valère's arms*) Ah!, my friend, thank Heaven: these victims shall not perish. Madame de Saint-Frémont promised me they would be pardoned.

VALÈRE: (*With joy*) Almighty God! What supreme happiness!

ZAMOR: Ah! I recognize her fair soul in these proceedings. (*To Valère*) Generous foreigners, may Heaven gratify your wishes! The Supreme Being will never abandon those who seek his likeness in good works.

VALÈRE: Ah! How happy you make our days!

MIRZA: How fortunate we are to have succored these French citizens! They owe us much; but we owe them even more.

SOPHIE: Madame de Saint-Frémont has assembled her best friends. I have instructed her of their innocence; she exerts all possible zeal in saving them. I had no trouble interesting her on their behalf; her soul is so fair, so sensitive to the troubles of the unfortunate.

ZAMOR: Her respectable husband equals her in merit and goodness.

SOPHIE: I did not have the good fortune of seeing him.

ZAMOR: (*Alarmed*) What do I see! A throng of soldiers arriving! Ah! All is over! You have been deceived, generous Frenchman; we are lost.

SOPHIE: Do not become alarmed; we must first find out . . .

VALÈRE: I shall risk my life to defend them. Alas! They were going to run away when you came to reassure them. I am going to ask the Officer in charge of this detachment what his mission is.

(A Company of Grenadiers and one of French Soldiers line up in the back of the Theatre, their bayonets extended. A troop of Slaves with bows and arrows stands in front of them; the troop is headed by the Major, the Judge, and M. de Saint-Frémont's Slave Steward.)

SCENE V

The Same, Major, Judge, Indian, *Grenadiers and French Soldiers, several Slaves*

VALÈRE: Monsieur, may I ask you what matter brings you here?

MAJOR: A cruel function. I come to execute the death sentence pronounced against these wretches.

SOPHIE: *(Upset)* You are going to have them put to death?

MAJOR: Yes, Madame.

VALÈRE: No, this frightful sacrifice will not be carried out.

SOPHIE: Madame de Saint-Frémont promised me they would be pardoned.

JUDGE: *(Harshly)* That is not within her power, the Governor himself could not grant them their pardon. Desist therefore in your stubborn wish to save them. You make their punishment more terrible. *(To the Major)* Major, sir, execute the order that you were given. *(To the Slaves)* And you, lead the criminals to the top of the rock.

INDIAN COMMANDER: Draw your bows!

VALÈRE: Stop! *(The Slaves listen only to Valère)*

JUDGE: Obey. *(The Major signals to the Soldiers; they run with their bayonets, which they point at the Slaves' chests; not one Slave budges)*

ZAMOR: *(Rushing up to meet them)* What are you doing? Only I deserve to die. What have my poor comrades done to you? Why slaughter them? Turn your arms against me. *(He opens his jacket)* Here is my breast! Cleanse their disobedience in my blood. The Colony asks only my death. Is it necessary that so many innocent victims who were not parties to my crime perish?

MIRZA: I am as guilty as Zamor; do not separate me from him: take my life out of pity; my days are bound to his destiny. I want to die first.

VALÈRE: *(To the Judge)* Monsieur, grant a stay of execution, I beg of you. I assure you they are to be pardoned.

MAJOR: *(To the Judge)* Monsieur, we can take this up ourselves; let us await the Governor.

JUDGE: *(Harshly)* I listen to nothing save my duty and the law.

VALÈRE: *(Furious)* Barbarian! Though your position makes the soul callous, your being even more cruel than the laws have prescribed, degrades what you do.

JUDGE: Major, sir, have this impudent man taken away to the Citadel.

MAJOR: He is a Frenchman: he will answer to the Governor for his conduct; I am not required to take orders from you in this matter.

JUDGE: Then execute those you were given.

SOPHIE: *(With heroism)* This excess of cruelty gives me courage. *(She runs and places herself between Zamor and Mirza, takes them both by the hand, and says to the Judge)* Barbarian! Dare to have me assassinated with them; I shall not leave them; nothing can wrench them from my arms.

VALÈRE: *(Transported)* Ah! My dear Sophie, this act of courage makes you even dearer to my heart.

JUDGE: *(To the Major)* Monsieur, have this impudent woman removed: you are not fulfilling your duty.

MAJOR: *(Indignant)* You demand it; but you will answer for the consequences. *(To the Soldiers)* Separate these foreigners from these slaves.

(Sophie screams while clasping Zamor and Mirza to her breast)

VALÈRE: *(Furious, running after Sophie)* If there is the slightest violence against my wife, then I cannot be held responsible for my actions. *(To the Judge)* And You, Barbarian, tremble, you may be sacrificed to my righteous fury.

A SLAVE: Were they to put us all to death, we would defend them.

(The Slaves line up around them, forming a rampart, the Soldiers and Grenadiers approach with their bayonets)

MAJOR: *(To the Soldiers)* Soldiers, stop. *(To the Judge)* I was not sent here to order carnage and bloodshed, but, rather to restore order. The Governor will not be long, and his prudence will best indicate what we must do. *(To the Foreigners and the Slaves)* Take heart; I will not use force; your efforts would be useless if I wanted to exercise it. *(To Sophie)* And you, Madame, you may stand aside with these wretches; I await the Governor. *(Sophie, Zamor and Mirza, exit with several Slaves)*

SCENE VI

Valère, Major, Judge, Indian, Grenadiers and Soldiers, Slaves

VALÈRE: I cannot abandon my wife in this state. Do your utmost to sway M. de Saint-Frémont. I do not need to recommend clemency to you; it must reign in your soul. Warriors have always been generous.

MAJOR: Rely upon me; withdraw and appear when it is time. *(Valère exits)*

SCENE VII

The Same, Except Valère

MAJOR: *(To the Judge)* There, Monsieur, is the fruit of too much harshness.

JUDGE: We are losing the Colony today because of your moderation.

MAJOR: More exactly; moderation is what may save the Colony. You know only your cruel laws, but I know the art of war and human nature. These are not our enemies whom we are fighting; these are our Slaves, or rather our Farmers. You would have them put to the sword to drive them to defeat, but, in this instance, imprudence would take us further than you think.

SCENE VIII

The Same, M. de Saint-Frémont, *entering from one side of the stage and Valère from the other. Two Companies of Grenadiers and Soldiers escort several Slaves in irons.*

VALÈRE: *(To M. de Saint-Frémont)* Ah! Monsieur, hear our prayers: you are a Frenchman, you will be just.

M. DE SAINT-FRÉMONT: I approve of your zeal; but in these climes zeal becomes indiscreet; it has even caused much trouble. I have just witnessed the most frightful attempt on a Magistrate. I had to use violence, contrary to my nature, to stop the slaves in their cruelty. I know all that you owe to these wretched creatures; but you do not have the right to defend them, nor to change the laws and manners of a country.

VALÈRE: I have at least the right that gratitude gives to all fair souls: whatever harshness you feign, my heart appeals to your heart.

M. DE SAINT-FRÉMONT: Cease your entreaties, it pains me too much to refuse you.

VALÈRE: Your worthy wife had made us hope against hope.

M. DE SAINT-FRÉMONT: She herself, Monsieur, is convinced of the absolute impossibility of what you ask.

VALÈRE: If it is a crime to have killed a monster who made nature shudder, this crime, at least, is excusable. Zamor was defending his own life, and that is his natural right.

JUDGE: You abuse the Governor's complaisance: you have already been told this. The laws condemn them as homicides; can you change the laws?

VALÈRE: No; but the laws could be tempered in favor of an involuntary crime.

JUDGE: Do you really think that? Temper the law in favor of a slave! We are not here in France; we need examples.

M. DE SAINT-FRÉMONT: The worst has happened; the general order must be executed.

VALÈRE: These words make my blood run cold and lie heavy on my heart . . . Dear wife, what will become of you? Ah! Monsieur, if you knew her sensibility, her misfortunes, you would be moved; she had placed all her hopes in your goodness; she even flattered herself that you would give her some particulars on the fate of a parent, her sole support, of whom she has been deprived since childhood, and who must be settled in some part of this Continent.

M. DE SAINT-FRÉMONT: Be assured that I shall do everything in my power to help you; but, as for the criminals, I can do nothing for them. Unhappy Stranger! Go and console her: she interests me without my knowing her. Deceive her even, if need be, so that she does not witness this frightful torture: tell her that they want to interrogate these wretches, that they must be left alone, and that their pardon depends perhaps upon this wise precaution.

VALÈRE: (Weeping) How we are to be pitied! I shall not survive their loss. (He exits)

SCENE IX

The Same, Except Valère

M. DE SAINT-FRÉMONT: How this Frenchman grieves me! His regrets on behalf of these unfortunates increase mine. They must die, and in spite of my leaning towards clemency . . . (With reflection) Zamor saved this foreigner; she is a French woman, and if I believe her husband, she is searching for a parent who lives in these climes. Would he be afraid to explain himself? His sorrow, his searches, his misfortunes . . . Unfortunate, if it were she . . . where is nature going to mislead me! And why am I surprised? This Foreigner's adventure is so much like my daughter's . . . and my cankered heart would like to rediscover my daughter in her. It is the fate of the wretched to cherish hope and to find consolation in the slightest connections.

JUDGE: Major, sir, advance your Soldiers. *(To the Indian)* Commander, sir, escort the Slaves, and line them up as customary.
(The Indian exits with the armed Slaves, while a troop of the others throw themselves at the feet of M. de Saint-Frémont)

SCENE X

The Same, Except the Indian

(Armed Slaves are replaced by unarmed Slaves)

A SLAVE: *(Kneeling)* Monseigneur, we have not been among the rebels' number. May we be permitted to ask for the pardon of our comrades! To redeem their lives we would suffer the most terrible chastisements. Increase our arduous toil; reduce our food rations; we would endure this punishment with courage. Monseigneur, you are moved to tears, I see the tears in your eyes.

M. DE SAINT-FRÉMONT: My children, my friends, what are you proposing? *(To the Judge)* How do you want me to respond to this act of heroism? Ah! Heavens! They show such greatness of soul, and we dare to regard them as the meanest of men! Civilized men! You believe yourselves superior to Slaves! From infamy and the vilest state, equity and courage raise them in one instant to the ranks of the most generous mortals. You see the example before your eyes.

JUDGE: They know your heart well; but you cannot yield to your inclination without compromising your dignity. I know them better than you; they promise everything in these moments; besides, these criminals are no longer in your power; they are delivered to the rigor of the law.

M. DE SAINT-FRÉMONT: Well, then, I abandon them to you. Alas! Here they are. Where can I hide? How cruel this duty is!

SCENE XI

The Same, Indian, Zamor, Mirza

ZAMOR: There is no longer any hope; our benefactors are surrounded by soldiers. Embrace me for the last time, my dear Mirza!

MIRZA: I bless my fate, since the same torment reunites us. *(To an old man and an old Slave woman)* Adieu, dear authors of my days; do not cry for your dear Mirza; she is no longer to be pitied. *(To the Slaves of her sex)* Adieu, my companions.

ZAMOR: Slaves, Colonists, listen to me: I have killed a man; I deserve to die. Do not regret my punishment, it is necessary for the good of the Colony. Mirza is innocent; but she cherishes her death. *(To the Slaves, in particular)* And you, my dear friends, listen to me in my last hour. I leave this life, I die innocent but fear rendering yourself guilty by defending me: fear especially this factious spirit, and never deliver yourselves into excess to escape slavery; fear breaking your irons with too much violence; time and divine justice are on your side; stand by the Governor and his respectable spouse. Pay them by your zeal and your attachment for all that I owe them. Alas! I cannot fulfill my obligation to them. Cherish this good Master, this good father, with a filial tenderness as I have always done. I shall die happy if I can believe at least that he will miss me! *(He throws himself at his feet)* Ah! My dear Master, am I still permitted to name you thus?

M. DE SAINT-FRÉMONT: *(With intense sorrow)* These words wring my heart. Wretched man! What have you done? Go, I no longer hold it against you; I suffer enough from the fatal duty that I fulfill.

ZAMOR: *(Bows and kisses his feet)* Ah! My dear master, death holds nothing frightful for me. You still cherish me; I die happy. *(He takes his hands)* May I kiss these hands for the last time!

M. DE SAINT-FRÉMONT: *(Full of pity)* Leave me, leave me, you are breaking my heart.

ZAMOR: *(To the armed Slaves)* My friends, do your duty. *(He takes Mirza in his arms and climbs upon the rock with her, where they both kneel. The Slaves aim their arrows)*

SCENE XII

The Same, Mme de Saint-Frémont, *with her Slaves, Grenadiers and French Soldiers*

MME DE SAINT-FRÉMONT: Stop, Slaves, and respect your governor's wife. *(To her husband)* Mercy, my friend, mercy!

SCENE XIII AND LAST

The Same, Valère, Sophie

SOPHIE: *(To Valère)* You restrain me in vain. I absolutely want to see them. Cruel one! You deceived me. *(To Mme de Saint-Frémont)* Ah! Madame, my strength abandons me. *(She falls into the arms of the Slaves)*

MME DE SAINT-FREMONT: *(To her husband)* My friend, you see this French woman's despair; would you not be moved?

SOPHIE: *(Recovering herself and throwing herself at the feet of M. de Saint-Frémont)* Ah Monsieur! I shall die of sorrow at your feet if you do not grant their pardon. It is within your heart and depends upon your power. Ah! If I cannot obtain it life no longer matters to me! We have lost everything. Deprived of a mother and of my fortune, abandoned at the age of five by a father, my consolation was in saving two victims who are dear to you.

M. DE SAINT-FRÉMONT: *(Aside, in the keenest agitation)* My memory . . . these features . . . that time . . . her age . . What confusion stirs my soul. *(To Sophie)* Ah Madame! Respond to my marked attention; may I ask you the names of those who gave you birth?

SOPHIE: *(Leaning on Valère)* Alas!

VALÈRE: Oh my dear Sophie!

M. DE SAINT-FRÉMONT: *(More warmly)* Sophie . . . *(Aside)* She was named Sophie. *(Aloud)* What name did you utter . . . Speak, answer me, for pity's sake, Madame, who was your mother?

SOPHIE: *(Aside)* What confusion agitates him, the more I examine him . . . *(Aloud)* The unfortunate Clarisse de Saint-Fort was my mother.

M. DE SAINT-FRÉMONT: Ah! My daughter, recognize me. Nature did not deceive me. Recognize the voice of a father too long absent from you and from your mother.

SOPHIE: Ah! My father! I am dying. *(She falls into the arms of the Soldiers)*

M. DE SAINT-FRÉMONT: O my daughter! O my blood!

SOPHIE: What did I hear? Yes, yes it is he . . . His features are still etched in my soul . . . What good fortune makes me find myself in your arms once more! I cannot express all the feelings that agitate me. But these wretched creatures, O my father, their fate is in your hands. Without their help your daughter would have perished. Grant to nature the first favor that she asks of you. Planters, Slaves, fall at the knees of the most generous of men; one finds clemency at the feet of virtue. *(All kneel, except the Judge and the Soldiers)*

SLAVES: Monseigneur!

PLANTERS: Governor, sir!

M. DE SAINT-FRÉMONT: What do you demand of me?

ALL: Their pardon.

M. DE SAINT-FRÉMONT: (Moved) My children, my wife, my friends, I grant it to you.

ALL: What happiness! *(The Grenadiers and soldiers genuflect)*

MAJOR: Brave warriors, do not blush at this show of sensibility; it purifies, not vilifies, courage.

MIRZA: Bless me! You change our unhappy fate; our happiness runneth over; manifestations of your justice never cease.

M. DE SAINT-FRÉMONT: My friends, I give you your liberty and shall look after your fortune.

ZAMOR: No, my master; keep watch over your kindnesses. The most precious kindness for our hearts would be to live in your midst along with all that you hold most dear.

M. DE SAINT-FRÉMONT: What! I have found my daughter again! I clasp her in my arms. A cruel fate thus ends its pursuit of me! O my dear Sophie! How I fear to learn of your mother's cruel fate.

SOPHIE: Alas! My poor mother is no longer! But, dear father, how sweet it is for me to see you. *(To Valère)* Dear Valère!

VALÈRE: I share your happiness.

MME DE SAINT-FRÉMONT: My daughter, see in me only a tender mother. Your father knows my intentions, and you will soon learn them yourself. Let us concern ourselves only with the marriage of Zamor and Mirza.

MIRZA: We are going to live to love each other. We shall live happily ever after.

ZAMOR: Yes, my dear Mirza; yes, we shall live happily ever after.

M. DE SAINT-FRÉMONT: My friends, I have just granted you your pardon. Would that I might also give liberty to all your fellow men, or at least temper their fate! Slaves, listen to me; if ever your destiny were to change, do not lose sight of the love of the public good, which until now has been unknown to you. Know that man, in his liberty, needs still to submit to wise and humane laws, and without disposing yourselves to reprehensible excesses, place all your hopes in a benevolent and enlightened Government. Let us go, my friends, my children, so that a general holiday may be the happy presage of this sweet liberty.

END.

DECLARATION OF THE RIGHTS OF WOMAN (EXCERPT)
Translated by Maryann DeJulio

It is essential that I say a few words about the public disturbances supposedly caused by the decree in favor of men of color on our islands. It is there that Nature shudders in horror; there that reason and humanity have not yet moved indurate souls; there especially that dissention and discord agitate their planters. It is not hard to guess the instigators of these incendiary fermentations: they exist right in the bosom of the National Assembly: they light the fire in Europe, which is to emblaze America. The colonists claim the right to rule like despots over men whose fathers and brothers they are; and failing to recognize natural rights, they proceed against even those with the slightest tinge of their own blood. These inhuman colonists say: our blood runs in their veins, but we shall spill it all, if needs be, to sate our greed or our blind ambition. It is in these places, where one is closest to nature, that father fails to recognize son; deaf to the cries of blood, he stifles all its charms. What can be expected of resistance against this? Suppressing it with violence renders it frightful; leaving it still in chains dispatches every calamity to America. A divine hand seems to spread man's appanage everywhere—liberty; the law alone has the right to repress this liberty if it degenerates into license, but it must be equal for all; it is liberty especially which the National Assembly must include in its decree, dictated by prudence and justice. May it work equally for the state of France, and be as attentive to new abuses as it has been to the old abuses which become daily more appalling! My opinion would still be to reconcile the executive and the legislative powers, for it seems to me that the one is everything, and the other nothing; from which shall be born, perhaps unfortunately, the loss of the French Empire. I consider these two powers like man and woman who must be united, but equal in strength and virtue, in order to live happily together.

RESPONSE TO THE AMERICAN CHAMPION
Translated by Maryann DeJulio

Since we are no longer fighting in France, Sir, I agree with you that we sometimes assassinate each other; that it is imprudent to provoke assassins; but it is even more indiscreet, more indecent, and more unjust, to attack people of honor, to attack them in the most inept way, and yet the most calumnious, by imputing a lack of courage to M. de La Fayette, whom you fear, perhaps, at the bottom of your heart. I shall tell you that I do not know this magnanimous hero as you claim. I know only that his reputation is intact, his worth known, like Bayard's heart,[4] his is fearless and unimpeachable; we shall perhaps owe him France's good fortune and her power as a nation. I shall not undertake to justify the famous men whom you provoke; they are all military men and French, and this title suffices for me to believe them worthy.

But, if I imitate you, Sir, by this kind of challenge, I stray a bit too far from my aim and blunder into the same gross error as you with respect to me. It is not the philosophers' cause, the cause of the Amis des Noirs, that I undertake to defend; it is my own, and you shall kindly permit me to use the only weapons that are within my power. We are going then to wage war, and this single combat, thanks to my *jeanlorgnerie*,[5] will not be murderous. Yet you grant me virtues and courage beyond my sex. I could acknowledge them without too much pride; but you do not credit me less gratuitously with the ambition to consult academicians, learned men and women of letters, and all the Muses, which protect more than one fool, and on which I set very little value, except for the writers, who have respected talent with honor and integrity, about language and my feeble productions. Literary merit amounts to very little when it is stripped of these two advantages: but let us pass on to that which is important for me to tell you, and of which you are completely unaware.

You claim, Sir, that the Amis des Noirs used a woman to provoke the colonists. It is certainly much more extraordinary that a man who evinces some spirit, some aptitude, and even gallantry, should charge a woman with being the bearer of a cartel, and want, by a venture as singular as it is cowardly, to prove her courage. I can appreciate your merit only as a kind of Don Quixote, and regard you as a slayer of giants and phantoms, which do not exist. Yet I want, by bringing you round to reason, to laugh with you at the troubles for which I see no remedy. You have to battle the Société des Amis des Noirs, and I, I have to confound something even more terrible, that is. . . . Time, which destroys everything, which changes the arts, manners and human justice at will, shall never change the corporate feeling of those of whom I have very strong reason to complain.

For several months now in France, we have seen error, imposture, and injustice unveiled, and finally we have seen the walls of the Bastille fall; but we have not yet seen the fall of the despotism that I attack. I therefore see myself reduced to trying to overthrow it. Despotism is a tree in the middle of a thickly wooded maze, bristling with thorns and prickles: to prune its branches I need all of Medea's magic. The retrieval of the golden fleece cost Jason less care and skill than the torment and snares it is going to cost me to avoid these poisonous branches that damage the celebrated tree and man's genius. To destroy them, I must lay low twenty dangerous dragons who, turning sometimes into zealous citizens, sometimes into supple serpents, creep everywhere and spread their venom over my works and my staff.

But, in my turn, must I not, Sir, rightfully suspect you of putting yourself *honorably* forward in this rampant faction which protested against *L'esclavage des nègres,* With what do you charge this work? With what do you charge the author? Is it to have sought to have the colonists in America slaughtered and to have been the agent of men whom I know less than you, who perhaps do not value all of my productions since I have shown that the abuse of liberty had born much evil? You know me very little. I was the apostle of a sweet liberty in the midst of despotism. But a true French woman, I idolize my country: I have sacrificed everything for her; I cherish my king to the same degree, and I would shed my blood to restore all that to which his virtues and his paternal tenderness entitle him. I would sacrifice neither my king to my country, nor my country to my king, but I would sacrifice myself to save them both together, persuaded as I am that the one cannot exist without the other. Man is known, so we claim, by his writings. Read me, Sir, from my *Lettre au peuple* to my *Lettre à la nation,* and you will recognize, dare I flatter myself, a heart and spirit that are truly French. Extreme parties have always feared and detested my productions. These two parties, divided by contrary interests, are always unmasked in my writings. My invariable maxims, my incorruptible sentiments, there are my principles. Royalist and true patriot, in life and in death, I show myself such as I am.

Since I have the courage to sign this written document, do likewise to show you are my equal and obtain my esteem, which is not perhaps indifferent to a gallant man: for I grant it with as much difficulty as Jean-Jacques. I may elevate myself to the level of this great man with respect to the righteous mistrust that he had of men: I have met few who are just and truly estimable. I do not reproach them minor faults, but their vices, their duplicity, and their remorseless inhumanity toward the weakest among us. May this revolution regenerate the spirit and the conscience of men, and reproduce the true French character! Permit me a word more, please.

I am not well informed though it pleased you to bestow this glory upon me. One day, perhaps, my memory will be well-known because of my ignorance. I know nothing, Sir; nothing, I tell you, and I have learned nothing from anyone. Student of simple nature, abandoned to her care alone, she thus enlightened me, since you think me completely informed. Without knowing the history of America, this odious Negro slave trade has always stirred my soul, aroused my indignation. The first dramatic ideas that I set down on paper were on behalf of this class of men tyrannized with cruelty for so many centuries. This feeble production may suffer perhaps a little too much from its being a dramatic career's debut. Our great men themselves did not all begin as they finished, and an attempt always deserves some indulgence. I can thus bear witness, Sir, that the Amis des Noirs did not exist when I conceived this subject, and you had rather assume, if prepossession has not blinded you, that this society is perhaps based on my drama, or that I have had the happy talent of nobly coming upon it. May they form a more general society, and inveigle it more often with its own representation! I did not try to chain public opinion to my patriotism; I patiently awaited its felicitous return in behalf of this drama. With what satisfaction I have heard myself say on all sides, that the changes that I had made generated wide-spread interest in this play, which can only increase when the public learns that, for four months now, I have dedicated this work to the nation, and that I have assigned its proceeds to the coffers of the patriots, whose establishment I presented in my *Lettre au peuple*, in print for 18 months. This priority justifies perhaps my considering myself, without vanity, the author. This pamphlet caused quite a stir at the time, was likewise criticized, and the plan that it offered has not been the less successfully effected. I should inform you, as well as the public, of these deeds that characterize the love that I have for the true French character and the efforts that I make for its preservation. I do not doubt that the Comedy, moved by these zealous acts, conspires to give the most propitious days* to the performance of this drama; I cannot dissemble their boundless interest in my play. The Comedy has given me proof thereof, which I cannot call in question. While multiplying their pleasures, the author, the Comedy, and the public will all contribute to increasing the stock of the patriots' coffers, which alone can save the state, if all citizens recognize this truth.

I must further note that in these patriotic performances a number of persons have often paid beyond the price of their seats. If this one moves them in the same way, then we must distinguish between the patriot's profits and the Comedy's rights. An accurate list, remitted to the nation by the Comedians, will give proof of these new citizens' zeal and fiat.

I hope, Sir, and I dare flatter myself, that after my enlightening you on *L'esclavage des nègres*, you will no longer proceed against it, and that you will become on the contrary the zealous protector of this drama; in having it even performed in America, it shall always bring black men round to their duties, while expecting the abolition of the black slave trade and a happier fate from colonists and the French nation. There are the attitudes that I have displayed in this work. I have not sought, under the circumstances, to make my play a banner of discord, a signal for insurrection; I have, on the contrary, since tempered its effect. If ever you doubt this assertion, read, I beseech you, *L'heureux naufrage,* in print for three years; and if I have made some allusion to men dear to France, these allusions are not at all harmful to America. The performance of my play will convince you of this, should you honor me by coming to see it. It is in this sweet hope that I beseech you to believe me, Sir, in spite of our little literary discussion, in accordance with accepted convention, your very humble servant,

DeGouge.

Paris, 18 January 1790.

POST-SCRIPTUM.

I would have thought to have compromised myself, if I had responded in the body of this letter to all the filth that an infamous lampoonist has just spread about me in his mercenary rag. It is sufficient for me to remind the public, in order to confound this abominable calumniator, of *La lettre écrite à M. le duc d'Orléans, La motion,* or *Séance royale.* The public will recognize that I employed the voice of honor with this prince in order to bring him round to his duty, if he had strayed from it; but at the same time these writings unmasked him, if he were guilty. I do not know if he were in fact, but that of which I am convinced, is that my son was sacrificed and has just lost his position in the house of this prince. There is my justification.

*Everyone knows that when the Comedians do not take every possible interest in an author, they grant her only the worst days for the performance of her work, that is, Tuesdays, Thursdays, and Fridays, and furthermore, that her work is most often performed only with hackneyed plays, which are not liable to draw a crowd.

On Translating Olympe de Gouges

Maryann DeJulio

Olympe de Gouges wrote the Preface to *L'esclavage des noirs* to vindicate herself and her play. She hoped to convince the public that she had not produced an incendiary work in *L'esclavage des noirs,* and, furthermore, that the Colonists and the Comedians had sabotaged her play for financial and political gain. Like all good rhetoricians, Gouges relies upon "emotional persuasion to excite her public to pity, indignation, contempt, horror, and conviction."[1] She makes full use of the melodramatic potential of the contents of her own story in order to establish her rights as a citizen by explaining them to the judges and to the public. It is therefore not at all surprising that Gouges's writing recalls the *mémoires judiciares* of her day, printed versions of lawyers' defenses of their clients, which developed in the later eighteenth century into a highly popular form of pamphlet literature.[2]

My translation of the Preface to *L'esclavage des noirs* emphasizes the legal conventions and the popular style of pamphletism, which influenced Gouges's writings; she herself wrote a number of pamphlets devoted to the Revolution.[3] Whenever possible, my portrait of Gouges stresses the fact that her ideas derive from sensations, a commonplace in an era impressed with Lockean epistemology, and that these sensations are particular to a woman writer and activist who seeks to accord public consciousness with her own experiences.

Key terms in my translation, which relate to legal conventions, include the following: *témoin auriculaire* (earwitness); *en état d'arrestation* (under arrest); *plaider ma cause* (plead my own case); *Tribunal* (Tribunal); *au scrutin des consciences* (a vote of conscience); *pluralité des voix* (majority); *preuve* (proof); and *droits incontestables* (incontestable right). I have maintained the cognate *force majeure* and inserted terms such as "thereof" and "whereby" to effect a language of contract law, thus underscoring Gouges's bold appropriation of an idiom exercised by professionals openly hostile to women inasmuch as they found women "incapable of covenanting for want of sufficient reason or independence."[4] Certain collocations such as *principes bienfaisants de la nature* (good principles of Nature) and *douces lois* (gentle laws), which convey the ethos of an era heavily influenced by Rousseau's writings on nature and society, were relatively equivalent in English; however, the abstract noun *bonheur,* also reminiscent of Rousseau, and the phrase *belle âme* proved more problematic insofar as their elusiveness suggests a range of possible solutions. My decision to translate *bonheur* as "pleasure," "happiness," or "good fortune" depended upon its context; whereas, I translate *belle âme* as "fair soul" to emphasize the judicious nature of woman, the "fair sex," as presented by Gouges.

In the Preface to *L'esclavage des noirs,* Gouges creates a set of oppositions, which she hopes to resolve in her favor: she contrasts metaphysical observations with personal experience; and men with herself, a woman. Gouges stages her personal drama throughout the Preface, always careful to cast herself as a woman writer, friend of the Truth, whose modest resources are but her soul and her words. She opens the Preface with a comparison between the *siècle de l'ignorance,* the standard French expression for the Dark Ages, and *le siècle le plus éclairé,* a so-called Enlightened Age. By not translating *le siècle le plus éclairé* with the stock phrase "the Age of Enlightenment," I suggest that Gouges herself did not share conventional views about her century, and that the mixture of preconceived notions and originality in her use of language was calculated to shape public opinion to her own ends.[5]

Gouges links questions of gender and race in the Preface by asserting that her works, that is, works written by a woman who does not figure among the Learned (*les Savants*),[6] bear but the color of human nature (*la couleur de l'humanité*). Gouges's use of the term "color" to evoke a range of human characteristics, which are observable through personal experience, thus serves two purposes: first, Gouges dissociates the term "color" from a strictly racial context; and, second, Gouges endows her own perspective with universality, a quality heretofore denied her as a woman writer. In this way, Gouges integrates notions of gender and race into what, for her, a French woman writing at the end of the eighteenth century, is a more natural point of view.[7]

My translation takes full advantage of the grammatical aspect of the gender question by feminizing all possessive adjectives and pronouns that relate to abstract notions of justice and compassion. Similarly, I have feminized the construct of Nature, but unlike the Nature of convention, often presented in a feminine guise, Nature in Gouges's writing acquires universally reasonable principles: "[Nature] has placed the laws of humanity and wise equality in my soul." In addition, my translation feminizes the generic term "author," along with the fruits of authorial productivity ("her writings"), in order to strike a clearer difference between Gouges, the writer whose gender here allies her with representations of virtue and goodness; and men, even men of color,[8] when they seek to imitate tyrants or are condemned to servitude by their "Fatherland." I have translated *patrie* as "Fatherland" rather than "motherland" or "mother country" to emphasize the negative context in this instance.

Of course, Gouges's writings were also subject to literary conventions and influences, and these are felt especially in my translation of the dialogue from the play *L'esclavage des noirs*. The hyperbolic language, strong emotions, and moral polarization, which characterized the melodramatic writing that first appeared in France in the 1750s and 1760s in the *drame* or *genre sérieux* of such writers as Denis Diderot, Pierre-Augustin Caron de Beaumarchais, and Louis-Sébastien Mercier,[9] convey the complex interplay of oppression and resistance throughout Gouges's work.

My translation of the title *L'esclavage des noirs* (*Black Slavery*) represents the moral polarization in Gouges's play: on the one hand, her play asserts that the concept of slavery itself is reprehensible; on the other, it shows that the enslavement of blacks in the French colonies serves a particular financial and political purpose. By transposing the French noun *noirs* and the English adjective *black,* I am able to connote the evil consequences of slavery, as well as the fact that Gouges is a European writer who does not truly individuate black slaves as characters in her writing, but rather, uses them as vehicles for the expression of her ideas. At the time, it was not uncommon, in fact, to find a certain misrepresentation everywhere in antislavery writing as is suggested by the British habit of calling yellow, brown, or red people "black."[10] The usage of the term "black" now has a long history that is sometimes tainted by racism; however, I have opted to use the term "black" in my fairly literal translation of Gouges's play because I do not believe that its effect in the eighteenth century was racist.[11]

Expressions and terms that indicate the historical moment in which the play was written provide other instances of moral polarization. My translation of *étranger* depends, for example, on varying perceptions of difference: "stranger" connotes sensitivity to a character's otherness; whereas, "foreigner" indicates a situation in which political distinctions prevail. Similarly, the general terms used to designate the protagonists (*ce bon Français* [this good Frenchman]; *camarades* [comrades]; *semblables* [fellowmen]; *habitants* [planters]; *esclaves* [slaves]; *cultivateurs* [farmers]) position the characters one against the other depending upon who is addressing whom. When the term *espèce*, pronounced by Mirza and Zamor, the two slaves, is translated as "kind" or "species," it is meant to be both objective and, for the modern reader or spectator, somewhat reminiscent of Darwinian genetics. In this way we see that Mirza and Zamor differentiate between themselves, people of color, and the Europeans and Planters whose advantage over them is clearly racist. I have translated *Négresse* as Negress, though considered pejorative in current parlance, to show the bias and confusion regarding people of color in late eighteenth-century France. When Valère, a Frenchman, attempts to flatter Mirza, a slave from the Indies, by saying "Je n'ai pas vu de plus jolie Négresse," it appears that he conflates Africans and Indians.

In order to elicit the range of strong emotions called for in Gouges's play, I have relied especially upon the translation procedure of componential analysis, namely, "[the comparison of] a source language word [in this instance, in French] with a target language word [in English], which has a similar meaning, but is not an obvious one-to-one equivalent, by demonstrating first their common and then their differing sense components."[12] My translation of *malheureux* as "wretch," "wretched creature," "wretched man," "unfortunate," and "unhappy"; and of *supplice* as "punishment," "torment," and "torture" can illustrate this procedure. I use the term "wretch" in situations in which an empathetic speaker's social status is superior to that of those he or she addresses; the pejorative connotations of "wretch" in twentieth-century English underscore differences in social class. "Wretched creature" and "wretched man" are used similarly; however, they exact greater emotional intensity from the speaker and are allied with the speaker's sense of responsibility toward the victim. Both Sophie and M. de Saint-Frémont, her father, refer to the slaves in this manner. Sophie's description of Zamor and Mirza to M. de Saint-Frémont, "wretched creatures," recalls the themes of nature and natural rights associated with female personae throughout the play; whereas, M. de Saint-Frémont's use of "wretched man" when addressing Zamor, one of his slaves who has just pledged undying loyalty to him, his master, suggests that to treat Zamor as anything less than a man greatly pains M. de Saint-Frémont.

My use of "unfortunate" and "unhappy" as translations for "malheureux" shifts emphasis from the more corporeal aspects of wretchedness to those aspects that relate to the heart or soul, the seat of feelings or sympathies. When Sophie declares that she had no trouble interesting Mme de Saint-Frémont on the slaves' behalf, she states that Madame is "so fair, so sensitive to the troubles of the unfortunate." Likewise, Mirza is "unhappy Mirza" when she confides to Zamor that her love has rendered him guilty.

In translating *supplice* as "punishment," "torment," or "torture," I have been especially attentive to the function of the word in the line as well as to the emotional tone that it conveys. Generally speaking, the move from "punishment," to "torment," to "torture" marks an increase in emotional intensity either on the part of a character or on the part of the reader or spectator. Characters may be reacting to a specific situation or to a series of situations that have accumulated during the course of the play, while the reader or spectator is then incited to react in turn. Thus, Mirza speaks to Zamor, her lover, of the "same torment that reunites [them]"; M. de Saint-Frémont tells Valère that he should not let Sophie witness "this frightful torture"; and the Judge observes, without passion, that Sophie only makes "their punishment more terrible." By act III, "torture" has become the most frequent translation for *supplice* despite one instance in which I substitute a legal convention for the expression: "Monsieur, suspendez, je vous prie, leur supplice." (Monsieur, grant a stay of execution, I beg of you.)

Questions of gender and race are formulated in the hyperbolic language of melodrama that Gouges uses throughout her play. The redundant qualifiers, exclamatory comments, and affected *a-parte* represent an eighteenth-century melodramatic style whose very awkwardness attests to its emotional poignancy. Though all the characters speak in the same register, be they slave, governor, or French citizen, class differences based on race and gender are made apparent by means of social titles, a common practice of the period. In most cases, I have kept the French title, *Monsieur, Madame, Monseigneur,* etc. to reflect the original context; however, I have been careful to use a juridical language in instances where the social relationship emphasizes its contractual nature as, for example, when I have translated *époux* or *épouse* by "spouse" rather than "husband" or "wife."

Thomas Holcroft's translation of *Coelina* (1800) by Pixérécourt, the first play to be designated a bona fide melodrama, provided me with a parallel text or model in English for the many stock phrases, exclamations, and terms of endearment scattered throughout Gouges's play.[13] Though I do not use exactly the same expressions found in Holcroft's translation, my solutions approximate the affected tone of his language, which has a slight biblical tinge. I use such apostrophes as "Divine Providence!", "Almighty God!", "Ah! Gods! Hey!" as well as the more secular "Dear Spouse! O half of myself!" and "O Louis! O adored Monarch!", plus the phrases "Adieu, dear authors of my days" and "our happiness runneth over." While I continue to represent Nature as female and compassionate ("Benevolent Mother!"), I have female characters blur gender distinctions in their speech. In the last two scenes of the play, for example, when Mme de Saint-Frémont entreats her husband to act judiciously and pardon Mirza and Zamor, she calls him "mon ami," which I translate quite literally as "my friend" although it usually means "my dear" in a domestic context.

Of the many qualifiers in Gouges's play, her use of *sauvage* is among the most interesting. Each time she uses the word *sauvage*, she recalls nature and the origins of liberty and equality. Similarly, my translation of *sauvage* recalls nature with the epithet "rude," that is, primitive or natural. I only use the cognate "savage," which connotes bestiality, to emphasize misunderstood racial tensions: "Compassionate being to whom I owe my life and my spouse's life! you are not a Savage; you have neither the language nor the manners of one. Are you the master of this Island?" (Valère to Zamor, [I, 6]).

My aim in the translations of *Réponse au champion américain* (1790) and the last section of *Déclaration des droits de la femme* (1791) is to emphasize the connection between knowledge and equality for women. Although the occasion for Gouges's writing *Réponse* is, of course, the slave trade, as she tells us herself: "It is not the philosophers' cause, the cause of the *Amis des Noirs,* that [she] undertake[s] to defend; it is [her] own." Likewise, in *Déclaration des droits de la femme,* Gouges feels compelled to "say a few words about the public disturbances supposedly caused by the decree in favor of men of color on our islands"; however, she closes her document with the image of man and woman "united, but equal in strength and virtue."

It is arguable that in both *Réponse* and *Déclaration des droits de la femme* Gouges moves from abolitionist remarks regarding the plight of slaves to analogous remarks concerning women's situation. In the one instance in *Réponse* in which Gouges uses the term *espèce,* my translation generalizes the slaves' plight by using the word "class" to designate them as a group rather than a race that has been "tyrannized with cruelty for so many centuries." In this way, it becomes easier to identify women as another group that has been similarly oppressed.

Throughout *Réponse* Gouges is keen on demonstrating the apparent contradiction of a situation in which one would accuse her of being well informed but not at all learned. In order to highlight the illogicality of her circumstances, I juxtapose the two contrary notions of knowledge and ignorance in the same line: "One day, perhaps, my memory will be well-known because of my ignorance." There is, in fact, a pattern of alternating images in which Gouges insists that she has learned nothing from anyone and that she must enlighten her opponent on this matter, which my translation would stress. In the line, "Since I have the courage to sign this written document, do likewise to show you are my equal," I introduce the principle of equality into a literate context.

In 1792, a year after Gouges's *Déclaration des droits de la femme,* Mary Wollstonecraft's *Vindication of the Rights of Woman* would champion women's rights and women's education. Though Wollstonecraft's and Gouges's political views differ considerably, they share similar opinions concerning a woman's right to prove herself intellectually equal to men.[14] Thus, it is helpful to compare Wollstonecraft's prose with Gouges's despite the fact that Wollstonecraft was supposedly unaware of her contemporary.[15]

As we have seen above, Gouges's writing is a mixture of received notions and originality, and she uses language to shape public opinion to her own ends. There is a parallel tendency in Wollstonecraft to rely on "personal observation, repetition, forceful comparisons (especially metaphors from ordinary life), and use of autobiographical reference, in a sentimental mode."[16] If Wollstonecraft and Gouges were both accused at times of poor literary style and sometimes faulty grammar, closer inspection of their images reveals an urgency of conviction that transcends lack of formal education and the stress under which they wrote. In *Réponse,* for example, in reply to her challenger, Gouges modifies the standard expression *tomber dans l'erreur grossière* to turn it in her favor: "But if I imitate you, Sir, . . . I stray a bit too far from my aim and blunder into the same gross error as you with respect to me." Since Gouges insists that she is a student of simple nature, and that nature alone has enlightened her, I translate references to her own work with images drawn from the material world whenever possible. I have, at times, used figures of conception, birth, and generation to feminize Gouges's political and creative activities: "May this revolution regenerate the spirit and the conscience of men, and reproduce the true French character!" Similarly, the changes that Gouges made to her play "generated widespread interest."

Recent attention to Olympe de Gouges's work and her life has prompted new editions of her oeuvre, including an English translation of *Déclaration des droits de la femme* by Val Stevenson.[17] I have not hesitated to borrow from Stevenson's excellent translation; however, my translation of the last line of Gouges's text is significantly different from the Stevenson translation. In keeping with my aim to emphasize woman's natural rights in Gouges's view of the world, I translate *pour faire un bon ménage* quite literally as "in order to live happily together" rather than "in perfect marriage," which is Stevenson's solution, because I do not want to subject Gouges's figure to what was at the time a socially repressive institution for women. It is well to remember that Gouges compares the executive and legislative powers of the French Empire to a "man and woman who must be united, but equal in strength and virtue."

PART THREE
Germaine de Staël (1766–1817)

Staël, Translation, and Race

Françoise Massardier-Kenney

Germaine de Staël (1766–1817) is the only major woman author of the nineteenth century, with the exception of George Sand, who has managed to break through the silence in literary history surrounding women's writing during that time. Still, until recently her reputation has rested mostly on having introduced German Romanticism in France in *De l'Allemagne* (1810), on her opposition to Napoleon, and on her affair with Benjamin Constant, which he fictionalized in *Adolphe*. Her works have been hard to find and her major pieces had not been available in current re-editions. The last two decades have seen a flurry of revisionist studies, of critical editions and translations,[1] which bear witness to the considerable interest that Staël's *oeuvre* holds for anyone interested in nineteenth-century intellectual movements and literature. Yet, her important connection to race and to translation has been ignored, except for Avriel Goldberger's pioneering article on the translation of *Corinne*.[2] The 1934 description of Staël's lifelong interest in the question of slavery by her descendant Comtesse Jean de Pange—"Mme de Staël et les nègres"—gives useful facts but does not analyze either her particular sensitivity as a woman author to the plight of slaves or her idea of culture based on differences and cross-influences. Staël's connection to race, gender, and translation needs to be examined.

Germaine de Staël is the quintessential figure of the translator; she embodies the ideal of translation. She is that "voice from the other side" who throughout her life and works forced her audience to become aware of their own culture through an appeal to the culture of others, be they German, English, or African. Her subtle but unrelenting questioning of the values of French culture through a discourse describing different discourses present in other cultures makes her an "exemplary intellectual," as Pierre Barbéris has called her.[3] She provides us with the point of view of one who is on the margin of mainstream culture and public life.

Staël and her family were, in a subtle way, outsiders. She was born in 1766 to Suzanne Curchod Necker, a Swiss-born, highly educated woman who had visited Rousseau and Voltaire during her years as governess to the children of the Swiss pastor Moulton. Suzanne Curchod married the Protestant Swiss banker Jacques Necker who became famous as finance minister under Louis XVI and as a financial innovator who used massive borrowings to restore French finances. Mme Necker's Parisian salon was one of the most famous of the times. Germaine Necker thus entered the world in a prominent family, and from her earliest years benefitted from the company of the most famous men; but the Neckers were Swiss and Protestant in a French Catholic society, and of course they were commoners.

The primacy of the spoken voice was to be a prominent feature of Staël's fiction. Suzanne Necker, a Rousseau disciple, devoted much time to her daughter's education and kept her with her in her salon. She was apparently unable to show her affection or approval, and her relations with her daughter were strained, both women focusing their love on Jacques Necker, the "patriarchal God of the household."[4] However, through her mother, Germaine Necker first encountered the life of the intellect in conversations, and she herself became a conversationalist well before she became a writer. The importance of the oral is obvious in the poetic improvisations of her famous heroine Corinne, but also, among the readings in this volume, in the early hymns of her Jolof character Mirza. Very early in her life and in her writing career, Staël abstains from valorizing the values of Western Europe, of "civilization." Her emphasis on the oral rather than on the written made her particularly suited to accept cultures from Africa and to appreciate their oral traditions. Her partial exclusion from written discourse because of her gender allowed her to be inclusive racially, and her early concern about the question of slavery would last throughout her life.

This privileging of the spoken voice also came as a transformation of an all too real denial of access to the written word. Germaine Necker's mother Suzanne had started a non-fictional work that she had to abandon at her husband's request. Jacques Necker disapproved of women writing. Later, when the Neckers' daughter began to write, both parents made light of her efforts, and the father reiterated that writing was to be the sole province of men. Between a father whom she adored but who disapproved of her writing, and a mother whom she disliked and who had suppressed her own writing, Staël would have little space in which to maneuver, and her literary strategies would tend to be indirect.

Staël's entry into the world of letters coincided with her gaining some distance from her father. In 1786 Germaine Necker married the Swedish ambassador to France, Eric-Magnus de Staël, and opened a Parisian salon that would soon become famous. Her first work titled *Lettres sur les ouvrages et le caractère de Jean-Jacques Rousseau* (1788) was published anonymously, but everyone knew she was the author. This first act of writing already bore the marks of Staël's strategy: seeming to obey the paternal injunction not to write (she published the work anonymously, she was no longer Mademoiselle Necker, and the work is a praise to another male role model), while nonetheless engaging in the act of writing (she did write and publish, and her authorship was known). This work was to attract a great deal of attention and be re-edited a number of times. Composed of five letters (a borderline genre between the oral and the written), it is a defense of Rousseau and approves of his views on women (i.e., that they should not play a role in public life.)[5] Thus in her first publication of nonfiction Staël took a firm position as a liberal[6] (her subject is a philosopher who questions the most basic institutions of the monarchy), but she also endorsed the paternalistic views of her male model, an endorsement which prefigured the Revolution's relegating women to the private sphere. A radical activist like Olympe de Gouges could publish a *Déclaration des droits de la femme et de la citoyenne* (1791), and women formed clubs of their own (Les Amies de la Vérité, and Citoyennes révolutionnaires), but the Convention abolished them in October 1793 and Gouges's efforts on women's behalf were to end on the guillotine. What we can learn from comparing Staël to Gouges is that Gouges's efforts on behalf of women and of people of color were more direct and urgent, and immediately thwarted. Her play *L'esclavage des noirs* was immediately brought down by the powerful colonists' club Massiac while Staël's more timorous, but perhaps more timely efforts (more specifically her intervention on behalf of the Guadeloupean Pelasge in 1803,[7] her preface to Wilberforce's essay against slavery in 1814), would go unimpeded.

Staël's paradox was to be that having accepted the paternal male denial of women's involvement in writing and in public life, she would, perhaps indirectly but steadily, write and make for herself a place in public life by using her writing differently from more radical figures like Gouges. A major strategy of Staël's (a major one, but by no means a conscious one), was the timing of the publication of her works so that she would avoid being silenced the way women like Gouges had been. It is perhaps not by chance that a work like *Lettres* (a work not concerned with gender or race) was the first piece she published. It gave her a public voice which she would later use to disseminate her more unsettling works, those sensitive to women, slaves, and cultural differences. Throughout her career she would interspace essays and works of fiction from which a dialogue of different voices would be heard. At the time she published *Lettres*, she had already written three short stories, the publication of which was delayed until 1795 with the *Essai sur les fictions* in a book titled *Recueil de morceaux détachés*. (It is noticeable that it is her short stories that Staël chose to have "détaché" [removed, cut off] while Gouges had her head "détachée.") The short stories not published earlier include *Mirza, ou lettre d'un voyageur, Adélaïde et Théodore,* and *Histoire de Pauline.* In her preface to *Mirza,* Staël indicated that the stories were written before the Revolution and when "she was not twenty yet."[8] Although these stories have not been dated with certainty, if we take Staël's word, we are led to conclude that they were written before she married, and before she published the *Lettres.* They can be read as a counterpoint to *Lettres,* or at least as another point of view, one Staël seemingly did not choose to make public when she was still Mademoiselle Necker.

During the revolution, Staël became active politically in a perhaps limited but real way. At the beginning of the revolution, she returned to Paris with her parents, her father having been recalled to the ministry of finance by public acclaim. She stayed in Paris until 1792 when the Terror forced her to take refuge in Switzerland. She spent the rest of the revolution in exile in England and in Coppet, the family estate in Switzerland Necker had bought previously. In 1795 the Convention freed slaves in the colonies, and that same year Staël returned to Paris where she became active politically. She publicly espoused republicanism, and in 1797 founded the Club Constitutionnel with Benjamin Constant among others. She soon became disenchanted with the government of Napoleon, who banned several of her works and exiled her from Paris. It is only in 1815 after the fall of Napoleon that she would be free to come back to Paris.

During the years of the revolution, Staël experimented with a number of forms and developed a theory of literature grounded on the necessity of cross influences from foreign literatures. She first published several plays (*Sophie, Jane Gray,* both written in 1786) depicting women's sacrificial love, as well as several newspaper articles: "Réflexions sur le procès de la reine" (1793), "Réflexions sur la paix" (published in 1794 in Switzerland and in 1795 in France). At the same time she published *Zulma,* another short story probably written a few years earlier, and an essay on politics entitled *De l'influence des passions* (1796). She expressed her views of literature both in the *Essai sur les fictions* (1795) and in *De la littérature considérée dans ses rapports avec les institutions sociales* (1800), where she argues that the revolution has changed the conditions in which literature is produced. It is no longer a matter of entertaining, of writing according to the rules and taste of a privileged class, but of expressing "the situation of the individual in modern society."[9] Her ideal is one of the republican novel, "the novel, in republican France, shall depict personalities, personal feelings, teaching man about himself and his relations with his fellowmen and with society [la collectivité]."[10] This republican novel will benefit from "graftings" from other, foreign literatures. Such a program could not endear her to Napoleon whose ambition was to forge a unified France that would be inwardly turned and would shun enemy influences coming from the countries around it (or "surrounding" it, as Napoleonic ideology would have phrased it).

Staël practiced in her own works the kind of intralingual translation that she advocated in her theoretical works. In 1802 she published *Delphine*, a fictional reworking of the themes of *De la littérature*, and which rekindled the controversy created by that work, with the result that Bonaparte forbade her to stay in Paris. As Pierre Barbéris has insightfully noted, Staël constituted the "legitimization of another language."[11] Her militant cosmopolitanism is but a way to question the unexamined values of French culture, what Barbéris calls "francocentrism" and "voltairo-centrism."[12] Thus the Germany she appeals to in *De la littérature* is used not as a historical reference, but as a utopian antidote to France, an open culture "which, because of its versatility, lends itself to antagonistic exchanges."[13] This appeal to the foreign in order to acknowledge and question the limits of one's culture and language is original: Staël is not interested in describing the picturesque or the exotic. She focuses on the essential: how sentiments are expressed and how power is exercised. In order to do so, she moves between fiction and essays, between what is French and what is foreign in a movement that makes her an exemplary practitioner of intralingual translation. She is interested in the ways in which cultural hybridization can be apprehended as a gain for the culture that lets in influences from the outside. In fact, she seems to sense that culture is "cultural capital," to use Pierre Bourdieu's term,[14] but that it should not be immobilized by trade barriers.

During the years 1803–13, Staël traveled to Germany and Italy and would write her major works. The outcome of her travels to Italy was the publication of *Corinne* (1807), which became an immediate success. In 1810 she published *De l'Allemagne*, which was immediately banned by Napoleon (before it was even distributed) and caused her to be sent back to her Swiss retreat at Coppet. *De l'Allemagne* finally appeared in 1813 in London (still in French). During this same decade, she published two antislavery pieces: "Préface pour la traduction d'un ouvrage de M. Wilberforce" (1814), written in London and translated into English by her daughter Albertine; and "Appel aux Souverains" (1814), in which she went back in nonfictional form to the concerns expressed at the beginning of her career in *Mirza* and *Histoire de Pauline*. Her abolitionist pleas were already voiced in the opening of *Pauline* written some twenty years earlier: "These scorching climates where men, solely occupied with a barbaric trade and gain, seem, for the most part, to have lost the ideas and feelings which could make them recoil in horror from such a trade."[15]

She spent her last years actively fighting Napoleon's regime, and during these years of political opposition, perhaps not accidentally, she published her last work *De l'esprit des traductions* (1816) in Milan where it was to create a major debate and to influence the development of Italian Romanticism. In this essay Staël advocates translation as the necessary condition to keep national literatures alive. She conceives of translation not as an imitation of what is foreign, but as a way to move free from obsolete literary conventions. She argues that it is through the influence of translation that a national literature can learn and develop new forms.[16] Staël's conception of translation is political, or rather, ideological in that she perceives that literature is a cultural product that functions like a commodity. She herself uses the term "circulation of ideas" and links translation to "other forms of commerce." In a very modern way, she perceives that translation is the agent of change which acknowledges that culture is determined by the society and the times in which it thrives, and that translation is a sort of ideological distancing from and criticism of existing national modes of writing. Her repeated use of the metaphor of gold to represent literature emphasizes that literature is a form of capital, and like a good liberal, she wants that capital to circulate freely between countries.

Her survey of the situation of translation in different countries emphasizes that literatures, without or with little translation, are dead literatures, precisely because they are severed from the influence and the test of other literatures. For Staël, a literature can thrive only if it is part of the great chain of other signifying practices. In her conclusion she calls for the practitioners of Italian literature to turn outward and to let translation rejuvenate their writing.

When it has been mentioned at all, *Mirza* has been dismissed absent-mindedly as "an awkward work,"[17] or patronizingly as "strictly a curiosity, of merely marginal interest."[18] Yet *Mirza*'s depiction of gender and race makes it an important text in the tradition of women's writing and antislavery. It may even be that it is this very conjunction of race and gender that has placed *Mirza* in the "margins," that space in established discourse which Staël was to use and appropriate to create a theory of cultural identity based on maintaining oppositions and differences, not on erasing them. As Pierre Macherey has observed, "it became possible for her to think about cultures, not from within, but from the gaps that, separating them from themselves, projected them outside of their own constitution."[19] From this perspective, Switzer's charges that "she is incapable of reacting to any kind of beauty that is not strictly within the scope of Western European standards,"[20] that she "indulges in the same kind of stereotypes adopted by Hugo in *Bug Jargal*,"[21] are unfounded. Whereas *Bug Jargal* presents stereotypical descriptions of people of color (i.e., childlike, violent, or overly physical figures), *Mirza*'s black characters are intellectual, sensitive, and their sexuality is not emphasized. Moreover, the title character Mirza is endowed with qualities which historical accounts tell us characterize the author. This identification of the implied author with the black character is the opposite of what happens in a work like *Bug Jargal*. Last, these characters are not simply "African"; they belong to two different tribes, a distinction of importance.

Anyway, Staël does not depict "real" Africans any more than she would later depict "real" Germans. She is using the depiction of the other, of the foreigner, to bring out particularities and deficiencies in her own culture. In a perhaps extremely perceptive and honest move, she seems to know that the other point of view can be used to place in question her own culture; but that its representation is inevitably mediated by the gender, the class, the culture, in brief, the ideology of the author, that the recognition of the limits of such a representation is at the center of her refusal to endorse culturocentrism.

Mirza clearly links antislavery sentiments and women. First, the preface, written several years after Staël wrote the story but before it was published in 1895, reclaims the narrative and its authorship. The presence of the preface provides a frame for the narrative, made by a male European to an unknown woman, so that, although the narrator is male, both the author and the addressee are women. This story of women and slavery is thus doubly gendered. Secondly, the title character Mirza, the African heroine, is first presented as the eloquent voice of antislavery. The character Ximeo first hears her speak: "The love of freedom, the horror of slavery were the subjects of the noble hymns that filled me with a rapturous admiration." Moreover, it is made clear in the story that Mirza, an orphan member of the Jolof tribe,[22] opposes the male warriors' custom of selling their war prisoners as slaves. The female character is thus the only one not ideologically implicated in the slave system. Revealingly, after offering herself as a substitute slave to save Ximeo[23] and after being saved by the French Governor, Mirza chooses to die. The superficial reason is her broken heart over Ximeo's faithlessness; but another motive, more indirect but still significant, is the impossibility for the independent woman to owe her life and her freedom to a European colonialist, generous as he may be. Thus Mirza dies while Ximeo heads a European-style plantation, answering the naive and patronizing questions of the European narrator about his superior ability to speak French and to run a smooth plantation. Ximeo only escapes the power structure master/slave, superior/inferior, European/African which links him to the European visitor through the retelling of Mirza's story (her story of abandonment and death, but also of rebellion): indeed, while the author carefully avoids using direct discourse between the European male narrator and Ximeo, thus sidestepping the question of using "tu" (the usual form for an intimate or an inferior) or "vous" (the form reserved for equality or formality), Ximeo finally addresses the narrator as "tu," an astonishing "tu" that acknowledges the significance of telling Mirza's story as a way to undermine confidence in the value, let alone superiority, of the European.

Lest this significant use of "tu" be interpreted as a sign of Ximeo's lack of mastery of the French language (the enduring stereotype was that Africans spoke "petit nègre," the French version of Pidgin English), the narrator had earlier emphasized Ximeo's native command of French. One sees here that, although superficially correct, the charge of Franco-centrism waged against Staël or other women writers for making their African characters speak perfect French needs to be reexamined. If a French author depicts foreign characters (be they Jolof like Mirza or Italian as in *Corinne*), their language will inevitably be a translation. The question is whether this translation will emphasize their lack of control of language through a stereotypical distortion of standard French or whether the translation will be transparent[24] (i.e., emphasize what they say rather than how inadequately they express themselves or how peculiar they sound). Thus Staël shifts the difference of her characters away from the grammatical forms of their language (from *langue*) to voice, a more individual, less collectively determined language (to *parole*); she is engaged in the representation of different modes of thinking and speaking. And speak is precisely what Mirza does, unlike Ximeo who is left speechless when Mirza improvises on the theme of freedom. Throughout the narrative, Staël emphasizes the power of Mirza's voice. When, at the end, she speaks up to the slave traders in favor of Ximeo, he is again speechless. Staël is here suggesting that Mirza's kind of voice, the voice of passion, of antislavery, of female difference, of the spoken, can silence and counterbalance—for a moment—the discourse of the male, patriarchal, European colonialism and deceit. When asked by Ximeo to speak about love, Mirza opposes herself to the other tribe. She tells Ximeo "do not expect me to speak with the artfulness of the women of your country." Mirza opposes the "naturalness" of her speech, which is the sincere outpouring of feelings, to a language which is deceitful. Through Mirza Staël criticizes the classical, regulated language of traditional French literature as well as the oppressive language of Ximeo. Mirza's language is a utopian language which is opposed to patriarchal language. At the same time, Staël refuses to create a mythical figure of an "African" who would speak a "pure" language; she distinguishes between Ximeo from Cayor and Mirza, the Jolof.

The link between patriarchy, political division, and deceit is made clear by Ximeo who, after writing a letter to Mirza about his departure and his alleged trip, attempts to justify himself: "my father would never have called daughter a woman from the Jolof country." The inability of one culture to accept an exterior element is directly linked to the father's discourse. *Mirza* does present a series of oppositions— Mirza/Ximeo, Africa/Europe, woman/man, voice/written discourse, antislavery/patriarchy—but these oppositions are not static binary oppositions. Shifts occur, change is possible, the language from without can enter and rejuvenate the culture from within. The male Ximeo shifts from the weak listener and writer position to that of speaker: "But I have wished to speak of her." The male character redeems himself by telling the woman's story, by learning to understand and speak her language. The link between race and gender is made once again.

Ximeo the African prince is to the European colonialist as woman is to man. Ximeo's feminization is suggested early in the story. The European male narrator describes him in ways which emphasize, not so much his Europeanness, but his feminine aspect. His features are "ravissantes" (beautiful), he is "trop mince pour un homme" (too thin for a man), he has "beaux yeux" (beautiful eyes), he has more "déli-catesse" (frailty) than "force" (strength). Staël's description of Ximeo's physical appearance, which runs counter to the stereotype of the black man as threatening because of his size and his physicality, is in fact one of her indirect ways of connecting race and gender. Ximeo is black and thus feminine in the eyes of the European (and it is the narrator who comments on Ximeo's lack of the "defects of the men of his race").[25] Revealingly, the female heroine Mirza is hardly de-scribed at all; rather, she is situated in a utopian elsewhere outside of the economy of static subject/object positions. The European male gaze of the narrator has not seen her and Ximeo has been subjugated by her voice.

Staël's strong liberal position and the indirect strategies she used to link gender and race, and to present the oppression of Africans and women by the French male patriarchy, seem to be the salient features which would direct the "siting" of the translation of *Mirza*. While Staël could not transcend the limits placed on her by her times and place, her opposition to Francocentrism, to slavery, and to patri-archy should not be minimized and decontextualized. In the same way as Staël used transparency yet allowed for the voice of difference, the translator translating *Mirza* for a modern American audience has to both work with a tone and a vocabulary that seem at home in English, and give an indication that the text comes from a culture which is different from ours but which can be apprehended without "cannibalizing" the source text, without erasing its difference. Avriel Goldberger has similarly stated about her translation of *Corinne*, "[t]he translator has sought as 'timeless' a language as possible, avoiding both an imitation of nineteenth-century English which can so easily sound like a parody, and the obviously twentieth-century which would give a false modernity to the text."[26] This transparency, which none-theless admits to the existence of a distance between the French and the English text, is a working in translation of the circulation of a specific cultural capital, a capital whose value determines how the translation is sited. This notion of transparency is quite different from the "bad" transparency described by Tejaswini Niranjana.[27] It does not aim at fixing a colonized discourse but at showing the modernity of Staël's notion of culture as something that should not be fixed by national boundaries.

In specific terms, the passionate, Romantic voice of Mirza could have been toned down to adapt to our contemporary mode of writing and to avoid skirting the ridiculous, but its dissident force would have been lost or trivialized. To keep the distance, yet to "familiarize" the text in English (to reuse the well-known Russian formalist notion of "defamiliarization"), I turned to the English romantics for texts of a similar sensibility but also remote in time. Perhaps not unsurprisingly, the most useful parallel text turned out to be Mary Shelley's *Frankenstein*.

For that same "familiarization" effect, Staël's careful feminization of Ximeo, her use of the passive voice to render his lack of agency, had to be kept without pushing her text in the direction of parody. Similarly, the terms used to describe Africans (nègre, nègresse) had to be carefully thought out since they now have a negative connotation which was not necessarily present in the original French text.[28] However, since the term Negro was endorsed by African Americans until recently, and since the translated text is obviously sited as an older text, not as a modernization, the term was kept.[29] A more ideologically loaded issue was Staël's reference to the African share of responsibilities in the slave trade (in the same way as Aphra Behn had done previously in English). The choice was either to tone down the statement so as to fit our expected audience's ideological expectations (i.e., to focus on the responsibility of the colonizer not on the complicity of the victims), or to keep it in as an integral part of the liberal antiabolitionist argument of the time. Since Staël also refers again to the African custom of slavery in her later piece on slavery, "Appel aux souverains," the statement was kept as is.

Other syntactic issues such as Ximeo's sudden use of "tu" have been handled in the "margin" of the translation, i.e., the introduction, which, like Staël's preface, is a necessary part of the text since it contextualizes the translated text and brings attention to its status as translation. I have noted earlier Staël's valorization of the oral over the written, and I would argue that her whole *oeuvre* is a valorization of the process of translation over original "pure," "uncontaminated" texts, that she optimistically emphasizes that it is in the retelling of the story in another language or from another point of view that cultures can be revitalized.[30]

SEVEN

Translations of Staël

MIRZA, OR LETTERS OF A TRAVELER

Translated by Françoise Massardier-Kenney

Preface

The reader will readily understand, I think, that the preceding *Essay on Fictions* was written after the three short stories I publish here: none deserves the title of novel; situations are sketched rather than developed, and their only merit lies in the depiction of a few sentiments of the heart. I was barely twenty years old when I wrote them, and the French revolution had not yet occurred. I should think that, since then, my mind has acquired enough strength to devote itself to more useful works. It is said that misfortunes hasten the development of all moral faculties, but sometimes I fear that it has the opposite effect, that it throws you into a state of melancholy which makes you indifferent both to yourself and to others. The greatness of the events around us makes us feel the emptiness of general thoughts and the impotence of individual feelings to such a degree that, lost in the midst of life, we no longer know what road hope should follow, what motive must arouse our efforts, what principle will henceforth guide public opinion through the mistakes caused by blind allegiance to a party, what principle will mark again, in all carriers, the brilliant aim of true glory.

*   *   *

Allow me, Madam, to apprise you of an anecdote from my trip, which you may find interesting. A month ago, in the town of Gorée,[1] I heard that the governor had persuaded a Negro[2] family to come and live a few miles away so as to establish a plantation[3] similar to the one found in Santo Domingo. He had imagined, surely, that such an example would incite Africans to grow sugarcane, and that, by drawing to their territory the free trade of this sugar, Europeans would no longer take Africans away from their homeland and make them suffer under the hideous yoke of slavery. In vain have the most eloquent writers attempted to obtain this revolution by appealing to the goodness of men. Thus, the enlightened administrator despairing to overcome selfish interest, would like to make it stand on the side of humanity, by no longer having this personal interest find its advantage in braving humanity; but the Negroes, who do not think of providing for their own future, are even more incapable of thinking about generations to come, and they refuse a present evil without comparing it to the fate from which it could free them. One single African, freed from slavery through the generosity of the governor, had agreed to take part in his project. A prince in his own country, he had been followed by a few Negroes of a lower station who farmed his land under his orders.

I asked to be taken there. I walked part of the day, and at dusk I arrived near a house which, I was told, had been built in part by French people, but which still had a primitive quality. When I drew near the Negroes were enjoying their moment of rest: for relaxation they were shooting with bows and arrows, perhaps longing for the times when this pleasure was their only occupation. Ourika, the wife of Ximeo (the Negro who was the head of the settlement), was sitting at some distance away from the games, and she looked distractedly at her two year old daughter who was playing at her feet.

My guide walked up to her and told her that I was seeking shelter for the night in the name of the governor. "Ha-Governor moo koo yooni. Doogoo silwaay da laal jam! Keurgui sa Keuria," she cried.[4] ["The governor sends him! Let him come in, welcome! Everything we have is his."] She came toward me with hurried steps, her beauty dazzled me; she had the true charm of her sex, that is, everything suggestive of delicacy and gracefulness. "Mo anaa zimeo?" my guide inquired. "He is not back," she replied, "he is taking his evening walk; when the sun is no longer on the horizon, when the very sunset no longer suggests light, he will come back, and it will no longer be night for me." After uttering these words, she let out a sigh, walked away, and, when she came back toward us, I could see streaks of tears down her cheeks. We went into the hut; we were served a meal composed of all the local produce. I tasted everything with pleasure, eager that I was to feel new sensations. Someone knocked at the door; startled, Ourika sprang up, opened the door, and threw herself in the arms of Ximeo, who kissed her without seeming to be conscious of what he was doing or seeing. I went up to him. You cannot imagine a more beautiful face; his features had none of the defects of the men of his color. His eyes produced an effect that I had never experienced before: they took hold of your soul, and the melancholy they expressed went directly into the heart of those he beheld. The proportions of the statue of the Apollo Belvedere[5] could not have been more perfect than his: perhaps he could have been considered too thin for a man, but the sorrowful grief that every one of his movements indicated, that his face depicted, was more in keeping with frailty than with strength.

He was not surprised to see us; he seemed impervious to any other emotion than his dominant idea. We told him who had sent us and what the aim of our journey was. "The governor earned the right to my gratefulness," he replied. "Can you believe that in my present state I still have a benefactor?" He talked to us for a while about the reasons which had led him to run a plantation, and I was surprised at how sharp-witted and articulate he was. He became aware of my surprise. "You are surprised," said he,—"when we are not at the level of sheer brutes, although you treat us as such."

"I am not surprised," I replied, "but even a Frenchman would not speak French better than you do."

"Ah, you are right," he added,—"one still retains a few rays when one has lived for a long time near an angel." And his beautiful eyes looked down and ceased to see anything that was outside him. Ourika was crying, and Ximeo finally noticed her. "Baalma," he cried and took her hand,—"Baalma! Tay sabisla sa-biis-la vaante maay noo nu fatiikoo." ["Forgive me; the present is yours, bear with my memories."] "Tomorrow," he said, turning toward me,—"tomorrow, we shall visit my plantation together; you will see if I can flatter myself that it meets the expectations of the governor. Our best bed will be readied for you; sleep peacefully. I would like you to feel comfortable here. Men whose heart is broken by misery," he told me in a low voice, "do not fear, and even long for, the spectacle of another's happiness."

I went to bed, but I could not sleep. I was full of sadness. Everything I saw carried its stamp. I did not know its cause, but I felt moved as one is when contemplating a painting that depicts melancholy. At dawn, I got up; I found Ximeo even more dejected than the previous day. I asked him what the cause of his sadness was and he answered: "my grief, fixed in my heart, can neither grow nor wither; but the uniformity of life makes it go away faster, and new incidents, whatever they may be, give rise to new thoughts, which always give rise to new tears." He showed me his entire plantation with the utmost care. I was surprised at the order that reigned there. The land yielded at least as much as a like surface farmed in Santo Domingo by as many men, and the happy Blacks were not overwhelmed with work. I saw with pleasure that in addition to everything else cruelty was unnecessary. I asked Ximeo who had advised him about the farming of the land, about the organization of the workers' day. "I was given little advice," he replied,—"but reason can lead to what reason has already discovered: since death was forbidden me, I had to dedicate my life to others; how else could I have lived? I abhorred slavery; I could not understand the barbarous purpose of the men of your color. I sometimes thought that their god, enemy of our god, had ordered them to make us suffer, but when I realized that a product of our country, neglected by us, was the sole cause of the cruel suffering endured by these unfortunate Africans, I accepted the offer to give them the example of growing sugarcane. May free trade be established between the two parts of the world! May my unfortunate compatriots renounce primitive life, devote themselves to work in order to satisfy your greed, and help save a few of them from the most horrible destiny! May those who could flatter themselves that they had avoided slavery apply themselves with an equal zeal to protect their fellow beings from such a fate." As he was talking to me thus, we reached a door that led to a forest on one side of the plantation. I thought that Ximeo was going to open it, but he turned away in order to avoid it. "Why," I said, "don't you show me?"

"Stop," he cried, "you seem sensitive, will you be able to hear the long story of my woes? It has been two years since I conversed with anyone. What I usually say is not really speaking. You can see it, I need to confide in someone. You should not be flattered by my trust; but still, it is your kindness which encourages me and makes me count on your pity."

"Ah! have no fear," I replied; "you will not be betrayed."

"I was born in the kingdom of Cayor.[6] My father, of royal blood, was the chief of several tribes that had been committed to his care by the monarch. I was trained early in the art of defending my country and I had been familiar with archery and javelin throwing since I was a child. At that time I was promised in marriage to Ourika, the daughter of my father's sister. I loved her as soon as I could love, and this faculty developed within me for her and through her. Her beautiful perfection struck me even more when I compared her to other women, and I came back by choice to my first inclination.

We were often at war against the Jolofs, our neighbors, and as we both had the atrocious custom of selling our prisoners of war to the Europeans, a deeply rooted hate that even peace could not abate allowed no communication between us. One day, while hunting in the mountain, I was led further than I intended; a woman's voice, remarkably beautiful, reached my ears. I listened to her song and I could not recognize the words that our maidens enjoy repeating. The love of freedom, the horror of slavery were the subjects of the noble hymns that filled me with a rapturous admiration. I drew near: a young person rose. Struck by the contrast between her age and the subject of her meditations, I looked in her face for something supernatural that might reveal the inspiration which can be a substitute for the long reflections of old age. She was not beautiful, but her noble and regular stature, her enchanting eyes, her animated countenance left love nothing to wish for in her face. She came forward and spoke to me at length without my being able to answer her. Finally I managed to express my surprise; it became more pronounced when I learned that she had composed the verse I had just heard. "There is no need to be surprised," she said, "a Frenchman who settled in Senegal, discontented with his lot and unhappy in his own country, retired among us. This old man was so good as to tend to my youthful years, and he gave me what the Europeans have that is worthwhile: the knowledge that they misuse and the philosophy whose lessons they follow so poorly. I learned the language of the French, I read a few of their books, and, for my own delight, I come to these mountains and reflect in solitude."

My interest, my curiosity, increased with every word she said; she was no longer a woman that I was hearing, she was a poet. Never had those of my countrymen who devote themselves to the cult of the gods seemed filled with such a noble enthusiasm. When leaving her, I obtained her permission to see her again: her memory followed me everywhere. I left with more admiration than love, and trusting this difference for a long time, I saw Mirza (as this young Jolof was named) without meaning to offend Ourika. One day, at length, I asked Mirza if she had ever loved. I asked this question with trepidation, but her ready wit and open mind made all answers easy for her: "No, I have not," she said,—"I have been loved sometimes; I may have wanted to feel; I wanted to know the feeling that takes over your whole life and rules every instant of the day, but I have reflected too much, I think, to feel this illusion. I feel all the movements of my heart and I can see them all in others. I could not to this day deceive nor be deceived." Her last words troubled me. "Mirza," I said, "how sorry I feel for you! The pleasures of the mind are not all absorbing; only those of the heart satisfy all the faculties of the soul." She taught me all the while with an inexhaustible kindness; in a short time, I learned everything that she knew. When I interrupted her with my praise, she would not listen; as soon as I stopped, she would proceed, and I could see by what she said that while I was praising her I had been the only object of her thoughts. Finally, intoxicated by her charm, her mind, and her eyes, I could feel that I loved her, and I dared tell her: what did I not say to transpose in her heart the exaltation I had found in her mind! I was dying of passion and fear at her feet. "Mirza," I repeated to her, "bring me into the world by telling me that you love me; open up the heavens for me so that I may soar with you." As she listened to me, she lost her composure and tears filled her beautiful eyes in which, until now, I had only seen the expression of genius. "Ximeo," she said, "I shall answer you tomorrow. Do not expect from me the art of the women of your country. Tomorrow, you will read in my heart; in the meantime, think about yours." After saying these words, she left me well before sunset, the usual signal of her retreat. I did not attempt to detain her; the power of her personality bound me to her will. Since I had met Mirza, I saw less of Ourika. I deceived her. I invoked trips as pretexts. I delayed the moment of our union. I postponed the future instead of planning it.

At last, the following day, which seemed like an eternity, I went to her. Mirza moved first toward me; she looked dejected, either because of foreboding or tender thoughts. She had spent that day in tears. "Ximeo," she said to me with a soft but steady voice, "are you quite sure that you love me? Is it certain that in your vast country no object has fixed your heart?" I answered with promises. "Ah, I believe you; surrounding nature is the only witness to your promises. Everything that I know about you, you yourself told me. The isolation, the neglect in which I live provide all my security. What distrust, what obstacle have I opposed to your will? In me, you could only deceive the regard I have for you, Ximeo; you could only avenge yourself of my love. My family, my friends, my fellow citizens, I banished all to depend on you only. To you, I must be sacred as the weak, the young, and the wretched are. No, I have nothing to fear, nothing." I interrupted her: I was at her feet; I thought I was sincere; the force of the present had made me forget past and future. I had deceived; I had convinced her; she believed me. Gods! What passionate expressions she found! What happiness she felt in loving! Oh, during the two months that passed thus, all that exists of love and happiness met in her heart. My wishes were gratified, but my excitement was fading. How strange is human nature! I was so struck by the pleasure she had seeing me that I soon began going for her sake rather than for my own: I was so sure of her welcome that I no longer trembled when approaching her. Mirza did not realize this; she spoke, she answered, she cried, she brought herself solace, and her active soul acted upon itself. Ashamed of myself, I needed to go away. War broke out in another part of the Cayor kingdom; I resolved to go there directly. I had to tell Mirza. Oh, at that moment I felt again how dear she was to me; because of her trust and sweet feeling of security, I did not have the strength to reveal my plan to her. She seemed so much to live by my presence that my tongue froze when I attempted to tell her that I was leaving. I resolved to write to her; this art that she had taught me was to be used to bring her misery. Twenty times I left her; twenty times I went back. The unfortunate soul enjoyed this and mistook my pity for love. Finally, I left; I informed her that my duty was forcing me to leave her, but that I would come back at her feet feeling more tender than ever. What response did she give me! Ah, language of love, how charming you become when you are embellished by thought! What a despair at my absence! What passionate desire to see me again! Thinking then of the excesses to which her heart could go in loving made me shudder; but my father would never have called by the name of daughter a woman from the Jolof country. All sorts of obstacles were offered to my thoughts when the veil that hid them was lifted. I saw Ourika again; her beauty, her tears, the power of a first inclination, the entreaties of an entire family, and all sorts of things, everything that seems insurmountable when one no longer draws one's strength from one's heart, made me unfaithful, and my vows with Ourika were taken in the presence of the Gods.

In the meanwhile, the time that I had given to Mirza for my return was drawing near; I wanted to see her again; I hoped to soften the blow that I was going to strike; I thought it was possible. When one no longer feels love, one no longer suspects its effects. One cannot even rely on one's memories. Oh! I was filled with such feelings when walking over the very spot that had been witness to my promises and my happiness! Nothing had changed but my heart, and I could hardly recognize them! As for Mirza, as soon as she saw me I think she experienced in a single moment the happiness that one barely feels at different moments in the whole of one's life, and it was thus the Gods repaid her. Ah! How can I tell you through what horrible degrees I led the unfortunate Mirza to know the state of my heart? My trembling lips uttered the word friendship. "Your friendship," she cried out,—"your friendship! You barbarian! Is it to my soul that such a feeling must be offered? Give me death, that is all you can do for me now." The excess of her grief did seem to lead her to her death; she fell unconscious at my feet. What a monster I was! It was then that I should have deceived her; but it was then that I spoke true.

"You are without feelings! Go now," she said to me. "The old man who took care of me when I was a child and who was a father to me may live longer. I must live for him. I am already dead here," she said, pointing to her heart with her hand. "But he needs my care, go away."—"I cannot," I cried out, "cannot bear your hatred."

"My hatred!" she answered,—"have no fear Ximeo, some hearts can only love and all their passion only turns against themselves. Farewell, Ximeo; you will thus belong to another woman."

"No, never, never," I said.

"I do not believe you now," she replied,—"yesterday your words would have made me doubt the light of day. Ximeo, hold me against you, call me your dearest mistress, let your voice find again the tone of the past, let me hear it again, not to enjoy it, but to remember it again: but it is impossible. Farewell, I will find it again alone, my heart will always hear it. It is the cause of death that I bear and keep in my heart; Ximeo, farewell." The touching sound of this last word, the effort she made when moving away, I remember everything; she is before my eyes. "Gods! Make this illusion stronger! Let me see her an instant so that—if it is still possible—I may feel more strongly what I have lost." For a long time, I remained motionless where she had left, distraught, troubled like a man who has just committed a great crime. Night overtook me before I thought of moving homeward; the remorse, the memory, the sense of Mirza's misery preyed on my soul; her shadow came back to me as if the end of her happiness had been the end of her life.

War against the Jolofs broke out; I had to fight against Mirza's countrymen. I wanted to shine with glory in her eyes, to justify her choice, and to deserve still the happiness I had given up. I had little fear of dying. I had made of my life such a cruel use that perhaps I risked that life with a secret pleasure. I became seriously wounded. While recovering, I learned that a woman came every day to the threshold of my door. Standing still, she would tremble at the slightest noise. Once I grew worse; she fainted. She was restored to animation, and said: "Do not let him know of the state in which you saw me. I am far from being a stranger to him; my interest will distress him." Finally one day, horrible day, I was weak still, my family and Ourika were with me. I was calm when I banished the memory of the one whose despair I had caused; I thought I was anyway; fate had driven me. I had acted like a man governed by it, and I feared so much the moment of repentance that I used all my strength to restrain my thoughts, which were all too ready to brood over the past. Our enemies, the Jolofs, struck the village where I lived: we were defenseless;

we sustained a fairly long attack, however, although at last they defeated us and took several prisoners. I was among them. What a moment for me when I saw myself in shackles. The cruel Hottentots only reserve death for the vanquished; but we, being more cowardly barbarians, we serve our common enemies and justify their crime by becoming their accomplices. A troop of Jolof soldiers made us walk all night; when day came to give us light, we found ourselves on the bank of the Senegal River; boats had been readied; I saw some white men, and I became certain of my fate. Soon my drivers began discussing the vile conditions of their heinous exchange: the Europeans checked with curiosity our youth and our strength to find there the hope of making us bear longer the wrongs that they held in store for us. Already I was determined; I was hoping that when passing onto this fateful boat my chains would loosen enough to let me throw myself into the river, and that despite the swift rescue of my greedy owners, the weight of my shackles would drag me to the bottom of the abyss. My eyes were fixed on the ground, my thoughts attached to the terrible thing I was hoping to do. I was detached from the objects around me. All of a sudden, a voice that happiness and sorrow had taught me to recognize made my heart beat faster and shook me out of my immobile meditation: I looked up. I saw Mirza, beautiful, unlike a mortal, but like an angel, for her face was irradiated by the soul within. I heard her ask the Europeans to listen to her: her voice was moved, but it was not fright or emotion that altered it; a supernatural movement transformed her whole appearance. "Europeans," she said, "it is to cultivate your land that you condemn us to slavery; it is your interest which makes our misfortune necessary; you do not seem to be evil gods, and tormenting us is not the goal of the suffering you will have us bear. Look at this young man weakened by his wounds; he will neither be able to withstand the long march nor the work that you will require of him; yet look at me, see my strength and my youth; my sex has not sapped my courage; let me be a slave in Ximeo's place. I will live, since it is at this price that you will have granted me Ximeo's freedom. I shall no longer think slavery degrading. I shall respect my masters' power, since I will have given it to them, and their benevolence will have sanctified it. Ximeo must cherish life; Ximeo is loved. I do not love anyone in this world; I may depart from it without leaving any void in a heart that would feel that I no longer exist. I was on the verge of taking my own life; a new happiness makes me outlive my heart. Ah, allow yourselves to be moved and, at a time when your pity is not at odds with your interest, do not resist my plea." As she finished speaking, this proud Mirza—

whom the fear of death would not have forced to kneel before the kings of the earth—humbly bowed her knee; but in this attitude, she still kept all her dignity, and admiration and shame were the lot of those whom she was imploring. For a moment she may have thought I could accept her generosity. I was tongue-tied and it was torture to be thus speechless. These Europeans all cried out in unison, "We accept the exchange, she is beautiful, she is young, she is courageous; we want the Negress and we let her friend go." I regained my strength; they were going to approach Mirza when I cried, "Barbarians, slavery is mine. Never, never; respect her sex, her weakness. Jolof Naax Naanguene Naagoo, weco seen none bu sax ak jigueenoo goxbi!" ["You Jolofs, will you allow a woman of your country to be enslaved in place of your cruelest enemy?"]

"Stop," cried Mirza," stop being generous. You are accomplishing this act of virtue for your sake only; if you had cared about my happiness, you would not have abandoned me. I prefer you guilty when I know you insensitive; leave me the right to complain when you cannot take my pain away; don't take away from me the only happiness that I have left, the sweet thought of being bound to you at least by the good I will have done you: I followed your destinies, I shall die if my days are of no use to you. This is your only means of saving my life; dare persist in your refusals."

Since, I have remembered every one of her words, and at the time I thought I did not hear them. I shuddered at Mirza's resolve; I feared that those vile Europeans would approve of it. I dared not declare that nothing separated me from her. These greedy merchants would have taken us both: perhaps, heartless as they were, they already counted on the effects of our hearts; even, they already promised themselves to choose for captives those whom love or duty could cause to be bought or followed; they studied our virtues to use them for their vices. But the governor, informed of our struggles, of Mirza's devotion, and of my despair, advanced like an angel of light: Who would not have thought that he was bringing us happiness! "Be free, both of you," he said to us. "I return you to your country and to your love. So much nobility of soul would have shamed the European who would have called you his slaves." My shackles were removed; I kissed his knees; I blessed his goodness in my heart, as if he had sacrificed legitimate rights. Ah, usurpers may thus attain the rank of benefactors by renouncing their injustices. I stood up; I thought that Mirza was at the feet of the governor like me. I saw her at some distance, leaning against a tree, caught in a deep reverie. I ran toward her: love, admiration, gratefulness, I felt all, I expressed all at once. "Ximeo," she said to me,—"it is too late; my grief is writ too deeply for your hand to even touch it: I can no longer hear your voice without wincing, and your presence freezes in my veins the blood that once flowed impetuously for you. Passionate souls can only know extremes; they cross the distance between the two without ever stopping. When you told me of my fate, I doubted it for a long time: you could still have come back. I would have believed that I had dreamed of your fickleness; but now, to destroy this memory, I have to cut through the heart from which it cannot be erased."

As she was speaking thus, the fatal arrow was in her heart. Oh, Gods who stopped my life at that moment, did you give it back to me only to avenge Mirza by the long agony of my suffering! The chain of my memories and my thoughts was broken during an entire month; I sometimes think that I am in another world made into hell by the memory of the first one. Ourika made me promise not to attempt suicide. The governor convinced me that I must live in order to serve my unfortunate compatriots, to respect the last wishes of Mirza who beseeched him, he said, on her death bed, to look after me, to bring me solace in her name: I obey, I have shut in a tomb the sad remains of the one I love when she no longer is, of the one I failed to appreciate when she lived. There, in solitude, when the sun sets, when all of nature seems to be overcast with my mourning, when universal silence lets me hear my thoughts, then only can I feel, prostrate before this tomb, the enjoyment of grief, the full feeling of its sorrows. My exalted imagination sometimes creates ghosts; I think I see her, but she never appears to me as an angry lover. I hear her consoling me and attending to my grief. Finally, uncertain of the fate awaiting us after life, I respect in my heart the memory of Mirza, and I fear that, by ending my life, I would destroy everything that remains of her. You are the only person with whom I have shared my sorrow. I don't expect you to feel pity; should a barbarian who caused the death of the woman he misses be of concern? But I wanted to speak of her. Ah! promise me that you will not forget the name of Mirza, that you will say it to your children, and that you will preserve after my death the memory of this angel of love, this victim of misfortune."

When he finished his story, a dark reverie spread over Ximeo's charming face. My eyes streamed with tears; I tried to speak to him: "Do you think," he said to me, "that you should attempt to console me? Do you think it is possible to have one single thought about my misfortune that my heart would not have already found? I have wanted to tell you my sorrows, only because I was quite sure that you could not ease my pain; I would die if it were removed from me;

remorse would take its place; it would occupy my whole heart, and the pains of remorse are barren and burning. Adieu, I thank you for listening to me." His somber calm, his tearless despair, easily convinced me that all my efforts would be pointless. I no longer dared speak to him; misfortune inspires respect. I left him, my heart full of bitterness, and I tell his story to fulfill my promise and sanctify, if I can, the sad name of his Mirza.

An Appeal to the Sovereigns Convened in Paris to Grant the Abolition of the Slave Trade
Translated by Sharon Bell

Despite the violent crisis in which England has been embroiled for twenty-five years, that nation has never used the dangers she faced as an excuse for neglecting the good that was within her power. Constantly concerned about humanity in the midst of war, and about the common good at the very moment her political existence was under threat, she abolished the slave trade at the time she was waging the most vigorous fight against the doctrine of a perverse liberty.[7] The opposing parties among the English came together for a goal as much moral as it was religious. Mr. Pitt and Mr. Fox collaborated on its behalf with equal ardor; and Mr. Wilberforce, a Christian orator, lent to this great work a perseverance the like of which is usually seen only among those working to further their personal interests.

The abolition of the slave trade, which took place seven years ago, did not affect the prosperity of the English colonies. The Negroes have sufficiently multiplied among themselves to supply the needed labor; and as always happens in the case of an act of justice, the public was ceaselessly alarmed over the possible disadvantages of this measure before it was enacted. But once it was, none of these supposed disadvantages were ever heard of again. Thus, thousands of lives and entire nations were preserved, without the financial interests of commerce having suffered.

Since that time, England, on signing the peace treaty with Denmark, made the abolition of the slave trade one of the articles of the treaty. The same condition was put to Portugal, which, up to now, has conceded only to restrictions. But today, since the confederation of sovereigns has met to enact the treaty and thus confirm the peace it has won with its might, it seems that nothing would be more worthy of the august congress about to open than to consecrate the triumph of Europe through an act of benevolence. The Crusaders of the Middle Ages never left for the Holy Land without binding themselves by some vow on their return. The sovereigns now meeting in France promised the good fortune of Africa to that propitious Heaven from which they obtained Europe's deliverance.

Many political interests will be discussed, but a few hours given to such a great religious interest would not be useless even to the affairs of this world. Thereafter, people would say: "It was at this Paris peace accord that the slave trade was abolished by all of Europe; thus, this accord is blessed, since it follows such an act of thanksgiving to the God of Hosts."

It has been proposed that a monument be raised to consecrate the fall of the oppressor who lay like a pall over the human race. Here we have it, a monument that can be raised with one word: the slave trade abolished by the kings who overthrew the tyranny of the conquest of Europe.

The sufferings these hapless Negroes are made to endure as they are transported from their homeland to the colonies almost make the very slavery which awaits them a relief. We provoke war in the countries of Africa to make the victors surrender their war captives; to be sold into slavery is the accepted punishment along the coasts of Africa for all kinds of misdeeds. The black chiefs who take part in this vile traffic excite the Negroes to crime by inciting them to drunkenness or by any other means, in order to claim the right to have them transported to America. Often, under the ridiculous pretext of sorcery, these unfortunates are exiled forever from the shores where they were born, far from that land even dearer to primitive than to civilized men. "Long coffins," to borrow an expression from a French writer, carry them across the seas; the captives are stacked in the ship in such a way that they would take up more space if they were dead, for their bodies would then at least be stretched out on the wretched plank they are allowed.

In his address against the slave trade, Mr. Pitt said in so many words: "I know of no evil which has ever existed, and I cannot imagine any, worse than 80,000 people annually snatched from their native land by the concerted action of the most civilized nations of Europe." Mr. Pitt's principles were well-known, as was the part he played in the present triumph of the allied nations because of his convictions. Should his authority not be counted? And that of the three powers of England, the House of Commons, the House of Lords, and the king: does their authority not confirm the truth of the facts and principles now submitted to the monarchs' attention?

Finally, one cannot hide the fact that Europe owes a great deal to England, who has often resisted alone during the course of these twenty-five years; and nowhere has there been a battle which was not seconded by English soldiers or English aid. How does one repay the richest and most fortunate nation in the universe? A warrior receives from his sovereign a token of honor, but what can be done for an entire nation who has played the warrior's role? The great humanitarian act that England is commending to all the governments of Europe must be adopted: good must be done for its own sake, but also for the sake of the English nation who requests it and to whom it is just to grant this noble token of gratitude.

The same advocate of humanity, Mr. Wilberforce, is in England as head of the society of missionaries which must carry the enlightenment of Christianity into Asia and Africa. But how could one be called Christian if one is cruel? Could not the king of France, that pious heir of St. Louis and of Louis XVI, be asked to agree to the abolition of the slave trade so that this humanitarian act might persuade the hearts of those to whom the gospel is to be preached? Could one not ask this same agreement of Spain, who awakened national spirit on the continent? of Portugal, who fought like a great state? of Austria, whose sole concern was the well-being of the German empire? of Prussia, where both nation and king proved so simply heroic? Let us also ask this great gift of the Russian emperor, who limited his own ambition when there was no longer any outside obstacle to check it. An absolute sovereign fought to found the wise principles of political liberty; the crown of such a monarch should be composed of every kind of glory: the emperor of Russia rules peoples of diverse degrees of civilization within the confines of Asia; he tolerates all religions, he permits all customs, and the scepter, in his hands, is as equitable as law. Asia and Europe bless the name of Alexander. May that name resound as well on the savage shores of Africa! There is no country on earth unworthy of justice.

Preface to the Translation of a Work by Mr. Wilberforce on the Slave Trade
Translated by Sharon Bell

Mr. Wilberforce is the author of the following essay on the slave trade.

This distinguished orator in the House of Commons, remarkably well-versed in everything pertaining to literature and that lofty philosophy based on religion, has devoted thirty years of his life to making Europe ashamed of a great moral outrage and to liberating Africa from a horrible misfortune. When he had amassed all the evidence of the cruelties which worsened the horror of an act of tyranny; when he thought he had the means to convince both great and small, in 1787 he made a motion in Parliament that the slave trade be abolished.

Mr. Pitt, Mr. Fox, Mr. Burke supported him. No truly superior man in England, no matter what his political opinions, would want to lend his support to opinions that would stain his reputation as a thinker and friend of humanity. Mr. Pitt may be suspected of having for some time allowed his followers to support the slave trade, but he held his glory too dear not to separate from his party in this instance. Still, the protests of all those who divide the human species into two groups, one of which, in their opinion, must be sacrificed to the other—these protests prevented Mr. Wilberforce's motion from being carried. The colonists claimed that the abolition of the slave trade would bankrupt them; the English trading cities declared that their prosperity depended on that of the colonists; last, there arose on every side that resistance which is always heard when decent people decide to defend the oppressed against the oppressors.

The excesses of the French revolution, which caused a certain order of ideas to be viewed with great disfavor, harmed the cause of the poor Negroes. Those who objected to the provocation of war among the peoples of Africa so that their prisoners might be enslaved were called anarchists; those whose actions had no other motives than religion and humanity were called Jacobins. But in a country like England enlightenment is so widespread, and the circulation of ideas so free, that one can calculate with certainty the very short time required for a truth to become established in public opinion.

Every year Mr. Wilberforce renewed the same motion, which had been defeated the first time, and through this perseverance Reason won new ground each time. The most religious men in England seconded Mr. Wilberforce's efforts; Mr. Clarkson, Mr. Macaulay, and several others must be mentioned in this honorable struggle. A subscription was taken up to establish, in Sierra Leone, all the means proper to civilize the Negroes, and this honorable enterprise cost the individuals who supported it over 200,000 pounds sterling. One can scarcely see how that mercantile spirit for which we reproach the English can explain such sacrifices. The motives which impelled the abolition of the slave trade are every bit as disinterested.

It was in 1807 that this great humanitarian act was realized. Its advantages and its disadvantages had been debated for twenty years. Mr. Fox and his friends were ministers then, but the cabinet changed during the period between the act and its passage into law. Nevertheless, the successors adopted the same principles in this regard, for among the new ministers, Mr. Perceval, Mr. Canning, and Lord Har-rowby—all three of them friends of Mr. Pitt's—proved to be ardent champions of this admirable cause. As he died, Mr. Fox had commit-ted it to his nephew, Lord Holland, and this noble heir, along with his friends, was allowed to carry the king's sanction to the House of Lords, even though he was no longer minister. "A ray of sunlight," said Clarkson, "broke through the clouds the moment the decree ending the slave trade was proclaimed." Indeed, this act deserved Heaven's favor, and at what moment did it take place? At a time when all the colonies were in the hands of the English, and when their self-interest, crudely considered, should have led them to maintain the degrading commerce which they were renouncing.

Today it is widely maintained that the English fear the reestablish-ment of the colony of Santo Domingo, to the advantage of the French; but in 1807 what chance was there for France to regain mastery of that colony, if indeed that chance exists even today? The party which impelled the abolition of the slave trade in England is that of those zealous Christians commonly called Methodists. In the interests of humanity they display energy, industry, and party spirit; and as they are numerous, they affect public opinion, and public opinion affects the government. Politicians and speculators likely to envy the prosper-ity of France were by no means neutral parties in the abolition of the trade—they mounted arguments against it similar to those that we see invoked in France today among the colonists and the merchants; they predict the same dire consequences. Yet, in the seven years since England has prohibited the slave trade, the experience has amply proven that all the fears that were manifested in this regard were illusory, that the maritime cities are presently in agreement with the rest of the nation on this subject. We have seen in this instance the same moral phenomenon one always observes under circumstances of a like nature. When it is proposed that some abuse of power be eliminated, those who benefit from that abuse are certain to declare that all the benefits of the social order are attached to it. "This is the keystone," they say, while it is only the keystone to their own advan-tages; and when at last the progress of enlightenment brings about the long-desired reform, they are astonished at the improvements which result from it. Good sends out its roots everywhere; equilibrium is effortlessly restored; and truth heals the ills of the human species, as does nature, without anyone's intervention.

Some Frenchmen were annoyed that the English ministers had made the abolition of the slave trade one of the conditions of peace, but in this regard the English ministers were nothing more than the interpreters of their nation's will. But the time when nations required humanitarian acts of each other would be a grand age indeed in history. These generous negotiations will meet no obstacle in the heart of a monarch as enlightened by religion as is the king of France, but the prejudices of nations can sometimes act against the very enlightenment of their kings.

Thus, it is the great good fortune of France, of England, and of distant Africa that glory like that of the Duke of Wellington should strengthen the cause he defends. The Marquis of Wellesley, his elder brother, had already suppressed the trade in black slaves in India, where he was governor, even before the decree which abolished it was proclaimed by the Parliament of England. The opinions of this illustrious family are well known. Let us hope, then, that Lord Wellington will triumph through reason in the Negroes' cause, just as he powerfully served the cause of the Spanish with his sword; for it is to this valiant hero that these famous words of Bossuet's should be applied: "His was a name which never appeared except in actions whose justice was unquestionable."

THE SPIRIT OF TRANSLATIONS
Doris Y. Kadish

No loftier service can be rendered to literature than transporting the masterpieces of the human mind from one language to another. There are so few works of the highest order; genius of any kind is such a rare phenomenon that if each modern nation were reduced to its own riches it would always be poor. Besides, circulating ideas is the most clearly profitable of all kinds of commerce.

At the time of the Renaissance in literature, scholars and even poets had the idea that they should all write in a single language, Latin, so that they could understand each other without the need for translation. That idea could have been profitable for the sciences, in which the development of ideas does not rely on the charm of style. But the result was that much of the wealth produced by Italians in Latin was unknown to Italians because most readers only knew the vernacular. Besides, to write in Latin on science and philosophy requires creating words that ancient writers never used. Thus scholars used a language that was both dead and artificial, while poets limited themselves to purely classical expressions. It is true that when Latin was still heard on the banks of the Tiber, Italy had writers such as Fra-Castor, Politien, Sannazar, whose style was said to resemble that of Virgil and Horace; but if the reputation of those Italian writers has endured, their works are only read as examples of a period of erudition; and a literary glory based on imitation is a sorry glory indeed. These medieval Latin poets were translated into Italian in their own country; and that proves how natural it is to favor a language that reminds you of the emotions of your own life instead of one that you can only recover through study.

The best way to dispense with translations, I agree, would be to know all the languages in which the works of the greatest poets were written: Greek, Latin, Italian, French, English, Spanish, Portuguese, German; but such work requires a great deal of time and assistance; and one can never be confident that knowledge that is so difficult to acquire will be universally attained. Ultimately, it is the universal to which one must aspire in attempting to do good for the human race. I would go even further: even if one had a good understanding of foreign languages, a successful translation of a work into one's own language would provide a more familiar and intimate pleasure than the original. The imported beauty that a translation brings with it gives the national style new turns of phrase and original expressions. To preserve a country's literature from banality, a sure sign of decadence, there is no more effective means than translating foreign poets.

But to draw a real profit from translation one should not follow the French, who give their own color to everything they translate. Even if in doing so one were to change everything one touches to gold, it would still be impossible to derive any nourishment or new food for thought; although the finery might be slightly different, one would always see the same face again. This criticism, which the French well deserve, derives from the fact that the art of poetry in their language is invariably kept in shackles. The scarcity of rhyme, the uniformity of verse structure, the difficulty of inversions, all imprison the poet in a fixed circle which necessarily leads back to the same hemistichs, if not the same thoughts, to a certain monotony in French poetic language, which genius escapes when it soars high but from which it cannot free itself in the transitions, in developments, in brief, in everything that leads up to and unites those poetic high points.

It would thus be difficult to find an example in French literature of a good translation of poetry, except for Abbé Delille's translation of Virgil's *Georgics*. There are beautiful imitations, which are conquests that have contributed to the wealth in the nation's coffers, but it would be difficult to name a work of poetry which in any way retained its foreign nature, and I truly doubt whether any such effort could ever succeed. If Delille's *Georgics* have been justifiably admired, it is because the French language has more than any other language been capable of assimilating to Latin, from which French derives, and whose pomp and majesty it retains; but modern languages contain so much diversity that French poetry cannot gracefully yield to Latin's rule.

The English, whose language allows for inversion, and whose versification is subject to laws that are far less severe than in French, could have enriched their language by translations both precise and natural; but their great authors did not undertake this labor of translation. Pope, the only one who did, made the *Iliad* and the *Odyssey* into two beautiful poems, but failed to retain the ancient simplicity which makes us sense the secret of Homer's superiority.

It is indeed improbable that for three thousand years one man's genius has surpassed that of all other poets; but there was something primitive about traditions, customs, opinions, and the air itself in his time that possessed endless charm. When we read Homer, we have a sense of the beginning of time and the youth of the human race, which renews in our souls the sort of emotion we feel in recalling our own childhood. Because that emotion blends with his dreams of a golden age, we prefer the most ancient poet to all his successors. If you subtract from his composition the simplicity of the first days of the world, it loses its uniqueness.

In Germany several scholars have claimed that the works of Homer were not composed by a single individual, and that one should consider the *Iliad*, and even the *Odyssey*, as a collection of heroic songs which celebrated the Greek conquest of Troy and the return of the victors. It is easy to refute that view, it seems to me, mainly because the unity of the *Iliad* does not allow one to adopt it. Why would several authors have limited themselves to the story of Achilles's anger? Subsequent events culminating in the capture of Troy would normally have formed part of the collection of rhapsodies that supposedly belonged to diverse authors. Only a single person could have conceived a plan focused on one unified event, Achilles's anger. But even without a discussion of the whole theory of multiple authorship, which would require an incredible erudition, it should at least be acknowledged that Homer's principal greatness stems from his century: why else would people believe that Homer's contemporaries, or at least a great number of them, collaborated on the *Iliad*? Here is added proof that this poem is the image of human society at a certain stage of civilization, proof that it bears the imprint of its time even more than that of its author.

The Germans did not limit themselves to these scholarly inquiries into Homer's existence. They attempted to make him come to life again among them, and Voss's translation is recognized as the most exact translation in existence in any language. He used the rhythm of the ancients, and it is said that his German hexameter almost follows the Greek hexameter word for word. Such a translation effectively provides a precise knowledge of the ancient poem; but is it certain that the charm of the original poem, accessible neither through rules nor through erudition, has been thoroughly transported into the German language? The number of syllables has been retained, but the harmony of sounds has not remained the same. When German poetry follows, step by step, the traces of the Greek original, it both loses its natural charm and fails to acquire the beauty of the musical language that was accompanied on the lyre.

Of all the modern languages, Italian is the one that most lends itself to rendering all the sensations produced by the Greek of Homer. It is true that Italian does not have the same rhythm as the original. The hexameter can hardly be introduced into our modern languages, in which long and short syllables are not sufficiently marked to copy the ancient poets. But Italian words have a harmony that can dispense with the symmetry of dactyls and spondees; and the grammatical construction of Italian lends itself to a perfect imitation of Greek inversions. Because the *versi sciolti* stand outside of the rhyme system, they impede the expression of ideas no more so than prose, yet they retain the grace and measure of poetry.

Among all the translations of Homer that exist in Europe, Monti's surely comes closest to producing the same pleasure as the original. It has both pomp and simplicity. The most ordinary practices of daily life such as clothes or dinners are enhanced by the natural dignity of Monti's expressions, and the most solemn events are made accessible to us through the realism of his scenes and the fluency of his style. No one in Italy will ever translate the *Iliad* again. There, Homer will forever be clothed in Monti's apparel; and it seems to me that even in the other European countries, whoever cannot rise to reading Homer in the original will have an idea of the pleasure that he can produce by reading the Italian translation. Translating a poet is not like taking a compass and measuring the dimensions of a building. It is making a different instrument vibrate with the same breath of life as the one we normally hear. A translation should provide as much pleasure as the original, not just duplicate its features.

It seems highly desirable to me for Italians to take the trouble to provide careful translations of various new works of English and German poetry; their compatriots would thus acquire a new genre instead of limiting themselves to images drawn from ancient mythology.

Those mythological images are becoming barren; paganism in poetry hardly exists anywhere else in Europe. To make intellectual progress glorious Italy must often look beyond the Alps, not to borrow, but to know: not to imitate, but to achieve emancipation from those conventional forms that persist, in literature as in society, and prevent the expression of any natural truth.

If poems in translation enrich the arts, the translation of plays can exercise an even greater influence; for theater is truly the executive branch of literature. By joining precision with inspiration, A. W. Schlegel did a translation of Shakespeare that has a truly German flavor. Thus transmitted, English plays are performed on the German stage, and Shakespeare and Schiller have become compatriots. Similar results could be obtained in Italy. French playwrights come as close to the Italian taste as Shakespeare does to the German. It would perhaps be possible to perform *Athalie* successfully on the beautiful stage in Milan, letting the admirable Italian music accompany the chorus. It may be true that Italians go to the theater to talk and meet their friends in the loges rather than to listen; but it is still the case that routinely spending more or less five hours every day listening to what Italian opera-goers call words is a sure way to diminish the intellectual faculties of a nation. When Casti wrote comic operas, when Métastase wrote musical adaptations filled with charming and elevated thoughts, entertainment lost nothing, and reason gained a great deal. If, in the midst of the habitual frivolity of society, when people rely on others to forget about themselves, you, as artists, could transmit not only pleasure but also a few ideas and feelings, you could train minds to appreciate serious works that give them real value.

Italian literature is now divided between scholars who comb through the ashes of the past, trying to dredge up a few flecks of gold, and writers who rely on the harmony of their language to produce harmonies without ideas, to string together exclamations, declamations, invocations in which not one word either stems from or touches the heart. Would it not be possible to emulate actively the success achieved on the stage, and, thereby, to restore gradually that originality of thought and truth of style without which there is no literature at all, nor perhaps even any of those qualities necessary for literature to exist?

Italian theater has become enthralled with sentimental drama. Instead of the gay, lively spirit that used to exist, instead of those dramatic characters that have been classics throughout Europe, we now see from the very beginning of these plays what I would describe, if I may say so, as the most insipid assassinations it is possible to present

on stage. What a poor education the constant repetition of such pleasures gives to a considerable number of people! Italian taste in the
arts is as simple as it is noble. But language too is an art, and it too
must be treated artistically. Language is integral to our human nature; and we can more easily dispense with paintings and monuments
than with those feelings that language should strive to convey.

Italians are extremely enthusiastic about their language. Great
writers have shown it to advantage, and intellectual distinction has
been the unique pleasure, and often the only consolation, of the
Italian nation. If all those capable of thought are to feel motivated to
reach their full development, all nations must have an active principle
of self-interest. Some countries are militaristic; others are political.
Italy's reputation should be based on its literature and its art; otherwise that country will fall into a sort of apathy from which even the
sun will not be enough to arouse it.

EIGHT

Black on White

Translation, Race, Class, and Power

Sharon Bell and Françoise Massardier-Kenney

The following dialogue represents an attempt to compensate for the importance of the written in the translation of *Mirza,* an importance which goes against the valorization of orality present in the story. This dialogue is also meant to document the kinds of thought processes the translator goes through as he or she is translating, the kinds of "roads not taken" which nonetheless led to the final version, the kinds of issues which were important for the translators. The two speakers both translated pieces by Germaine de Staël. Françoise Massardier-Kenney (identified as "F") translated *Mirza* and Sharon Bell (identified as "S") translated the two abolitionist pieces presented in this volume, "Appel aux Souverains" and "Préface pour la traduction d'un ouvrage de M. Wilberforce." Bell is an African American who has translated the Haitian writer Jacques-Stéphen Alexis. Massardier-Kenney is a French native who has translated Lacanian psychoanalytic texts.

The issues the dialogue raises include the influence of the translator's background (be it cultural or racial) on reading and on the translating process, and power (the superiority/inferiority of the translator over the author, of the narrator over the characters, of the cultures involved by the translation). This dialogue is meant more as a mediating ground for asking questions pertinent to translation than as a place to provide answers.

F: You read my translation of *Mirza;* what did you think, of the work or its translation?

S: I thought the translation was very well done; in fact, I was amazed that in places you managed to preserve aspects of tone and certain features of language in the English that I would have thought very difficult to do. But my reaction to the story itself was very ambivalent. I found the narrator's comments offensive. If you remember, the narrator of *Mirza* establishes a clear difference between the characters of Ximeo and his wife and those of the blacks who serve them—in fact, between Ximeo and Ourika and the bulk of Africans. These latter are represented as being playful, as having no concept of planning for the future, as being unable to weigh a present evil against a posterior one. Though by the end of the story the narrator is left marveling at the nobility of Ximeo and Mirza, I felt that he looked down on blacks in general (and I myself certainly fall into that category). I had to wonder if Staël had been able to articulate his views so convincingly because she shared them too. But I concluded that these comments represented an obvious case of distance between the narrator and the implied author of this story. In any case, whereas it's possible that a nineteenth-century reader could have accepted those initial comments without question, as twentieth-century readers we distance ourselves from the things he says. I found that I was so aghast at them that it put me in a position of superiority over him because I could see through his argument. But his comments also tempered my reaction to the rest of the story, in a rather negative way.

F: Absolutely. Yes.

S: And I think that it is interesting that Staël has a male narrator say these things.

F: Yes, he says it to a woman listener, but, again, the narrator might be representing the discourse of the male European who is sympathetic but has those general ideas, like blacks are incapable of providing for their future, but doesn't analyze why it is that they don't plan for their future. It is interesting that there is this distance between the narrator, the author, and the characters.

S: I wonder what the reaction of the public was when it was first published. Did they think like this narrator? Or did they distance themselves from him the way we twentieth-century readers, especially women do?

F: It depends on the readers. If the reader is a racist, one who endorses the stereotypes, there probably would be very little distance. The biggest distance might have to do with Ximeo and Mirza. For one thing, they are exceptional characters, and the reader is not. Was I shocked by the narrator's comments? No, I wasn't; it might have to do with the fact that I am white, but within the framework of the story when the narrator says "those people were given a chance to grow sugarcane but they didn't want to do it because they didn't think about the future!" I disagree with his analysis, but I can see why he would say that. I don't think it says anything about blacks, that it is a statement specifically about blacks.

S: But it appears to be exactly that.

F: True, but all I am saying is that this is a discourse that was used against the working class, that the working class does not plan for the future, that they squander their money, etc.; it's a discourse that was current among the middle class in the nineteenth century, at least in France, but we know why the lower class did not plan for the future. They had no future. They had nothing to plan for. So when I hear that, I don't hear it as a racial statement. I hear it as a class statement. The bourgeois very much in control of his life speaking against the behavior of the lower class. But I do think that in our reactions there is a racial element; you take it personally, whereas I don't. What do you think?

S: Yes, this is the argument I heard all my life, you know, "Blacks are shiftless, lazy, never serious; they're always happy, they don't plan for the future; they squander."

F: Then I have a problem. Since I am not American, I am not quite aware of that discourse; I did not recognize it the way you did. I didn't think "oh yeah, the same old thing." What I found most interesting in what Staël was doing is her refusal to endorse essential differences, racial differences, and I think that at the time it was a radical move. And that's where I had a big problem in translating the story. You have a woman at the beginning of the nineteenth century whose main character is a black woman who is extremely articulate and who completely masters language. In the context of the nineteenth century this is a radical gesture. Then most people thought that blacks could not do that. To show a character who is the equal, probably the superior, of the reader is a radical gesture, but I have a problem as a translator because that gesture does not work in modern English; to have a black character speak perfect English is not radical. Everybody assumes that there is equality in this regard.

S: Not necessarily. In fact in the seventies, there were times when I had to go and speak on white campuses to student groups. People would run up to me after my talk and say, "Your English is so beautiful!" And another time at a conference a man said "Wow, you speak such good French, and your English is so good too!"

F: So, in thinking that I had not adapted the radical gesture, maybe I was wrong; maybe there is still a need to do that.

S: There is another thing. The lower-class blacks of the story never speak. You don't have to establish a contrast between these two superior individuals and the mass who is not superior by the way they talk because the mass never speaks. To have Mirza and Ximeo speak absolutely literate English is, in a way, a gesture. Most blacks don't speak that way with each other in informal contexts. It's more of a gesture than you realize.

F: When I thought about it, I thought if I really change the way they speak, I am also rewriting Staël, in a way which destroys the project, which is to unearth a tradition of some radicalness, of resistance; of course, these authors were not all revolutionaries, let's not fool ourselves, but they made that gesture, and it needs to be uncovered, especially in light of the fact that the canonical white male tradition did not do that. So, for historical reasons I wanted to keep it; but as you suggest, by keeping it we are still making that radical claim.

S: What else could you have done?

F: Staël presents a character who is "in translation" because Mirza's native language is not French, and yet she speaks in French, so I don't know what I could have done. One thing is to look at some works by contemporary authors from Africa or the West Indies who write in English, or works that have been translated into English and try to follow the rhythms, the metaphors, in a sense to completely rewrite it so as not to give the translation of a translation, but it's very hard to do because it is an early nineteenth-century voice, and we have no idea of what that voice was actually like, and maybe the idea is to emphasize that it is a translation, that's the only way those voices came to us, in translation. If it hadn't been for translation, they would be silent, or silenced. So the fact that it is in translation might be positive. Because it is only through this project that these texts on race by women will be available. They are not available in their native language at the moment.

S: There's another point too. And it's just this: she has created two characters who have learned French perfectly, who can express poetry, the deepest longings of the soul, in a language that isn't theirs, and we, as teachers of language, know that is a significant accomplishment. Furthermore, Ximeo has learned to speak French from Mirza. She learned from a native speaker; he learned from her. That makes his accomplishment that much greater. But I don't think there is a problem in making them speak perfect English. You don't have to worry about the fact that their French might have been a little foreign. The point is they completely absorbed a language that was believed at the time to be the language of civilization.

F: But to have characters extremely powerful with language now— although as you say the situation with blacks may not be as positive as I would like to think—but in the early nineteenth century, that was a radical gesture, which we can assess in the introduction, in the footnotes, but somehow in the text itself, I was unable to do that.

S: There's a tradition in American movies, in several movies where you have a superior black hero, who not only speaks absolutely standard English, but also listens to classical music, knows fine arts—you know the sort of things. A class difference, too, is being expressed. But in the sixties, when I saw some of these movies, nobody would have thought of class. The thing that hit you in the face was the racial difference.

F: But I think it is offensive to legitimize a black by the fact that he is only using high culture.

S: Absolutely. In fact, this was part of the motif of the tragic mulatto in black American literature. Often this type of character was not only light-skinned, but his or her superiority was seen in the fact that he or she participated in high culture and spoke standard English.

F: So I guess that's what I am fighting against. I thought of a solution for my narrative gesture after seeing the film *Daughters of the Dust*, where people speak English, but a very different kind of English. You understood—well, being French, I did not understand; I didn't recognize some of the words and the sentences, but it was clear to me that it was different from standard English, and I thought if we were doing a movie of *Mirza*, that's what we could do, use that kind of language, with subtitles so that you could both get that sense of extremely high accomplishment and yet of difference, so that you would go to the source language rather than just having the character already speaking in translation.

S: Don't you think that Staël's whole point is that they are not different, or that they are different to the extent that they are superior; it's not a horizontal difference, it's a vertical difference.

F: In terms of the translation of *Mirza*, once we tried as an experiment to both translate a part of *Mirza*. What is your reaction to the differences?

S: The problems that I had came from a slightly different source, and it was this: I really wanted to reproduce the English of the early nineteenth century.

F: I looked at our translations. I found that there was very little difference. I expected differences; I don't know what. Maybe I am essentializing nationalities or race!

S: Well, I am not an essentialist, and I really wonder if social class in
America doesn't wind up having more to do with people's discourse
than race does, to a certain extent. As for the two of us as readers,
our experience has sensitized us to certain kinds of things, and
your observation that this story is about class, to me, makes good
sense. I first saw it as being solely about race. The negative comments about blacks made by the narrator apply to blacks of a different class from Mirza and Ximeo, but I saw them as racial, pure and
simple. It didn't occur to me that these were things people were also
saying about lower class white people or the lumpenproletariat. But
aside from being sensitized to different kinds of issues, and in my
case having a vernacular language that's not standard English,
aside from that, I really wonder if things like social class and education don't influence the way we think and the way we write more
than things like race. And you have lived in America for a number
of years; you are becoming bicultural.

F: Then, to go back to *Mirza,* are you saying that we need to translate
it, to have a text acknowledging, or not even acknowledging, assum-
ing that there is complete equality?

S: Yes, and in fact, this text assumes that nobility and greatness of
spirit can belong to anybody. Black American literature also has
this message quite a lot, but, strikingly, not tied to social class. Celie
in *The Color Purple* comes immediately to mind. But I think it's
fascinating that you find this same message, if you know how to
look, how to decode the text, from a woman who lived in eighteenth-century France. I think that's a very interesting addition to
the general discourse about race that goes on in America right now.

F: So, my feeling about Staël's contribution was that she refuses to
take race as an ultimate difference. She says basically race is a mark
of difference which is used against people, but that's all it is. It is
something which is used. It is not something that's essential, and
that does not disturb you? You endorse that too; is this what you
are saying? The question I am trying to ask is: do I think it is a
contribution because I am white or a Western intellectual? Did you
react differently?

S: See, I didn't pick up that reading. Readers bring to a text their
own experiences, and their own presuppositions, so I did not read
it that way. But when I hear you explain it, I thought "Of course!"
Perhaps the fact that I found this text offensive in some ways

stopped me from seeing beyond the things that offended me. I think you are absolutely right, that it is a reading where race is not a matter of essential difference, that people are alike everywhere. She creates these two characters who prove that black people are just like white people, though that's an extremely offensive way to put it.

F: Well, let's put it this way, white people are like black people.

S: Or like this: Qualities like intelligence, nobility, goodness, and badness are equally distributed among the human race. Things like genius and stupidity, all these are universal characteristics of human beings.

F: There is no essential difference, but she does recognize some cultural differences, like orality as opposed to writing; and even though this is a written story, it's a written story about somebody who communicates orally. So, because the frame is written, you could say that the power structure is such that the Western tradition (writing) wins; at the same time, the writing is a translation of, a transcription of, the oral; but the oral is present, and that presence, the presence of that voice is very important. Without Staël, we wouldn't have it. There would be no voice of that Jolof woman, Mirza. At the same time our reactions were very different, and they seem to be different along racial lines. When you first read the text, you found offensive the passages where the narrator made generalizations about black behavior.

S: And I found offensive the fact that these two were given special status because they were superior. In other words, blacks didn't have any value unless they were superior; nobody considered the mass of blacks at all.

F: But at the same time, it's the same for French workers. In Staël's novels, you don't hear about what the maid thinks. All you have represented is the extremely educated woman. You are right, the lower class is not given a voice. I have another question. You translated the Wilberforce piece, and I would like to speak about it to see if you think that somehow you made certain changes because the issue was race, and you are an African American.

S: There was a place where I very deliberately changed the sentence because she said something I found shocking; she called blacks "savages," or something like that. You also have this thing with "sauvage, primitif, rustique" in French, words whose English cognates have very negative connotations, but which are much less emotionally loaded in French. I deliberately softened that one sentence, and yet, because of the difference between what words like "primitif," "sauvage" mean in French and English, it may be that my refraction would pass unnoticed. I remember that the statement offended me so much I could not put down what the sentence actually said.

F: My next question is: If, in my translation, when you read it, you still have that reaction of distaste, then there is a sense in which I failed because—

S: No, I don't think you, as a translator, failed. I think readers help create texts, and we create them by bringing our baggage, rightly or wrongly, to the text. Scholars are supposed to be able to distance themselves from their own emotional baggage. We are supposed to have the capacity to look at the background out of which a text arose and judge it a little more dispassionately. I'm really talking about two different readings, and in the translation you translated very much the spirit of the text. But I read it according to my own presuppositions, shaped in part by the racial discourse of America, and by the fact that I've personally been a victim of that discourse.

F: My first reaction to this text, as a naive reader, was that I was a little annoyed by the romantic excesses of Mirza. I must say that in my translation, I tried to soften the excesses and wanted to valorize her speech. I wanted to make sure that people reading only the English would get from the text a sense of the power of that voice, as opposed to the quaint or romantic.

S: I think that the power of the voice comes through. But a lot of times, our reactions to "old" literature are cultural reactions shaped by the fact that cultural values have changed. One example I think of is Dickens's *The Old Curiosity Shop,* where one of the most touching scenes in the novel is the death of Little Nell. All these people came to weep at her bedside for days and days. This is obviously a climactic point in this novel, but for a modern reader it's just embarrassing. We just don't look at death in the same way.

F: But maybe that's where the translator can change things. Is there a voice in English which would allow *Mirza* to come through closer to us and more effective?

S: Well, that brings up another concern of mine as I translated. And that was trying to maintain the sound of an early nineteenth-century text. Was it an option not to do that?

F: I think it's always an option. The question is: why are you translating? The reason for translating, for me, was to really reconstitute the tradition of women writing about race, a tradition which is a generous tradition that is not part of the racist discourse. So I was very much pulled to the source text. And again, I thought that some of the options discussed, like using English from an African writer, were as questionable as this one. But, I do think that there are other options.

S: I wonder if African writers writing at that time, except for subject matter, might not be indistinguishable from European ones. I don't know the writings of Equiano or Gustavus Africanus, two very early African writers who wrote in English. For Phyllis Wheatley that was certainly true, if you didn't know it was the writing of a slave.

F: So that's also a problem. Or choose somebody contemporary. For example, English from the West Indies. But again, who is the audience? The audience will not probably recognize that it's that kind of English. You spoke about the background of the readers. We are basically addressing a middle-class, academic readership; so it's very circumscribed by the circumstances. And our readers will be likely to read the discussion or introduction.

S: And another thought occurs to me. If the first gut level of the reading in French is going to be offensive, to what extent do you expect the translation to bring out another reading? When I translated Staël, I wanted my reader in English to get what the reader in French got. I don't want to bring out the subtext. If it's there, let them dig for it the way I have to dig for it in French. But it's also valid to translate in such a way that you do bring out alternate readings. In fact, your translation has to bring out some reading.

F: Do you think that the race of the translator is a determining factor in translating those kinds of texts or do you think that an informed translator is what you need, regardless of race?

S: You need an informed translator. But, on the other hand, I think race is intimately tied to culture in this country because of segregation, and culture has everything to do with values you absorb growing up. There is also the fact that translators have to decide what they are going to do with the text. Do we translate this as nineteenth-century English, or do we come up with a really modern translation? Do we soften ideas offensive to modern sensibilities in an otherwise sympathetic writer, or do we let them speak freely, for better or worse? A translator has to make those decisions, and again, you almost have to privilege one reading, and the translator chooses which reading to privilege. As a translator, I take the text very seriously and I don't want deliberately to slant the text in a direction in which I don't feel that it was already going; so I stay close to what the surface meaning of the text appears to be. That means that if other readings exist maybe a reader who closely analyzes the text can pull them out, but I'm very reluctant to try to do that as part of the act of translation. But you've got to translate one reading or another, so in a way, whether or not to translate these subtexts becomes a false problem. And if a translator arrives at a reading that the text can be seen to support, then it's valid to render that reading in the translation, even if it seems radical, different from what you first perceived when you read the French. When you translated, you didn't think of trying to translate this in very contemporary English?

F: No, I did not think that was an option. But it wasn't an option because my goal was to allow the voice of Staël and Mirza to sound, and if I'd done that there's a sense in which it wouldn't have been Staël's voice. So, that is why I went back to the English romantics, and the most consonant was Mary Shelley, another woman, and the work which helped me the most was *Frankenstein,* the story of the monster.

F: On another topic, does the inclusion of discourses that are opposed to her position in her two abolitionist pieces make you rethink your reaction to *Mirza*? She has listened to the proponents of the slave trade and she addresses their arguments so their arguments are a part of her discourse, like her references to Christianity? In *Mirza,* she does the same. The narrator is not the radical that she is. Therefore, he comes up with those stereotypes about what he expects the Africans to be. I'm just wondering, in terms of your translating those two pieces, whether that affected retrospectively your reaction to *Mirza,* or not.

S: It didn't because I still didn't get it. To look at Mirza and Ximeo in light of what was then current racist discourse, never hit me. I looked at it in the light of present-day racist discourse. That's why I couldn't really see what Staël had accomplished in that story.

F: One of the contributions that Staël makes is that she endorses orality rather than justifying black equality or superiority. What do you think of that? Do you think it's significant or that making her characters express themselves orally is closer to African traditions, although she can't get back to the African voice; is the fact that she insists on the oral tradition a positive thing as people like Chamoiseau would argue?

S: The fact that the story is recounted orally didn't really hit me one way or the other. And privileging the oral didn't strike me as harking back to African tradition. Orality turns out to be important in a lot of other cultures, too. I think of the salon in France, for example.

F: But the salon is woman's stuff; compared to the written production of the males, it was considered secondary.

S: And yet, the salons were probably the catalyst for the creative output of both men and women in the eighteenth century. And furthermore, the art of conversation was probably raised to a very high level and given a great deal of prestige. Well, that's the connection I made with the oral discourse and the fact that the story is actually presented orally and orality is given such a privileged position.

F: So you tied orality to the salon, that is to the origin of the white writer, as opposed to tying it to the tradition of a number of African countries where the oral transmission of culture was primary.

S: Yes. I'm wondering what eighteenth- and nineteenth-century Europe even knew about African traditions and orality.

F: Well, they knew they didn't use the written word to transmit their tales, myths, and philosophy.

S: I'm not sure they knew about their tales, myths, and philosophies then.[1] When anthropologists started going to Africa in the mid-nineteenth century, a lot of those things began to be revealed to the rest of the world for the first time. What the discourse we heard here in North America said was that there was no culture. Africans were basically wild people who hunted, who had unbridled sexual mores, and who were incapable of founding families. There was an assumption that there was no culture to be transmitted orally.

F: Even if the French at large didn't know it, showing that their culture privileges the oral would be a fairly advanced gesture. As opposed to saying that the only way to do culture is through the written word.

S: After all, *Bug Jargal* is oral too. The whole thing is an oral recitation; the oral recitation within a novelistic frame was a device a lot of people used in nineteenth-century fiction.

F: Yes, but in *Bug Jargal* they don't have the black character going up to the top of a hill and spouting off poetry. Do you see what I'm saying? That there's an insistence here on cultural skills that are oral. These characters know how to write, so it's not that they can't write, it's that they *won't* write. Actually, when Ximeo writes, it's to tell Mirza lies. So writing is devalorized. I stated that the use of pidgin French or pidgin English used by other writers like Maupassant in *Timbouctou* was more racist than what Staël does. Do you agree with that?

S: I think I agree, because Africans were thought not to be able to acquire a language. And so for her to depict these characters as capable of using French to express great depths of feeling with eloquence definitely makes a statement.

F: So you think it's a more racist technique to have black characters use non-standard English as opposed to standard English?

S: Well, you know, the one example I remember is in *Bug Jargal,* and I feel that to portray inferiority is absolutely its purpose in *Bug Jargal.* Although it seems Bug spoke a mixture of French and Spanish, and what you see is command of two languages. But, with Jean François, Biassou, and the dwarf, I suspect that their mixture of French, Spanish, and Creole was a manifestation of their inferiority: it's as if they're incapable of learning one language right.

F: I agree. Again, inferiority, and class inferiority as well, because you can't imagine educated people speaking pidgin French or pidgin English.

F: The historical survey in chapter 2 mentions La Place's translation of a text on blacks where he adapts and does something much more radical with the racial elements and completely rewrites it. That's not acceptable nowadays to completely rewrite, to remove some episodes, or add some. But if we said it was acceptable at the moment, how would *Mirza* be rewritten through radical translation? As a translator, how would you do it?

S: I really have trouble accepting that liberal a standard. I wouldn't do it.

F: You wouldn't do it? Well, I have the same reaction in a sense. I know that Phyllis Wheatley translated a work like *Mirza, Le nègre comme il y a peu de blancs* and that the work has the kinds of limitations that *Mirza* has; there's a sense in which people can argue that translating those kinds of texts is being co-opted or used by abolitionists. The question is: can you preserve a non-hegemonic voice when translating literature or expository essays like Staël's? My reaction is when the translator is a woman there's a sense of deference to the authority of the text. And then you have somebody like La Place, who is the male and is going to come up and make everything right. I find such an attitude offensive.

S: And with the translations of *Bug Jargal* that we examined one of the translators did exactly that. But we found another translation that kept very closely to the text, and that was the work of a woman translator.

F: You just reacted the same way when I asked you how you would do a radical translation, and you said, "well, I wouldn't." Because there is a sense in which it is a very arrogant position to take something which is radical and say it isn't radical enough, let's completely change it. To what?

S: That tends to be my feeling. However, we mentioned the idea that often you have subtexts that perhaps you could bring to the surface depending on how you translate. I really do believe that different readers, because of their different experiences, preconceptions, and ideals, will legitimately create different texts. So why is it not possible, as these translators work, to produce quite different translations of the same originals, but still to operate within limits?

F: When you did your translation of Alexis, you did a radical translation because you used black English very often when the text was in standard French. So, you radicalized it.

S: Actually, it wasn't standard French. In one place that I have just looked at again, the register was very familiar, and it dawns on me now as I'm thinking about this, that I don't have that register in standard English myself. But I think, too, that it was a case of trying to bring out a subtext that actually did exist. I know of one white scholar who is translating Alexis, and, in fact, I've seen the Spanish translation of the same work I've translated. The Spanish one was very direct. Whereas I use a lot of the popular register in English, which is black English, the Spanish translator didn't use the vernacular at all. I haven't seen any of the work of the American translator I've mentioned, but I'm very curious to see what he comes up with when his translation comes out.

F: But for *Mirza,* how could we do it? I just thought about one way to radicalize it. We could find a person who speaks the language of the Wolof and who could supply us with a translation into Wolof of the passage when the narrator comes to Ximeo's plantation. The guide could then say to the narrator, "Oh, of course you don't speak Wolof, so let me translate this for you."

S: That's wonderful!

F: So that would be a way to radicalize it, to give the characters back their voice, in a sense. Instead of presenting them in translation, you would also have the original language so that your text would contain whatever African language was spoken specifically in that region, plus the French translation. The reader would be put in the position of the French narrator, which is, you understand one thing, but you don't understand the other one. Another thing I thought about, where you wouldn't really need to change the story. Near the end, when Mirza speaks to herself, she would speak in another language. In a footnote, you could translate it into French or into English. It would be a way to put the voice back in again.

S: But the idea of having them speak something else in front of the Frenchman and excluding him is a wonderful idea. I thought of other things one can do. In the discourse between Ximeo and Mirza, you could do code mixing with African languages. Why would it be improbable that they had not given each other their own languages, as well as the French? You drop a word here and there. And maybe you don't explain it, or you put it in a footnote. That's a way it could be done too.

F: And that would be a way to bring the issue of translation to the fore, which is a major issue. Even when you have those well-meaning French abolitionists, their black characters are in translation already; their natural language is already lost. So that would be a way to make sure the reader perceives that loss and maybe make the reader reexperience the loss.

S: When we originally began working on this text, we were dealing with ideological translation. And we were considering it fairly negatively. We were considering those instances in *Bug Jargal* where the translator had changed things around very obviously, deleted things favorable to blacks and added things that weren't in the text which were favorable to whites. From the standard of our times, that's a very obvious misuse of translation. And having started this project discussing incidents like that, that's one of the things that made me especially careful to try not to refract Staël, at least not deliberately.

F: The reason why we've all stayed fairly close to the text was because we were aware of all the negative ideological implications of changing it. If you do it yourself, under another agenda, is it legitimate or not?

S: Well, take the example of the passages in the Staël pieces that I translated, where we deliberately tried to bring out feminist subtexts. I don't know where Staël was coming from as a feminist. And I was very uncomfortable doing some of it, simply because I was so conscious of not changing things ideologically. Yet going from one language to another is complicated because languages are not equal; it's not an algebraic equation. So you take a term like "maîtresse" in "There was no chance France could become mistress of that colony again." It's actually legitimate to say in English, "There was no chance France would again regain mastery of that island." That seems to fit with the way we think in English a little bit better. I think translating to bring out subtexts that a reader legitimately sees in a text, in order to bring them out, not to create them where the translator wishes they existed, I don't think that's an illegitimate act of interpretation.

S: Well, I think this brings us back to where we started, considering the quality of the story as well as that of the translation. Your reading of *Mirza* has uncovered some significant subtexts. To propose a different answer to your very first question, I'd say that, while your translation doesn't make them obvious—any more than they are "obvious" in the French—it definitely preserves them and makes it possible for an informed reader to discover them in English.

PART FOUR
Claire de Duras (1777–1828)

NINE

Duras, Racism, and Class

Françoise Massardier-Kenney

About twenty-five years after the publication of *Mirza* by Germaine de Staël, another novel about a black person, *Ourika* (1823), was published in Paris by another woman, the Duchess Claire de Duras, who had the most prestigious salon of the Restoration. However, if, as women, Staël and Duras shared a particular sensitivity to the plight of people of color, they differed to a significant extent in their assessment of the issue of race. The utopian cosmopolitanism of Staël and her open endorsement of translation was replaced by Duras's pessimistic description of the inevitable alienation of the colonized and by her skepticism of translation as a viable cultural paradigm.

This shift from optimism to pessimism is understandable in light of the changes in historical circumstances. During the years separating these two works, Napoleon had reestablished slavery (1802) and the black rebellion of Santo Domingo (Haiti) (1791) fueled racial prejudices in France. It was not until the period of the Restoration in the 1820s that the question of slavery and of people of color in general attracted interest once again. In 1826 Victor Hugo published *Bug Jargal;* in 1822 the subject of the poetry prize offered by the conservative governmental institution l'Académie-Française was the abolition of the slave trade. In 1821, Duras told the story of Ourika to the members of her salon and published it in 1823.

Ourika was one of the four novels that the famous *salonnière* would compose at the age of forty-five during 1821–22. While *Ourika* would see publication, the others would remain unpublished until well after her death. Although the publication history of *Ourika* suggests that the novel was quite popular—it saw two reeditions the year of publication; nine reeditions between 1826 and 1878, two almost immediate translations into Spanish (1824 and 1825, both published in Paris); it was adapted for the theater and into the world of fashion in the form of a hat; and was admired by people as different as Sainte-Beuve,

Chateaubriand, Talleyrand, Goethe, and von Humbolt—it was virtually ignored for much of the twentieth century. It was only in 1979 that a reedition of *Ourika* by Editions des femmes made the text accessible and sparked a renewal of interest about the author, about the reasons for the success of the novel, and about what it reveals concerning nineteenth-century French attitudes toward race.

It may seem surprising that an aristocratic woman, wife of the Chamberlain of the court of Louis XVIII, host of the most prominent royalist salon of the Restoration, would write works uncovering the prejudices which characterized the class to which she belonged. As *Ourika* exposes race prejudices, *Edouard,* written the same year, describes class prejudices. However, if, by marriage, the author Claire de Kersaint became a Duras, her father Guy de Coëtnempren, Count of Kersaint, had been an advocate of political and social reforms and was considered by conservative members of the nobility as a traitor to his class. He was a liberal, author of *Le bon sens,* a pamphlet attacking privileges and the rigid class distinctions marked by the three orders. A Girondin who supported the revolution, he was guillotined in 1793 after having voted against the death sentence of Louis XVI and resigned from the assembly. Thus, in denouncing the privileges and abuses of her class, Duras was following the tradition of her father.

Her interest in the fate of people of color, besides the fact that it was an interest widespread at the time, can also be linked to her mother, a Creole born in the French colony of Martinique. Through her mother, Claire Louise Françoise de Paul d'Alesso d'Eragny, Claire de Kersaint had direct access to knowledge about the economic and political situation in Martinique, i.e., a world of sugar plantations worked by slaves and owned by Europeans. Moreover, while the slave trade was the enterprise of the bourgeoisie and, as such, could be the target of opposition by the nobility, the Kersaints had great financial interests in Martinique and were, like members of the bourgeoisie, economically linked to it. Claire de Kersaint, whose parents had separated, and then divorced during the revolution, heard in the street about her father's death on June 12, 1793, in Bordeaux as she was ready to embark for Martinique with her mother to recover "a great fortune she had inherited" and she later managed this fortune herself in Martinique, her mother "being sick and weak of mind."[1] One cannot help speculate about the nature of this fortune since the major source of income in Martinique was land (sugarcane fields), and thus slaves.

Through both her parents, Duras found herself both implicated in and distanced from the other members of her class. This distance was

Duras's ambivalence about language and identity is expressed by her rejection of authorship and her refusal to be implicated in the commercial circuit of publishing. Similarly, she published *Edouard* the following year after having it printed in fifty copies. Before the publication of this novel she loaned a proof to her friend Rosalie de Constant, but requested that she loan it only to trustworthy people because she "fears nothing more than a counterfeit edition and publicity against my will."[6] In an attempt to shun the gossip and the sneers brought on after she read it in her salon, she would never print, let alone publish for the public, *Olivier*, written the same year as *Ourika*.[7] Similarly, *Ourika* may have been appreciated by her fellow authors (Goethe, Sainte Beuve, von Humbolt), but the novel was a source of notoriety and ridicule in the salons of the Faubourg Saint Germain. Actually, the crowd of the other salons nicknamed her Ourika (and in this, they were perhaps more perceptive than they knew), and her two daughters Bourgeonika and Bourika.[8] The Faubourg Saint Germain's ridicule is a reminder to the modern reader that, for all its objectionable characteristics (a novel with a protagonist who, although black, has adopted all the prejudices of the aristocratic world, and who is almost abject in her self-hatred), *Ourika* was a radical work that uncovered the foundations of the racist prejudices of the aristocracy.

This ideological complexity of *Ourika* reflects, in some ways, the complexity of the times; it mirrors more specifically the complexity of the real anecdote that was the basis for Duras's narrative. Ourika was the name of an actual young black girl who died at sixteen of a mysterious illness and who had been "given" to the Princess of Beauvau by the Chevalier de Boufflers, governor of Senegal, who has been called one of the most enlightened administrators in the French colonies.[9] His enlightenment, however, went hand in hand with the kind of unconscious prejudice displayed in his correspondence. On one hand, he could write about a child, "I feel moved to tears when I think that this poor child was sold to me like they would a lamb"[10] while also writing to Mme de Sabran in 1788, "I still have a parakeet for the queen, a horse for the Maréchal de Castries, a little captive for Mme de Beauvau, a sultan hen for the Duke of Laon, and an ostrich for M. de Nivernois."[11] The little captive in question was Ourika, whose story Duras was to tell. It is precisely this contradictory position (sympathy but inability to really treat the Africans as equal human beings) that Duras was to describe and question in *Ourika*. The Boufflers letters were read in Mme de Sabran's salon, and the anecdote repeated in aristocratic circles, so that by the time Duras told the story it must have been common knowledge.

The reason why the story of Ourika drew Duras's interest is both historical and personal. It described a common pattern of gifts from Africa exchanged among the members of the nobility and came from Boufflers, who was very informative about Africa. On the personal side, the theme of an isolated individual excluded by society because of race or class was to be a constant in her work, and the depression of the character seems to have reflected Duras's own state as it is documented in the accounts of the times.

David O'Connell has recognized that *Ourika* is the first novel in French to describe the effects of racism on a black person and that the psychological disintegration of Ourika (her depression and self-hatred) corresponds to the stages described by Frantz Fanon in his seminal *Peau noire masques blancs*.[12] At first Ourika lives in the world of childhood where her color is of no significance. She is "fussed over" and loved by her benefactress and her grandson: "my black color did not prevent him from loving me." When Ourika first realizes that she can only have a life of solitude (actually, not quite, only a life without husband or child), she becomes very depressed and attempts to hide from herself the signs of what she comes to call her "mal" (her illness, her disease). "When I caught sight of my black hands, I thought I saw those of a monkey, I exaggerated my ugliness to myself." However, as Chantal Bertrand-Jennings has argued, the alienation felt by Ourika is characteristic of women in general, who adopt the values of the group that oppresses them.[13]

This overlap of race and gender is present from the beginning of Ourika's story. A girl (Ourika) is given by a man (the Chevalier de B.) to a woman (Mme de B.), and for all of its ambiguities, Ourika's integration into the world of the French aristocracy is facilitated and encouraged by her patron in a way possible only in a *gynécée*. It is noticeable that there seem to be no adult males in the entourage of Mme de B., who claims that she loves Ourika like a daughter and has her educated as other aristocratic young women would be: reading, painting, dancing, foreign languages.

The feminine world of Mme de B. allows a cohabitation of two worlds, and the effects of colonization (a patriarchal process), the alienation and erasure of the collective memory of the colonized, are suspended. As long as Ourika is young enough to remain in the maternal haven of Mme de B., she is protected from racism. Ourika's rejection of her color and her self-hatred are a rejection of her "difference" as it is defined by the white male European world; whereas this same "difference" was accepted and valorized by Mme de B. Ourika later recounts with bitterness the ball organized by Mme de B. to allow her talents to shine and, if the incident can be read as an example of the patronizing European attitude toward black Africans, it can also be seen as an attempt to learn about Africa, to appreciate it, and to bring it in contact with the Parisian world of the salon. Mme de B. organizes a dance where the four parts of the world are represented, and Ourika represents Africa. To prepare for the ball, "we consulted travelers, we poured over books of costumes, we consulted scholarly works on African music, finally we chose a Comba, the national dance of my country." The desire to give Ourika an opportunity to be herself, i.e., someone of African origin, proud of the country of her birth, by consulting serious documentation about Africa, is the positive aspect of the incident, and reveals a more enlightened attitude toward Africa than the interest tainted with the disdain of Boufflers.[14]

However, the maternal world of Mme de B. is a fragile one, and it may not be accidental that the eruption of racism in Ourika's life takes place shortly after the ball, the most pronounced example of symbolic attempts at integrating different cultures. When Mme de B. is confronted by the anonymous marquise (whom we presume represents public opinion) with the fact that Ourika has no future, Mme de B. shows her anxiety, but also her hope, that Ourika will keep living "in her intimate circle."

The outside world represented by the marquise, however, states the matter bluntly, "Who will ever want to marry a negress?" The revelation of white racism is intimately connected with patriarchal values: the reproduction of economic interests through marriage. Mme de B., like the Chevalier de B., may have saved Ourika from the terrible fate of slavery, but she cannot achieve her integration into the French world. The message is pessimistic: there is no place where Ourika can live; the white world can only accommodate her as long as she does not reproduce. We are now back to Duras's pessimistic view of translation: the foreign text (or the foreign body) cannot be transferred to and integrated into the dominant culture without being distorted or smothered.

The impact of white prejudice on Ourika is all the stronger because she, as well as the other characters in the novel, can only conceive of herself as a woman in the most traditional sense of the word, i.e., as a supporting spouse and mother, roles which inevitably place women in the realm of the circulation of property within specific classes.

Thus Mme de B. can protect Ourika only as long as she is not yet a woman, but, once Ourika does become a woman, Mme de B. cannot ensure her a place in her class system. Ourika's race is also linked to social class. Not born an aristocrat, she cannot join the ranks of aristocracy. What Duras shows is that whatever the reason, class or color, it is not the semantic content that is central; it is the sign, the fact of the difference existing between the class that wants to protect its purity and the rest of the world. However, color figures a difference that is ineradicable. Black Ourika discovers that she is alone, and, in a sense, so would any member of the working class alienated from his or her own culture, yet forbidden to be part of the aristocracy. But although it is conceivable that a class difference could be erased, color cannot, and the class barriers described by Duras, unlike color, are all the more impenetrable that they are part of the unconscious ideology of the aristocratic class. Mme de B., who has enlightened views, cannot even conceive of marrying Ourika to her grandson, for instance. Although it is not clear that she knows of Ourika's feelings for him, she would have certainly considered them if Ourika had been an aristocrat who belonged to her circle. Charles's marriage is presented like a strategic alliance, and the possibility that Ourika could have feelings is never considered.

This presentation of class and racial prejudices by Duras is accompanied by a very modern description of what Joan Scott calls "the process of subject construction."[15] Duras shows how Ourika's very experience of her own identity as a black woman is mediated by a white male world. First, the story of Ourika is framed by the narrative of a young doctor who visits her at the convent and who will tease out her story by asserting that her "illness" lies in the past and that "the past must be cured. I can't cure it without knowing it." This scientific version of Ourika's "malheur" (misfortune), as she herself first calls it, will be adopted by Ourika, who will then call her color an "ill," a "disease." The very experience of telling her story is thus already mediated through the discourse of science, a bourgeois discourse in the process of displacing the concept of normality from the social realm to the more inescapable realm of the physical. The doctor's confidence in his ability to "cure" Ourika by treating her physically ("my treatment seemed to be effective") is, of course, belied by the last lines of the narrative, "unfortunately they [my cares] were useless; she died at the end of October." Science cannot cure social prejudice.

Secondly, Ourika's sense of herself comes to her mediated as well. Her origin and her history as a captive become known to her well after she is enculturated as a member of Mme de B.'s entourage. "It is only later that I learned about the history of the first days of my childhood." Although she starts the narrative of her story with the scene where she is rescued from slavery, she, in fact, has no memory of the experience; it is only because she has been told the circumstances that she can recount them.

Likewise, until the age of fifteen, she does not experience racial prejudices. What she calls her "blindness" to her color is suddenly revealed to her (indirectly again) by the anonymous marquise, but her own realization of the significance of her color is limited by the terms of the marquise. Like her, Ourika does not see that racial and social prejudices are intertwined. As Mme de B. and the marquise discuss Ourika's predicament, it is evident that her color is a problem because she is not a "common person"; because of her education she is like an aristocrat and would be happy only in a refined environment. Unfortunately, this aristocratic world is defined by the strict rules of exclusion that protect its members from grafts from the outside world. Ourika latches onto the fact of her color because it is the most visible marker of her rejection, but it is very far from being the most significant one.

Far from diminishing the importance of race, Duras links it to a whole system of exclusion based on the difference, the "otherness" of those excluded. She takes racial equality as a given. Her heroine has all the qualities and the defects of a young aristocratic woman; it is only her color that marks her as different. Although considering equality as a given may not seem much nowadays, we must remember that it was an extraordinary achievement. At the time, American abolitionists were still fighting against the notion of the racial inferiority of Africans by showing that they could be as educated and intelligent as white Americans. That Ourika is intelligent and educated (in fact critics have faulted Mme de Duras for the fact that Ourika talks like a *salonnière*) is obvious. Duras shows that prejudice is not rooted in the belief that a race is superior or inferior to another, but that it stems from the desire to exclude what is different.

Translation of Duras

OURIKA
Translated by Françoise Massardier-Kenney and Claire Salardenne
This is to be alone, this, this, is solitude!
Lord Byron

INTRODUCTION

I had come from the town of Montpellier a few months before, and I was practicing medicine in Paris when, one morning, I was summoned to a convent in the Faubourg Saint-Jacques on the Left Bank, to visit a young nun who was ill. The emperor Napoleon had recently allowed a few of these convents to reopen: the one where I was going was devoted to the education of young girls and belonged to the Ursuline order. The revolution had destroyed part of the building. The cloister had one side without walls as the ancient church adjacent to it had been destroyed; the only remnants were a few arches. A nun let me in this cloister, and we walked on large flagstones which provided a path in the galleries. I realized these were tombs because they were all marked by inscriptions which had been, for the most part, blurred by the abrasion of time. A few of these stones had been broken during the revolution: the nun pointed them out to me, saying that they had not yet had time to repair them. I had never been inside a convent before: this spectacle was a novelty for me. From the cloister we went into the garden, where the nun told me they had carried the sister who was ill: indeed, I could see her at the end of a long path shaded by a bower. She was seated, and her long black veil covered her entirely. "Here is the doctor," said the nun as she left. I came forward with some apprehension; the sight of these tombs had wrung my heart, and I thought I was to behold yet another victim of the cloisters. The prejudices of my youth had awakened, and my interest in the woman whom I had come to visit was doubled by the misfortune that I attributed to her.

She turned toward me, and I was strangely surprised when I saw a Negress. My surprise became greater because of the politeness with which she greeted me and the kinds of expressions she used. "You are visiting a person who is quite ill," she said to me, "now I want to get well; but I did not always wish it so, and this perhaps is what did me so much damage." I asked her a few questions about her illness. "I feel," she said, "a constant oppression, I cannot sleep, and I have an unrelenting fever." Her appearance only confirmed this sad description of her state of health: she was excessively thin, her large and shiny eyes, her brilliant white teeth were the only light in her face. Her soul was still alive, but her body was destroyed, and she showed all the marks of a long and acute grief. Touched beyond words, I decided to do everything that was possible to save her. I began by mentioning the necessity to calm her imagination, to think of other things, to avoid painful feelings. "I am happy," she said, "I have never felt such serenity." Her tone of voice was sincere; this soft voice could not deceive; but my surprise increased at every moment. "You haven't always thought so," I told her, "and you bear the trace of a very long lasting grief." "It is true," she said, "My heart found peace quite late, but now I am happy." "Well, if this is the case," I went on, "it is the past that we must cure; let us hope that we shall overcome it: but I cannot cure this past without knowing what it is." "Alas," she answered, "this is foolishness!" When she said these words, her eyes moistened. "Ah, you say that you are happy!" I cried out. "Yes, I am," she added firmly, "and I would not exchange my happiness for the destiny which I used to so desire. I have no secret: the story of my whole life is my misfortune. I suffered so much until I entered this house, that, little by little, my health was destroyed. I welcomed the decline of my health because I saw no hope in the future. This was a guilty thought! As you can see, I have been punished for it; and when at last I wish to live, I may no longer be able to do so."

I reassured her; I gave her hope that she would recover soon, but when I said these consoling words, when I promised her that she would live, a sad sense of foreboding warned me that it was too late and that death had marked its victim.

I saw this young nun again several times; the interest that I showed her seemed to touch her. One day, she came back of her own to the subject to which I wanted to lead her. "The sorrows that I have felt," she said, "must seem so strange that I have always been quite reluctant to share them: One cannot judge other people's afflictions, and confidants are almost always accusers." "Do not fear this from me," I said, "I can see well enough the havoc that sorrow has wreaked in you not to believe it is sincere." "You will find it sincere," she said, "but you will find it unreasonable." "Still, granting what you say," I resumed, "does it exclude sympathy?" "Almost always," she replied, "however, if, in order to cure me, you need to know the sorrows that destroyed my health, I shall confide in you when we are better acquainted."

I visited the convent more and more often; the treatment which I proposed seem to have an effect. Finally, one day last summer, I found her alone in the same arbor, on the same bench where I had seen her for the first time; we resumed the same conversation, and she told me what follows:

OURIKA

I was brought back from Senegal, at the age of two, by monsieur le chevalier de B., the governor of that colony. He took pity on me one day when he saw slaves being taken aboard a slave ship which was about to leave the harbor: my mother was dead, and they were taking me away despite my cries. M. de B. bought me, and, upon his arrival in France, gave me to his aunt Mme la maréchale de B., the most amiable person of her time, and the person who was able to combine the most elevated qualities with the most touching kindness.

My rescue from slavery, my being given Mme de B. as benefactress, were like two gifts of life: I was ungrateful to Providence by not being happy; and, yet, does happiness always result from the gifts of intelligence? I tend to believe the contrary: one must pay for the gift of knowledge by wishing not to know, and legend does not say whether Galatea found happiness after receiving life.

I did not learn the story of the first days of my childhood until much later. My earliest memories take me back only as far as Mme de B.'s salon; I spent all my time there, loved by her, cherished, pampered by all her friends, showered with presents, praised, exalted as the wittiest and the most amiable child.

The tone of that society was enthusiastic; yet good taste did exclude from this enthusiasm anything that resembled exaggeration: everything that lent itself to praise was praised, everything that lent itself to blame was excused, and frequently, with an even more amiable tactfulness, weaknesses themselves were turned into qualities. Success gives courage; with Mme de B. people were worth as much as they could be worth, and perhaps a little more, since she lent some of her own qualities to her friends without being aware of it: seeing her, or listening to her, led them to think that they resembled her.

Dressed in Oriental attire, I would sit at Mme de B.'s feet and listen to the conversation of the most distinguished men of that time without understanding it yet. I was not boisterous like most children; I was thoughtful before I could reflect; I was happy by Mme de B.'s side: love, to me, meant being there, hearing her, obeying her, and, above all, watching her. I wanted nothing more. Living in luxury, being surrounded only by the wittiest and the most amiable people, could not surprise me: I knew nothing else; yet, unbeknownst to me, I was beginning to disdain everything that was not part of the world where I was spending my life. Good taste is to the mind what a good ear is to sounds. When I was still a young child, tastelessness would offend me; I intuitively knew what good taste was before I could even define it, and habit had made it almost a necessity for me. Had I had a future, this inclination would have been dangerous; but I had no future, and I did not know it.

When I reached the age of twelve, it still had not occurred to me that there could be a different way of being happy. Being a Negress did not bother me. People told me I was charming; besides, nothing warned me that my color was a disadvantage. I hardly saw any other children; only one was my friend, and my blackness did not keep him from loving me.

My benefactress had two grandsons, the children of a daughter who had died young. Charles, the younger grandson, was about my age. Brought up with me, he was my protector, my guide, and my supporter in all my little faults. At the age of seven, he went to school. I cried when he left; this was my first sorrow. I often thought about him, but I hardly ever saw him. He was studying, and for my part, I was learning, in order to please Mme de B., everything required for a perfect education. She wanted me to have every talent: I had a good voice, the most skilled masters trained it; I had a disposition for painting, and a famous painter, a friend of Mme de B., undertook to direct my efforts; I learned English, Italian, and Mme de B. herself supervised my readings. She was guiding my mind, forming my judgement. By talking with her, by discovering all the treasures of her soul, I felt mine rise, and it was admiration that opened my mind to intelligence. Alas! I could not foresee that those sweet hours of instruction would be followed by such bitter days; I thought only of pleasing Mme de B.; a smile of approbation on her face was all my future.

In the meantime, repeated readings, poets especially, were beginning to occupy my young imagination; but, without a goal, without a plan, my thoughts wandered aimlessly, and, with the confidence of my young age, I thought that Mme de B. would know how to make me happy. Her affection for me, the life I was leading, everything aggravated my error and justified my blindness. Let me give you an example of the care and attention of which I was the object.

You will perhaps find it hard to believe, when you see me today, that I was renowned for the elegance and beauty of my figure. Mme de B. often praised what she called my grace, and she had wanted me to become a perfect dancer. To allow this talent of mine to shine, my benefactress gave a ball, supposedly for her grandsons, but actually to show me at my best in a quadrille of the four parts of the world, in which I was to represent Africa. We consulted travelers, pored over books on costumes, read erudite works on African music, and finally we chose a *comba*, the national dance of my country. My partner put a veil on his face. Alas! I did not need one on mine; yet, at that time I did not have this thought. Completely captivated by the pleasure of the ball, I danced the *Comba* and had all the success that could be expected from the novelty of the show and the choice of the audience, mostly friends of Mme de B.'s who were infatuated with me and who wanted to please her by letting this exuberance show. The dance, as a matter of fact, was striking; it consisted of a mixture of gestures and measured steps; love, pain, triumph, and despair were depicted. I was not yet aware of all these violent movements of the soul; yet some instinct made me guess them, and I succeeded. I received applause, attention, and much praise: my pleasure was unalloyed; nothing then troubled my security. It was only a few days after the ball that a conversation, overheard by chance, opened my eyes and ended my youth.

There was a large lacquered screen in Mme de B.'s salon. This screen hid a door; it also extended near a window, and between the screen and the window stood a table at which I sometimes sat to draw. One day, I was carefully finishing a miniature; absorbed by my work, I had remained still for a long time, and Mme de B. probably thought that I had left, when one of her friends was announced, the Marquise de—. The marquise was a person of cold reason, peremptory, rational to the point of being harsh; her friendship was of the same nature: sacrifices cost her nothing for the good and the benefit of her friends; but the price that she exacted for this great attachment was high. Inquisitive and rough, as demanding as she was devoted, she was the least amiable of Mme de B.'s friends. I feared her even though she was good to me; she treated me well in her way: for her, to scrutinize, even sternly, was a sign of interest. Alas! I was so accustomed to benevolence, that justice always seemed threatening to me. "While we are alone," Mme de — told Mme de B., "I want to speak to you about Ourika: She is becoming delightful; her mind is quite formed; her conversation will be as witty as yours. She is very talented; she is piquant, natural; but what will become of her? and in the end what will you do with her?" "Alas!" Mme de B. said, "this thought is often on my mind, and, I must admit, always painfully so: I love her as if she were my own daughter; I would do anything to make her happy; and yet, when I think of her situation, I cannot find a remedy. Poor Ourika! I see her alone, forever alone in life!"

I could not possibly recount to you the effect that these few words produced in me. It was as swift as thunder; I saw it all; I saw myself a Negress, dependent, despised, without fortune, without support, without a human being of my own kind with whom I could join my destiny; until then I had been but a toy, an amusement for my benefactress, and I was soon to be cast out of a world in which I could not be admitted. A dreadful palpitation overtook me, my eyes grew dim, the pounding of my heart was so loud that I could not hear; eventually, I recovered enough to hear the rest of the conversation.

"I fear," Mme de — was saying, "that you will make her unhappy. What could satisfy her, now that she has spent her life in your inner circle?" "But she will stay with me," Mme de B. said. "She will," continued Mme de—, "as long as she is a child: but she is fifteen years old; to whom will you marry her, with her intelligence and the education you have given her? Who will ever want to marry a Negress? Even if you can find a man who, for a large dowry, will consent to be the father of Negro children, this man will be of a lower condition, and she will be unhappy. She can only want those men who cannot want her." "All this is true," Mme de B. said; "but fortunately, she is not aware of it yet, and she has for me an attachment which, I do hope, will keep her from judging her situation for a long time. To make her happy, I would have had to have made her a common person: I sincerely believe this was impossible. Well! Perhaps she will be distinguished enough to rise above her position, since she could not stay below it." "This is mere fantasy on your part," Mme de — said: "philosophy puts us above the evils of destiny, but it is powerless against the evils that stem from breaching the natural order of things. Ourika did not fulfill her destiny; she has entered society without its permission; society will have its revenge." "Assuredly," Mme de B. said, "she is innocent of this crime; but you are judging the poor child so severely." "I want to do her more good than you do," Mme de — continued; "I want her happiness, and you are ruining her." Mme de B. answered with impatience, and I was about to be the cause of a quarrel between the two friends, when another visitor was announced: I slipped behind the screen; I escaped; I ran to my room where a flood of tears temporarily soothed my wretched heart.

This loss of the prestige that had surrounded me until then was such a great change in my life! Some illusions are like daylight; when you lose them, everything else disappears with them. In the confusion of the new ideas which assailed me, I could not find anything that had occupied me until then: this was an abyss with all its terrors. The contempt which pursued me; the society in which I was out of place; the man who, for a large dowry, would perhaps consent to his children being Negroes! All these thoughts arose successively like ghosts and attached themselves to me like furies: isolation especially; the conviction that I was alone, forever alone in life, as Mme de B. had said. And at every moment I repeated to myself, alone! forever alone! Until the day before, what did it matter to me to be alone? I was not aware of being alone; I could not feel it. I needed those I loved, it did not occur to me that those I loved did not need me. But now my eyes were open, and misfortune had already let mistrust enter my soul.

When I came back to Mme de B.'s, everybody was struck by the change in me; I was questioned: I said that I was ill; I was believed. Mme de B. sent for Barthez, who examined me carefully, felt my pulse, and said abruptly that there was nothing wrong with me. Mme de B. felt reassured and tried to divert and entertain me. I dare not say how ungrateful I was for the care given by my benefactress. It was as if my soul had closed in on itself. Only the favors that the heart can repay are sweet to accept: My heart was filled with too much bitterness to open up. Infinite combinations of the same thoughts occupied all my time; they kept coming back under a thousand different forms: my imagination gave them the gloomiest colors; I often spent my entire nights in tears. I could pity only myself; my face filled me with horror; I no longer dared look at myself in a mirror; when I looked at my black hands, I thought they were those of a monkey; I exaggerated my ugliness, and this color seemed to me the sign of my reprobation. Only my color separated me from those of my kind, only my color condemned me to be alone, forever alone! "Never loved! Some man, for a large dowry, would perhaps consent to his children being Negroes!" This thought made all my being tremble with indignation. For a moment, I thought of asking Mme de B. to send me back to my country; but there again, I would have been isolated: who would have heard me, who would have understood me? Alas! I no longer belonged to anybody; I was a stranger to the entire human race!

I did not understand the possibility of submitting to such a fate until much later. Mme de B. was not religious. I owed the few religious feelings I had to a respectable priest who had instructed me for my first communion. These feelings were as sincere as my entire character; I did not know, however, that to be beneficial, piety needs to be associated to all the deeds of one's life. My piety had occupied a few moments of my days, but it had remained separate from everything else. My confessor was a saintly old man whose heart harbored few suspicions; I saw him once or twice a year, and since I did not imagine that sorrows could be sins, I did not tell him of my torments. These considerably altered my health; yet the strange thing is that they perfected my mind! A wise man from Orient once said: "What does he know, He who has not suffered?" I saw that before my misfortune I knew nothing; my impressions were all mere feelings. I did not judge. I lived. My heart enjoyed or did not enjoy discussions, actions, people. Now, my mind had emptied itself of these involuntary movements: sorrow is like distance, it makes you judge objects in their entirety. Since I had been feeling estranged from everything, I had become more particular, and scrutinized almost everything I had been enjoying until then.

This disposition could not escape Mme de B.; I never learned whether she guessed its cause. She may have feared to deepen my sorrow by allowing me to confide in her. She nonetheless talked to me without any reserve, and, to divert me from my sorrows, occupied me with her own. She judged my heart well; my ties to life could only be restored through thinking that I could be necessary or at least useful to my benefactress. The thought that haunted me the most was that I was alone on earth, and that I could die without being missed in anyone's heart. I was unfair to Mme de B.; she loved me, and had sufficiently proved it; but, she had other interests that were much more important than I was. I did not envy her tenderness for her grandsons, especially Charles; yet I would have liked to be able to call her "my mother" as they did!

Family ties, especially, made me look back on myself with much pain, I who was never to be the sister, the wife, the mother of anyone! I imagined in these ties more tenderness than they may actually have, and because I could not partake of them, I neglected those that I was allowed to have. No one was my friend, no one had my trust. What

I felt for Mme de B. was closer to worship than to affection; but, I think that I felt for Charles everything one feels for a brother.

Charles was still in school, but was soon to leave and start his travels. He was leaving with his elder brother and his tutor; they were to visit Germany, England, and Italy. Their absence was to last two years. Charles was delighted to go; and for my part, I was not distressed until the last moment; for I was always very happy to see him pleased. I had told him nothing about all the ideas that had been occupying me. I never saw him alone, and I would have needed a long time to explain my sorrow: I am sure that back then he would have understood me. Yet, with all his gentle and serious manner, he tended to be sarcastic, which made me shy: it is true that he used sarcasm only on the ridiculous ways of affectation; all that was sincere disarmed him. I told him nothing anyhow. Besides, his leaving was a distraction, and I think that it was doing me good to grieve over something that was not my usual grief.

Shortly after Charles's departure, the revolution took a more serious turn: I heard people speak all day long, in Mme de B.'s salon, about nothing but the great moral and political interests that the revolution shook to their very roots; these interests were related to everything that had occupied superior minds of all times. Nothing was more capable of extending and forming my ideas than the sight of that arena where, everyday, distinguished people questioned everything that could have been considered settled until then. They would thoroughly study every subject, go back to the origins of every institution, but, too often, to unsettle and destroy everything.

Would you believe that, young as I was, a stranger to all interests of society, nursing my secret wound in solitude, the revolution brought a great change in my ideas, gave rise to a few hopes in my heart, and suspended my griefs for a moment? One is so quick to seek consolation! I thus foresaw that, in that great chaos, I could find my place; that all the fortunes overthrown, all the distinctions of ranks dissolved, all the prejudices having vanished, would perhaps bring a state of things in which I would be less of a stranger; and that, if I had some superiority of mind, some hidden quality, it would be appreciated when my color would no longer isolate me in the middle of the world, as had been the case so far. But, these very qualities that I could find in myself soon opposed my illusion: I soon had to give up the desire of a great evil for a little personal good. Moreover, I saw how ridiculous these persons who wanted to control events were; I judged the pettiness of their character; I guessed their secret goals. Soon their false philanthropy stopped deceiving me, and I abandoned hope when I saw that there would still be enough contempt left against me amidst such adversity. Still, I always took an interest in these lively discussions; but, they soon lost their greatest charm. Gone was the time when one only thought of being charming, and when forgetting one's proud accomplishments was the foremost condition to please, when the revolution stopped being an attractive theory and interfered with the intimate interests of each and every one, conversations degenerated into quarrels, and bitterness, sourness, and personalities took the place of reason. Sometimes, despite my sadness, I was amused by all these violent opinions, which were, in the end, almost always nothing but pretentions, affectations, or fears: but, the joy that comes from observing ridicule does no good; there is too much malice in this joy to cheer the heart that only enjoys innocent pleasures. One may feel this mocking gaiety, without ceasing to be unhappy; perhaps unhappiness even makes one more likely to feel this pleasure, for the bitterness on which the soul feeds is the usual food of this sad pleasure.

The promptly ruined hope which the revolution had given me had not changed the state of my soul; I was still dissatisfied with my fate, and my sorrows were only softened by Mme de B.'s trust and kindness. Sometimes, in the midst of those sour political conversations which she could not seem to sweeten, she looked at me sadly; this look was a balm to my heart; it seemed to say: Ourika, only you can understand me.

People were beginning to talk about freedom for Negroes: it was impossible for me not to be deeply affected by this question; it was an illusion that I still liked to cherish, that elsewhere, at least, there were people like me: Because they were unhappy, I thought them to be good, and I became interested in their condition. Alas! I promptly discovered my mistake! The Santo Domingo massacres caused me a new, excruciating pain: Until then, I had been distressed at belonging to a proscribed race; now I was ashamed of belonging to a race of barbarians and murderers.

Meanwhile, the revolution was making rapid progress; people were frightened to see the most violent men take over all places. It soon appeared that these men were determined to respect nothing: during the dreadful days of June 20 and August 10, people had to prepare themselves for any eventuality. What was left of Mme de B.'s society scattered at that time: some fled from persecutions to foreign countries; the others went into hiding or retired into the country. Mme de B. neither fled nor retired; she was bound to her home by the constant preoccupation of her heart; she stayed there with a memory and near a tomb.

We had been living in seclusion for a few months when, at the end of 1792, the decree seizing émigré property was issued. In the midst of this general disaster, Mme de B. would not have minded the loss of her fortune, had it not belonged to her grandsons; but, according to family arrangements, she only had the trust of that fortune. She thus decided to have the younger of her two grandsons, Charles, come back, and to send the elder, who was almost twenty, to join Condé's army. The two brothers were in Italy at that time, finishing the long journey undertaken two years before under very different circumstances. Charles arrived in Paris at the beginning of February 1793, a short time after the king's death.

This heinous crime had caused Mme de B. the most violent grief; she gave way completely to it, and her soul was strong enough to proportion the horror she felt for the crime to its very immensity. Great sorrows, in old people, have something striking: they have the authority of reason. Mme de B. was suffering with all the energy of her character; her health was affected, but I could not imagine anyone trying to comfort or even divert her. I cried, I joined in her feelings; I tried to elevate my soul to bring it closer to hers, to suffer with her and at least as much as she did.

I almost did not think about my sorrows as long as the Terror lasted; I would have been ashamed to find myself unhappy in the presence of those great misfortunes: as a matter of fact, I no longer felt isolated since everybody was unhappy. Opinion is like a mother-country; it is something that people enjoy together; people are united as a family to support and defend it. I sometimes said to myself that I, a poor Negress, nonetheless was like all elevated souls, and had in common with them the need for justice: the day when virtue and truth would triumph would be a day of triumph for me as well as for them: but, alas! that day was far ahead.

As soon as Charles arrived, Mme de B. left for the country. All her friends were hiding or fleeing; her society was almost reduced to an old priest whom I had heard mocking religion everyday for ten years, and who now was angry that the property of the clergy had been sold, because it would deprive him of an income of twenty thousand francs. This priest went to Saint-Germain with us. His company was sweet, or rather, it was quiet: for his calmness had nothing sweet; it came from the turn of his mind rather than from the peace of his heart.

All her life, Mme de B. had been in the position of doing many favors: being a close friend of M. de Choiseul had enabled her, during his long ministership, to be useful to many people. Two of the most influential men during the Terror had obligations towards Mme de B.; they remembered these and showed gratitude. They constantly watched her, and did not allow her to be harmed. They risked their lives several times to conceal her from revolution's fury: one must admit that in those gloomy days even the leaders of the most violent parties could not do any good without putting themselves in danger. It seemed that, on this desolated earth, one could only reign by evil, because only evil could give and take power. Mme de B. did not go to prison; she was put under house arrest with the excuse of her poor health. Charles, the priest, and I stayed by her side and gave her all our care.

Nothing could depict the state of anxiety and terror of the days that we spent then, reading every night, in the newspapers, about the condemnation and the death of Mme de B.'s friends, and fearing at every moment that her protectors would no longer have the power to protect her from sharing such a fate. And, indeed, we learned that she was about to perish, when Robespierre's death put an end to such horror. We could breathe again; the guards left Mme de B.'s house. We remained, all four of us in the same solitude, as people find themselves, I suppose, after a great calamity from which they have escaped together. It seemed as if misfortune had made these ties stronger: I had felt that there, at least, I was no stranger.

If I have known a few happy moments in my life, since the loss of the illusions of my childhood, it is during the time that followed these disastrous days. Mme de B. possessed, to a supreme degree, what makes domestic life so attractive: she had an indulgent and easy disposition. You could say anything in front of her; she could guess what you meant. Never would a severe or inaccurate interpretation chill the trust between her and her friends. Thoughts were taken for what they were worth; one was responsible for nothing. This quality alone would have made Mme de B.'s friends happy, had it been her only quality. Still, she had so many other charms! One never felt any gaps or dull moments when she talked; everything was matter for her conversation. The interest that one takes in small things, which is vanity in ordinary people, is the source of a thousand pleasures in a distinguished person; it is characteristic of superior minds to make something out of nothing. The most ordinary idea became fecund, through Mme de B.'s mouth; her spirit and her mind knew how to dress an idea with a thousand new colors.

Charles's character was closely related to Mme de B.'s, and his mind too was similar to hers, that is to say that it was what Mme de B.'s must have been, just, firm, extensive, but with no modifications. Young people ignore such modifications: to them, everything is right or wrong, whereas the danger of old age is often to find that nothing is quite right, and nothing quite wrong. Charles had the two passions of his age, justice and truth. I have said that he hated even the shadow of affectation; he had the defect of sometimes seeing affectation where there was none. He was habitually reserved and his trust, when he gave it, was flattering; it was the result of his regard, not the inclination of his character: all that he granted had a value, for almost nothing in him was involuntary, and yet everything was natural. He counted so much on me, that he did not have a thought that he would not immediately tell me. At night, sitting around a table, conversations were limitless: our old priest had his place; he had built such a chain of false ideas, and he maintained them with such good faith, that he was an inexhaustible source of amusement for Mme de B., whose just and brilliant mind admirably brought out the absurdities of the poor priest, who was never angry. She thrust into his order of ideas great strokes of good sense that we compared to the parries of Roland or Charlemagne.

Mme de B. liked to walk: every morning she took a walk in the Saint-Germain woods, on the arm of the abbé. Charles and I would follow her at a distance. It was then that he would tell me about everything that concerned him, his plans, his hopes, but mostly his ideas about mankind, about the world. He kept nothing hidden from me; yet he did not realize that he was telling me anything. He had counted on me for such a long time that for him my friendship was like his life; he enjoyed it without being aware of it. He did not ask for my interest or my attention; he knew quite well that when he spoke to me about himself he was speaking about me, and that I was more he than he himself. Ah! the charm of such a trust can replace everything; it can even replace happiness.

I never thought of talking to Charles about what had caused me so much suffering! I would listen to him, and these conversations had some kind of magical effect on me that led me to forget my sorrows. If he had asked questions he would have made me remember. Then, I would have told him everything; but he could not imagine that I also had a secret. People were accustomed to seeing me unwell, and Mme de B. did so much for my happiness that she must have fancied I was happy. I should have been happy; I often told myself I should have been. I blamed myself for being ungrateful and deranged; I do not know if I would have dared to admit how wretched the incurable ill of my color made me. There is something humiliating about not being able to submit to necessity: thus, when it dominates your soul, this grief has all the characteristics of despair. What intimidated me also about Charles was the somewhat rigid turn of his ideas. One evening the conversation had settled on the subject of pity, and we were wondering if sorrows draw our interest more through their results than through their causes. Charles thought it was their causes; he thought all sorrows had to be reasonable. But who can tell what reason is? Is it the same for everybody? Does every heart need the same thing? Is unhappiness not the lack of what your heart needs? It was rare, however, that our evening conversations would turn my mind back to myself. I endeavored to think of myself as little as I could. I had removed all the mirrors from my bedroom. I always wore gloves, my attire hid my neck and my arms, and to go out I donned a large hat with a veil that I often even wore inside. Alas! I was deceiving myself: like a child, I would close my eyes and hope nobody would see me.

Near the end of the year 1795, the Terror came to an end. People started to regroup; the remains of Mme de B.'s society gathered around her, and with sadness I watched the circle of her friends widen. My position in the world was so false that the more society returned to its natural order, the more excluded I felt. Every time I saw new people join Mme de B., I felt a new pang of torment. The expression of surprise mixed with disdain that I could see on their countenances began to trouble me. I was sure to be the subject of a whispered comment or of a private conversation by a window: they had to be told how a Negress could be admitted to the circle of Mme de B.'s close friends. I suffered martyrdom during these explanations: I wished I had been transported to my barbarous fatherland, amid the savages who live there, a place less fearful for me than this cruel society which held me responsible for the harm it itself had done. I was haunted, for days in a row, by the memory of these faces full of disdain; I saw them in my dreams; I saw them at every moment. They would appear before me like my own image. Alas! I allowed myself to be obsessed with the face of chimeras! You had not yet taught me, O Lord, to ward off these ghosts. I did not know that you are the only haven.

Then, it was in Charles's heart that I was looking for a haven. I was proud of his friendship, and even more so of his virtues. I admired him as the most perfect being on this earth. Before, I had thought that I loved Charles like a brother, but since my health had deteriorated, I felt older, and it seemed that my affection for him was more like a mother's affection. Only a mother, indeed, could feel such a passionate desire for his happiness, for his success. I would have willingly given my life to spare him a moment of grief. I saw well before he did the impression he made on others. He was happy enough not to care about it. It was quite simple: he had nothing to fear; nothing had given him the constant worry that I felt about what others might think. In his lot, everything was harmony; in mine, everything was discord.

One morning, an old friend of Mme de B. came to visit; he was entrusted with a marriage proposal for Charles. Mlle de Thémines had become, quite cruelly so, a rich heiress; she had lost her entire family to the scaffold on the same day. She only had a great-aunt left, a former nun who, now that she was the guardian of Mlle de Thémines, considered it her duty to have her marry. She wanted to hurry because she was over 80 years old, and she feared that she would die and leave her niece alone and without protection in the world. Mlle de Thémines had all the advantages of birth, fortune, and education. She was 16. She was beautiful as daylight. It was impossible to hesitate. Mme de B. spoke to Charles, who, at first, was a little frightened by the idea of marrying so young. Soon he agreed to see Mlle de Thémines; they met and then he no longer hesitated. Anais de Thémines had everything to please Charles: she was pretty but did not know it; she had such a quiet modesty that this charming virtue seemed quite natural. Mme de Thémines gave Charles permission to visit, and he fell passionately in love. He described to me the progress of his feelings. I was impatient to see the beautiful Anais who was destined to make Charles happy. At last she came to Saint-Germain. Charles had told her about me; I did not have to endure from her the disdainful and scrutinizing glance that always hurt me so: she looked like an angel of kindness. I promised her that she would be happy with Charles; I reassured her about his young age. I told her that at 21 he had the solid reason of a much more mature person. I answered all her questions. She asked many because she knew that I had known Charles since childhood; and I so enjoyed telling her about his qualities that I never tired of speaking about them.

Financial matters delayed the conclusion of the wedding for a few weeks. Charles kept going to Mme de Thémines's, and he often stayed in Paris two or three days in a row: these absences saddened me, and I was displeased with myself when I realized that I preferred my happiness to Charles's. This was not the way I was accustomed to love. The days when he came back were like holidays; he would tell me what he had done, and whether he had made some progress in

Anais's heart. I felt happy for him. One day, however, he told me about the way he wanted to live with her: "I want her to trust me completely," he told me, "and give her all my trust. I shall not hide anything from her; she will know my every thought; she will know all the secret movements of my heart; I want the trust between her and me to be like ours, Ourika." Like ours! This word hurt me terribly. It reminded me that Charles did not know the only secret in my life, and I lost any desire to tell him. Little by little Charles's absences became more prolonged; he was in Saint-Germain only very briefly. He would make his journey on horseback to come more quickly and return to Paris after dinner, so that all our evenings were spent without him. Mme de B. often made light of these long absences; I wished I too had been able to take them lightly.

One day, we were walking in the forest. Charles had been gone almost all week; all of a sudden I saw him at the end of the path where we were walking; he was riding his horse, very fast. When he approached the spot where we were, he dismounted and proceeded to walk with us. After a few minutes of general conversation, he stayed behind with me, and we started to talk as before. I remarked on it. "As before!" he exclaimed; "ah, what a difference. Did I have anything to say at that time? It seems that I only started to live two months ago. Ourika, I shall never be able to tell you what I feel for her! Sometimes, I feel as if my whole soul were about to fuse into hers. When she looks at me, I stop breathing. When she blushes, I would lie at her feet to adore her. To think that I shall be the protector of this angel, that she entrusts me with her life, her destiny! Ah, how proud I am of mine! Ah, how happy I shall make her! I shall be for her the father, the mother that she has lost; but I shall also be her husband, her lover! She will give me her first love; her whole heart will pour out unto mine. We shall partake of the same life; during the course of our long life, I do not want her to be able to say she was unhappy for a single hour. What a delight, Ourika, to think that she will be the mother of my children, that they will draw their life at Anais's bosom! Ah, they will be sweet and beautiful like her. Ah, Lord, what have I done to deserve such happiness!"

Alas! At that moment I was asking heaven the opposite question! For a few moments, I had been listening to these passionate declarations with an indefinable feeling. Lord! You are witness that I was happy for Charles's happiness: but why did you give life to poor Ourika? Why did she not die on the slave ship from which she was torn, or in her mother's arms? A few grains of Africa's sand would have covered her body, and this burden would have been very light!

What importance for the world that Ourika lived? Why was she condemned to live? Was it to live alone, always alone, never loved! O Lord, do not allow this to be! Remove poor Ourika from the earth! No one needs her: is she not alone in life? This terrible thought assailed me with more violence than it had hitherto done. I felt that my legs were giving way, I sank to my knees, my eyes closed, and I thought I was going to die.

As the poor nun uttered these words, her oppression seemed to increase, her voice faltered, and a few tears ran down her wrinkled cheeks. I urged her to stop her story; she refused. "It is nothing," she said, "sorrow no longer lasts in my heart; its root has been severed. God took pity on me; he himself removed me from the abyss where I fell for lack of knowing and loving him. Do not forget that I am happy; but, alas," she added, "then, I was not."

Until the time I have just mentioned, I could bear my sorrows; they had impaired my health, but I had kept my sanity and some sort of control. My grief, like a canker eating up a fruit, had started with my heart; I carried within me the germ of destruction while outwardly I was still full of life. I liked to converse; discussions animated me. I had even kept a sort of lightheartedness; but I had lost the joys of the heart. Finally, until the time I have just mentioned, I was stronger than my sorrows. Now I felt that my sorrows would be stronger than I.

Charles carried me home in his arms; there, I was attended to, and I recovered my recollection. When I opened my eyes, I saw Mme de B. by my bed. Charles held my hand; they had tended me themselves, and I saw on their faces a mixture of anxiety and pain which touched me profoundly. I felt life coming back to me. I began to cry. Mme de B. wiped my tears gently; she did not say anything; she did not ask any questions. Charles asked many. I do not know what I replied; I said that my accident had been caused by the heat, the length of the walk. He believed me, and I was overwhelmed by bitterness when I saw that he did. My tears stopped; I told myself that it was quite easy to deceive those whose interest lay elsewhere. I withdrew the hand he still held, and I tried to look composed. Charles left, as usual, at five o'clock. I was hurt. I wished that he had worried about me; I was suffering so much! He would have left just the same. I would have made him leave; but I would have told myself that he owed me the happiness of his evening, and this thought would have cheered me. I refrained from showing Charles this movement of my heart. Delicate feelings have a kind of modesty; if they are not shared, they are incomplete. It is as if they require two persons to be felt.

Charles had hardly left when a soaring fever overtook me. The fever worsened during the next two days. Mme de B. took care of me with her usual kindness; she despaired of my condition and of the impossibility of having me carried to Paris, where she had to go the following day for Charles's wedding. The doctors told Mme de B. that I would live if she left me in Saint-Germain. She resolved to do so, and she showed me such a tender affection when she left that for a moment she calmed my feelings. But, after her departure, the complete, real isolation in which I found myself for the first time in my life threw me in a deep despair. I could see the situation that my imagination had so often pictured coming true: I died far away from those I loved and my anguished moanings did not even reach their ears. Alas, my sufferings would have troubled their joy. I could see them succumbing to the rapture of happiness, far from the dying Ourika. They were the only presence in Ourika's life; but they did not need Ourika. Nobody needed her! This horrible feeling of the uselessness of life is what stabs the heart the most cruelly: it gave me such a distaste for life that I sincerely wished to die of the illness which had attacked me. I did not speak. I gave almost no sign of consciousness, and one thought only was quite distinct in me: "I want to die." At other times, I was more agitated. I remembered every word of the last conversation I had had with Charles in the forest; I saw him in the middle of the sea of joys he had pictured for me. Why was I dying, alone in death as in life? This idea tormented me even more still than pain. I imagined new chimeras to satisfy this new feeling. I imagined Charles arriving in Saint-Germain; he was told "she is dead." If you can believe it, I enjoyed his grief; it was my revenge. Revenge for what, O Lord? For his having been the guardian angel of my life? This horrible feeling soon filled me with horror: I saw that if grief was not a sin, to indulge in it as I did could be a crime. My ideas took another course: I endeavored to conquer myself, to find within me the strength to fight the feelings that troubled me. But I did not look for this strength where it was. I berated myself for being ungrateful. I shall die, I said to myself. I want to die; but I do not want to let hatred near my heart. Ourika is a disinherited child; but her innocence remains. I shall not let it wither through ungratefulness. I shall pass over the earth like a shadow; but in the tomb, I shall have peace. O Lord! They already have much happiness: let them have still Ourika's share, and let her die as the leaf falls in autumn. Have I not suffered enough already?

I came out of the illness which had put my life in danger only to fall into a languorous state in which grief played a large part. Mme de B. settled in Saint-Germain after Charles's wedding; he went there often with Anais, never without her. I always suffered more when they were present. I do not know if the image of happiness made me more aware of my own misfortune or if Charles's presence awakened the memory of our former friendship. I sometimes endeavored to find him again, and I no longer recognized him. He, however, told me almost everything he had told me before; but his present friendship resembled his past friendship like an artificial flower resembles a real flower: it is the same, but it has no life or scent.

Charles attributed the change in my disposition to my declining health; I think that Mme de B. knew the sad state of my soul better, that she guessed my secret torments and that she was quite grieved. But the time when I could console others was gone; the only pity I had left was for myself.

Anais was with child, and we went back to Paris. My sadness increased daily. This domestic happiness so peaceful, these family ties so sweet, this innocent love, always so tender, passionate, what a sight for an unfortunate woman destined to spend her life in isolation and to die without having been loved, without having known other ties besides that of dependency and pity! Thus days, months, went by; I did not take part in any conversation; I had abandoned all my accomplishments. If I could bear to do some reading, it was reading the books in which I thought I would find the imperfect depiction of the grief that devoured me. I turned my reading into a new poison. I became inebriated with my own tears, and, alone in my room for hours on end, I would succumb to my grief.

The birth of a son crowned Charles's happiness; he rushed to tell me, and in the movements of his joy, I recognized some of the accents of his former trust. How this hurt me! Alas! it was the voice of the friend I no longer had! And all the past, when I heard his voice, would tear my wound open.

Charles's child was as beautiful as Anais; the picture of this young mother with her son moved everyone. I alone, through a strange twist of fate, was condemned to see him with bitterness. My heart devoured this image of a happiness that would always be foreign to me, and envy, like a vulture, fed in my breast. What had I done to those who thought they were saving me by bringing me to this island of exile? Why did they not let me follow my fate? So what if I had been the negress slave of some rich colonist; burnt by the sun, I would have farmed the land for another, but I would have had my own humble hut to go to at night. I would have had a companion to share my life and children of my color who would have called me "Mother!" They would press their little lips on my forehead without disgust; they would rest their head on my shoulder, and they would fall asleep in my arms! What have I done to be condemned to never feel the only affections for which my heart was meant! O Lord! Remove me from this world; I feel I can no longer bear to live.

I was on my knees in my room, addressing this blasphemous prayer to the creator when I heard the door open: it was Mme de B.'s friend, the Marquise de—, who had recently returned from England where she had spent several years. With terror, I saw her approach me. Seeing her always reminded me that she had been the first to apprise me of my fate, that she had opened this well of sorrows from which I had drawn so much. Since her return to Paris, I only saw her with a feeling of uneasiness. "I have come to see you and to speak with you, my dear Ourika," she said. "You know how much I have cared for you since you were a child, and I cannot see the melancholy in which you are sinking without sincere grief. With a mind like yours, is it possible that you cannot face your situation better?" "The mind, Madam," I answered, "only serves to increase real ills; it makes you see them under so many varied forms!" "But," she resumed, "when ills are without remedy, is it not foolish to refuse to accept them, and to fight thus against necessity? For, in the end, we are not the strongest." "This may be true," I said, "but it seems to me that, in this case, necessity is one more ill." "You will admit, however, Ourika, that reason advises to submit and to seek diversions." "Yes, Madam, but to have diversions, one must see hope in another direction." "You could at least develop new tastes and occupations to fill your time." "Ah, Madam, the tastes that one creates are an effort, not a pleasure." "But," she added, "you have many talents." "For talents to be a resource, Madam," I answered, "one needs a purpose; my talents would be like the flower of the English poet, which lost its scent in the desert." "You forget your friends who will enjoy them." "I do not have any friends, Madam, I have protectors, and that is quite a different matter." "Ourika," she said, "you are making yourself quite unhappy, and quite unnecessarily so." "Everything is useless in my life, Madam, even my grief." "How can you utter such bitter words? You, Ourika, whose attendance on Mme de B. was so exemplary when you were the only one left for her during the Terror!" "Alas! Madam, I am like the evil genie who is powerful only during times of calamities and whom happiness scares off." "Tell me your secret, my dear Ourika, open up your heart to me, nobody is more interested in you than I am, and perhaps I shall do you some good." "I do not have any secret, Madam," I answered, "my position and my color are my only ills, as you know." "Come," she replied, "can you deny that you harbor in your innermost soul a great sorrow? One only needs to behold you for an instant to be convinced of it." I persisted in telling her what I had already said. She became impatient, raised her voice; I saw that the storm was going to burst. "Is this your good faith?" said she, "the truthfulness for which you are known? Ourika, beware; sometimes reserve leads to duplicity." "But what could I tell you, Madam," I said, "to you especially who foresaw a long time ago how unhappy my situation would be? To you, of all people, I have nothing new to say on this topic." "You will never convince me of that," she replied, "but since you refuse to give me your trust and you claim that you have no secret, well, Ourika, I shall take upon myself to inform you that you do have a secret. Yes, Ourika, all your regrets, all your sorrows stem only from an unfortunate, irrational passion, and if you were not beside yourself with love for Charles, you would readily accept being a Negress. Adieu, Ourika, I am leaving and, I must tell you, with much less interest in you than I had when I arrived here." She departed uttering these words. I was stunned. What had she revealed to me! What terrible light had she thrown on the abyss of my sorrows! O Lord, it was like the light that once reached the bottom of hell and made its unfortunate inhabitants wish for darkness. What! I harbored a criminal passion! That is what, until now, had devoured my heart! This desire to hold my place in the chain of beings, this need for nature's affections, this grief of loneliness, these were the regrets of a guilty love! And when I thought I envied the image of happiness, it was happiness itself that was the object of my blasphemous wish. But what had I done that would have made people think I suffered from this hopeless passion! Is it impossible to love more than one's life with innocence? The mother who threw herself in the lion's mouth to save her child, what feeling moved her? The brothers and sisters who wished to die together on the scaffold, and who prayed to God before climbing the steps, was it a culpable affection that thus united them? Does not humanity alone produce acts of sublime devotion daily? Why could I not in this way love Charles, my childhood companion, the protector of my youth? And yet, a faint voice cries, from the bottom of my soul, that they are right, and that I am a criminal. O Lord! I shall also receive remorse in my distressed heart! Ourika must know every kind of bitterness, she must exhaust all pain. What! Henceforth my tears will be guilty! I will be forbidden to think of him! What! I will no longer dare suffer!

These terrible thoughts threw me in a state of prostration which resembled death. The same night fever overtook me and, in less than three days, it was believed I would not live. The doctor declared that if they wanted to perform the last offices, it should be done immediately. My confessor was sent for, but he had died a few days before. Then Mme de B. had a priest from the parish notified. He came and gave me extreme unction, for I was not in a state to receive the last sacrament. I had lost all consciousness, and I was expected to die at any moment. It must have been then that God took pity on me: He began by saving my life; against all hope, my strength held up. I struggled thus for about a fortnight, then recovered myself. Mme de B. never left my side, and Charles seemed to have regained his former affection for me. The priest continued to visit me every day, because he wanted to take advantage of the first possible moment to confess me. I wished to do so myself; I know not what movement carried me toward God and gave me the urge to throw myself into His arms and find peace. The priest received the confession of my sins; he was not frightened by the state of my soul. Like an old sailor, he knew every storm. He began by reassuring me about the passion of which I was accused: "Your heart is pure," said he, "it is only yourself that you have hurt, but you are guilty nonetheless. God will ask you for an account of your own happiness, which he had entrusted to you. What did you do with it? This happiness was in your hands, for it consists in the doing of our duties. Did you even know what they were? God is the goal of Mankind: what was yours? But do not lose heart. Pray to God, Ourika. He is here; He is holding out his arms to you. For Him, there are no Negroes and no whites; all hearts are equal before Him, and yours deserves to become worthy of Him." This is how that respectable man encouraged poor Ourika. These simple words brought to my soul a kind of peace that I had never known; I thought about them all the time, and, like from a rich source, I would always draw some new reflection. I saw that indeed I had not known my duties: God has assigned them to those who are alone as to those who have ties to the world. He may have deprived them of the ties of kindred, but he gave them the whole of humanity for a family. The sister of charity, I reflected, is not alone in life, even though she has renounced everything. She has created a family for herself; she is the mother of all the orphans, the daughter of all the poor old people, the sister of all the wretched. Have not men of the world often sought isolation of their own accord? They wanted to be alone with God; they renounced all pleasures to worship, in solitude, the pure source of all good and all happiness. In the recesses of their thoughts, they worked to make their souls ready to appear before the Lord. It is for you, my Lord, that it is sweet to adorn one's heart in this way, to embellish it, as for a holiday, with all the virtues that please You. Alas!

What had I done? The foolish plaything of the involuntary movements of my soul, I had searched after the joys of life and I had
neglected its happiness. But it is not too late yet; when throwing me
on this foreign land, God may have wanted to claim me for Himself.
He tore me away from barbarity and ignorance. Through a miracle
of His goodness, He rescued me from the vices of slavery and let me
know His Law: this Law shows me what all my duties are; it shows
me my way: I shall follow it, O Lord; I shall not use Your gifts to
offend You; I shall no longer accuse You of my sins.

This new light in which I considered my position restored tranquil-
lity to my heart. I was surprised by the peace that came after so many
storms. An outlet from the stream that wreaked havoc on its banks
had been opened, and now it carried its appeased waters into a
tranquil sea.

I decided to enter the convent. I mentioned it to Mme de B.; she
was grieved but she said "I did you so much harm while meaning to
do you good that I do not feel I have the right to oppose your decision." Charles was stronger in his resistance; he entreated me, he
beseeched me to stay. I told him, "Let me go, Charles, to the only
place where I may think of you constantly."

At this point, the young nun abruptly ended her story. I kept on
giving her medical care; unfortunately, it was useless. She died at the
end of October; she fell with the last leaves of Autumn.

ELEVEN

Ourika's Three Versions
A Comparison

Doris Y. Kadish

This analysis contextualizes the translation of *Ourika* that has been provided here by comparing it with two previous translations of that work: an anonymous translation that was published in 1829 and a translation by the British novelist John Fowles that was published in 1977.[1] It needs to be pointed out that both of these previous translations are hard to locate[2] and that, as explained in chapter 1, the translators of *Ourika* for this volume chose not to consult those earlier translations, preferring to produce a completely new and independent text. It is worth looking at those earlier translations now, however: not to judge their accuracy, or to evaluate comprehensively their translation strategies, but rather to discover representative examples in them of the complex mixture of ideological effects that inevitably arise in translating gender and race. These effects vary interestingly, according to the historical moment when the translation is produced as well as to the gender, race, class, or ethnicity of the translator or reader. Looking at those earlier translations of *Ourika* and comparing them with the one provided in this volume makes it possible to reflect about the choices that translators make and thus to open up the process of translation to the kind of interrogation and dialogue that needs to be practiced by translators, translation critics, and readers alike. A comparative analysis will also help readers to assess the success and the possible limitations of the translation provided here.

We can begin by focusing on the anonymous 1829 translation and by drawing attention to a representative sample of its "resistant" and "compliant" features: that is, features that seem, from our vantage point in the 1990s, to be indicative of either resistance against or compliance with stereotypical or regressive notions of gender or race. Although only a small sample of such features can be examined here,

218 / CLAIRE DE DURAS

that sample has been chosen from among many other ideological elements that together form a consistent pattern within the translations that will be discussed. The first such feature occurs, curiously, before the narration of Ourika's story even begins. The title page of the 1829 translation reads *Ourika; A Tale, From the French*, with no mention of Claire de Duras, whose name is similarly absent from the title page of the original. What does appear on the title page in both the translation and the original is an epigraph, in English in both cases, bearing the words and signature of Byron. That epigraph from a male poet, placed before and outside of a novel by and about a woman, anticipates the role of the male voice within the novel: in the opening pages of the story, a male doctor introduces, and in some sense legitimizes, Ourika's narration in the rest of the novel. An interesting difference between the original and the 1829 translation occurs, and a significant resistant effect is produced in the translation on the page following the title page. In addition to the name of the woman author, Duras, that appears in the original and the 1829 translation, the translation additionally contains a quotation from the *Mémoires* of Mme de Genlis. Through its evocation of a woman writer, that quotation could be said to counterbalance the authority of Byron and the English poetic tradition evoked on the title page by introducing a competing authority, that of feminine writing and the French narrative tradition, in which Mme de Genlis played an important role. And although the anonymity of the 1829 translation of course precludes any knowledge about the intentions or gender of the translator, the additional epigraph raises the distinct possibility that the translator may have been attentive to issues of gender and may have sought to capture or even enhance in the translation some of the resistant force of the woman writer's original work.

Another resistant feature of the 1829 translation is its tendency to accentuate the relatively muted abolitionist thrust of the original. That tendency can undoubtedly be explained in part by the publication of this translation at a time when abolitionism was an active force both in France and the United States, especially in Boston where this work was published. The abolitionist tendencies of the translation could also derive from the possible feminine gender of the translator. For, as the numerous examples of women translators and authors provided in this volume demonstrate, there has been a long tradition of women's special interest in the issue of antislavery and sensitivity in treating that issue.

To demonstrate the kind of abolitionist tone present in the 1829 translation and to illustrate the differences that occur in translating

racially charged passages it will be useful to look at the first sentence
of Ourika's first-person narration, which occurs after the frame narration by the doctor, and to subject that sentence to a kind of microscopic analysis that will enable us to perceive and assess the
significance of small and subtle differences.[3] The distinctive features
of the 1829 translation can be illuminated by comparing the four
numbered elements in the following passages with those same elements in the 1977 and 1993 translations.

> *Je fus rapportée* [1] du Sénégal, à l'âge de deux ans, par M. le chevalier
> de B., qui en était gouverneur. *Il eut pitié de moi* [2], *un jour qu'il voyait
> embarquer des esclaves sur un bâtiment négrier* [3] qui allait bientôt quitter
> le port: ma mère était morte, et *on m'emportait* [4] dans le vaisseau,
> malgré mes cris. (1824, 25–26)
>
> *I was carried away* [1] from Senegal at the age of two years, by the
> Chevalier de B., who was a Governor of that place. *He pitied my miseries*
> [2], when *he one day saw some slaves carried on board a negro vessel* [3]
> which was soon to leave the port: my mother was dead, and *they forced
> me on board* [4], notwithstanding my cries. (1829, 13–14)
>
> *I was brought here* [1] from Senegal when I was two years old by the
> chevalier de B. who was then governor there. *One day he saw me being
> taken aboard a slaver* [3] that was soon to leave port. My mother had
> died and in spite of my cries *I was being carried to the ship* [4]. *He took
> pity* [2] and bought me. . . . (1977, 17)
>
> "*I was brought back* (1) from Senegal, at the age of two, by Monsieur
> le chevalier de B., the governor of that colony. *He took pity on me* (2) *one
> day when he saw slaves being taken aboard a slave ship* (3) which was about
> to leave the harbor: my mother was dead, and *they were taking me away*
> (4) despite my cries. (1993)

The four elements underlined in these passages reveal the subtle
ways in which an intensification of abolitionist sentiment can occur in
translation. In the case of the first element, a neutral term—"rap-
porté" (1824), "brought here" (1977), "brought back" (1993)—is
heightened to a small degree in the 1829 version by the rendering
"carried away," which suggests less of a voluntary compliance with the
voyage on the part of the natives than in the other versions and which
duplicates the word "carried" also used for the deportation of slaves.
Similarly for the second element, "il eut pitié de moi" (1824), the
choice made in the 1829 translation—"He pitied my miseries"—is
considerably stronger and more emotionally charged than in either
the original or the other translations: "He took pity" (1977) and "He
took pity on me" (1993). Fowles chooses to further downplay the
emotional effect of this expression by shifting it to the end of the

passage. In the case of the third element, in the original slaves embark on a slave ship ("il voyait embarquer des ésclaves"), which creates an ambiguity as to whether they were coerced or whether, as in Mérimée's *Tamango*, they participated in their own enslavement by being drunk or overly trusting of the slave dealers who lured them on board. All three translations remove that ambiguity by specifying that Ourika was "carried on board" or "taken aboard" a slave ship. Only the 1829 and 1993 versions specify, however, that the context for Ourika's voyage was that slaves were being carried on board the slave ship, whereas Fowles's "one day he saw me being taken aboard" places the emphasis on her personal fate rather than on the more general situation of transporting slaves. For the fourth element, finally, the phrase "on m'emportait" (1824) is exaggerated in "they forced me on board" (1829), rendered fairly literally in "I was being carried" (1977), and articulated as an abolitionist issue but in a less emotional way than in the 1829 translation by "they were taking me away" (1993).

Along with the more resistant elements of the 1829 translation that have just been observed, other elements bearing on the closely intertwined issues of race and gender indicate that translation's ideological limitations and compliance with the social institutions of its time. Those limitations are especially apparent with the issue of interracial coupling, or what has been referred to historically as miscegenation. That issue is raised in a revealing passage in which Ourika overhears a friend of her benefactress' say that as an African woman Ourika has no hopes of marrying because no man would agree to have negro children:

> Qui voudra jamais épouser une négresse? Et si, à force d'argent, vous trouvez *quelqu'un qui consente à avoir des enfants nègres,* ce sera un homme d'une condition inférieure. . . . (1824, 48–49)
>
> Who would wish to marry a negress? And if, by the gift of wealth, you can find *one who will bear the relation of father to her children,* he must be one of a condition inferior to her own. . . . (1829, 25)
>
> What kind of man would marry a negress? Even supposing you could bribe *some fellow to father mulatto children,* he could only be of low birth. . . . (1977, 22)
>
> Who will ever want to marry a negress? Even if you can find a man who, for a sum, will consent to be *the father of Negro children,* this man will be of a lower condition. . . . (1993)

A revealing change occurs in the 1829 translation in the shift from the white man's willingness to have black children ("qui consente à avoir *des enfants nègres*") to his willingness to "bear the relation of *father to her children.*" By translating "des enfants" as "her children," the 1829 translator shifts the responsibility for interracial children from the couple to the black woman.

That same shift is repeated later when Ourika reflects upon what the friend of her benefactress said about a man's willingness to bear Negro children. In her reflections, Ourika repeats the friend's words twice, almost word for word:

> cet homme qui, à prix d'argent, *consentirait peut-être que ses enfants fussent nègres!* (1824, 53); Un homme, à prix d'argent, *consentirait peut-être que ses enfants fussent nègres!* (1824, 58)
>
> the man, who for the price of gold, might perhaps consent to call *my children* his own. . . . (1829, 27); For the reward of gold one may perhaps consent that *my children* should call him father! (1829, 29)
>
> I saw myself . . . destined to be the bride of some venal "fellow" who might condescend *to get half-breed children on me.* . . . (1977, 23); A fellow would be paid and might condescend *to give me mulatto children!* (1977, 24)
>
> the man who, for a large dowry, would perhaps consent to *his children* being Negroes! . . . (1993); Some man, for a large dowry, would perhaps consent to *his children* being Negroes! (1993)

In the original, Duras uses the possessive pronoun "ses," which, although it can mean "his" or "her," clearly denotes "his" in this context: "cet homme qui . . . consentirait peut-être que *ses enfants* fussent nègres!"; "Un homme . . . consentirait peut-être que *ses enfants* fussent nègres." By translating "ses" as "her," the 1829 translator shifts the responsibility for the practice of interracial coupling away from white men, who by virtue of their control over black women were historically the perpetrators of that practice. The translator also promotes and endorses the stereotypical identification of women as mothers and their primary association with reproduction. This example shows that although the translator endorsed abolition on the political level, he or she was still thinking on the personal level along the traditional racist or sexist lines of the dominant ideology of the times.

To further emphasize the ideological limitations at work in the 1829 translation it is helpful to compare it to Fowles's 1977 and our 1993 translations. Fowles translation of the friend's comment—"What kind of man would marry a negress? Even supposing you could bribe some fellow *to father mulatto children,* he could only be of low birth" (1977, 22)—does not go as far as the 1829 version in attributing the children to her alone. However, it introduces a social class distinction ("some fellow," "of low birth"), and it fails to capture the sense of shared and consensual parenthood contained in the original. Ourika's repeated versions of that comment accentuate that classist element and firmly place the accent on her as carrying the burden and responsibility of bearing children: "I saw myself . . . destined to be the bride of *some venal 'fellow'* who might condescend to get half-breed children *on me*" (1977, 23); "A *fellow* would be paid and might condescend *to give me* mulatto children!" (1977, 24). In contrast, the translators of this volume's *Ourika* captured the sense of the white man's fathering multiracial children that is contained in the original by translating the initial comment as "Who will ever want to marry a negress? Even if you can find a man who, for a large dowry, will consent to be *the father of Negro children,* this man will be of a lower condition" (1993). That same sense is captured in the translations of Ourika's reflections: "the man who, for a large dowry, would perhaps consent to *his children* being negroes!"; "Some man, for a large dowry, would perhaps consent to *his children* being negroes!" (1993).

Having seen examples of the mixture of resistant and compliant effects in the 1829 version of *Ourika,* we now turn our attention directly to Fowles's translation, which similarly displays a combination of resistance and compliance. As I showed in the first example, Fowles's translation often tends either to downplay the issue of race or to diminish the resistant thrust of Duras's treatment of that issue. An interesting example that can be added to those already mentioned occurs when the doctor, seeing Ourika for the first time, observes that "son grand voile noir l'enveloppait presque tout entière" (10), which Fowles translates as her being "almost entirely hidden by her large black veil" (13). Whereas Duras thematically foregrounds color by using the active voice to attribute agency to the symbolic black veil that envelops Ourika's physical and social existence, Fowles minimizes the importance of the veil by the use of the passive voice, as does the translator of the 1829 version. In contrast, the 1993 translation retains the sense of agency in the original with the phrase "her long black veil covered her entirely." Fowles's translation of this small detail is revealing because it is part of a larger pattern of paying less attention to race than either the original or the other translations.

It is indeed apparent from the remarks in the foreword and epilogue of Fowles's *Ourika* that he had some awareness of his own ideological limitations with respect to race, although he did not connect them specifically to his practice of translation. Speculating that *Ourika* may have had a profound effect on his writing of *The French Lieutenant's Woman,* he calls attention to having chosen the name of Ourika's beloved Charles for his male protagonist; and he observes, moreover, that "though I could have sworn I had never had the African figure of Ourika herself in mind during the writing of *The French Lieutenant's Woman*, I am now certain in retrospect that she was very active in my unconscious" (1977, 7). He goes on to explain that when, some years after writing that novel, he along with other novelists were asked to comment on the origins of their works, he replied that "the seed of mine had come in a half-waking dream and consisted of an image of a woman standing with her back to me. She was in black, and her stance had a disturbing mixture of both rejection and accusation" (8). That his preoccupation with this "woman who had been unfairly exiled from society" (8) had little to do with race becomes apparent to him at the moment when he writes the foreword to the translation of *Ourika*. At that moment, he realizes that in his earlier response to the question about the origins of his novel he had failed to recognize that the woman in black standing with her back to him was Ourika, an African woman: "I'm afraid it has revealed to me a remnant of colour prejudice, since something in my unconscious cheated on the essential clue. The woman in my mind who would not turn had black clothes, but a white face" (8).

With regard to gender, Fowles's translation also contains a mix of resistant and compliant elements. From a feminist perspective, the ideological effects are mixed when Fowles targets religion as an oppressive institution for women and accentuates the antireligious, materialist sense of the novel. To return to the microscopic analysis of small details practiced earlier in this essay, we can look at some sentences from the doctor's frame narrative at the beginning of the novel, several sentences after his first glimpse of the black veil.

> Je me figurais que j'allais contempler une nouvelle victime des cloîtres; *les préjugés de ma jeunesse* [1] venaient de se réveiller, et mon intérêt s'exaltait pour celle que j'allais visiter, en proportion *du genre de malheur que je lui supposais* [2]. Elle se tourna vers moi, et je fus étrangement surpris en apercevant une négresse! . . . Je la questionnai sur *sa maladie* [3]. J'éprouve, me dit-elle, une oppression continuelle, je n'ai plus de sommeil, et la fièvre ne me quitte pas. Son aspect ne confirmait que trop *cette triste description de son état* [4]: sa maigreur était excessive, *ses yeux brillants et fort grands* [5], ses dents d'une blancheur éblouissante, éclairaient seuls sa physionomie . . . et elle portait toutes les marques d'*un long et violent chagrin* [6]. (1824, 11–13)

> "I supposed I was about to behold a new victim of the cloisters. *All the prejudices of my youth* [1] were revived; and my interest in her whom I came to visit was the more increased, as I thought on *the malady with which I supposed she was afflicted* [2]. She turned herself toward me, and how great was my surprise at beholding a *negress!* I questioned her

upon the nature of *her complaints* [3]. "I suffer," said she, "a constant oppression, my fever never leaves me, and I cannot sleep." Her appearance but too well confirmed *what she had told me* [4]. She was extremely emaciated, *her eyes were very bright and large* [5], and her teeth, of a dazzling whiteness, of themselves lit up her countenance . . . and she bore all the marks of *a long and violent sorrow* [6]. (1829, vii–ix)

"I imagined I was about to meet a new victim of the convent system. *The anticlerical prejudices of my early years* [1] had been reawakened; and my concern for the woman I was to treat rose in sympathy with my views on *the kind of injustice I supposed her to have suffered* [2]. She turned towards me. I had a strange shock. I was looking at a negress. I asked her for *her symptoms* [3]. "I experience a constant feeling of being weighed down," she said. "I can't sleep any more. And I have a persistent fever." Her appearance only too exactly confirmed *this unpromising syndrome* [4]. She was excessively thin. The sole things that gave light to her face were *her abnormally large and luminous eyes* [5] and her dazzingly white teeth. . . . She showed every sign of having suffered from *prolonged and acute melancholia* [6]. (1977, 13–14)

"I thought I was to behold yet another victim of the cloisters. *The prejudices of my youth* [1] had awakened, and my interest in the woman whom I came to see was doubled by *the misfortune that I attributed to her* [2]. She turned toward me, and I was strangely surprised when I saw a Negress. . . . I asked her a few questions about *her illness* [3]. "I feel," she said, "a constant oppression, I cannot sleep, and I have an unrelenting fever." Her appearance only confirmed *this sad description of her state of health* [4]: she was excessively thin, *her large and shiny eyes* [5], her brilliant white teeth were the only light in her face. Her soul was still alive, but her body was destroyed, and she showed all the marks of *a long and acute grief* [6]. (1993)

In the first element, the doctor acknowledges the ambivalent feelings he has upon visiting a cloistered nun due to "les préjugés" (1824) of his youth. That expression, which is translated simply as "the prejudices of my youth" in the 1829 and 1993 versions, is intensified in Fowles's translation of it as the "anticlerical prejudices of my early years" (1977). In the same vein, in the case of the second element, the doctor states that his interest in the sick nun was triggered by the "genre de malheur que je lui supposais" (1824), with "malheur" connoting vaguely either physical, mental, or moral illness. In contrast with translations of that phrase that capture the vagueness of the original—"the malady with which I supposed she was afflicted" (1829) and "the misfortune that I attributed to her" (1993)—Fowles specifies that convents functioned as oppressive institutions for women in his translation of the phrase as "the kind of injustice I supposed her to have suffered" (1977). With respect to gender, however, the ideological effect of Fowles's translation of these elements is not clearcut. It is undeniable that convents functioned historically as oppressive institutions where women were in many cases confined against their will. It is also the case, however, that, as observed in chapter 2, religion was an integral part of, and driving force behind, the antislavery movement and antislavery writings by women. For Gouges, Staël, and Duras as well as the other women discussed earlier in this volume such as Behn, Sand, and Stowe, injustice to blacks was one piece in the larger picture of issues that humanitarian and evangelical groups within religious institutions addressed. From a historical perspective, then, religion was in many ways an empowering institution in the nineteenth century for women of color and their allies in the antislavery movement.

A similarly mixed ideological effect results from Fowles's use of scientific and medical terms in a far more explicit way than in the original or either the 1829 or the 1993 translations and his general downplaying of the importance of religion for Ourika in the novel. In the description of the doctor's first visit to the convent discussed above, for example, one finds a series of terms that are far more clinical in Fowles's translation than in the original or the other translations: [3] "sa maladie" becomes "her symptoms" (1977), in contrast with "her complaints" (1829) or "her illness" (1993); [4] "cette triste description de son état" is translated as "this unpromising syndrome" (1977), as compared to "what she had told me" (1829) or "this sad description of her state of health" (1993); [5] "ses yeux brillants et fort grands" turns into "her abnormally large and luminous eyes" (1977), unlike "her eyes were very bright and large" (1829) and "her large and shiny eyes" (1993); [6] "un long et violent chagrin," finally, is rendered as "prolonged and acute melancholia" (1977), in opposition to "a long and violent sorrow" (1829) and "a long and acute grief" (1993). From a feminist perspective, privileging the scientific over the religious as Fowles does can be a resistant strategy inasmuch as religion often functioned historically as a repressive force which blocked the liberatory effects of scientific and medical discoveries that helped women and prolonged their and their children's lives. From that same perspective, however, Fowles's insistence on science and medicine can be said to produce a compliant effect inasmuch as science and medicine have also often functioned as repressive, patriarchal institutions that have been insensitive to women's needs and desires. In addition, his use of details that emphasize Ourika's clinical abnormality suggests a psychoanalytic discourse about hysteria and neurosis that has often been repressively applied to women.

It is also worth noting with regard to gender that Fowles's antireligious ideology at times results in the silencing of the feminine voice in *Ourika*. Fowles modifies the direct addresses to God in the second person that appear increasingly as the novel draws to an end and Ourika finds her chief consolation in religion. In the original, Duras accentuates the closeness of the second-person address and enables us to hear Ourika's voice in speaking to God:" Grand Dieu! vous êtes témoin que j'étais heureuse du bonheur de Charles" (1824). The 1829 and 1993 translations similarly capture that closeness: "Great God! thou dost bear witness that I rejoiced in the happiness of Charles" (1829); "Lord! You are witness that I was happy for Charles's happiness" (1993). Fowles, in contrast, uses a more impersonal third-person construction that mutes Ourika's voice: "God will bear witness, I was happy for Charles" (1977). A comparison of his translation of the following passage with the original and the other translations also shows that at times he omits the mention of God altogether:

> Quelle lumière affreuse avait-elle jetée sur l'abîme de mes douleurs! *Grand Dieu!* c'était comme la lumière qui pénétra une fois au fond des enfers, et qui fit regretter les ténèbres à ses malheureux habitants. (1824, 157)
>
> What she had just revealed to me threw a terrifying illumination over the depths of my suffering. It was like the shaft of light that once penetrated to the bottom of hell and made the miserable beings there weep for the darkness of their existence. (1977, 46)
>
> What frightening light had been darted into the abyss of my sorrows! 'Great God! such light didst thou once cast into the depths of hell, and the darkness mourned for its miserable inhabitants.' (1829, 77)
>
> What terrible light had she thrown on the abyss of my sorrows! *O Lord;* it was like the light that once reached the bottom of hell and made its unfortunate inhabitants wish for darkness. (1993)

It is also important to stress, however, that Fowles also often demonstrates a distinct sensitivity to the modalities of translating gender. Indeed, his translation of *Ourika* at times reveals the seeds of the feminist outlook that appears fully grown in *The French Lieutenant's Woman,* in which plot and thematic meaning revolve around the birth of feminism in the nineteenth century. That sensitivity can be illustrated specifically through a small but striking detail: the translation of "patrie" in the following key passage from *Ourika:*

L'opinion est comme *une patrie;* c'est un bien dont on jouit ensemble; on est frère pour la soutenir et pour la défendre. Je me disais quelquefois, que moi, pauvre négresse, je tenais pourtant à toutes les âmes élevées, par le besoin de la justice que j'éprouvais en commun avec elles. (1824, 84)

A view of life is like *a motherland.* It is a possession mutually shared. Those who uphold and defend it are like brothers. Sometimes I used to tell myself that, poor negress though I was, I still belonged with all the noblest spirits, because of our shared longing for justice. (1977, 30)

One's opinions, like *one's native country,* to bring happiness must be enjoyed with others; he who supports, who defends them, is a brother. I said sometimes to myself, that I, a poor negress, was bound to the most exalted minds by the unjust sufferings we equally endured. (1829, 42)

Opinion is like *a mother-country;* it is something that people enjoy together; people are united as a family to support and defend it. I sometimes said to myself that I, a poor negress, nonetheless was like all elevated souls, and had in common with them the need for justice. (1993)

What is special in this passage according to Fowles's comments in the epilogue is its egalitarian message, to wit, that "Mankind has only one true frontier, that of our common humanity—be it black, brown or white in face. This is the subversive proposition at the heart of *Ourika.*" (1977, 64) What is interesting is the way in which in the practice of translation Fowles uses gender rather than race to express that message. The choice of translating "patrie" as "motherland" (or "mother-country," as in our 1993 translation, as opposed to "native country" in the 1829 version) is an example of the kind of choices that translators are called on to make. It is an intelligent and effective choice which restores the feminine quality that stems in the original from the presence of numerous feminine nouns (opinion, patrie, âme, justice) and numerous articles, pronouns, and adjectives indicating feminine gender (*une* patrie, pour *la* soutenir et pour *la* défendre, âmes *élevées, la* justice, avec *elles.*) In order to make that choice, however, the translator has to possess sensitivity to the role of gender in the novel and the ideological implications of translation.

In closing, there have been numerous occasions in the comparison of versions of *Ourika* presented here and throughout the volume *Translating Slavery* to observe the benefits that translators derive from an awareness of ideology. Consider one salient example highlighted in this essay, the translation in our 1993 version of "consentirait que ses enfants fussent nègres" as "will consent to be the father of negro children." What is important is not only the improvement that the

1993 version makes upon such earlier versions as "will bear the relation of father to her children" or "might condescend to give me mulatto children." Equally important is the fact that that improvement reflects the translators' understanding of the theoretical, practical, and historical issues relevant to translating sexually or racially charged passages such as this one. Undoubtedly other ideological issues exist to which the translators have not been equally attuned. It is up to our readers to discover the compliant elements in the version of *Ourika* and the other translations that appear in this volume, as we have sought to uncover those compliant elements along with the resistant features of the translations produced by Fowles, La Place, La Bédollière, Belloc, and the other translators discussed here. If there is no escaping ideology, there is at least a way of developing an awareness of its effects on translation.

Olympe de Gouges

RÉFLEXIONS SUR LES HOMMES NÈGRES
(Février 1788)[1]

L'espèce d'hommes nègres m'a toujours intéressée à son déplorable sort. A peine mes connaissances commençaient à se développer, et dans un âge où les enfants ne pensent pas, que l'aspect d'une Négresse que je vis pour la première fois, me porta à réfléchir, et à faire des questions sur sa couleur.

Ceux que je pus interroger alors, ne satisfirent point ma curiosité et mon raisonnement. Ils traitaient ces gens-là de brutes, d'êtres que le Ciel avait maudits; mais, en avançant en âge, je vis clairement que c'était la force et le préjugé qui les avaient condamnés à cet horrible esclavage, que la Nature n'y avait aucune part, et que l'injuste et puissant intérêt des Blancs avait tout fait.

Pénétrée depuis longtemps de cette vérité et de leur affreuse situation, je traitai leur Histoire dans le premier sujet dramatique qui sortit de mon imagination. Plusieurs hommes se sont occupés de leur sort; ils ont travaillé à l'adoucir; mais aucun n'a songé à les présenter sur la Scène avec le costume et la couleur, tel que je l'avais essayé, si la Comédie-Française ne s'y était point opposée.

Mirza avait conservé son langage naturel, et rien n'était plus tendre. Il me semble qu'il ajoutait à l'intérêt de ce drame, et c'était bien de l'avis de tous les connaisseurs, excepté les Comédiens. Ne nous occupons plus de ma Pièce, telle qu'elle a été reçue. Je la présente au Public.

Revenons à l'effroyable sort des Nègres; quand s'occupera-t-on de le changer, ou au moins de l'adoucir? Je ne connais rien à la Politique des Gouvernements; mais ils sont justes, et jamais la Loi Naturelle ne s'y fit

---

1. We have chosen for our base document the French language edition of "Réflexions sur les hommes nègres" which appears in Olympe de Gouges, *Oeuvres,* présenté par Benoîte Groult. Paris: Mercure de France, 1986.

mieux sentir. Ils portent un oeil favorable sur tous les premiers abus. L'homme partout est égal. Les Rois justes ne veulent point d'esclaves; ils savent qu'ils ont des sujets soumis, et la France n'abandonnera pas des malheureux qui souffrent mille trépas pour un, depuis que l'intérêt et l'ambition ont été habiter les îles les plus inconnues. Les Européens avides de sang et de ce métal que la cupidité a nommé de l'or, ont fait changer la Nature dans ces climats heureux. Le père a méconnu son enfant, le fils a sacrifié son père, les frères se sont combattus, et les vaincus ont été vendus comme des boeufs au marché. Que dis-je? c'est devenu un Commerce dans les quatre parties du monde.

Un commerce d'hommes! . . . grand Dieu! et la Nature ne frémit pas! S'ils sont des animaux, ne le sommes-nous pas comme eux? et en quoi les Blancs diffèrent-ils de cette espèce? C'est dans la couleur . . . Pourquoi la blonde fade ne veut-elle pas avoir la préférence sur la brune qui tient du mulâtre? Cette tentation est aussi frappante que du Nègre au mulâtre. La couleur de l'homme est nuancée, comme dans tous les animaux que la Nature a produits, ainsi que les plantes et les minéraux. Pourquoi le jour ne le dispute-t-il pas à la nuit, le soleil à la lune, et les étoiles au firmament? Tout est varié, et c'est là la beauté de la Nature. Pourquoi donc détruire son Ouvrage?

L'homme n'est-il pas son plus beau chef-d'oeuvre? L'Ottoman fait bien des Blancs ce que nous faisons des Nègres: nous ne le traitons cependant pas de barbare et d'homme inhumain, et nous exerçons la même cruauté sur des hommes qui n'ont d'autre résistance que leur soumission.

Mais quand cette soumission s'est une fois lassée, que produit le despotisme barbare des habitants des Isles et des Indes? Des révoltes de toute espèce, des carnages que la puissance des troupes ne fait qu'augmenter, des empoisonnements, et tout ce que l'homme peut faire quand une fois il est révolté. N'est-il pas atroce aux Européens, qui ont acquis par leur industrie des habitations considérables, de faire rouer de coups du matin au soir les infortunés qui n'en cultiveraient pas moins leurs champs fertiles, s'ils avaient plus de liberté et de douceur?

Leur sort n'est-il pas des plus cruels, leurs travaux assez pénibles, sans qu'on exerce sur eux, pour la plus petite faute, les plus horribles châtiments? On parle de changer leur sort, de proposer les moyens de l'adoucir, sans craindre que cette espèce d'hommes fasse un mauvais usage d'une liberté entière et subordonnée.

Je n'entends rien à la Politique. On augure qu'une liberté générale rendrait les hommes Nègres aussi essentiels que les Blancs: qu'après les avoir laissés maîtres de leur sort, ils le soient de leurs volontés:

qu'ils puissent élever leurs enfants auprès d'eux. Ils seront plus exacts aux travaux, et plus zélés. L'esprit de parti ne les tourmentera plus, le droit de se lever comme les autres hommes les rendra plus sages et plus humains. Il n'y aura plus à craindre de conspirations funestes. Ils seront les cultivateurs libres de leurs contrées, comme les Laboureurs en Europe. Ils ne quitteront point leurs champs pour aller chez les Nations étrangères.

La liberté des Nègres fera quelques déserteurs, mais beaucoup moins que les habitants des campagnes françaises. A peine les jeunes Villageois ont obtenu l'âge, la force et le courage, qu'ils s'acheminent vers la Capitale pour y prendre le noble emploi de Laquais ou de Crocheteur. Il y a cent Serviteurs pour une place, tandis que nos champs manquent de cultivateurs.

Cette liberté multiplie un nombre infini d'oisifs, de malheureux, enfin de mauvais sujets de toute espèce. Qu'on mette une limite sage et salutaire à chaque Peuple, c'est l'art des Souverains, et des Etats Républicains.

Mes connaissances naturelles pourraient me faire trouver un moyen sûr: mais je me garderai bien de le présenter. Il me faudrait être plus instruite et plus éclairée sur la Politique des Gouvernements. Je l'ai dit, je ne sais rien, et c'est au hasard que je soumets mes observations bonnes ou mauvaises. Le sort de ces infortunés doit m'intéresser plus que personne, puisque voilà la cinquième année que j'ai conçu un sujet dramatique, d'après leur déplorable Histoire.

Je n'ai qu'un conseil à donner aux Comédiens-Français, et c'est la seule grâce que je leur demanderai de ma vie: c'est d'adopter la couleur et le costume nègre. Jamais occasion ne fut plus favorable, et j'espère que la Représentation de ce Drame produira l'effet qu'on en doit attendre en faveur de ces victimes de l'ambition.

Le costume ajoute de moitié à l'intérêt de cette Pièce. Elle émouvra la plume et le coeur de nos meilleurs Ecrivains. Mon but sera rempli, mon ambition satisfaite, et la Comédie s'élèvera au lieu de s'avilir, par la couleur.

Mon bonheur sans doute serait trop grand, si je voyais la Représentation de ma Pièce, comme je la désire. Cette faible esquisse demanderait un tableau touchant pour la postérité. Les peintres qui auraient l'ambition d'y exercer leurs pinceaux, pourraient être considérés comme les Fondateurs de l'Humanité la plus sage et la plus utile, et je suis sûre d'avance que leur opinion soutiendra la faiblesse de ce Drame, en faveur du sujet.

Jouez donc ma Pièce, Mesdames et Messieurs, elle a attendu assez longtemps son tour. La voilà imprimée, vous l'avez voulu; mais toutes les Nations avec moi vous en demandent la représentation, persuadée qu'elles ne me démentiront pas. Cette sensibilité qui ressemblerait à l'amour-propre chez tout autre que chez moi, n'est que l'effet que produisent sur mon coeur toutes les clameurs publiques en faveur des hommes nègres. Tout Lecteur qui m'a bien appréciée sera convaincu de cette vérité.

Enfin passez-moi ces derniers avis, ils me coûtent cher, et je crois à ce prix pouvoir les donner. Adieu, Mesdames et Messieurs; après mes observations, jouez ma pièce comme vous le jugerez à propos, je ne serai point aux répétitions. J'abandonne à mon fils tous mes droits; puisse-t-il en faire un bon usage, et se préserver de devenir Auteur pour la Comédie-Française. S'il me croit, il ne griffonnera jamais de papier en littérature.

L'ESCLAVAGE DES NOIRS[2]
1786

Préface

Dans les siècles de l'ignorance les hommes se sont fait la guerre; dans le siècle le plus éclairé, ils veulent se détruire. Quelle est enfin la science, le régime, l'époque, l'âge où les hommes vivront en paix? Les Savants peuvent s'appesantir et se perdre sur ces observations métaphysiques. Pour moi, qui n'ai étudié que les bons principes de la Nature, je ne définis plus l'homme, et mes connaissances sauvages ne m'ont appris à juger des choses que d'après mon âme. Aussi mes productions n'ont-elles que la couleur de l'humanité.

Le voilà enfin, ce Drame que l'avarice et l'ambition ont proscrit, et que les hommes justes approuvent. Sur ces diverses opinions quelle doit être la mienne? Comme Auteur, il m'est permis d'approuver cette production philanthropique; mais comme témoin auriculaire des récits désastreux des maux de l'Amérique, j'abhorrerais mon Ouvrage, si une main invisible n'eût opéré cette révolution à laquelle je n'ai participé en rien que par la prophétie que j'en ai faite. Cependant on me blâme, on m'accuse sans connaître même l'*Esclavage des Noirs*, reçu en 1783 à la Comédie Française, imprimé en 1786, et représenté en

---

2. The text of *L'Esclavage des noirs* and its preface is a transcription of the original imprint from the Bibliothèque Nationale, Paris. The preface was written at the time of the play's publication in 1792.

Décembre 1789. Les Colons, à qui rien ne coûtait pour assouvir leur cruelle ambition, gagnèrent les Comédiens, et l'on assure ... que l'interception de ce Drame n'a pas nui à la recette; mais ce n'est point le procès des Comédiens ni des Colons que je veux faire, c'est le mien.

Je me dénonce à la voix publique; me voilà en état d'arrestation: je vais moi-même plaider ma cause devant ce Tribunal auguste, frivole ... mais redoutable. C'est au scrutin des consciences que je vais livrer mon procès; c'est à la pluralité des voix que je vais le perdre ou le gagner.

L'Auteur, ami de la vérité, l'Auteur qui n'a d'autre intérêt que de rappeler les hommes aux principes bienfaisants de la Nature, qui n'en respecte pas moins les lois, les convenances sociales, est toujours un mortel estimable, et si ses écrits ne produisent pas tout le bien qu'il s'en était promis, il est à plaindre plus qu'à blâmer.

Il m'est donc important de convaincre le Public et les détracteurs de mon Ouvrage, de la pureté de mes maximes. Cette production peut manquer par le talent, mais non par la morale. C'est à la faveur de cette morale que l'opinion doit revenir sur mon compte.

Quand le Public aura lu ce Drame, conçu dans un temps où il devait paraître un Roman tiré de l'antique féerie, il reconnaîtra qu'il est le tableau fidèle de la situation actuelle de l'Amérique. Tel que ce Drame fut approuvé sous le despotisme de la presse, je le donne aujourd'hui sous l'an quatrième de la liberté. Je l'offre au Public comme une pièce authentique et nécessaire à ma justification. Cette production est-elle incendiaire? Non. Présente-t-elle un caractère d'insurrection? Non. A-t-elle un but moral? Oui sans doute. Que me veulent donc ces Colons pour parler de moi avec des termes si peu ménagés? Mais ils sont malheureux, je les plains, et je respecterai leur déplorable sort; je ne me permettrai pas même de leur rappeler leur inhumanité: je me permettrai seulement de leur citer tout ce que j'ai écrit pour leur conserver leurs propriétés et leurs plus chers intérêts: ce Drame en est une preuve.

C'est à vous, actuellement, esclaves, hommes de couleur, à qui je vais parler; j'ai peut-être des droits incontestables pour blâmer votre férocité: cruels, en imitant les tyrans, vous les justifiez. La plupart de vos Maîtres étaient humains et bienfaisants, et dans votre aveugle rage vous ne distinguez pas les victimes innocentes de vos persé-cuteurs. Les hommes n'étaient pas nés pour les fers, et vous prouvez qu'ils sont nécessaires. Si la force majeure est de votre côté, pourquoi exercer toutes les fureurs de vos brûlantes contrées? Le poison, le fer, les poignards, l'invention des supplices les plus barbares et les plus atroces ne vous coûtent rien, dit-on. Quelle cruauté! quelle inhumanité! Ah! combien vous faites gémir ceux qui voulaient vous préparer, par des moyens tempérés, un sort plus doux, un sort plus digne d'envie que tous ces avantages illusoires avec lesquels vous ont égarés les auteurs des calamités de la France et de l'Amérique. La tyrannie vous suivra, comme le crime s'est attaché à ces hommes pervers. Rien ne pourra vous accorder entre vous. Redoutez ma prédiction, vous savez si elle est fondée sur des bases vraies et solides. C'est d'après la raison, d'après la justice divine, que je prononce mes oracles. Je ne me rétracte point: j'abhorre vos Tyrans, vos cruautés me font horreur.

Ah! si mes conseils vont jusqu'à vous, si vous en reconnaissez tout l'avantage, j'ose croire qu'ils calmeront vos esprits indomptés, et vous ramèneront à une concorde indispensable au bien de la Colonie et à vos propres intérêts. Ces intérêts ne consistent que dans l'ordre social, vos droits dans la sagesse de la Loi; cette Loi reconnaît tous les hommes frères; cette Loi auguste que la cupidité avait plongée dans le chaos est enfin sortie des ténèbres. Si le sauvage, l'homme féroce la méconnaît, il est fait pour être chargé de fers et dompté comme les brutes.

Esclaves, gens de couleur, vous qui vivez plus près de la Nature que les Européens, que vos Tyrans, reconnaissez donc ses douces lois, et faites voir qu'une Nation éclairée ne s'est point trompée en vous traitant comme des hommes et vous rendant des droits que vous n'eûtes jamais dans l'Amérique. Pour vous rapprocher de la justice et de l'humanité, rappelez-vous, et ne perdez jamais de vue, que c'est dans le sein de votre Patrie qu'on vous condamne à cette affreuse servitude, et que ce sont vos propres parents qui vous mènent au marché: qu'on va à la chasse des hommes dans vos affreux climats, comme on va ailleurs à la chasse des animaux. La véritable Philosophie de l'homme éclairé le porte à arracher son semblable du sein d'une horrible situation primitive où les hommes non seulement se vendaient, mais où ils se mangeaient encore entr'eux. Le véritable homme ne considère que l'homme. Voilà mes principes, qui diffèrent bien de ces prétendus défenseurs de la Liberté, de ces boutefeux, de ces esprits incendiaires qui prêchent l'égalité, la liberté, avec toute l'autorité et la férocité des Despotes. L'Amérique, la France, et peut-être l'Univers, devront leur chute à quelques énergumènes que la France a produits, la décadence des Empires et la perte des arts et des sciences. C'est peut-être une funeste vérité. Les hommes ont vieilli, ils paraissent vouloir renaître, et d'après les principes de M. Brissot, la vie animale convient parfaitement à l'homme; j'aime plus que lui la Nature, elle a placé dans mon âme les lois de l'humanité et d'une sage égalité; mais quand je considère cette Nature, je la vois souvent en contradiction avec ses principes, et tout m'y paraît subordonné. Les animaux ont leurs Empires, des Rois, des Chefs, et leur règne est paisible; une main invisible et bienfaisante semble conduire leur administration. Je ne suis pas tout-à-fait l'ennemie des principes de M. Brissot, mais je les crois impraticables chez les hommes: avant lui j'ai traité cette matière. J'ai osé, après l'auguste Auteur du *Contrat Social,* donner le *Bonheur Primitif de l'Homme,* publié en 1789. C'est un Roman que j'ai fait, et jamais les hommes ne seront assez purs, assez grands pour remonter à ce bonheur primitif, que je n'ai trouvé que dans une heureuse fiction. Ah! s'il était possible qu'ils pussent y arriver, les lois sages et humaines que j'établis dans ce contrat social, rendraient tous les hommes frères, le Soleil serait le vrai Dieu qu'ils invoqueraient; mais toujours variantes, le *Contrat Social,* le *Bonheur Primitif* et l'Ouvrage auguste de M. Brissot seront toujours des chimères, et non une utile instruction. Les imitations de Jean-Jacques sont défigurées dans ce nouveau régime, que seraient donc celles de Mme de Gouges et celles de M. Brissot? Il est aisé, même au plus ignorant, de faire des révolutions sur quelques cahiers de papier; mais, hélas! l'expérience de tous les Peuples, et celle que font les Français, m'apprennent que les plus savants et les plus sages n'établissent pas leurs doctrines sans produire des maux de toutes espèces. Voilà ce que nous offre l'histoire de tous les pays.

Je m'écarte du but de ma Préface, et le temps ne me permet pas de donner un libre cours à des raisons philosophiques. Il s'agissait de justifier l'*Esclavage des Noirs,* que les odieux Colons avaient proscrit, et présenté comme un ouvrage incendiaire. Que le public juge et prononce, j'attends son arrêt pour ma justification.

Personnages

Zamor, Indien instruit.
Mirza, jeune Indienne, amante de Zamor.
M. de Saint-Frémont, Gouverneur d'une Île dans l'Inde.
Mme de Saint-Frémont, son épouse.
Valère, Gentilhomme Français, époux de Sophie.
Sophie, fille naturelle de M. de Saint-Frémont.
Betzi, Femme de Chambre de Mme de Saint-Frémont.
Caroline, Esclave.
Un Indien, Intendant des Esclaves de M. de Saint-Frémont.
Azor, Valet de M. de Saint-Frémont.
M. de Belfort, Major de la Garnison.

Un Juge.
Un Domestique de M. de Saint-Frémont.
Un Vieillard Indien.
Plusieurs Habitants Indiens des deux sexes, et Esclaves.
Grenadiers et Soldats Français.

La Scène se passe, au premier Acte, dans une Ile déserte; au second, dans une grande Ville des Indes, voisine de cette Île, et au troisième, dans une Habitation proche cette ville.

L'ESCLAVAGE DES NOIRS, OU L'HEUREUX NAUFRAGE

Acte I

Le Théâtre représente le rivage d'une Ile déserte, bordée et environnée de rochers escarpés, à travers lesquels on aperçoit la pleine mer dans le lointain. Sur un des côtés en avant est l'ouverture d'une cabane entourée d'arbres fruitiers du climat: l'autre côté est rempli par l'entrée d'une forêt qui paraît impénétrable. Au moment où le rideau se lève, une tempête agite les flots: on voit un navire qui vient se briser sur la côte. Les vents s'apaisent et la mer se calme peu à peu.

SCÈNE PREMIÈRE

Zamor, Mirza

ZAMOR: Dissipe tes frayeurs, ma chère Mirza; ce vaisseau n'est point envoyé par nos persécuteurs: autant que je puis en juger il est Français. Hélas! il vient de se briser sur ces côtes, personne de l'équipage ne s'est sauvé.

MIRZA: Zamor, je ne crains que pour toi; le supplice n'a rien qui m'effraie; je bénirai mon sort si nous terminons nos jours ensemble.

ZAMOR: O ma Mirza! Que tu m'attendris!

MIRZA: Hélas! qu'as-tu fait? mon amour t'a rendu coupable. Sans la malheureuse Mirza tu n'aurais jamais fui le meilleur de tous les Maîtres, et tu n'aurais pas tué son homme de confiance.

ZAMOR: Le barbare! il t'aima, et ce fut pour devenir ton tyran. L'amour le rendit féroce. Le tigre osa me charger du châtiment qu'il t'infligeait pour n'avoir pas voulu répondre à sa passion effrénée. L'éducation que notre Gouverneur m'avait fait donner ajoutait à la sensibilité de mes moeurs sauvages, et me rendait encore plus insupportable le despotisme affreux qui me commandait ton supplice.

MIRZA: Il fallait me laisser mourir; tu serais auprès de notre Gouverneur qui te chérit comme son enfant. J'ai causé tes malheurs et les siens.

ZAMOR: Moi, te laisser périr! ah! Dieux! Eh! pourquoi me rappeler les vertus et les bontés de ce respectable Maître? J'ai fait mon devoir auprès de lui: j'ai payé ses bienfaits, plutôt par la tendresse d'un fils, que par le dévouement d'un esclave. Il me croit coupable, et voilà ce qui rend mon tourment plus affreux. Il ne sait point quel monstre il avait honoré de sa confiance. J'ai sauvé mes semblables de sa tyrannie; mais, ma chère Mirza, perdons un souvenir trop cher et trop funeste: nous n'avons plus de protecteurs que la Nature. Mère bienfaisante! tu connais notre innocence. Non, tu ne nous abandonneras pas, et ces lieux déserts nous cacheront à tous les yeux.

MIRZA: Le peu que je sais, je te le dois, Zamor; mais dis-moi pourquoi les Européens et les Habitants ont-ils tant d'avantage sur nous, pauvres esclaves? Ils sont cependant faits comme nous: nous sommes des hommes comme eux: pourquoi donc une si grande différence de leur espèce à la nôtre?

ZAMOR: Cette différence est bien peu de chose; elle n'existe que dans la couleur; mais les avantages qu'ils ont sur nous sont immenses. L'art les a mis au-dessus de la Nature: l'instruction en a fait des Dieux, et nous ne sommes que des hommes. Ils se servent de nous dans ces climats comme il se servent des animaux dans les leurs. Ils sont venus dans ces contrées, se sont emparés des terres, des fortunes des Naturels des Îles, et ces fiers ravisseurs des propriétés d'un peuple doux et paisible dans ses foyers, firent couler tout le sang de ses nobles victimes, se partagèrent entr'eux ses dépouilles sanglantes, et nous ont faits esclaves pour récompense des richesses qu'ils ont ravies, et que nous leur conservons. Ce sont ces propres champs qu'ils moissonnent, semés de cadavres d'Habitants, et ces moissons sont actuellement arrosées de nos sueurs et de nos larmes. La plupart de ces maîtres barbares nous traitent avec une cruauté qui fait frémir la Nature. Notre espèce trop malheureuse s'est habituée à ces châtiments. Ils se gardent bien de nous instruire. Si nos yeux venaient à s'ouvrir, nous aurions horreur de l'état où ils nous ont réduits, et nous pourrions secouer un joug aussi cruel que honteux; mais est-il en notre pouvoir de changer notre sort? L'homme avili par l'esclavage a perdu toute son énergie, et les plus abrutis d'entre nous sont les moins malheureux. J'ai témoigné toujours le même zèle à mon maître; mais je me suis bien gardé de faire connaître ma façon de penser à mes camarades. Dieu! détourne le présage qui menace encore ce climat, amolis le coeur de nos Tyrans, et rends à l'homme le droit qu'il a perdu dans le sein même de la Nature.

MIRZA: Que nous sommes à plaindre!

ZAMOR: Peut-être avant peu notre sort va changer. Une morale douce et consolante a fait tomber en Europe le voile de l'erreur. Les hommes éclairés jettent sur nous des regards attendris: nous leur devrons le retour de cette précieuse liberté, le premier trésor de l'homme, et dont des ravisseurs cruels nous ont privés depuis si longtemps.

MIRZA: Je serais bien contente d'être aussi instruite que toi; mais je ne sais que t'aimer.

ZAMOR: Ta naïveté me charme; c'est l'empreinte de la Nature. Je te quitte un moment. Va cueillir des fruits. Je vais faire un tour au bas de la côte pour y rassembler les débris de ce naufrage. Mais, que vois-je! une femme qui lutte contre les flots! Ah! Mirza, je vole à son secours. L'excès du malheur doit-il dispenser d'être humain? *(Il descend du côté du rocher.)*

SCÈNE II

MIRZA: *(seule)* Zamor va sauver cette infortunée! Puis-je ne pas adorer un coeur si tendre, si compatissant? A présent que je suis malheureuse, je sens mieux combien il est doux de soulager le malheur des autres. *(Elle sort du côté de la forêt.)*

SCÈNE III

VALÈRE: *(seul, entre par le côté opposé à celui où Mirza est sortie)* Rien ne paraît sur les vagues encore émues. O ma femme! tu es perdue à jamais! Eh! pourrais-je te survivre? Non: il faut me réunir à toi. J'ai recueilli mes forces pour te sauver la vie, et j'ai seul échappé à la fureur des flots. Je ne respire qu'avec horreur: séparé de toi, chaque instant redouble mes peines. En vain je te cherche, en vain je t'appelle: Ta voix retentit dans mon coeur, mais elle ne frappe pas mon oreille. Je te fuis. (*Il descend avec peine et tombe au fond du Théâtre appuyé sur une roche.*) Un nuage épais couvre mes yeux, ma force m'abandonne! Grand Dieu, accorde-moi celle de me traîner jusqu'à la mer! Je ne puis plus me soutenir. (*Il reste immobile d'épuisement.*)

SCÈNE IV

Valère, Mirza

Mirza, accourant et apercevant Valère

MIRZA: Ah! Dieu! Quel est cet homme? S'il venait pour se saisir de Zamor et me séparer de lui! Hélas! que deviendrais-je? Mais, non, il n'a peut-être pas un si mauvais dessein; ce n'est pas un de nos persécuteurs. Je souffre . . . Malgré mes craintes, je ne puis m'empêcher de le secourir. Je ne puis plus longtemps le voir en cet état. Il a l'air d'un Français. (*A Valère.*) Monsieur, Monsieur le Français . . . Il ne répond point. Que faire! (*Elle appelle.*) Zamor, Zamor. (*Avec réflexion.*) Montons sur le rocher pour voir s'il vient. (*Elle y court et en redescend aussitôt.*) Je ne le vois pas. (*Elle revient à Valère.*) Français, Français, réponds-moi? Il ne répond pas. Quels secours puis-je lui donner? Je n'ai rien, que je suis malheureuse! (*Prenant le bras de Valère et lui frappant dans la main.*) Pauvre étranger, il est bien malade, et Zamor ne revient pas: il a plus de force que moi; mais allons chercher dans notre cabane de quoi le faire revenir. (*Elle sort.*)

SCÈNE V

Valère, Zamor, Sophie

Zamor, entrant du côté du rocher, et portant sur ses bras Sophie qui paraît évanouie, vêtue d'une robe blanche à la lévite, avec une ceinture et les cheveux épars

ZAMOR: Reprenez vos forces, Madame, je ne suis qu'un esclave Indien, mais je vous donnerai du secours.

SOPHIE: (*d'une voix expirante*) Qui que vous soyez, laissez-moi. Votre pitié m'est plus cruelle que les flots. J'ai perdu ce que j'avais de plus cher. La vie m'est odieuse. O Valère! O mon époux! qu'es-tu devenu?

VALÈRE: Quelle voix se fait entendre? Sophie!

SOPHIE: (*l'aperçoit*) Que vois-je . . . C'est lui!

VALÈRE: (*se levant et tombant aux pieds de Sophie*) Grand Dieu! vous me rendez ma Sophie! O chère épouse! objet de mes larmes et de ma tendresse! Je succombe à ma douleur et à ma joie.

SOPHIE: Providence divine! tu m'as sauvée! achève ton ouvrage, et rends moi mon père.

SCÈNE VI

Valère, Zamor, Sophie, Mirza, apportant des fruits et de l'eau; elle entre en courant, et surprise de voir une femme, elle s'arrête

ZAMOR: Approche, Mirza, ne crains rien. Ce sont deux infortunés comme nous; ils ont des droits sur notre âme.

VALÈRE: Etre compatissant à qui je dois la vie et celle de mon épouse! tu n'es point un Sauvage; tu n'en as ni le langage ni les moeurs. Es-tu le maître de cette Ile?

ZAMOR: Non, mais nous l'habitons seuls depuis quelques jours. Vous me paraissez Français. Si la société d'esclaves ne vous semble pas méprisable, c'est de bon coeur qu'ils partageront avec vous la possession de cette Ile, et si le destin le veut, nous finirons nos jours ensemble.

SOPHIE: *(à Valère)* Que ce langage m'intéresse! *(Aux Esclaves.)* Mortels généreux, j'accepterais vos offres, si je n'allais plus loin chercher un père que peut-être je ne retrouverai jamais! Depuis deux ans que nous errons sur les mers, nous n'avons pu le découvrir.

VALÈRE: Eh bien! restons dans ces lieux: acceptons pour quelquel temps l'hospitalité de ces Indiens, et sois persuadée, ma chère Sophie, qu'à force de persévérance nous découvrirons l'auteur de tes jours dans ce Continent.

SOPHIE: Cruelle destinée! nous avons tout perdu, comment continuer nos recherches?

VALÈRE: Je partage ta peine. *(Aux Indiens.)* Généreux mortels, ne nous abandonnez pas.

MIRZA: Nous, vous abandonner! Jamais, non, jamais.

ZAMOR: Oui, ma chère Mirza, consolons-les dans leurs infortunes. *(A Valère et à Sophie.)* Reposez-vous sur moi; je vais parcourir tous les environs du rocher: si les pertes que vous avez faites sont parmi les débris du vaisseau, je vous promets de vous les apporter. Entrez dans notre cabane, Etrangers malheureux; vous avez besoin de repos; je vais tâcher de rendre le calme à vos esprits agités.

SOPHIE: Mortels compatissants, que de grâces nous avons à vous rendre! vous nous avez sauvé la vie, comment m'acquitter jamais envers vous?

ZAMOR: Vous ne me devez rien, en vous secourant je ne fais qu'obéir à la voix de mon coeur. *(Il sort.)*

SCÈNE VII

Mirza, Sophie, Valère

MIRZA: *(à Sophie)* Je vous aime bien, quoique vous ne soyiez pas esclave. Venez, j'aurai soin de vous. Donnez-moi votre bras. Ah! la jolie main, quelle différence avec la mienne! Asseyons-nous ici. *(Avec gaieté.)* Que je suis contente d'être avec vous! Vous êtes aussi belle que la femme de notre Gouverneur.

SOPHIE: Oui? vous avez donc un Gouverneur dans cette Ile?

VALÈRE: Il me semble que vous nous avez dit que vous l'habitiez seule?

MIRZA: *(avec franchise)* Oh! c'est bien vrai, et Zamor ne vous a point trompés. Je vous ai parlé du Gouverneur de la Colonie, qui n'habite pas avec nous. *(A part.)* Il faut prendre garde à ce que je vais dire; car s'il savait que Zamor a tué un blanc, il ne voudrait pas rester avec nous.

SOPHIE: *(à Valère)* Son ingénuité m'enchante, sa physionomie est douce, et prévient en sa faveur.

VALÈRE: Je n'ai pas vu de plus jolie Négresse.

MIRZA: Vous vous moquez, je ne suis pas cependant la plus jolie; mais, dites-moi, les Françaises sont-elles toutes aussi belles que vous? Elles doivent l'être, car les Français sont tous bons, et vous n'êtes pas esclaves.

VALÈRE: Non, les Français voient avec horreur l'esclavage. Plus libres un jour ils s'occuperont d'adoucir votre sort.

MIRZA: *(avec surprise)* Plus libres un jour, comment, est-ce que vous ne l'êtes pas?

VALÈRE: Nous sommes libres en apparence, mais nos fers n'en sont que plus pesants. Depuis plusieurs siècles les Français gémissent sous le despotisme des Ministres et des Courtisans. Le pouvoir d'un seul Maître est dans les mains de mille Tyrans qui foulent son Peuple. Ce Peuple un jour brisera ses fers, et reprenant tous ses droits écrits dans les lois de la Nature, apprendra à ces Tyrans ce que peut l'union d'un peuple trop longtemps opprimé, et éclairé par une saine philosophie.

MIRZA: Oh! bon Dieu! Il y a donc partout des hommes méchants!

SCÈNE VIII

Zamor, *sur le rocher,* **Sophie, Valère, Mirza**

ZAMOR: C'en est fait, malheureux Etrangers! vous n'avez plus d'espoir. Une vague vient d'engloutir le reste de l'équipage avec toutes vos espérances.

SOPHIE: Hélas! qu'allons-nous devenir?

VALÈRE: Un vaisseau peut aborder dans cette Ile.

ZAMOR: Vous ne connaissez pas, malheureux Etrangers, combien cette côte est dangereuse. Il n'y a que des infortunés comme Mirza et moi, qui aient osé s'en approcher et vaincre tout péril pour l'habiter. Nous ne sommes cependant qu'à deux lieues d'une des plus grandes villes de l'Inde; ville que je ne reverrai jamais à moins que nos tyrans ne viennent nous arracher d'ici pour nous faire éprouver le supplice auquel nous sommes condamnés.

SOPHIE: Le supplice!

VALÈRE: Quel crime avez-vous commis l'un et l'autre? Ah! je le vois; vous êtes trop instruit pour un esclave, et votre éducation a sans doute coûté cher à celui qui vous l'a donnée.

ZAMOR: Monsieur, n'ayez point sur moi les préjugés de vos semblables. J'avais un Maître qui m'était cher: j'aurais sacrifié ma vie pour prolonger ses jours; mais son Intendant était un monstre dont j'ai purgé la terre. Il aima Mirza; mais son amour fut méprisé. Il apprit qu'elle me préférait et dans sa fureur il me fit éprouver des traitements affreux; mais le plus terrible fut d'exiger de moi que je devinsse l'instrument de sa vengeance contre ma chère Mirza. Je rejettai avec horreur une pareille commission. Irrité de ma désobéissance, il courut sur moi l'épée nue; j'évitai le coup qu'il voulait me porter; je le désarmai, et il tomba mort à mes pieds. Je n'eus que le temps d'enlever Mirza et de fuir avec elle dans une chaloupe.

SOPHIE: Que je le plains, ce malheureux! Quoiqu'il ait commis un meurtre, son meurtre me paraît digne de grâce.

VALÈRE: Je m'intéresse à leur sort, ils m'ont rappelé à la vie, ils ont sauvé la tienne: je les défendrai aux dépens de mes jours. J'irai moi-même voir son Gouverneur: S'il est Français, il doit être humain et généreux.

ZAMOR: Oui, Monsieur, il est Français, et le meilleur des hommes.

MIRZA: Ah! si tous les Colons lui ressemblaient, nous serions moins malheureux.

ZAMOR: Je fus à lui dès l'âge de huit ans, il se plaisait à me faire instruire, et m'aimait comme si j'eusse été son fils; car il n'en a

jamais eu, ou peut-être en est-il privé: il semble regretter quelque
chose. On l'entend quelquefois soupirer; sûrement il s'efforce de
cacher quelque grand chagrin. Je l'ai surpris souvent versant des
larmes: il adore sa femme, et elle le paie bien de retour. S'il ne
dépendait que de lui, j'aurais ma grâce; mais il faut un exemple.
Il n'y a point de pardon à espérer pour un esclave qui a levé la
main sur son Commandeur.

SOPHIE: *(à Valère)* Je ne sais pourquoi ce Gouverneur m'intéresse.
Le récit de ses chagrins oppresse mon coeur; il est généreux,
clément: il peut vous pardonner. J'irai moi-même me jeter à ses
pieds. Son nom? Si nous pouvions sortir de cette Ile.

ZAMOR: Il se nomme Monsieur de Saint-Frémont.

SOPHIE: Hélas! ce nom ne m'est point connu; mais n'importe, il est
Français: il m'entendra, et j'espère le fléchir. *(A Valère.)* Si avec la
chaloupe qui les a sauvés, nous pouvions nous conduire au port,
il n'y a point de péril que je n'affronte pour les défendre.

VALÈRE: Je t'admire, ma chère Sophie! j'approuve ton dessein: nous
n'avons qu'à nous rendre auprès de leur Gouverneur. *(Aux Esclaves.)* Mes amis, cette démarche nous acquitte faiblement envers
vous. Heureux si nos prières et nos larmes touchent votre généreux Maître! Partons, mais que vois-je? des esclaves qui nous exa-
minent et qui viennent avec précipitation vers nous. Ils apportent
des chaînes.

SOPHIE: Malheureux, vous êtes perdus!

ZAMOR: *(se retourne, et voyant les Esclaves)* Mirza, c'en est fait! nous
sommes découverts.

SCÈNE IX

Les Précédents, un Indien, *plusieurs Esclaves qui descendent du rocher
en courant*

L'INDIEN: *(à Zamor)* Scélérat! enfin, je te trouve; tu n'échapperas pas
au supplice.

MIRZA: Qu'on me fasse mourir avant lui!

ZAMOR: O ma chère Mirza!

L'INDIEN: Qu'on les enchaîne.

VALÈRE: Monsieur, écoutez nos prières! Qu'allez-vous faire de ces
Esclaves?

L'INDIEN: Un exemple terrible.

SOPHIE: Vous les emmenez pour les faire mourir? Nous nous ôterez
plutôt la vie, avant de les arracher de nos bras.

Valère: Que fais-tu? ma chère Sophie! Nous pouvons tout espérer de l'indulgence du Gouverneur.

L'Indien: Ne vous en flattez pas. Monsieur le Gouverneur doit un exemple à la Colonie. Vous ne connaissez point cette maudite race; ils nous égorgeraient sans pitié si la voix de l'humanité nous parlait en leur faveur. Voilà ce qu'on doit toujours attendre même des Esclaves qu'on instruit. Ils sont nés pour être sauvages, et domptés comme les animaux.

Sophie: Quel affreux préjugé! La Nature ne les a point faits esclaves; ils sont hommes comme vous.

L'Indien: Quel langage tenez vous-là, Madame?

Sophie: Le même que je tiendrais à votre Gouverneur. C'est par reconnaissance que je m'intéresse à ces infortunés, qui connaissent mieux que vous les droits de la pitié, et celui dont vous tenez la place était sans doute un homme atroce.

Zamor: Ah! Madame, cessez de le prier; son âme est endurcie et ne connaît point l'humanité. Il est de son emploi de signaler tous les jours cette rigueur. Il croirait manquer à son devoir, s'il ne la poussait pas jusqu'à la cruauté.

L'Indien: Malheureux!

Zamor: Je ne te crains plus. Je connais mon sort et je le subirai.

Sophie: Que leur malheur les rend intéressants! Que ne ferais-je point pour les sauver!

Valère: (à l'Indien) Emmenez-nous, Monsieur, avec eux. Vous nous obligerez de nous retirer d'ici. (A part.) J'espère fléchir le Gouverneur.

L'Indien: J'y consens avec plaisir, d'autant plus que le danger pour sortir de cette Ile n'est pas le même que pour y arriver.

Valère: Mais, Monsieur, comment avez-vous pu y aborder?

L'Indien: J'ai tout risqué pour le bien de la Colonie. Voyez s'il est possible de leur faire grâce. Nous ne sommes plus les Maîtres de nos Esclaves. Les jours de notre Gouverneur sont peut-être en danger, et ces deux misérables ne seront pas plutôt punis, que le calme renaîtra dans les habitations. (Aux Nègres.) Nègres, qu'on tire le canon, et que le signal convenu annonce au Fort que les criminels sont pris.

Zamor: Allons, Mirza, allons mourir.

Mirza: Ah! Dieu! je suis cause de ta mort.

Zamor: La bonne action que nous avons faite en sauvant ces Etrangers jettera quelques charmes sur nos derniers moments, et nous goûterons au moins la douceur de mourir ensemble.

On emmène Zamor et Mirza; les autres personnages les suivent, et tous vont s'embarquer. Un instant après on voit passer le navire qui les porte.

Fin du premier Acte.

Acte II

Le Théâtre change et représente un Salon de Compagnie meublé à l'Indienne.

SCÈNE PREMIÈRE

Betzi, Azor

BETZI: Eh bien, Azor, que dit-on de Mirza et de Zamor? On les fait chercher partout.

AZOR: On parle de les faire mourir sur le rocher de l'habitation; je crois même qu'on fait les préparatifs de leur supplice. Je tremble qu'on ne les trouve.

BETZI: Mais, Monsieur le Gouverneur peut leur faire grâce. Il en est le maître.

AZOR: Il faut que cela soit impossible; car il aime Zamor, et il dit qu'il n'a jamais eu à se plaindre de lui. Toute la Colonie demande leur mort, et il ne peut la refuser sans se compromettre.

BETZI: Notre Gouverneur n'était point fait pour être un tyran.

AZOR: Comme il est bon avec nous! Tous les Français sont de même; mais les Naturels du pays sont bien plus cruels.

BETZI: L'on m'a assuré que dans les premiers temps nous n'étions pas esclaves.

AZOR: Tout nous porte à le croire. Il y a encore des climats où les Nègres sont libres.

BETZI: Qu'ils sont heureux!

AZOR: Ah! nous sommes bien à plaindre.

BETZI: Et personne ne prend notre défense! On nous défend même de prier pour nos semblables.

AZOR: Hélas! le père et la mère de la malheureuse Mirza seront témoins du supplice de leur fille.

BETZI: Quelle férocité!

AZOR: Voilà comme on nous traite.

BETZI: Mais, dis-moi, Azor, pourquoi Zamor a-t-il tué l'Intendant?

AZOR: On m'a assuré que c'était par jalousie. Tu sais bien que Zamor était l'amant de Mirza.

BETZI: Oui, c'est toi qui me l'as appris.

AZOR: Le Commandeur l'aimait aussi.

BETZI: Mais il ne devait point le tuer pour cela.

AZOR: Il est vrai.

BETZI: Il y avait d'autres raisons.

AZOR: Cela se peut bien, mais je les ignore.

BETZI: Si on pouvait les faire échapper, je suis sûre que Monsieur et Madame de St-Frémont n'en seraient pas fâchés.

AZOR: Je le crois bien, mais ceux qui les serviraient s'exposeraient beaucoup.

BETZI: Sans doute, mais il n'y aurait pas punition de mort.

AZOR: Peut-être, je sais bien toujours que je ne m'y exposerais pas.

BETZI: Il faudrait du moins parler à leurs amis; il pourraient gagner les autres esclaves. Ils aiment tous Zamor et Mirza.

AZOR: On parle de faire mettre le régiment sous les armes.

BETZI: Il n'y a plus d'espoir.

AZOR: Nous devons au contraire, pour le bien de nos camarades, les exhorter à l'obéissance.

BETZI: Tu as raison; fais-le si tu peux, car je n'en aurais jamais la force.

SCÈNE II

Les Précédents, Coraline

CORALINE: *(en courant)* O mes chers camarades! quelle mauvaise nouvelle je viens vous apprendre! On assure qu'on a entendu le canon et que Zamor et Mirza sont pris.

AZOR: Allons donc, cela n'est pas possible, Coraline.

BETZI: Grand Dieu!

CORALINE: J'étais sur le port au moment qu'on annonçait cette malheureuse nouvelle. Plusieurs Colons attendaient avec impatience un navire qu'on découvrait dans le lointain. Il est enfin entré au port, et aussitôt tous les habitants l'ont entouré, et moi, toute tremblante, je me suis enfuie. Pauvre Mirza! malheureux Zamor! nos tyrans ne leur feront pas grâce.

AZOR: Oh! je t'en réponds bien; ils seront bientôt morts.

BETZI: Sans être entendus? sans être jugés?

CORALINE: Jugés! il nous est défendu d'être innocents et de nous justifier.

AZOR: Quelle générosité! et on nous vend par-dessus au marché comme des boeufs.

BETZI: Un commerce d'hommes! O Ciel! l'humanité répugne.

AZOR: C'est bien vrai, mon père et moi avons été achetés à la Côte de Guinée.

CORALINE: Bon, bon, mon pauvre Azor, va, quelque soit notre déplorable sort, j'ai un pressentiment que nous ne serons pas toujours dans les fers, et peut-être avant peu...

AZOR: Eh bien! qu'est-ce que nous verrons? Serons-nous maîtres à notre tour?

CORALINE: Peut-être; mais non, nous serions trop méchants. Tiens, pour être bon, il ne faut être ni maître ni esclave.

AZOR: Ni maître, ni esclave; oh! oh! et que veux-tu donc que nous soyons? Sais-tu, Coraline, que tu ne sais plus ce que tu dis, quoique nos camarades assurent que tu en sais plus que nous?

CORALINE: Va, va, mon pauvre garçon, si tu savais ce que je sais! J'ai lu dans un certain Livre, que pour être heureux il ne fallait qu'être libre et bon cultivateur. Il ne nous manque que la liberté, qu'on nous la donne, et tu verras qu'il n'y aura plus ni maîtres ni esclaves.

AZOR: Je ne t'entends pas.

BETZI: Ni moi non plus.

CORALINE: Mon Dieu, que vous êtes bons l'un et l'autre! Dites-moi, Zamor n'avait-il pas sa liberté? A-t-il pour cela voulu quitter notre bon Maître; nous ferons tous la même chose. Que les Maîtres donnent la liberté, aucun Esclave ne quittera les ateliers. Insensiblement les plus sauvages d'entre nous s'instruiront, reconnaîtront les lois de l'humanité et de la justice, et nos supérieurs trouveront dans notre attachement, dans notre zèle, la récompense de ce bienfait.

AZOR: Tu parles comme un homme! Je crois entendre M. le Gouverneur... Oh! qu'il faut avoir de l'esprit pour retenir tout ce que les autres disent. Mais, voici Madame.

BETZI: Voici Madame, taisons-nous!

CORALINE: Il ne faut pas dire à Madame que l'on craint que Zamor ne soit pris. Cela lui ferait trop de peine.

AZOR: Oh! oui.

SCÈNE III

Les Précédents, Mme de Saint-Frémont

MME DE SAINT-FRÉMONT: Mes enfants, j'ai besoin d'être seule. Laissez-moi, et n'entrez point que je ne vous appelle, ou que vous n'ayez quelque nouvelle à m'annoncer. *(Ils sortent.)*

SCÈNE IV

MME DE SAINT-FRÉMONT: *(seule)* Mon époux est sorti pour cette malheureuse affaire: il est allé dans une des habitations où l'on demandait sa présence. Depuis cette catastrophe la révolte règne dans l'esprit de nos esclaves. Tous soutiennent que Zamor est innocent, et qu'il n'a tué le Commandeur que parce qu'il s'y est vu forcé; mais les Colons se sont réunis pour demander la mort de Mirza et de Zamor, et on les fait chercher partout. Mon mari voudrait bien faire grâce à Zamor, quoiqu'il ait prononcé son arrêt, ainsi que celui de la pauvre Mirza, qui doit périr avec son amant. Hélas! l'attente de leur supplice me jette dans une tristesse profonde. Je ne suis donc pas née pour être heureuse! En vain je suis adorée de mon époux: mon amour ne peut vaincre la mélancolie qui le consume. Depuis plus de dix ans il souffre, et je ne puis deviner la cause de sa douleur. C'est le seul de ses secrets dont je ne sois pas dépositaire. Il faut, lorsqu'il sera de retour, que je redouble d'efforts pour le lui arracher. Mais je l'entends.

SCÈNE V

Mme de Saint-Frémont, M. de Saint-Frémont

MME DE SAINT-FRÉMONT: Eh bien! mon ami, votre présence a-t-elle dissipé cette fermentation?

M. DE SAINT-FRÉMONT: Tous mes esclaves sont rentrés dans leur devoir; mais ils me demandent la grâce de Zamor. Cette affaire est bien délicate, *(A part.)* et pour comble de malheurs, je viens de recevoir de France des nouvelles qui me déchirent le coeur.

MME DE SAINT-FRÉMONT: Que dis-tu, mon ami, tu sembles te faire des reproches. Ah! si tu n'es coupable qu'envers moi, je te pardonne tout pourvu que ton coeur me reste. Tu détournes les yeux; je vois couler tes larmes. Ah! mon ami, je n'ai plus votre confiance; je vous deviens importune; je vais me retirer.

M. DE SAINT-FRÉMONT: Toi, me devenir importune! jamais, jamais. Ah! si j'avais pu m'écarter de mon devoir, ta seule douceur me ramènerait à tes pieds, et tes grandes vertus me rendraient encore plus amoureux de tes charmes.

MME DE SAINT-FRÉMONT: Mais tu me caches un secret ennui. Avoue-le moi. Tes soupirs étouffés me le font soupçonner. La France te fut chère; c'est ta Patrie . . . Peut-être une inclination . . .

M. DE SAINT-FRÉMONT: Arrête, arrête, chère épouse, et ne viens point rouvrir une plaie qui s'était fermée auprès de toi. Je crains de t'affliger.

MME DE SAINT-FRÉMONT: Si je te fus chère, il faut m'en donner une preuve.

M. DE SAINT-FRÉMONT: Laquelle exiges-tu?

MME DE SAINT-FRÉMONT: Celle de me révéler les causes de ton affliction.

M. DE SAINT-FRÉMONT: Tu le veux?

MME DE SAINT-FRÉMONT: Je l'exige; fais-toi pardonner, par cette complaisance, ce secret que tu m'as gardé si longtemps.

M. DE SAINT-FRÉMONT: J'obéis. Je suis d'une Province où des lois injustes et inhumaines privent les enfants cadets du partage égal que la Nature donne aux enfants nés du même père et de la même mère. J'étais le plus jeune de sept; mes parents m'envoyèrent à la Cour pour y demander de l'emploi; mais comment aurais-je pu réussir dans un pays où la vertu est une chimère, et où l'on n'obtient rien sans intrigue ni bassesse. Cependant, j'y fis la connaissance d'un brave Gentilhomme Ecossais qui y était venu dans le même dessein. Il n'était pas riche, et avait une fille au Couvent: il m'y mena. Cette entrevue nous devint funeste à tous les deux. Le père, au bout de quelques mois, partit pour l'armée: il me recommanda d'aller voir sa fille, et dit même qu'on pouvait me la confier quand elle voudrait sortir. Ce brave ami, ce bon père, ne prévoyait pas les suites que son imprudence occasionna. Il fut tué dans une bataille. Sa fille resta seule dans le monde, sans parents et sans connaissances. Elle ne voyait que moi, et paraissait ne désirer que ma présence. L'amour me rendit coupable: Epargne-moi le reste: je fis le serment d'être ton époux; voilà mon crime.

MME DE SAINT-FRÉMONT: Mais, mon ami, vous êtes-vous déterminé vous-même à l'abandonner?

M. DE SAINT-FRÉMONT: Qui, moi? avoir abandonné une femme si intéressante? Ah! la plus longue absence ne me l'aurait jamais fait oublier. Je ne pouvais l'épouser sans le consentement de tous mes parents. Elle devint mère d'une fille. On découvrit notre liaison; je fus éloigné. On obtint pour moi un brevet de Capitaine dans un régiment qui partait pour l'Inde, et l'on me fit embarquer. Peu de temps après on me donna la fausse nouvelle que Clarisse était morte, et qu'il ne me restait que ma fille. Je te voyais tous les jours; ta présence affaiblit avec le temps l'impression que l'image de Clarisse faisait encore sur mon coeur. Je sollicitai ta main, tu acceptas mes voeux, et nous fûmes unis; mais par un raffinement de barbarie, le cruel parent qui m'avait trompé m'apprit que Clarisse vivait encore.

MME DE SAINT-FRÉMONT: Hélas! à quel funeste prix j'ai le bonheur d'être ton épouse! mon ami, tu es plus malheureux que coupable.

Clarisse elle-même te pardonnerait, si elle était témoin de tes remords. Il faut faire les plus vives recherches, pour que ton bien et le mien puissent t'acquitter envers ces infortunés. Je n'ai point d'autres parents que les tiens. Je fais ta fille mon héritière; mais ton coeur est un trésor qu'il n'est pas en mon pouvoir de céder à une autre.

M. DE SAINT-FRÉMONT: Ah! digne épouse, j'admire tes vertus. Hélas! je ne vois que Clarisse qui fut capable de les imiter. C'est donc aux deux extrémités du monde que j'étais destiné à rencontrer ce que le sexe a de plus vertueux et de plus aimable!

MME DE SAINT-FRÉMONT: Tu mérites une compagne digne de toi; mais, mon ami, songe qu'en t'unissant avec moi tu consentis à prendre le nom de mon père, qui, en te donnant son nom, n'avait d'autre but que de te céder sa place comme à son fils adoptif. Il faut écrire à tes parents, surtout à tes plus fidèles amis, qu'ils fassent de nouvelles recherches, et qu'ils nous donnent promptement des nouvelles de ces infortunés. Je crois, mon ami, que j'aurai la force de m'éloigner de vous pour aller chercher moi-même celle à qui vous avez donné le jour. Je sens que j'ai déjà pour elle des entrailles de mère; mais en même temps je frémis! O mon ami, mon ami! s'il fallait me séparer de vous! Si Clarisse t'arrachait de mes bras! . . . Ses malheurs, ses vertus, ses charmes . . . Ah! pardonne, pardonne à mon désespoir, pardonne-moi, cher époux, tu n'es pas capable de m'abandonner et de faire deux victimes pour une.

M. DE SAINT-FRÉMONT: Chère épouse! O moitié de moi-même! Cesse de déchirer ce coeur déjà trop affligé. Clarisse ne vit plus sans doute, puisque depuis deux ans on me fait repasser tous les fonds que j'envoie en France pour elle et pour ma fille. On ignore même ce qu'elles sont devenues. Mais l'on vient; nous reprendrons cette conversation.

SCÈNE VI

M. et Mme Saint-Frémont
Un Juge

LE JUGE: Monsieur, je viens vous apprendre que les criminels sont pris.

MME DE SAINT-FRÉMONT: Comment! si tôt! le temps aurait pu effacer leur crime.

M. DE SAINT-FRÉMONT: *(affligé)* Quel affreux exemple je suis obligé de donner!

Le Juge: Rappelez-vous, Monsieur, dans cette circonstance la dis-
grâce de votre beau-père. Il fut contraint de quitter sa place pour
l'avoir exercée avec trop de bonté.

M. de Saint-Frémont: *(à part)* Malheureux Zamor, tu vas périr!
Je n'ai donc élevé ton enfance que pour te voir un jour traîner au
supplice. *(Haut.)* Que mes soins lui deviennent funestes! Si je
l'avais laissé dans ses moeurs sauvages, il n'aurait peut-être pas
commis ce crime. Il n'avait point dans l'âme des inclinations vici-
euses. L'honnêteté et la vertu le distinguaient dans le sein de
l'esclavage. Elevé dans une vie simple et laborieuse, malgré l'instruction qu'il avait reçue, il n'oubliait jamais son origine. Qu'il
me serait doux de pouvoir le justifier! Comme simple habitant,
j'aurais pu peut-être adoucir son arrêt; mais, comme Gouverneur,
je suis forcé de le livrer à toute la rigueur des lois.

Le Juge: Il est nécessaire qu'on exécute sur-le-champ leur arrêt,
d'autant plus que deux Européens ont excité une révolte générale
parmi les Esclaves. Ils ont dépeint votre Commandeur comme un
monstre. Les Esclaves ont écouté avec avidité ces discours sédi-
tieux, et tous ont promis de ne point exécuter les ordres qui leur
ont été donnés.

M. de Saint-Frémont: Quels sont ces étrangers?

Le Juge: Ce sont des Français qu'on a trouvés sur la côte où ces
criminels s'étaient réfugiés. Ils prétendent que Zamor leur a conservé la vie.

M. de Saint-Frémont: Hélas! ces malheureux Français sans doute
ont fait naufrage, et la reconnaissance a produit seule ce zèle
indiscret.

Le Juge: Vous voyez, Monsieur le Gouverneur, qu'il n'ya point de
temps à perdre, si vous voulez éviter la ruine totale de nos habitations. C'est un mal désespéré.

M. de Saint-Frémont: Je n'ai point le bonheur d'être né dans vos
climats; mais quel empire n'ont point les malheureux sur les âmes
sensibles! Ce n'est point votre faute si les moeurs de votre pays
vous ont familiarisé avec ces traitements durs que vous exercez
sans remords sur des hommes qui n'ont d'autre défense que leur
timidité, et dont les travaux, trop mal récompensés, accroissent
notre fortune en augmentant notre autorité sur eux. Ils ont mille
tyrans pour un. Les Souverains rendent leurs Peuples heureux:
tout Citoyen est libre sous un bon Maître, et dans ce pays d'esclavage il faut être barbare malgré soi. Eh! comment puis-je m'empêcher de me livrer à ces réflexions, quand la voix de l'humanité

crie au fond de mon coeur:«Sois bon et sensible aux cris des malheureux.» Je sais que mon opinion doit vous déplaire: l'Europe,
cependant, prend soin de la justifier, et j'ose espérer qu'avant peu
il n'y aura plus d'esclaves. O Louis! O Monarque adoré! que ne
puis-je en ce moment mettre sous tes yeux l'innocence de ces
proscrits! En accordant leur grâce, tu rendrais la liberté à des
hommes trop longtemps méconnus; mais n'importe: vous voulez
un exemple, il se fera, quoique les Noirs assurent que Zamor
est innocent.

LE JUGE: Pouvez-vous les en croire?

M. DE SAINT-FRÉMONT: Ils ne peuvent m'en imposer, et je connais
plus qu'eux les vertus de Zamor. Vous voulez qu'il meure sans être
entendu? J'y consens avec regret; mais vous n'aurez point à me
reprocher d'avoir trahi les intérêts de la Colonie.

LE JUGE: Vous le devez, Monsieur le Gouverneur, dans cette affaire
où vous voyez que nous sommes menacés d'éprouver une révolte
générale. Il faut donner des ordres pour faire mettre les troupes
sous les armes.

M. DE SAINT-FRÉMONT: Suivez-moi; nous allons voir le parti qu'il
faut prendre.

MME DE SAINT-FRÉMONT: Mon ami, je vous vois sortir avec peine.

M. DE SAINT-FRÉMONT: Ma présence est nécessaire pour rétablir
l'ordre et la discipline.

SCÈNE VII

MME DE SAINT-FRÉMONT: *(seule)* Que je plains ces malheureux!
C'en est fait! Ils vont mourir. Quel chagrin pour mon époux; mais
un plus grand chagrin m'agite de nouveau. Tout ce qui porte le
nom de Française m'épouvante! Si c'était Clarisse! Oh! malheureuse, quel serait mon sort. Je connais les vertus de mon époux,
mais je suis sa femme. Non, non! cessons de nous abuser! Clarisse,
dans le malheur, a de plus grands droits sur son âme! Cachons le
trouble qui m'agite.

SCÈNE VIII

Mme de Saint-Frémont, Betzi, *accourant*

MME DE SAINT-FRÉMONT: Qu'y-a-t-il de nouveau, Betzi?

BETZI: *(avec exaltation)* Monsieur le Gouverneur n'est point ici?

MME DE SAINT-FRÉMONT: Non, il vient de sortir, parle donc?

BETZI: Ah! laissez-moi reprendre mes sens ... Nous étions sur la terrasse; de temps en temps nous jetions tristement les yeux vers l'habitation. Nous voyons arriver de loin le père de Mirza avec un autre Esclave; au milieu d'eux était une étrangère, les cheveux épars et la douleur peinte sur son visage: ses yeux étaient fixés vers la terre, et quoiqu'elle marchât vite, elle avait l'air fort occupée. Lorsqu'elle a été près de nous, elle a demandé Mme de Saint-Frémont. Elle nous a appris que Zamor l'a sauvée de la fureur des flots. Elle a ajouté: je mourrai aux pieds de M. le Gouverneur, si je n'obtiens sa grâce. Elle veut implorer votre secours. La voici.

SCÈNE IX

Les Précédentes, Sophie, *suivie de tous les Esclaves*

SOPHIE: *(se jetant aux genoux de Mme de Saint-Frémont)* Madame, j'embrasse vos genoux. Ayez pitié d'une malheureuse étrangère qui doit tout à Zamor, et n'a autre espoir qu'en vos bontés.

MME DE SAINT-FRÉMONT: *(à part)* Ah! je respire. *(Haut, en la relevant.)* Levez-vous, Madame, je vous promets de faire tout ce qui sera en mon pouvoir. *(A part.)* Sa jeunesse, sa sensibilité, touchent mon coeur à un point que je ne puis exprimer. *(A Sophie.)* Etrangère intéressante, je vais tout employer pour vous faire accorder la grâce que vous exigez de mon époux. Croyez que je partage vos douleurs. Je sens combien ces infortunés vous doivent être chers.

SOPHIE: Sans le secours de Zamor, aussi intrépide qu'humain, je périssais dans les flots. Je lui dois le bonheur de vous voir. Ce qu'il a fait pour moi lui assure dans mon coeur les droits de la Nature; mais ces droits ne me rendent point injuste, Madame, et le témoignage qu'ils rendent à vos rares qualités fait assez voir qu'ils ne sont point reprochables d'un crime prémédité. Quelle humanité! Quel zèle à nous secourir! Le sort qui les poursuit devait plutôt leur inspirer la crainte que la pitié; mais, loin de se cacher, Zamor a affronté tout péril. Jugez, Madame, si avec ces sentiments d'humanité, un mortel peut être coupable; son crime fut involontaire, et c'est faire justice que de l'absoudre comme innocent.

MME DE SAINT-FRÉMONT: *(aux Esclaves)* Mes enfants, il faut nous réunir avec les Colons, et demander la grâce de Zamor et de Mirza. Nous n'avons pas de temps à perdre: *(A Sophie.)* et vous, que je brûle de connaître, vous êtes Française, peut-être pourriezvous . . . mais les moments nous sont chers. Retournez auprès de ces infortunés; Esclaves, accompagnez ses pas.

SOPHIE: *(transportée)* Ah! Madame, que de bienfaits à la fois! Hélas! je voudrais, autant que je le désire, vous prouver ma reconnaissance. *(Elle lui baise les mains.)* Bientôt mon époux viendra s'acquitter envers vous de son devoir. Cher Valère, quelle heureuse nouvelle je vais t'apprendre! *(Elle sort avec les Esclaves.)*

SCÈNE X

Mme de Saint-Frémont, Betzi, Coraline

MME DE SAINT-FRÉMONT: *(à part)* Je trouve dans les traits de cette Etrangère une ressemblance . . . Quelle chimère! . . . *(Haut.)* Et vous, Coraline, faites venir le Secrétaire de M. de Saint-Frémont.

CORALINE: Ah! Madame, vous ignorez ce qui se passe: il vient de faire fermer vos portes par ordre de M. le Gouverneur. Tout est livré aux flammes . . . Entendez, Madame . . . On bat la générale . . . et le son des cloches . . . *(On doit entendre la générale dans le lointain.)*

MME DE SAINT-FRÉMONT: *(allant avec frayeur au fond du Théâtre)* Malheureuse! que vais-je devenir? Que fait mon mari?

BETZI: Je tremble pour mes camarades.

MME DE SAINT-FRÉMONT: *(livrée à la plus grande douleur)* Dieu, mon époux est peut-être en danger! Je vole à son secours . . .

CORALINE: Rassurez-vous, Madame, il n'y a rien à craindre pour M. le Gouverneur. Il est à la tête du régiment. Mais quand même il serait au milieu du tumulte, tous les Esclaves respecteraient ses jours. Il en est trop chéri pour qu'aucun voulût lui faire du mal. C'est seulement à quelques habitants que les Esclaves en veulent: ils leur reprochent le supplice de Zamor et de Mirza; ils assurent que sans eux on ne les aurait pas condamnés.

MME DE SAINT-FRÉMONT: *(agitée)* Comment! on va les faire mourir.

CORALINE: Hélas! bientôt mes pauvres camarades ne seront plus.

MME DE SAINT-FRÉMONT: *(avec empressement)* Non, mes enfants, ils ne périront point: mon mari sera touché de mes larmes, du désespoir de cette Etrangère, qui, peut-être mieux que moi, saura l'émouvoir. Son coeur n'a pas besoin d'être sollicité pour faire le bien; mais il peut tout prendre sur lui. *(A part.)* Et si cette Française lui donnait des renseignements sur sa fille! Grand Dieu! il devrait tout à ces victimes que l'on traîne au supplice. *(Haut.)* Allons, Betzi, il faut joindre mon mari, lui dire . . . Mais dans ce moment, comment entrer en explication? Il faut que je le voie moi-même. Où est-il maintenant?

CORALINE: Je ne sais précisément avec quel régiment il est: toute l'armée est dispersée. On dit seulement que M. de Saint-Frémont ramène le calme et remet l'ordre partout où il passe. Il serait bien difficile de le trouver dans ce moment. Il n'y a qu'à nous rendre dans l'habitation, si déjà on ne nous y a pas devancées. Mais les chemins sont rompus ou coupés. On conçoit à peine qu'on ait pu faire tant de dégâts en si peu de temps.

MME DE SAINT-FRÉMONT: N'importe; je ne crains ni le danger ni la fatigue, quand il s'agit de sauver les jours de deux infortunés.

Fin du deuxième Acte

Acte III

Le Théâtre représente un lieu sauvage où l'on voit deux collines en pointes, et bordées de touffes d'arbrisseaux qui s'étendent à perte de vue. Sur un des côtés est un rocher escarpé, dont le sommet est une plate-forme, et dont la base est perpendiculaire sur le bord de l'avant-scène. On y monte du côté d'une des collines, de manière que les Spectateurs y peuvent voir arriver tous les Personnages. On voit deçà et delà quelques cabanes de Nègres éparses.

SCÈNE PREMIÈRE

Valère, Zamor, Mirza

VALÈRE: Vous voilà libres! je vole à la tête de vos camarades. Mon épouse ne tardera pas longtemps à reparaître à nos yeux. Elle aura sans doute obtenu votre grâce de M. de Saint-Frémont. Je vous quitte pour un instant, et ne vous perds point de vue.

SCÈNE II

Zamor, Mirza

ZAMOR: Que notre sort est déplorable, ô ma chère Mirza! Il devient d'autant plus affreux, que je crains que le zèle de ce Français à vouloir nous sauver ne le perdre lui-même ainsi que son épouse. Quelle idée accablante!

MIRZA: Elle me poursuit aussi: mais peut-être sa digne épouse aura pu fléchir notre Gouverneur, ne nous affligeons point avant son retour.

ZAMOR: Je bénis mon trépas, puisque je meurs avec toi; mais, qu'il est cruel de perdre la vie en coupable! on m'a jugé tel, notre bon maître le croit; voilà ce qui me désespère.

MIRZA: Je veux voir moi-même M. le Gouverneur. Cette dernière volonté doit m'être accordée. Je me jetterai à ses pieds; je lui révèlerai tout.

ZAMOR: Hélas! que pourras-tu lui dire?

MIRZA: Je lui ferai connaître la cruauté de son Commandeur et de son amour féroce.

ZAMOR: Ta tendresse pour moi t'aveugle: tu veux t'accuser pour me rendre innocent! Si tu dédaignes la vie à ce prix, m'en crois-tu assez avare pour vouloir la conserver aux dépens de tes jours? Non, ma chère Mirza, il n'y a point de bonheur pour moi sur la terre, si je ne le partage avec toi.

MIRZA: Je pense de même, je ne pourrais plus vivre sans te voir.

ZAMOR: Qu'il nous aurait été doux de prolonger nos jours ensemble! Ces lieux me rappellent notre première entrevue. C'est ici que le tyran reçut la mort; c'est ici qu'on va terminer notre carrière. La Nature semble en ces lieux être en contraste avec elle-même. Jadis elle nous paraissait riante: elle n'a rien perdu de ses attraits; mais elle nous montre à la fois l'image de notre bonheur passé et de l'horrible sort dont nous serons les victimes. Ah! Mirza, qu'il est cruel de mourir quand on aime.

MIRZA: Que tu m'attendris! Ne m'afflige pas davantage. Je sens que mon courage m'abandonne; mais ce bon Français revient à nous; que va-t-il nous apprendre?

SCÈNE III

Zamor, Mirza, Valère

VALÈRE: O mes bienfaiteurs! Il faut vous sauver. Profitez de ces instants précieux que vos camarades vous procurent. Ils bouchent les chemins, répondez à leur zèle et à leur courage; ils s'exposent pour vous, fuyez dans un autre climat. Il se peut que mon épouse n'obtienne pas votre grâce. On voit plusieurs troupes de soldats s'approcher d'ici: vous avez le temps d'échapper par cette colline. Allez, vivez dans les forêts: vos semblables vous ouvriront leur sein.

MIRZA: Ce Français a raison. Viens, suis-moi. Il nous aime; profitons de ses conseils. Cours avec moi, cher Zamor; ne crains point de revenir habiter dans le fond des forêts. A peine tu te rappelles nos lois, et bientôt ta chère Mirza t'en retracera la douce image.

ZAMOR: Eh bien! je cède. Ce n'est que pour toi que je chéris la vie. (Il embrasse Valère.) Adieu, le plus généreux des hommes!

MIRZA: Hélas! il faut donc que je vous quitte sans avoir le bonheur de me jeter aux pieds de votre épouse!

VALÈRE: Elle partagera vos regrets, n'en doutez point; mais fuyez des lieux trop funestes.

SCÈNE IV

Les Précédents, Sophie, Esclaves

SOPHIE: *(se précipitant dans les bras de Valère)* Ah! mon ami, remercions le Ciel: ces victimes ne périront point. Madame de Saint-Frémont m'a promis leur grâce.

VALÈRE: *(avec joie)* Grand Dieu! quel comble de bonheur!

ZAMOR: Ah! je reconnais à ce procédé sa belle âme. *(A Valère.)* Etrangers généreux, que le Ciel comble vos désirs! L'Etre suprême n'abandonne jamais ceux qui cherchent à lui ressembler par la bienfaisance.

VALÈRE: Ah! que vous rendez nos jours fortunés!

MIRZA: Que nous sommes heureux d'avoir secouru ces Français! Ils nous doivent beaucoup; mais nous leur devons encore plus.

SOPHIE: Madame de Saint-Frémont a fait assembler ses meilleurs amis. Je l'ai instruite de leur innocence; elle met tout le zèle possible à les sauver. Je n'ai aucune peine à l'intéresser en leur faveur; son âme est si belle, si sensible aux maux des malheureux!

ZAMOR: Son respectable époux l'égale en mérite et en bonté.

SOPHIE: Je n'ai pas eu le bonheur de le voir.

ZAMOR: *(alarmé)* Que vois-je? des soldats qui arrivent en foule! Ah! c'en est fait! Vous vous êtes abusés, généreux Français, nous sommes perdus.

SOPHIE: Ne vous alarmez point, il faut savoir . . .

VALÈRE: Je les défendrai au péril de ma vie. Hélas! Ils allaient se sauver lorsque tu es venu les rassurer. Je vais savoir de l'Officier qui commande ce détachement, quelle est sa mission.

(Une Compagnie de Grenadiers et une de Soldats Français se rangent au fond du Théâtre, la baïonnette au bout du fusil. En avant d'eux se place une troupe d'Esclaves avec des arcs et des flèches; ils ont à leur tête le Major, le Juge et l'Intendant des Esclaves de M. de Saint-Frémont.)

SCÈNE V

Les Précédents, le Major, le Juge, L'Indien, *Grenadiers et Soldats Français, plusieurs Esclaves*

VALÈRE: Monsieur, puis-je vous demander quel sujet vous amène ici?

LE MAJOR: Une cruelle fonction. Je viens faire exécuter l'arrêt de mort prononcé contre ces malheureux.

SOPHIE: *(troublée)* Vous allez les faire mourir?

LE MAJOR: Oui, Madame.

VALÈRE: Non, cet affreux sacrifice ne s'exécutera point.

SOPHIE: Madame de Saint-Frémont m'a promis leur grâce.

LE JUGE: *(durement)* Cela n'est pas en son pouvoir, M. le Gouverneur lui-même ne pourrait la leur accorder. Ainsi, cessez de vouloir vous obstiner à les sauver. Vous rendriez leur supplice plus terrible. *(Au Major.)* Monsieur le Major, exécutez les ordres qui vous ont été donnés. *(Aux Esclaves.)* Et vous, menez les criminels sur le haut du rocher.

LE COMMANDEUR INDIEN: Tendez vos arcs!

VALÈRE: Arrêtez! *(Les Esclaves n'écoutent que Valère.)*

LE JUGE: Obéissez. *(Le Major fait signe aux Soldats, ils courent avec la baïonnette, qu'ils présentent à la poitrine de tous les Esclaves, dont aucun ne remue.)*

ZAMOR: *(accourant au-devant d'eux)* Que faites-vous? J'ai seul mérité la mort. Que vous ont fait mes pauvres camarades? Pourquoi les égorger? Tournez vos armes contre moi. *(Il ouvre sa veste.)* Voilà mon sein! Lavez dans mon sang leur désobéissance. La Colonie ne demande que ma mort. Est-il nécessaire de faire périr tant d'innocentes victimes qui ne sont pas complices de mon crime?

MIRZA: Je suis aussi coupable que Zamor, ne me séparez point de lui: par pitié ôtez-moi la vie; mes jours sont attachés à sa destinée. Je veux mourir la première.

VALÈRE: *(au Juge)* Monsieur, suspendez, je vous prie, leur supplice. Je puis vous assurer qu'on s'occupe de leur grâce.

LE MAJOR: *(au Juge)* Monsieur, nous pouvons prendre ceci sur nous; attendons le Gouverneur.

LE JUGE: *(durement)* Je n'écoute rien que mon devoir et la loi.

VALÈRE: *(furieux)* Barbare! Quoique ta place endurcisse l'âme, tu la dégrades en la rendant encore plus cruelle que les lois ne te l'ont prescrite.

LE JUGE: Monsieur le Major, faites conduire cet audacieux à la Citadelle.

LE MAJOR: C'est un Français: il rendra compte de sa conduite à M. le Gouverneur, et je n'ai pas, à cet égard, d'ordres à recevoir de vous.

LE JUGE: Exécutez donc ceux qui vous ont été donnés.

SOPHIE: *(avec héroïsme)* Cet excès de cruauté me donne du courage. *(Elle court se placer entre Zamor et Mirza, les prend tous les deux par la main, et dit au Juge.)* Barbare! ôse me faire assassiner avec eux; je ne les quitte point: rien ne pourra les arracher de mes bras.

VALÈRE: *(transporté)* Ah! ma chère Sophie, ce trait de courage te rend encore plus chère à mon coeur.

LE JUGE: *(au Major)* Monsieur, faites retirer cette femme audacieuse: vous ne remplissez pas votre devoir.

LE MAJOR: *(indigné)* Vous l'exigez; mais vous répondrez des suites. *(Aux Soldats.)* Séparez ces étrangers de ces esclaves.

SOPHIE: *(jette un cri perçant, en serrant Zamor et Mirza contre son sein)*

VALÈRE: *(furieux, courant après Sophie)* Si l'on emploie la moindre violence contre mon épouse, je ne respecte plus rien. *(Au Juge.)* Et toi, barbare, tremble d'être immolé à ma juste fureur.

UN ESCLAVE: Dût-on nous faire mourir tous, nous les défendrons.

(Les Esclaves se rangent autour d'eux, et forment un rempart, les Soldats et Grenadiers s'en approchent avec la baïonnette.)

LE MAJOR: *(aux Soldats)* Soldats, arrêtez. *(Au Juge.)* Je ne suis point envoyé ici pour ordonner le carnage et pour répandre du sang, mais pour ramener l'ordre. Le Gouverneur ne sera pas longtemps à paraître, et sa prudence nous indiquera mieux ce que nous devons faire. *(Aux Etrangers et aux Esclaves.)* Rassurez-vous; je n'emploierai pas la force; vos efforts seraient inutiles, si je voulais l'exercer. *(A Sophie.)* Et vous, Madame, vous pouvez vous retirer à l'écart avec ces malheureux; j'attends M. le Gouverneur. *(Sophie, Zamor et Mirza, sortent avec quelques Esclaves.)*

SCÈNE VI

Valère, le Major, le Juge, L'Indien, *Grenadiers et Soldats, Esclaves*

VALÈRE: *(au Major)* Je ne puis abandonner mon épouse dans cet état. Faites tous vos efforts auprès de M. de Saint-Frémont. Je n'ai pas besoin de vous recommander la clémence; elle doit régner dans votre âme. Un guerrier fut toujours généreux.

LE MAJOR: Reposez-vous sur moi; retirez-vous, et vous paraîtrez quand il en sera temps. *(Valère sort.)*

SCÈNE VII

Les Précédents, Excepté Valère

LE MAJOR, AU JUGE: Voilà, Monsieur, le fruit d'une trop grande sévérité.

LE JUGE: Votre modération perd aujourd'hui la Colonie.

LE MAJOR: Dites mieux; elle la sauve peut-être. Vous ne connaissez que vos lois cruelles, et moi, je connais l'art de la guerre et l'humanité. Ce ne sont point nos ennemis que nous combattons; ce sont nos Esclaves, ou plutôt nos Cultivateurs. Pour les réduire, il eût fallu, suivant vous, les faire passer au fil de l'épée, et dans cette circonstance, une imprudence nous mènerait sans doute plus loin que vous ne pensez.

SCÈNE VIII

Les Précédents, M. de Saint-Frémont, *entrant d'un côté et*
Valère de l'autre. Deux Compagnies de Grenadiers et Soldats
conduisent plusieurs Esclaves enchaînés.

VALÈRE: *(à M. de Saint-Frémont)* Ah! Monsieur, écoutez nos prières: vous êtes Français, vous serez juste.

M. DE SAINT-FRÉMONT: J'approuve votre zèle; mais dans ce climat il devient indiscret; il a même produit beaucoup de mal. Je viens d'être témoin de l'attentat le plus affreux exercé sur un Magistrat. Il a fallu, contre mon caractère, employer la violence pour arrêter la cruauté des esclaves. Je sais tout ce que vous devez à ces malheureux; mais vous n'avez pas le droit de les défendre, ni de changer les lois et les moeurs d'un pays.

VALÈRE: J'ai du moins le droit que la reconnaissance donne à toutes les belles âmes: quelque soit votre sévérité simulée, mon coeur en appelle au vôtre.

M. DE SAINT-FRÉMONT: Cessez de me prier, il m'en coûte trop pour refuser.

VALÈRE: Votre digne épouse nous avait fait tout espérer.

M. DE SAINT-FRÉMONT: Elle-même, Monsieur, est convaincue de l'impossibilité absolue de ce que vous demandez.

VALÈRE: Si c'est un crime d'avoir tué un monstre qui faisait frémir la nature, ce crime, au moins, est excusable. Zamor défendait sa propre vie, et la défense est de droit naturel.

LE JUGE: Vous abusez de la complaisance de M. le Gouverneur: on vous l'a déjà dit. Les lois les condamnent comme homicides, pouvez-vous les changer?

VALÈRE: Non, mais on pourrait les adoucir en faveur d'un crime involontaire.

LE JUGE: Y pensez-vous bien? les adoucir en faveur d'un esclave! Nous ne sommes pas ici en France, il nous faut des exemples.

M. DE SAINT-FRÉMONT: C'en est fait, il faut que l'arrêt s'exécute.

VALÈRE: Ces paroles glacent mon sang et mon coeur oppressé . . .
Chère épouse, que vas-tu devenir? Ah! Monsieur, si vous connais-
siez sa sensibilité, ses malheurs, vous en seriez touché; elle avait
mis toutes ses espérances dans vos bontés; elle se flattait même
que vous lui donneriez des renseignements sur le sort d'un parent, son unique appui, dont elle est privée depuis son enfance,
et qui doit être établi dans quelque partie de ce Continent.

M. DE SAINT-FRÉMONT: Soyez assuré que je vous servirai de tout
ce qui sera en mon pouvoir; mais, quant aux criminels, je ne puis
rien faire pour eux. Malheureux Etranger! allez la consoler: elle
m'intéresse sans la connaître. Trompez-la même, s'il est nécessaire, pour qu'elle ne soit pas témoin de cet affreux supplice:
dites-lui que l'on veut interroger ces malheureux, qu'il faut les
laisser seuls, et que leur grâce dépend peut-être de cette sage
précaution.

VALÈRE: *(pleurant)* Que nous sommes à plaindre! Je ne survivrai pas
à leur perte. *(Il sort.)*

SCÈNE IX

Les Précédents, Excepté Valère

M. DE SAINT-FRÉMONT: Que ce Français m'afflige! ses regrets en
faveur de ces infortunés augmentent les miens. Il faut donc qu'ils
meurent, et malgré mon penchant à la clémence . . . *(Avec réflexion.)* Zamor a sauvé cette étrangère; elle est Française, et si j'en
crois son époux, elle cherche un parent qui habite ce climat. Au-
rait-il craint de s'expliquer? Sa douleur, ses recherches, ses malheurs . . . Infortunée, si c'était . . . où la nature va-t-elle m'égarer!
Et pourquoi m'en étonner! L'aventure de cette Etrangère a tant de
rapport avec celle de ma fille . . . et mon coeur ulcéré voudrait la
retrouver en elle. C'est le sort des malheureux de se bercer d'espérance, et de trouver de la consolation dans les moindres rapports.

LE JUGE: Monsieur le Major, faites avancer vos Soldats. *(A l'Indien.)*
Monsieur le Commandeur, conduisez les Esclaves, et faites les
ranger suivant l'usage.

*(L'Indien sort avec les Esclaves armés, tandis qu'une troupe d'autres viennent
se jeter aux pieds de M. de Saint-Frémont.)*

SCÈNE X

Les Précédents Excepté L'Indien

Les Esclaves armés sont remplacés par les Esclaves sans armes

UN ESCLAVE: *(à genoux)* Monseigneur, nous n'avons pas été du nombre des rebelles. Qu'il nous soit permis de demander la grâce de

nos camarades! Que pour racheter leur vie on nous fasse éprouver les châtiments les plus terribles! qu'on augmente nos travaux pénibles, et qu'on diminue nos aliments; nous supporterions cette punition avec courage. Monseigneur, vous vous attendrissez, je vois couler vos pleurs.

M. DE SAINT-FRÉMONT: Mes enfants, mes amis, que me proposez-vous? *(Au Juge.)* Que voulez-vous que je réponde à ce trait d'héroïsme? Ah! Ciel! ils montrent tant de grandeur d'âme, et nous osons les regarder comme les derniers des humains! Hommes civilisés! vous vous croyez supérieurs à des Esclaves! De l'opprobre et de l'état le plus vil, l'équité, le courage, les élèvent en un instant au rang des plus généreux mortels. Vous en avez l'exemple devant les yeux.

LE JUGE: Ils connaissent bien votre coeur; mais vous ne pouvez céder à votre penchant sans compromettre votre dignité. Je les connais mieux que vous; ils promettent tout dans ces moments; d'ailleurs, ces criminels ne sont plus en votre puissance, ils sont livrés à la rigueur des lois.

M. DE SAINT-FRÉMONT: Eh bien! je vous les abandonne. Hélas! les voici. Où me cacher? Que ce devoir est cruel!

SCÈNE XI

Les Précédents, L'Indien, Zamor, Mirza, *les Esclaves armés*

ZAMOR: Il n'y a plus d'espérance; nos bienfaiteurs sont entourés de soldats. Embrasse-moi pour la dernière fois, ma chère Mirza!

MIRZA: Je bénis mon sort, puisque le même supplice nous réunit. *(A un vieillard et une vieille Esclave.)* Adieu, chers auteurs de mes jours; ne pleurez plus votre pauvre Mirza, elle n'est plus à plaindre. *(Aux Esclaves de son sexe.)* Adieu, mes compagnes.

ZAMOR: Esclaves, Colons, écoutez-moi: j'ai tué un homme, j'ai mérité la mort; ne regrettez point mon supplice, il est nécessaire au bien de la Colonie. Mirza est innocente; mais elle chérit son trépas. *(Aux Esclaves, particulièrement.)* Et vous, mes chers amis, écoutez-moi à mon dernier moment. Je quitte la vie, je meurs innocent; mais craignez de vous rendre coupables pour me défendre: craignez surtout cet esprit de faction, et ne vous livrez jamais à des excès pour sortir de l'esclavage; craignez de briser vos fers avec trop de violence; attendez tout du temps et de la justice divine, remplacez nous auprès de M. le Gouverneur, de sa respectable épouse. Payez-les par votre zèle et par votre attachement de tout ce que je leur dois. Hélas! je ne puis m'acquitter envers eux. Chérissez ce bon Maître, ce bon père, avec une tendresse filiale, comme je l'ai toujours fait. Je mourrais content si je pouvais croire du moins qu'il me regrette! *(Il se jette à ses pieds.)* Ah! mon cher Maître, m'est-il permis encore de vous nommer ainsi?

M. DE SAINT-FRÉMONT: *(avec une vive douleur)* Ces paroles me serrent le coeur. Malheureux! qu'as-tu fait? va, je ne t'en veux point, je souffre assez du fatal devoir que je remplis.

ZAMOR: *(s'incline et lui baise les pieds)* Ah! mon cher maître, la mort n'a plus rien d'affreux pour moi. Vous me chérissez encore, je meurs content. *(Il lui prend les mains.)* Que je baise ces mains pour la dernière fois!

M. DE SAINT-FRÉMONT: *(attendri)* Laisse-moi, laisse-moi, tu m'arraches le coeur.

ZAMOR: *(aux Esclaves armés)* Mes amis, faites votre devoir. *(Il prend Mirza dans ses bras, et monte avec elle sur le rocher, où ils se mettent à genoux. Les Esclaves ajustent leurs flèches.)*

SCÈNE XII

Les Précédents, Mme de Saint-Frémont, *avec ses Esclaves, Grenadiers et Soldats Français.*

MME DE SAINT-FRÉMONT: Arrêtez, Esclaves, et respectez la femme de votre Gouverneur. *(A son époux.)* Grâce, mon ami, grâce!

SCÈNE XIII ET DERNIÈRE

Les Précédents, Valère, Sophie

SOPHIE: *(à Valère)* Tu me retiens en vain. Je veux absolument les voir. Cruel! tu m'as trompée. *(A Mme de Saint-Frémont.)* Ah! Madame, mes forces m'abandonnent. *(Elle tombe dans les bras des Esclaves.)*

MME DE SAINT-FRÉMONT: *(à son mari)* Mon ami, vous voyez le désespoir de cette Française; pourriez-vous n'en être pas touché?

SOPHIE: *(revenant à elle, et se jetant aux pieds de M. de Saint-Frémont)* Ah Monsieur! je meurs de douleur à vos pieds si vous ne m'accordez leur grâce. Elle est dans votre coeur et dépend de votre pouvoir. Ah! si je ne puis l'obtenir, que m'importe ma vie! Nous avons tout perdu. Privée d'un père depuis l'âge de cinq ans, je mettais ma consolation à sauver deux victimes qui vous sont chères.

M. DE SAINT-FRÉMONT: *(à part, dans la plus vive agitation)* Quel souvenir ... quels traits ... quelle époque ... son âge ... Quel

trouble s'élève dans mon âme. *(A Sophie.)* Ah Madame! répondez
à mon empressement, puis-je vous demander les noms de ceux
qui vous ont donné le jour?

SOPHIE: *(s'appuyant sur Valère)* Hélas!

VALÈRE: O ma chère Sophie!

M. DE SAINT-FRÉMONT: *(plus vivement)* Sophie . . . *(A part.)* Elle fut
nommée Sophie. *(Haut.)* Quel nom avez-vous prononcé . . .
Parlez, répondez-moi, de grâce, Madame, quelle fut votre mère?

SOPHIE: *(à part)* Quel trouble l'agite, plus je l'examine . . . *(Haut.)* La
malheureuse Clarisse de Saint-Fort fut ma mère.

M. DE SAINT-FRÉMONT: Ah! ma fille, reconnais-moi. La nature ne
m'a point trompé. Reconnais la voix d'un père trop longtemps
séparé de toi et de ta mère.

SOPHIE: Ah! mon père! je me meurs. *(Elle tombe dans les bras des
Soldats.)*

M. DE SAINT-FRÉMONT: O ma fille! ô mon sang!

SOPHIE: Qu'ai-je entendu? Oui, oui c'est lui . . . Ses traits sont restés
gravés dans mon âme . . . Quel bonheur me fait retrouver dans
vos bras! Je ne puis vous rendre tous les sentiments qui m'agitent.
Mais ces malheureux, ô mon père, leur sort est dans vos mains.
Sans leur secours votre fille périssait. Accordez à la nature la première grâce qu'elle vous demande. Habitants, Esclaves, tombez
aux genoux du plus généreux des hommes; c'est aux pieds de la
vertu qu'on trouve la clémence. *(Tous se mettent à genoux, excepté le
Juge et les Soldats.)*

LES ESCLAVES: Monseigneur!

LES HABITANTS: Monsieur le Gouverneur!

M. DE SAINT-FRÉMONT: Qu'exigez-vous de moi?

TOUS: Leur grâce.

M. DE SAINT-FRÉMONT: *(attendri)* Mes enfants, mon épouse, mes
amis, je vous l'accorde.

TOUS: Quel bonheur! *(Les Grenadiers et Soldats fléchissent le genou, et
se remettent tout de suite.)*

LE MAJOR: Braves guerriers, ne rougissez point de ce mouvement
de sensibilité; il épure le courage et ne l'avilit pas.

MIRZA: Grand Dieu! vous changez notre malheureux sort; vous com-
blez notre félicité; votre justice ne cesse jamais de se manifester.

M. DE SAINT-FRÉMONT: Mes amis, je vous donne votre liberté, et
j'aurai soin de votre fortune.

ZAMOR: Non, mon maître; gardez vos bienfaits. Le plus précieux à
notre coeur est de nous laisser vivre auprès de vous et de tout ce
que vous avez de plus cher.

M. DE SAINT-FRÉMONT: Quoi! je retrouve ma fille! je la serre dans mes bras. Un sort cruel a donc fini de me poursuivre. O ma chère Sophie! que je crains d'apprendre le sort cruel de votre mère.

SOPHIE: Hélas! ma pauvre mère n'est plus! mais, mon père, qu'il m'est doux de vous voir. *(A Valère.)* Cher Valère!

VALÈRE: Je partage ta félicité.

MME DE SAINT-FRÉMONT: Ma fille, ne voyez en moi qu'une tendre mère. Votre père connaît mes intentions, et vous les apprendrez bientôt vous-même. Ne nous occupons plus que du mariage de Zamor et de Mirza.

MIRZA: Nous allons vivre pour nous aimer. Nous serons toujours heureux, toujours, toujours.

ZAMOR: Oui, ma chère Mirza; oui, nous serons toujours heureux.

M. DE SAINT-FRÉMONT: Mes amis, je viens de vous accorder votre grâce. Que ne puis-je de même donner la liberté à tous vos semblables, ou du moins adoucir leur sort! Esclaves, écoutez-moi; si jamais on change votre destinée, ne perdez point de vue l'amour du bien public, qui jusqu'à présent vous fut étranger. Sachez que l'homme, dans sa liberté, a besoin encore d'être soumis à des lois sages et humaines, et sans vous porter à des excès répréhensibles, espérez tout d'un Gouvernement éclairé et bienfaisant. Allons, mes amis, mes enfants, qu'une fête générale soit l'heureux présage de cette douce liberté.

FIN.

DÉCLARATION DES DROITS DE LA FEMME
(extraits)[3]
(1791)

Il était bien nécessaire que je dise quelques mots sur les troubles que cause, dit-on, le décret en faveur des hommes de couleur, dans nos îles. C'est là où la Nature frémit d'horreur; c'est là où la raison et l'humanité, n'ont pas encore touché les âmes endurcies; c'est là surtout où la division et la discorde agitent leurs habitants. Il n'est pas difficile de deviner les instigateurs de ces fermentations incendiaires: il y en a dans le sein même de l'Assemblée nationale: ils allument en Europe le feu qui doit embraser l'Amérique. Les Colons prétendent régner en despotes sur des hommes dont ils sont les pères et les frères; et méconnaissant les droits de la nature, ils en poursuivent la source

---

3. This text is based on the French edition of the *Oeuvres Complètes*.

266 / APPENDIX A

jusque dans la plus petite teinte de leur sang. Ces Colons inhumains disent: notre sang circule dans leurs veines, mais nous le répandrons tout, s'il le faut, pour assouvir notre cupidité ou notre aveugle ambition. C'est dans ces lieux, les plus près de la Nature, que le père méconnaît le fils; sourd aux cris du sang, il en étouffe tous les charmes. Que peut-on espérer de la résistance qu'on lui oppose? la contraindre avec violence, c'est la rendre terrible, la laisser encore dans les fers, c'est acheminer toutes les calamités vers l'Amérique. Une main divine semble répandre partout l'apanage de l'homme, *la liberté;* la loi seule a le droit de réprimer cette liberté, si elle dégénère en licence; mais elle doit être égale pour tous, c'est elle surtout qui doit renfermer l'Assemblée nationale dans son décret, dicté par la prudence et par la justice. Puisse-t-elle agir de même pour l'état de la France, et se rendre aussi attentive sur les nouveaux abus, comme elle l'a été sur les anciens qui deviennent chaque jour plus effroyables! Mon opinion serait encore de raccommoder le pouvoir exécutif avec le pouvoir législatif, car il me semble que l'un est tout, et que l'autre n'est rien; d'où naîtra, malheureusement peut-être, la perte de l'Empire français. Je considère ces deux pouvoirs, comme l'homme et la femme qui doivent être unis, mais égaux en force et en vertu, pour faire un bon ménage.

Réponse au Champion Américain[4]
(1790)

Depuis qu'on ne se bat plus en France, Monsieur, je conviens avec vous qu'on s'y assassine quelquefois; qu'il est imprudent de provoquer les assassins; mais il est encore plus indiscret, plus indécent, et plus injuste, d'attaquer les gens d'honneur, de les attaquer de la manière la plus inepte, et cependant la plus calomnieuse, en imputant un manque de courage à M. de la Fayette, que vous craignez, peut-être, au fond du coeur. Je vous dirai que je ne connais point ce héros magnanime comme vous le prétendez. Je sais seulement que sa réputation est intacte, sa valeur connue, son coeur, comme celui de Bayard, sans peur, sans reproches; à qui nous devrons peut-être le bonheur de la France et le pouvoir de la nation. Je n'entreprendrai point de justifier les hommes célèbres que vous provoquez; ils sont tous militaires et Français, et ce titre me suffit pour les croire braves.

---

4. This text is based on the French edition which appeared in *La révolution française et l'abolition de l'esclavage*, vol. 4, *Traite des noirs et esclavage* (Paris: EDHIS, 1968).

Mais, si je vous imite, Monsieur, par cette espèce de défi, je m'écarte un peu trop de mon but en tombant dans l'erreur grossière que vous avez commise à mon égard. Ce n'est pas la cause des philosophes, des amis des noirs, que j'entreprends de défendre; c'est la mienne propre, et vous voudrez bien me permettre de me servir des seules armes qui sont en mon pouvoir. Nous allons donc guerroyer, et ce combat singulier, grâce à ma *jeanlorgnerie,* ne sera pas meurtrier. Vous m'accordez cependant des vertus et du courage au-dessus de mon sexe. Je pourrais en convenir sans trop d'orgueil: mais vous ne me prêtez pas moins gratuitement l'ambition de consulter sur la langue et sur mes faibles productions les académiciens, les savants gens de lettres, et tout le sacré vallon qui protège plus d'un sot, et dont je fais fort peu de cas, excepté les écrivains, qui ont honoré les talents par l'honneur et la probité. Le mérite littéraire est bien peu de chose quand il est dénué de ces deux avantages: mais passons à ce qu'il m'est important de vous apprendre, et que vous ignorez parfaitement.

Vous prétendez, Monsieur, que les amis des noirs se sont servis d'une femme pour provoquer les colons. Certes il est bien plus extraordinaire qu'un homme qui annonce quelqu'esprit, de la facilité et même de la bravoure, charge une femme d'être le porteur d'un cartel, et veuille, par une entremise aussi singulière que poltrone, faire ses preuves de courage. Je ne puis donc apprécier votre valeur que comme une espèce de dom quichotade, et vous considérer comme un pourfendeur de géants et de fantômes qui n'existent pas. Je veux cependant, en vous ramenant à la raison, rire avec vous des maux où je ne vois point de remède. Vous avez à combattre la société des amis des noirs, et moi, j'en ai à confondre une bien plus terrible, c'est celle de . . . Le temps qui détruit tout, qui change à son gré les arts, les moeurs et la justice des hommes, ne changera jamais l'esprit de corps de ceux de qui j'ai si fortement à me plaindre.

On a vu tomber en France, depuis quelques mois, le voile de l'erreur, de l'imposture, de l'injustice, et enfin les murs de la Bastille; mais on n'a pas vu encore tomber le despotisme que j'attaque. Je me vois donc réduite à essayer de l'abattre. C'est un arbre au milieu d'un labyrinthe touffu, hérissé de ronces et d'épines: pour émonder ses branches, il faudrait toute la magie de Médée. La conquête de la toison d'or coûta moins de soins et d'adresse à Jason que ne vont me coûter de tourments et de pièges à éviter ces branches empoisonnées qui font du tort à l'arbre célèbre et au génie de l'homme. Pour les détruire, il faut terrasser vingt dragons dangereux qui, tantôt se transformant en citoyens zélés, tantôt en serpents flexibles, se glissent partout, et sèment leur venin sur mes ouvrages et mon personnel.

Mais, à mon tour, ne dois-je pas, Monsieur, avec plus de raison vous soupçonner de vous être mis vous-même *honorablement* en avant pour cette faction rampante qui s'est élevée contre l'*Esclavage des nègres*? Qu'imputez-vous à cet ouvrage? qu'imputez-vous à l'auteur? Est-ce d'avoir cherché à faire égorger en Amérique les colons, et d'avoir été l'agent d'hommes que je connais moins que vous, qui peut-être n'estiment pas toutes mes productions depuis que j'ai montré que l'abus de la liberté avait produit beaucoup de mal? Vous me connaissez bien peu. J'étais l'apôtre d'une douce liberté dans le temps même du despotisme. Mais véritable Française, j'idolâtre ma patrie: j'ai tout sacrifié pour elle; je chéris au même degré mon roi, et je donnerais mon sang pour lui rendre tout ce que ses vertus et sa tendresse paternelle méritent. Je ne sacrifierais ni mon roi à ma patrie, ni ma patrie à mon roi, mais je me sacrifierais pour les sauver ensemble, bien persuadée que l'un ne peut exister sans l'autre. On connaît l'homme, dit-on, par ses écrits. Lisez-moi, Monsieur, depuis ma *lettre au peuple* jusques à ma *lettre à la nation,* et vous y reconnaîtrez, j'ose m'en flatter, un coeur et un esprit véritablement Français. Les partis extrêmes ont toujours craint et détesté mes productions. Ces deux partis, divisés par des intérêts opposés, sont toujours démasqués dans mes écrits. Mes maximes invariables, mes sentiments incorruptibles, voilà mes principes. Royaliste et véritable patriote, à la vie à la mort, je me montre telle que je suis.

Puisque j'ai le courage de signer cet écrit, montrez-vous de même, et vous obtiendrez mon estime qui n'est pas peut-être indifférente pour un galant homme: car je l'accorde aussi difficilement que Jean-Jacques. Je puis m'élever jusqu'à ce grand homme par la juste défiance qu'il eut des hommes: j'en ai peu rencontré de justes et de véritablement estimables. Ce n'est pas de légers défauts que je leur reproche; mais leurs vices, leur fausseté et leur inhumanité exercées sans remords sur les plus faibles. Puisse cette révolution régénérer l'esprit et la conscience des hommes, et reproduire le véritable caractère Français! Deux mots encore, je vous prie.

Je ne suis point instruite comme il vous a plu de m'en accorder la gloire. Peut-être un jour mon ignorance attachera quelque célébrité à ma mémoire. Je ne sais rien, Monsieur; rien, vous dis-je, et l'on ne m'a rien appris. Elève de la simple nature, abandonnée à ses seuls soins, elle m'a donc bien éclairée, puisque vous me croyez parfaitement instruite. Sans connaître l'histoire de l'Amérique, cette odieuse traite des nègres a toujours soulevé mon âme, excité mon indignation.

Les premieres idées dramatiques que j'ai déposées sur le papier, furent en faveur de cette espèce d'hommes tyrannisés avec cruauté depuis tant de siècles. Cette faible production se ressent peut-être un peu trop d'un début dans la carriere dramatique. Nos grands hommes mêmes n'ont pas tous commencé comme ils ont fini, et un essai mérite toujours quelqu'indulgence. Je puis donc vous attester, Monsieur, que les amis des noirs n'existaient pas quand j'ai conçu ce sujet, et vous deviez plutôt présumer, si la prévention ne vous eût pas aveuglé, que c'est peut-être d'après mon drame que cette société s'est formée, ou que j'ai eu l'heureux mérite de me rencontrer noblement avec elle. Puisse-t-il en former une plus générale, et l'entraîner plus souvent à sa représentation! Je n'ai point voulu enchaîner l'opinion du public à mon patriotisme: j'ai attendu avec patience son heureux retour en faveur de ce drame. Avec quelle satisfaction je me suis entendu dire de toute part, que les changements que j'avais faits répandaient sur cette pièce un grand intérêt qui ne pourra que s'augmenter, quand le public va être instruit que, depuis quatre mois, j'ai dédié cet ouvrage à la nation, et que j'en ai consacré le produit à la caisse patriotique; établissement dont j'ai présenté le projet dans ma *lettre au peuple,* publiée depuis dix-huit mois! Cette priorité m'autorise peut-être, sans vanité, à m'en regarder comme l'auteur. Cette brochure fit beaucoup de bruit dans le temps, fut de même critiquée, et le projet qu'elle offrait n'a pas été moins réalisé avec succès. Je devais vous instruire, ainsi que le public, de ces faits qui caractérisent l'amour que j'ai pour le véritable caractère Français, et les efforts que je fais pour sa conservation. Je ne doute pas que la Comédie, touchée de ces actes de zèle, ne conspire à donner des jours favorables* à la représentation de ce drame, auquel je ne puis me dissimuler qu'elle s'intéresse infiniment. Elle m'en a donné des preuves que je ne puis révoquer en doute. L'auteur, la comédie et le public contribueront ensemble, en multipliant leurs plaisirs, à grossir les fonds de la caisse patriotique qui peut seule sauver l'état, si tous les citoyens reconnaissent cette vérité.

Je dois encore observer que dans ces représentations patriotiques, plusieurs personnes ont payé souvent au-dessus de leurs places. Si celle-ci produit la même disposition de coeur, il faudra distinguer les profits de la caisse patriotiques des droits de la comédie. Une liste exacte, remise à la nation de la part des Comédiens, donnera la preuve de l'ordre et du zèle de ces nouveaux citoyens.

J'espère, Monsieur, et j'ose m'en flatter, que d'après les éclaircissements que je vous donne sur l'*esclavage des nègres,* vous ne le poursuivrez plus, et que vous deviendrez au contraire le zélé protecteur de ce drame; en le faisant même représenter en Amérique, il ramènera toujours les hommes noirs à leurs devoirs, en attendant des colons et de la nation française l'abolition de la traite, et un sort plus heureux. Voilà les dispositions que j'ai montrées dans cet ouvrage. Je n'ai point prétendu, d'après les circonstances, en faire un flambeau de discorde, un signal d'insurrection; j'en ai, au contraire, depuis, adouci l'effet. Pour peu que vous doutiez de cette assertion, lisez, je vous prie, l'*heureux naufrage* imprimé depuis trois ans; et si j'ai fait quelqu'allusion à des hommes chers à la France, ces allusions ne sont point nuisibles à l'Amérique. C'est ce dont vous serez convaincu à la représentation de cette pièce, si vous voulez me faire l'honneur d'y venir. C'est dans ce doux espoir que je vous prie de me croire, Monsieur, malgré notre petite discussion littéraire, suivant le protocole reçu, votre très-humble servante,

DeGouge
Paris, le 18 janvier 1790.

POST-SCRIPTUM

J'aurais cru me compromettre, si j'avais répondu dans le corps de cette lettre à toutes les ordures qu'un infâme libelliste vient de répandre sur mon compte dans sa feuille mercenaire. Il me suffit de rappeler au public, pour confondre cet abominable calomniateur, *la lettre écrite à M. le duc d'Orléans, La motion,* ou *séance royale.* Le public reconnaîtra que j'employai auprès de ce prince la voix de l'honneur pour le ramener à son devoir, s'il s'en était écarté; mais en même temps ces écrits le démasquaient, s'il était coupable. J'ignore s'il l'est en effet, mais ce dont je suis convaincue, c'est que mon fils a été sacrifié et vient de perdre sa place dans la maison de ce prince. Voilà ma justification.

*Chacun sait que lorsque les comédiens ne prennent pas à un auteur tout l'intérêt possible, ils ne lui accordent pour la représentation de son ouvrage, que les mauvais jours, c'est-à-dire, les mardis, jeudis et vendredis, et encore ne représentent-ils le plus souvent qu'avec des pieces usées, et peu susceptibles d'attirer le concours et l'affluence. [This remark by Gouges appears in the original.]

Germaine de Staël

MIRZA, OU LETTRES D'UN VOYAGEUR[1]
(1795)

Préface

On comprendra bien, je pense, que l'Essai sur les fictions, qu'on vient de lire, a été composé après les trois Nouvelles que je publie ici; aucune ne mérite le nom de roman; les situations y sont indiquées plutôt que développées, et c'est dans la peinture de quelques sentiments du coeur qu'est leur seul mérite. Je n'avais pas vingt ans quand je les ai écrites, et la révolution de France n'existait point encore. Je veux croire que, depuis, mon esprit a acquis assez de force pour se livrer à des ouvrages plus utiles. On dit que le malheur hâte le développement de toutes les facultés morales; quelquefois je crains qu'il ne produise un effet contraire, qu'il ne jette dans un abattement qui détache et de soi-même et des autres. La grandeur des événements qui nous entourent fait si bien sentir le néant des pensées générales, l'impuissance des sentiments individuels, que, perdu dans la vie, on ne sait plus quelle route doit suivre l'espérance, quel mobile doit exciter les efforts, quel principe guidera désormais l'opinion publique à travers les erreurs de l'esprit de parti, et marquera de nouveau, dans toutes les carrières, le but éclatant de la véritable gloire.

Permettez que je vous rende compte, madame, d'une anecdote de mon voyage, qui peut-être aura le droit de vous intéresser. J'appris à Gorée, il y a un mois, que monsieur le gouverneur avait déterminé une famille nègre à venir demeurer à quelques lieues de là, pour y établir une habitation pareille à celle de Saint-Domingue; se flattant,

---

1. The texts by Germaine de Staël follow the French reprint of the *Oeuvres Complètes*, Geneva: Slatkine, 1967.

sans doute, qu'un tel exemple exciterait les Africains à la culture du sucre, et qu'attirant chez eux le commerce libre de cette denrée, les Européens ne les enlèveraient plus à leur patrie, pour leur faire souffrir le joug affreux de l'esclavage. Vainement les écrivains les plus éloquents ont tenté d'obtenir cette révolution de la vertu des hommes; l'administrateur éclairé, désespérant de triompher de l'intérêt personnel, voudrait le mettre du parti de l'humanité, en ne lui faisant plus trouver son avantage à la braver; mais les nègres, imprévoyants de l'avenir pour eux-mêmes, sont plus incapables encore de porter leurs pensées sur les générations futures, et se refusent au mal présent, sans le comparer au sort qu'il pourrait leur éviter. Un seul Africain, délivré de l'esclavage par la générosité du gouverneur, s'était prêté à ses projets; prince dans son pays, quelques nègres d'un état subalterne l'avaient suivi, et cultivaient son habitation sous ses ordres. Je demandai qu'on m'y conduisit. Je marchai une partie du jour, et j'arrivai le soir près d'une maison que des Français, m'a-t-on dit, avaient aidé à bâtir, mais qui conservait encore cependant quelque chose de sauvage. Quand j'approchai, les nègres jouissaient de leur moment de délassement; ils s'amusaient à tirer de l'arc, regrettant peut-être le temps où ce plaisir était leur seule occupation. Ourika, femme de Ximéo (c'est le nom du nègre chef de l'habitation), était assise à quelque distance des jeux, et regardait avec distraction sa fille âgée de deux ans, qui s'amusait à ses pieds. Mon guide avança vers elle, et lui dit que je lui demandais asile de la part du gouverneur. «C'est le gouverneur qui l'envoie! s'écria-t-elle. Ah! qu'il entre, qu'il soit le bienvenu; tout ce que nous avons est à lui.» Elle vint à moi avec précipitation: sa beauté m'enchanta; elle possédait le vrai charme de son sexe, tout ce qui peint la faiblesse et la grâce. «Où donc est Ximéo? lui dit mon guide.— Il n'est pas revenu, répondit-elle, il fait sa promenade du soir; quand le soleil ne sera plus sur l'horizon, quand le crépuscule même ne rappellera plus la clarté, il reviendra, et il ne fera plus nuit pour moi.» En achevant ces mots, elle soupira, s'éloigna, et quand elle se rapprocha de nous, j'aperçus des traces de pleurs sur son visage. Nous entrâmes dans la cabane; on nous servit un repas composé de tous les fruits du pays: j'en goûtais avec plaisir, avide de sensations nouvelles. On frappe: Ourika tressaille, se lève avec précipitation, ouvre la porte de la cabane, et se jette dans les bras de Ximéo, qui l'embrasse sans paraître se douter lui-même de ce qu'il faisait, ni de ce qu'il voyait. Je vais à lui; vous ne pouvez pas imaginer une figure plus ravissante: ses traits n'avaient aucun des défauts des hommes de sa couleur; son regard produisait un effet que je n'ai jamais ressenti; il disposait de l'âme, et la mélancolie qu'il exprimait passait dans le coeur de celui sur lequel il s'attachait; la taille de l'Apollon du Belvédère n'est pas plus parfaite: peut-être pouvait-on le trouver trop mince pour un homme; mais l'abattement de la douleur que tous ses mouvements annonçaient, que sa physionomie peignait, s'accordait mieux avec la délicatesse qu'avec la force. Il ne fut point surpris de nous voir; il paraissait inaccessible à toute émotion étrangère à son idée dominante; nous lui apprîmes quel était celui qui nous envoyait, et le but de notre voyage. «Le gouverneur, nous dit-il, a des droits sur ma reconnaissance; dans l'état où je suis, le croirez-vous, j'ai cependant un bienfaiteur.» Il nous parla quelque temps des motifs qui l'avaient déterminé à cultiver une habitation, et j'étais étonné de son esprit, de sa facilité à s'expliquer: il s'en aperçut. «Vous êtes surpris, me dit-il, quand nous ne sommes pas au niveau des brutes, dont vous nous donnez la destinée?—Non, lui répondis-je; mais un Français même ne parlerait pas sa langue mieux que vous.—Ah! Vous avez raison, reprit-il; on conserve encore quelques rayons lorsqu'on a long-temps vécu près d'un ange.» Et ses beaux yeux se baissèrent pour ne plus rien voir au dehors de lui. Ourika répandait des larmes: Ximéo s'en aperçut enfin. «Pardonne, s'écria-t-il en lui prenant la main, pardonne: le présent est à toi; souffre les souvenirs. Demain, dit-il en se retournant vers moi, demain nous parcourrons ensemble mon habitation; vous verrez si je puis me flatter qu'elle réponde aux désirs du gouverneur. Le meilleur lit va vous être préparé; dormez tranquillement: je voudrais que vous fussiez bien ici. Les hommes infortunés par le coeur, me dit-il à voix basse, ne craignent point, désirent même le spectacle du bonheur des autres.» Je me couchai, je ne fermai pas l'oeil; j'étais pénétré de tristesse, tout ce que j'avais vu en portait l'empreinte, j'en ignorais la cause; mais je me sentais ému comme on l'est en contemplant un tableau qui représente la mélancolie. A la pointe du jour je me levai; je trouvai Ximéo encore plus abattu que la veille; je lui en demandai la raison. «Ma douleur,» répondit-il, fixée dans mon coeur, ne peut s'accroître ni diminuer; mais l'uniformité de la vie la fait passer plus vite, et des événements nouveaux, quels qu'ils soient, font naître de nouvelles réflexions, qui sont toujours de nouvelles sources de larmes.» Il me fit voir avec un soin extrême toute son habitation; je fus surpris de l'ordre qui s'y faisait remarquer; elle rendait au moins autant qu'un pareil espace de terrain cultivé à Saint-Domingue par un même nombre d'hommes, et les nègres heureux n'étaient point accablés de travail. Je vis avec plaisir que la cruauté était inutile, qu'elle avait cela de plus. Je demandai à Ximéo qui lui avait donné des conseils sur la culture de la terre, sur la division de la journée des ouvriers. «J'en ai peu reçu, me répondit-il, mais la raison peut atteindre à ce que la raison a trouvé: puisqu'il était défendu de mourir, il fallait bien consacrer sa vie aux autres; qu'en aurais-je fait pour moi? J'avais horreur de l'esclavage, je ne pouvais concevoir le barbare dessein des hommes de votre couleur. Je pensais quelquefois que leur Dieu ennemi du nôtre leur avait commandé de nous faire souffrir: mais quand j'appris qu'une production de notre pays, négligée par nous, causait seule ces maux cruels aux malheureux Africains, j'acceptai l'offre qui me fut faite de leur donner l'exemple de la cultiver. Puisse un commerce libre s'établir entre les deux parties du monde! puissent mes infortunés compatriotes renoncer à la vie sauvage, se vouer au travail pour satisfaire vos avides désirs, et contribuer à sauver quelques-uns d'entre eux de la plus horrible destinée! puissent ceux même qui pourraient se flatter d'éviter un tel sort, s'occuper avec un zèle égal d'en garantir à jamais leurs semblables!» En me parlant ainsi, nous approchâmes d'une porte qui conduisait à un bois épais, dont un côté de l'habitation était bordé; je crus que Ximéo allait l'ouvrir, mais il se détourna pour l'éviter. «Pourquoi, lui dis-je, ne me montrez-vous pas . . . ?—Arrêtez, s'écria-t-il, vous avez l'air sensible; pourrez-vous entendre les longs récits du malheur? Il y a deux ans que je n'ai parlé; tout ce que je dis, ce n'est pas parler. Vous le voyez, j'ai besoin de m'épancher: vous ne devez pas être flatté de ma confiance; cependant, c'est votre bonté qui m'encourage, et me fait compter sur votre pitié.—Ah! ne craignez rien, répondis-je, vous ne serez pas trompé.—Je suis né dans le royaume de Cayor; mon père, de sang royal, était chef de quelques tribus qui lui étaient confiées par le souverain. On m'exerça de bonne heure dans l'art de défendre mon pays, et dès mon enfance l'arc et le javelot m'étaient familiers. L'on me destina dès lors pour femme Ourika, fille de la soeur de mon père; je l'aimai dès que je pus aimer, et cette faculté se développa en moi pour elle et par elle. Sa beauté parfaite me frappa davantage quand je l'eus comparée à celle des autres femmes, et je revins par choix à mon premier penchant. Nous étions souvent en guerre contre les Jaloffes nos voisins; et comme nous avions mutuellement l'atroce coutume de vendre nos prisonniers de guerre aux Européens, une haine profonde, que la paix même ne suspendait pas, ne permettait entre nous aucune communication. Un jour, en chassant dans nos montagnes, je fus entraîné plus loin que je ne voulais; une voix de femme, remarquable par sa beauté, se fit entendre à moi. J'écoutai ce qu'elle chantait, et je ne reconnus point les paroles que les jeunes filles se plaisent à répéter. L'amour de la liberté, l'horreur de l'esclavage, étaient le sujet des nobles hymnes qui me ravirent d'admiration. J'approchai: une jeune personne se leva; frappé du contraste de son âge et du sujet de ses méditations, je cherchais dans ses traits quelque chose de surnaturel, qui m'annonçât l'inspiration qui supplée aux longues réflexions de la vieillesse; elle n'était pas belle, mais sa taille noble et régulière, ses yeux enchanteurs, sa physionomie animée, ne laissaient à l'amour même rien à désirer pour sa figure. Elle vint à moi, et me parla longtemps sans que je pusse lui répondre: enfin, je parvins à lui peindre mon étonnement; il s'accrut quand j'appris qu'elle avait composé les paroles que je venais d'entendre. «Cessez d'être surpris, me dit-elle; un Français établi au Sénégal, mécontent de son sort et malheureux dans sa patrie, s'est retiré parmi nous; ce vieillard a daigné prendre soin de ma jeunesse, et m'a donné ce que les Européens ont de digne d'envie: les connaissances dont ils abusent, et la philosophie dont ils suivent si mal les leçons. J'ai appris la langue des Français, j'ai lu quelques-uns de leurs livres, et je m'amuse à penser seule sur ces montagnes.» A chaque mot qu'elle me disait, mon intérêt, ma curiosité redoublaient; ce n'était plus une femme, c'était un poète que je croyais entendre parler; et jamais les hommes qui se consacrent parmi nous au culte des dieux, ne m'avaient paru remplis d'un si noble enthousiasme. En la quittant, j'obtins la permission de la revoir; son souvenir me suivait partout; j'emportais plus d'admiration que d'amour, et me fiant longtemps sur cette différence, je vis Mirza (c'était le nom de cette jeune Jaloffe), sans croire offenser Ourika. Enfin, un jour je lui demandai si jamais elle avait aimé; en tremblant je faisais cette question, mais son esprit facile et son caractère ouvert lui rendaient toutes ses réponses aisées. «Non, me dit-elle: on m'a aimé quelquefois; j'ai peut-être désiré d'être sensible; je voulais connaître ce sentiment qui s'empare de toute la vie, et fait à lui seul le sort de chaque instant du jour; mais j'ai trop réfléchi, je crois, pour éprouver cette illusion; je sens tous les mouvements de mon coeur, et je vois tous ceux des autres; je n'ai pu jusqu'à ce jour ni me tromper, ni être trompée.» Ce dernier mot m'affligea. «Mirza, lui dis-je, que je vous plains! les plaisirs de la pensée n'occupent pas tout entier; ceux du coeur seul suffisent à toutes les facultés de l'âme.» Elle m'instruisait cependant avec une bonté que rien ne lassait; en peu de temps j'appris tout ce qu'elle savait. Quand je l'interrompais par mes éloges, elle ne m'écoutait pas; dès que je cessais, elle continuait, et je voyais, par ses discours, que pendant que je la louais, c'était à moi seul qu'elle avait toujours pensé. Enfin, enivré de sa grâce, de son esprit, de ses regards, je sentis que je l'aimais, et j'osai le lui dire: quelles expressions n'employai-je pas pour faire passer dans son coeur l'exaltation que j'avais trouvée dans son esprit! Je mourais à ses pieds de passion et de crainte. «Mirza, lui répétai-je, place-moi sur le monde en me disant que tu m'aimes, ouvre-moi le ciel pour que j'y monte avec toi.» En m'écoutant elle se troubla, et des larmes remplirent ses beaux yeux, où jusqu'alors je n'avais vu que l'expression du génie. «Ximéo, me dit-elle, demain je te répondrai; n'attends pas de moi l'art des femmes de ton pays; demain tu liras dans mon coeur; réfléchis sur le tien.» En achevant ces mots, elle me quitta longtemps avant le coucher du soleil, signal ordinaire de sa retraite; je ne cherchai point à la retenir. L'ascendant de son caractère me soumettait à ses volontés. Depuis que je connaissais Mirza, je voyais moins Ourika; je la trompais, je prétextais des voyages, je retardais l'instant de notre union, j'éloignais l'avenir au lieu d'en décider.

«Enfin, le lendemain, que des siècles pour moi semblaient avoir séparé de la veille, j'arrive: Mirza la première s'avance vers moi; elle avait l'air abattu; soit pressentiment, soit tendresse, elle avait passé ce jour dans les larmes. «Ximéo, me dit-elle d'un son de voix doux, mais assuré, es-tu bien sûr que tu m'aimes? est-il certain que dans tes vastes contrées aucun objet n'a fixé ton coeur?» Des serments furent ma réponse. «Eh bien, je t'en crois, la nature qui nous environne est seule témoin de tes promesses; je ne sais rien sur toi que je n'aie appris de ta bouche; mon isolement, mon abandon fait toute ma sécurité. Quelle défiance, quel obstacle ai-je opposé à ta volonté? tu ne tromperais en moi que mon estime pour Ximéo, tu ne te vengerais que de mon amour; ma famille, mes amies, mes concitoyens, j'ai tout éloigné pour dépendre de toi seul; je dois être à tes yeux sacrée comme la faiblesse, l'enfance et le malheur; non, je ne puis rien craindre, non.» Je l'interrompis; j'étais à ses pieds, je croyais être vrai, la force du présent m'avait fait oublier le passé comme l'avenir; j'avais trompé, j'avais persuadé; elle me crut. Dieux! que d'expressions passionnées elle sut trouver! qu'elle était heureuse en aimant! Ah! pendant deux mois qui s'écoulèrent ainsi, tout ce qu'il y a d'amour et de bonheur fut rassemblé dans son coeur. Je jouissais, mais je me calmais. Bizarrerie de la nature humaine! j'étais si frappé du plaisir qu'elle avait à me voir, que je commençai bientôt à venir plutôt pour elle que pour moi: j'étais si certain de son accueil, que je ne tremblais plus en l'approchant. Mirza ne s'en apercevait pas; elle parlait, elle répondait, elle pleurait, elle se consolait, et son âme active agissait sur elle-même; honteux de moi-même, j'avais besoin de m'éloigner d'elle. La guerre se déclara dans une autre extrémité du royaume de Cayor, je résolus d'y courir; il fallait l'annoncer à Mirza. Ah! dans ce moment je sentis encore combien elle m'était chère; sa confiante et douce sécurité m'ôta la force de lui découvrir mon projet. Elle semblait tellement vivre de ma présence, que ma langue se glaça quand je voulus lui parler de mon départ. Je résolus de lui écrire; cet art qu'elle m'avait appris devait

servir à son malheur; vingt fois je la quittai, vingt fois je revins sur
mes pas. L'infortunée en jouissait, et prenait ma pitié pour de l'amour.
Enfin, je partis; je lui mandai que mon devoir me forçait à me séparer
d'elle, mais que je reviendrais à ses pieds plus tendre que jamais.
Quelle réponse elle me fit! Ah! langue de l'amour, quel charme tu
reçois quand la pensée t'embellit! quel désespoir de mon absence!
quelle passion de me revoir! Je frémis alors en songeant à quel excès
son coeur savait aimer; mais mon père n'aurait jamais nommé sa fille
une femme du pays des Jaloffes. Tous les obstacles s'offrirent à ma
pensée quand le voile qui me les cachait fut tombé; je revis Ourika;
sa beauté, ses larmes, l'empire d'un premier penchant, les instances
d'une famille entière; que sais-je enfin? tout ce qui paraît insurmon-
table quand on ne tire plus sa force de son coeur, me rendit infidèle
et mes liens avec Ourika furent formés en présence des dieux. Cependant le temps que j'avais fixé à Mirza pour mon retour approchait; je
voulus la revoir encore: j'espérais adoucir le coup que j'allais lui porter, je le croyais possible; quand on n'a plus d'amour on n'en devine
plus les effets, l'on ne sait pas même s'aider de ses souvenirs. De quel
sentiment je fus rempli en parcourant ces mêmes lieux témoins de
mes serments et de mon bonheur! Rien n'était changé que mon coeur,
et je pouvais à peine les reconnaître. Pour Mirza, dès qu'elle me vit,
je crois qu'elle éprouva en un moment le bonheur qu'on goûte à peine
épars dans toute sa vie, et c'est ainsi que les dieux s'acquittèrent envers
elle. Ah! comment vous dirais-je par quels degrés affreux j'amenai
la malheureuse Mirza à connaître l'état de mon coeur? Mes lèvres
tremblantes prononcèrent le nom d'amitié «Ton amitié! s'écria-t-elle;
ton amitié, barbare! est-ce à mon âme qu'un tel sentiment doit être
offert? Va, donne-moi la mort. Va, c'est là maintenant tout ce que tu
peux pour moi.» L'excès de sa douleur semblait l'y conduire; elle
tomba sans mouvement à mes pieds: monstre que j'étais! c'était alors
qu'il fallait la tromper, c'était alors que je fus vrai. «Insensible, laisse-
moi, me dit-elle; ce vieillard qui prit soin de mon enfance, qui m'a
servi de père, peut vivre encore quelque temps; il faut que j'existe
pour lui: je suis morte déjà là, dit-elle en posant la main sur son
coeur; mais mes soins lui sont nécessaires; laisse-moi.—Je ne pourrais,
m'écriai-je, je ne pourrais supporter ta haine.—Ma haine! me répondit-elle; ne la crains pas Ximéo; il y a des coeurs qui ne savent
qu'aimer, et dont toute la passion ne retourne que contre eux-mêmes.
Adieu, Ximéo; une autre va donc posséder . . .—Non, jamais, non,
jamais, lui dis-je.—Je ne te crois pas à présent, reprit-elle; hier tes
paroles m'auraient fait douter du jour qui nous éclaire. Ximéo, serre-
moi contre ton coeur, appelle-moi ta maîtresse chérie; retrouve l'accent d'autrefois; que je l'entende encore, non pour en jouir, mais pour

m'en ressouvenir: mais c'est impossible. Adieu, je le retrouverai seule, mon coeur l'entendra toujours; c'est la cause de mort que je porte et retiens dans mon sein. Ximéo, adieu.» Le son touchant de ce dernier mot, l'effort qu'elle fit en s'éloignant, tout m'est présent; elle est devant mes yeux. Dieux! rendez cette illusion plus forte; que je la voie un moment, pour, s'il se peut encore, mieux sentir ce que j'ai perdu. Longtemps immobile dans les lieux qu'elle avait quittés, égaré, troublé comme un homme qui vient de commettre un grand crime, la nuit me surprit avant que je pensasse à retourner chez moi; le remords, le souvenir, le sentiment du malheur de Mirza s'attachaient à mon âme; son ombre me revenait comme si la fin de son bonheur eût été celle de sa vie.

«La guerre se déclara contre les Jaloffes; il fallait combattre contre les habitants du pays de Mirza; je voulais à ses yeux acquérir de la gloire, justifier son choix, et mériter encore le bonheur auquel j'avais renoncé; je craignais peu la mort; j'avais fait de ma vie un si cruel usage, que je la risquais peut-être avec un secret plaisir. Je fus dangereusement blessé: j'appris, en me rétablissant, qu'une femme venait tous les jours se placer devant le seuil de ma porte; immobile, elle tressaillait au moindre bruit: une fois j'étais plus mal, elle perdit connaissance; on s'empressa autour d'elle, elle se ranima, et prononça ces mots: «Qu'il ignore, dit-elle, l'état où vous m'avez vue; je suis pour lui bien moins qu'une étrangère, mon intérêt doit l'affliger.» Enfin un jour, jour affreux! faible encore, ma famille, Ourika, étaient auprès de moi: j'étais calme quand j'éloignais le souvenir de celle dont j'avais causé le désespoir; je croyais l'être du moins; la fatalité m'avait conduit, j'avais agi comme un homme gouverné par elle, et je redoutais tellement l'instant du repentir, que j'employais toutes mes forces pour retenir ma pensée prête à se fixer sur le passé. Nos ennemis, les Jaloffes, fondirent tout à coup sur le bourg que j'habitais: nous étions sans défense; nous soutînmes cependant une assez longue attaque; mais enfin ils l'emportèrent et firent plusieurs prisonniers: je fus du nombre. Quel moment pour moi quand je me vis chargé de fers! Les cruels Hottentots ne destinent aux vaincus que la mort; mais nous, plus lâchement barbares, nous servons nos communs ennemis, et justifions leurs crimes en devenant leurs complices. Un détachement de Jaloffes nous fit marcher toute la nuit; quand le jour vint nous éclairer, nous nous trouvâmes sur le bord de la rivière du Sénégal: des barques étaient préparées; je vis des blancs, je fus certain de mon sort. Bientôt mes conducteurs commencèrent à traiter des viles conditions de leur infâme échange: les Européens examinaient curieusement notre âge et notre force, pour y trouver l'espoir de nous faire supporter plus longtemps les maux qu'ils nous destinaient. Déjà j'étais déterminé; j'espérais qu'en passant sur cette fatale barque, mes chaînes se relâcheraient assez pour me laisser le pouvoir de m'élancer dans la rivière, et que, malgré les prompts secours de mes avides possesseurs, le poids de mes fers m'entraînerait jusqu'au fond de l'abîme. Mes yeux fixés sur la terre, ma pensée attachée à la terrible espérance que j'embrassais, j'étais comme séparé des objets qui m'environnaient. Tout à coup une voix que le bonheur et la peine m'avaient appris à connaître, fait tressaillir mon coeur, et m'arrache à mon immobile méditation; je regarde, j'aperçois Mirza, belle, non comme une mortelle, mais comme un ange, car c'était son âme qui se peignait sur son visage; je l'entends qui demande aux Européens de l'écouter: sa voix était émue, mais ce n'était point la frayeur ni l'attendrissement qui l'altéraient; un mouvement surnaturel donnait à toute sa personne un caractère nouveau. «Européens, dit-elle, c'est pour cultiver nos terres que vous nous condamnez à l'esclavage; c'est votre intérêt qui vous rend notre infortune nécessaire; vous ne ressemblez pas au dieu du mal, et faire souffrir n'est pas le but des douleurs que vous nous destinez: regardez ce jeune homme affaibli par ses blessures, il ne pourra supporter ni la longueur du voyage, ni les travaux que vous lui demandez; moi, vous voyez ma force et ma jeunesse, mon sexe n'a point énervé mon courage; souffrez que je sois esclave à la place de Ximéo. Je vivrai, puisque c'est à ce prix que vous m'aurez accordé la liberté de Ximéo; je ne croirai plus l'esclavage avilissant, je respecterai la puissance de mes maîtres; c'est de moi qu'ils la tiendront, et leurs bienfaits l'auront consacrée. Ximéo doit chérir la vie; Ximéo est aimé! Moi, je ne tiens à personne sur la terre; je puis en disparaître sans laisser de vide dans un coeur qui sente que je n'existe plus. J'allais finir mes jours, un bonheur nouveau me fait survivre à mon coeur. Ah! laissez-vous attendrir, et quand votre pitié ne combat pas votre intérêt, ne résistez pas à sa voix.» En achevant ces mots, cette fière Mirza, que la crainte de la mort n'aurait pas fait tomber aux pieds des rois de la terre, fléchit humblement le genou; mais elle conservait dans cette attitude encore toute sa dignité, et l'admiration et la honte étaient le partage de ceux qu'elle implorait. Un moment elle put penser que j'acceptais sa générosité; j'avais perdu la parole, et je me mourais du tourment de ne la pas retrouver. Ces farouches Européens s'écrièrent tous d'une voix: «Nous acceptons l'échange; elle est belle, elle est jeune, elle est courageuse; nous voulons la négresse, et nous laissons son ami.» Je retrouvai mes forces; ils allaient s'approcher de Mirza. «Barbares, m'écriai-je, c'est à moi, jamais, jamais; respectez son sexe, sa faiblesse. Jaloffes, consentirez-vous qu'une femme de votre contrée soit esclave à la place de votre plus cruel ennemi?—Arrête, me dit Mirza, cesse d'être généreux; cet acte de vertu, c'est pour toi seul que tu l'accomplis; si mon bonheur t'avait été cher, tu ne m'aurais pas abandonnée; je t'aime mieux coupable, quand je te sais insensible: laisse-moi le droit de me plaindre; quand tu ne peux m'ôter ma douleur, ne m'arrache pas le seul bonheur qui me reste, la douce pensée de tenir au moins à toi par le bien que je t'aurai fait: j'ai suivi tes destins, je meurs si mes jours ne te sont pas utiles; tu n'as que ce moyen de me sauver la vie; ose persister dans tes refus.» Depuis, je me suis rappelé toutes ses paroles, et dans l'instant je crois que je ne les entendais pas: je frémissais du dessein de Mirza; je tremblais que ces vils Européens ne le secondassent; je n'osais déclarer que rien ne me séparerait d'elle. Ces avides marchands nous auraient entraînés tous les deux: leur coeur, incapable de sensibilité, comptait peut-être déjà sur les effets de la nôtre; déjà même ils se promettaient à l'avenir de choisir pour captifs ceux que l'amour ou le devoir pourraient faire racheter ou suivre, étudiant nos vertus pour les faire servir à leurs vices. Mais le gouverneur, instruit de nos combats, du dévouement de Mirza, de mon désespoir, s'avance comme un ange de lumière; eh! qui n'aurait pas cru qu'il nous apportait le bonheur! «Soyez libres tous deux, nous dit-il. Je vous rends à votre pays comme à votre amour. Tant de grandeur d'âme eût fait rougir l'Européen qui vous aurait nommés ses esclaves.» On m'ôta mes fers, j'embrassai ses genoux, je bénis dans mon coeur sa bonté, comme s'il eût sacrifié des droits légitimes. Ah! les usurpateurs peuvent donc, en renonçant à leurs injustices, atteindre au rang de bienfaiteurs. Je me levai, je croyais que Mirza était aux pieds du gouverneur comme moi; je la vis à quelque distance, appuyée sur un arbre, et rêvant profondément. Je courus vers elle: l'amour, l'admiration, la reconnaissance, j'éprouvais, j'exprimais tout à la fois. «Ximéo, me dit-elle, il n'est plus temps; mon malheur est gravé trop avant pour que ta main même y puisse atteindre: ta voix, je ne l'entends plus sans tressaillir de peine, et ta présence glace dans mes veines ce sang qui jadis y bouillonnait pour toi; les âmes passionnées ne connaissent que les extrêmes; l'intervalle qui les sépare, elles le franchissent sans s'y arrêter jamais: quand tu m'appris mon sort, j'en doutai longtemps; tu pouvais revenir alors; j'aurais cru que j'avais rêvé ton inconstance; mais maintenant, pour anéantir ce souvenir, il faut percer le coeur dont rien ne peut l'effacer.» En prononçant ces paroles, la flèche mortelle était dans son sein. Dieux qui suspendîtes en cet instant ma vie, me l'avez-vous rendue pour mieux venger Mirza par le long supplice de ma douleur! Pendant un mois entier, la chaîne des souvenirs et des pensées fut interrompue pour moi; je crois quelquefois que je suis dans un autre monde, dont l'enfer est le souvenir du premier. Ourika m'a fait promettre de ne pas attenter à mes jours; le gouverneur m'a convaincu qu'il fallait vivre pour être utile à mes malheureux compatriotes, pour respecter la dernière volonté de Mirza, qui l'a conjuré, dit-il, en mourant, de veiller sur moi, de me consoler en son nom: j'obéis, j'ai renfermé dans un tombeau les tristes restes de celle que j'aime quand elle n'est plus, de celle que j'ai méconnue pendant sa vie. Là, seul quand le soleil se couche, quand la nature entière semble se couvrir de mon deuil, quand le silence universel me permet de n'entendre plus que mes pensées, j'éprouve, prosterné sur ce tombeau, la jouissance du malheur, le sentiment tout entier de ses peines; mon imagination exaltée crée quelquefois des fantômes; je crois la voir, mais jamais elle ne m'apparaît comme une amante irritée. Je l'entends qui me console et s'occupe de ma douleur. Enfin, incertain du sort qui nous attend après nous, je respecte en mon coeur le souvenir de Mirza, et crains, en me donnant la mort, d'anéantir tout ce qui reste d'elle. Depuis deux ans, vous êtes la seule personne à qui j'aie confié ma douleur: je n'attends pas votre pitié; un barbare qui cause la mort de celle qu'il regrette, doit-il intéresser? Mais j'ai voulu parler d'elle. Ah! promettez-moi que vous n'oublierez pas le nom de Mirza; nous le direz à vos enfants, et vous conserverez après moi la mémoire de cet ange d'amour, et de cette victime du malheur.» En terminant son récit, une sombre rêverie se peignit sur le charmant visage de Ximéo; j'étais baigné de pleurs, je voulus lui parler. «Crois-tu, me dit-il, qu'il faille chercher à me consoler? crois-tu qu'on puisse avoir sur mon malheur une pensée que mon coeur n'ait pas trouvée? J'ai voulu te l'apprendre, mais parce que j'étais bien sûr que tu ne l'adoucirais pas; je mourrais si on me l'ôtait, le remords en prendrait la place, il occuperait mon coeur tout entier, et ses douleurs sont arides et brûlantes. Adieu, je te remercie de m'avoir écouté.» Son calme sombre, son désespoir sans larmes, aisément me persuadèrent que tous mes efforts seraient vains; je n'osai plus lui parler, le malheur en impose; je le quittai le coeur plein d'amertume; et pour accomplir ma promesse, je raconte son histoire, et consacre, si je le puis, le triste nom de sa Mirza.

APPEL AUX SOUVERAINS RÉUNIS À PARIS POUR EN OBTENIR L'ABOLITION DE LA TRAITE DES NÈGRES
(1814)

Malgré la crise violente dans laquelle l'Angleterre s'est trouvée pendant vingt-cinq ans, elle ne s'est point servie des dangers qu'elle courait comme d'un prétexte pour négliger le bien qu'elle pouvait faire.

Constamment occupée de l'humanité au milieu de la guerre, et du bonheur général dans le moment même où son existence politique pouvait être menacée, elle a aboli la traite des nègres à l'époque où elle soutenait contre la doctrine d'une liberté perverse la lutte la plus acharnée. Les partis opposés parmi les Anglais se sont réunis pour un but aussi moral que religieux. M. Pitt et M. Fox y ont concouru avec une égale ardeur; et M. Wilberforce, un orateur chrétien, a mis à ce grand oeuvre une persévérance dont ordinairement on ne voit d'exemple que parmi ceux qui s'occupent de leurs intérêts personnels.

L'abolition de la traite des nègres, qui a eu lieu il y a sept ans, n'a porté aucune atteinte à la prospérité des colonies anglaises. Les nègres se sont assez multipliés entre eux pour suffire aux travaux nécessaires; et, comme il arrive toujours quand il s'agit d'un acte de justice, l'on ne cessait d'alarmer les esprits sur les inconvénients que pouvait avoir cette mesure avant qu'elle fût accomplie; mais lorsqu'elle l'a été, on n'a plus entendu parler de tous ces prétendus inconvénients. Ainsi, des milliers d'hommes et des nations entières ont été préservés, sans que les avantages pécuniaires du commerce en aient souffert.

L'Angleterre, depuis ce temps, en signant la paix avec le Danemark, a fait de l'abolition de la traite des nègres un des articles du traité: la même condition a été demandée au Portugal, qui, jusqu'à présent, n'a encore admis que des restrictions. Mais aujourd'hui que la confédération des souverains se trouve réunie pour affermir par la paix le repos qu'elle a conquis par les armes, il semble que rien ne serait plus digne de l'auguste congrès qui va s'ouvrir, que de consacrer le triomphe de l'Europe par un acte de bienfaisance. Les croisés, dans le moyen âge, ne partaient point pour la terre sainte sans se lier eux-mêmes par quelques voeux à leur retour. Les souverains, maintenant réunis en France, promettaient le bonheur de l'Afrique à ce ciel propice dont ils ont obtenu la délivrance de l'Europe.

Beaucoup d'intérêts politiques vont être discutés; mais quelques heures données à un si grand intérêt religieux ne seraient pas même inutiles aux affaires de ce monde. On dirait désormais: C'est à cette paix de Paris que la traite des nègres a été abolie par l'Europe entière; elle était donc sainte, cette paix, puisqu'on l'a fait précéder d'une telle action de grâces au Dieu des armées.

On a proposé d'élever un monument pour consacrer la chute de l'oppresseur qui pesait sur l'espèce humaine; le voilà, ce monument qu'une parole suffit pour élever: La traite des nègres est abolie par les rois qui ont renversé la tyrannie de la conquête en Europe.

Les souffrances qu'on fait éprouver à ces malheureux nègres pour les transporter de chez eux dans les colonies, font presque de l'esclavage même qui leur est destiné un soulagement pour eux. On excite la guerre dans leur propre pays pour qu'ils se livrent les uns les autres; être vendu comme esclave est la punition admise sur les côtes d'Afrique pour tous les genres de fautes. Les chefs noirs qui se permettent cet infâme trafic excitent les nègres au crime par l'ivresse, ou par tout autre moyen, afin d'avoir le droit de les faire exporter en Amérique. Souvent, sous le ridicule prétexte de la sorcellerie, ces infortunés sont pour jamais exilés des bords qui les ont vus naître, loin de cette patrie plus chère encore aux sauvages qu'aux hommes civilisés. *De longs cercueils,* pour me servir de l'expression d'un écrivain français, les transportent sur les mers; ils sont entassés dans le vaisseau de façon qu'ils occuperaient plus de place s'ils étaient morts, car leur corps serait du moins alors étendu sur la misérable planche qu'on leur accorde.

M. Pitt, dans son discours contre la traite des nègres, a dit en propres termes: «Je ne connais aucun mal qui ait jamais existé, et je ne puis en imaginer aucun qui soit pire que quatre-vingt mille personnes annuellement arrachées de leur terre natale par la combinaison des nations les plus civilisées de l'Europe.» On sait quels étaient les principes de M.Pitt et la part qu'il a eue par ses opinions inébranlables au triomphe actuel des alliés. Son autorité ne doit-elle pas être comptée? et celle des trois pouvoirs de l'Angleterre, la chambre des communes, la chambre des pairs, et le roi, ne consacre-t-elle pas la vérité des faits et des principes maintenant soumis à l'attention des monarques?

Enfin, l'on ne peut se le dissimuler, l'Europe doit beaucoup à l'Angleterre: elle a souvent résisté seule dans le cours de ces vingt-cinq années, et nulle part il n'a existé un combat qui ne fût secondé par ses soldats ou par ses secours. On ne sait de quelle manière récompenser une nation la plus riche et la plus heureuse de l'univers. Un guerrier reçoit de son souverain une marque d'honneur; mais une nation qui s'est conduite tout entière comme un guerrier, que peut-on faire pour elle? Il faut adopter le grand acte d'humanité qu'elle recommande à tous les gouvernements de l'Europe: il faut faire le bien pour lui-même, mais aussi pour la nation anglaise qui le sollicite, et à laquelle il est juste d'accorder cette noble marque de reconnaissance.

Le même avocat de l'humanité, M. Wilberforce, est en Angleterre à la tête de l'établissement des missionnaires qui doivent porter les lumières du christianisme dans l'Asie et dans l'Afrique. Mais comment se dire chrétien, si l'on était cruel? Ne peut-on pas demander au roi de France, à ce pieux héritier de saint Louis et de Louis XVI, d'accéder à l'abolition de la traite des nègres, afin que cet acte d'humanité persuade le coeur de ceux à qui l'on va prêcher l'Evangile? Ne peut-on pas demander aussi cette accession à l'Espagne, qui a réveillé l'esprit national sur le continent? au Portugal, qui s'est battu comme un grand Etat? à l'Autriche, qui n'a considéré que le salut de l'empire allemand? à la Prusse, où la nation et le roi se sont montrés si simplement héroïques? Demandons aussi ce grand bienfait à l'empereur de Russie qui a mis lui-même des limites à son ambition, quand elle ne rencontrait plus aucun obstacle au dehors. Un souverain absolu a combattu pour fonder les principes sages de la liberté politique; la couronne d'un tel monarque doit être composée de tous les genres de gloire: l'Empereur de Russie régit, sur les confins de l'Asie, des peuples dont les degrés de civilisation sont divers; il tolère toutes les religions; il permet toutes les coutumes; et le sceptre est, dans ses mains, équitable comme la loi. L'Asie et l'Europe bénissent le nom d'Alexandre. Que ce nom retentisse encore sur les bords sauvages de l'Afrique! Il n'est aucun pays sur la terre qui ne soit digne de la justice.

PRÉFACE POUR LA TRADUCTION D'UN OUVRAGE DE M. WILBERFORCE SUR LA TRAITE DES NÈGRES (1814)

M. Wilberforce est l'auteur de l'écrit qu'on va lire sur l'abolition de la traite des nègres.

Orateur distingué dans la chambre des communes, remarquablement instruit sur tout ce qui tient à la littérature et à cette haute philosophie dont la religion est la base, il a consacré trente ans de sa vie à faire rougir l'Europe d'un grand attentat, et à délivrer l'Afrique d'un affreux malheur. Lorsqu'il eut rassemblé toutes les preuves des cruautés qui ajoutaient encore à l'horreur d'un acte tyrannique, lorsqu'il crut avoir de quoi convaincre les faibles et les forts, il fit, en 1787, dans le parlement, la motion d'abolir la traite des nègres.

M. Pitt, M. Fox, M. Burke, l'appuyèrent; aucun homme vraiment supérieur en Angleterre, quelles que soient ses opinions politiques, ne voudrait prêter son nom à des opinions qui dégradent du nom de penseur et d'ami de l'humanité. On peut soupçonner M. Pitt d'avoir permis pendant quelque temps à ses adhérents de soutenir la traite des nègres; mais sa gloire lui était trop chère pour ne pas se séparer de son parti dans cette circonstance. Toutefois les réclamations de tous ceux qui font de l'espèce humaine deux parties, dont l'une, à leur avis, doit être sacrifiée à l'autre, ces réclamations empêchèrent que la motion de M. Wilberforce ne fût adoptée. Les colons prétendirent qu'ils seraient ruinés si la traite était abolie; les villes de commerce d'Angleterre affirmèrent que leur prospérité tenait à celle des colons:

enfin l'on rencontra de tous les côtés ces résistances qui recommencent toujours, quand les honnêtes gens s'avisent de défendre les opprimés contre les oppresseurs.

Les excès de la révolution de France, qui répandaient une grande défaveur sur un certain ordre d'idées, nuisirent à la cause des pauvres nègres. On criait à l'anarchie contre ceux qui ne voulaient pas qu'on excitât la guerre entre les peuples d'Afrique, pour faire leurs prisonniers esclaves; on appelait jacobins les hommes qui n'avaient pour motifs de leurs actions que la religion et l'humanité. Mais dans un pays tel que l'Angleterre, les lumières sont si universelles, et la circulation des idées si libre, qu'on peut calculer avec certitude le temps très court qu'il faut pour qu'une vérité s'établisse dans l'opinion.

M. Wilberforce renouvela toutes les années la même motion, qui avait été d'abord écartée, et cette persévérance faisait gagner chaque fois du terrain à la raison. Les hommes les plus religieux de l'Angleterre secondèrent les efforts de M. Wilberforce; M. Clarkson, M. Macauley, plusieurs autres encore doivent être nommés dans cette honorable lutte: on fit une souscription pour établir dans la Sierra-Léone tous les moyens propres à civiliser les nègres, et cette honorable entreprise coûta plus de deux cent mille livres sterling aux particuliers qui s'en chargèrent. On ne voit guère comment l'esprit mercantile que l'on reproche aux Anglais pouvait expliquer de tels sacrifices: les motifs qui décidèrent l'abolition de la traite des nègres sont d'une nature tout aussi désintéressée.

C'est en 1807 que ce grand oeuvre d'humanité fut accompli. On avait délibéré vingt ans sur ses inconvénients et sur ses avantages. M. Fox et ses amis étaient alors ministres; mais le ministère changea dans l'intervalle du projet de loi à sa sanction. Toutefois les successeurs adoptèrent à cet égard les mêmes principes; car parmi les nouveaux ministres, M. Perceval, M. Canning et lord Harrowby, tous les trois amis de M. Pitt, s'étaient montrés les champions ardents de cette belle cause. M. Fox, en mourant, l'avait recommandée à son neveu, lord Holland, et l'on permit à ce noble héritier, bien qu'il ne fût plus ministre, de porter lui-même avec ses amis la sanction du roi à la chambre des pairs. *Un rayon du soleil,* dit Clarkson, *perça les nuages au moment où le décret qui supprimait la traite des nègres fut proclamé.* En effet, cet acte méritait la faveur du ciel; et dans quel moment eut-il lieu? lorsque toutes les colonies étaient entre les mains des Anglais, et qu'ainsi leur intérêt, vulgairement considéré, devait les porter à maintenir l'indigne commerce qu'ils abjuraient.

Aujourd'hui l'on se plaît à soutenir que les Anglais craignent le rétablissement de la colonie de Saint-Domingue au profit des Français:

mais en 1807 quelle chance y avait-il pour que la France pût redevenir maîtresse de cette colonie, si toutefois cette chance existe maintenant? Le parti qui a déterminé l'abolition de la traite des nègres en Angleterre, c'est celui des chrétiens zélés, appelés communément *méthodistes*. Ils portent dans les intérêts de l'humanité les qualités de l'esprit de parti, l'énergie et l'activité; et comme ils sont en grand nombre, ils agissent sur l'opinion, et l'opinion sur le gouvernement. Loin que les politiques ou les spéculateurs qui peuvent être jaloux de la prospérité de la France fussent pour rien dans l'abolition de la traite, ils y opposaient les mêmes arguments qu'on voit reparaître en France aujourd'hui parmi les colons et les commerçants; ils menaçaient des mêmes maux, et néanmoins depuis sept ans que l'Angleterre a interdit la traite, l'expérience a si bien prouvé que toutes les craintes qu'on avait manifestées à cet égard étaient illusoires, que les villes maritimes de la nation sont à présent d'accord sur ce sujet avec le reste de la nation. L'on a vu, dans cette occasion, le même phénomène moral que l'on peut observer dans toutes les circonstances d'une nature analogue. Quand on propose de supprimer un abus quelconque du pouvoir, aussitôt ceux qui jouissent de cet abus ne manquent pas d'affirmer que tous les bienfaits de l'ordre social y sont attachés. «C'est la clef de la voûte,» disent-ils, tandis que c'est seulement la clef de leurs propres avantages; et lorsque enfin le progrès des lumières amène la réforme longtemps désirée, on est tout étonné des améliorations qui en résultent. Le bien jette des racines de toutes parts, l'équilibre se rétablit sans efforts, et la vérité guérit les maux de l'espèce humaine, comme la nature, sans que personne s'en mêle.

Quelques Français se sont irrités de ce que les ministres anglais avaient fait de l'abolition de la traite des nègres l'une des conditions de la paix: les ministres anglais n'ont été à cet égard que les interprètes du voeu de leur nation. Mais ce serait une belle époque dans l'histoire que celle où les peuples se demanderaient mutuellement des actes d'humanité. Cette négociation généreuse ne rencontrera pas d'obstacle dans le coeur d'un monarque aussi religieusement éclairé que celui de la France; mais les préjugés des pays peuvent quelquefois contrarier les lumières mêmes de leurs chefs.

C'est donc un grand bonheur pour la France, l'Angleterre et la lointaine Afrique, qu'une gloire telle que celle du duc de Wellington donne de la force à la cause qu'il défend. Déjà le marquis de Wellesley, son frère aîné, a supprimé dans l'Inde, dont il était gouverneur, la traite des nègres, avant même que le décret qui l'abolit eût été prononcé par le parlement d'Angleterre. Les opinions de cette illustre famille sont connues: espérons donc que lord Wellington triomphera par la raison dans la cause des nègres, comme il a puissamment servi la cause des Espagnols par son épée; car c'est à ce héros vertueux que l'on devrait appliquer ces paroles célèbres de Bossuet: *Il avait un nom qui ne parut jamais que dans des actions dont la justice était incontestable.*

DE L'ESPRIT DES TRADUCTIONS
(1816)

Il n'y a pas de plus éminent service à rendre à la littérature, que de transporter d'une langue à l'autre les chefs-d'oeuvre de l'esprit humain. Il existe si peu de productions du premier rang; le génie, dans quelque genre que ce soit, est un phénomène tellement rare, que si chaque nation moderne en était réduite à ses propres trésors, elle serait toujours pauvre. D'ailleurs, la circulation des idées est, de tous les genres de commerce, celui dont les avantages sont les plus certains.

Les savants et même les poètes avaient imaginé, lors de la renaissance des lettres, d'écrire tous dans une même langue, le latin, afin de n'avoir pas besoin d'être traduits pour être entendus. Cela pouvait être avantageux aux sciences, dont le développement n'a pas besoin des charmes du style. Mais il en était résulté cependant que plusieurs des richesses des Italiens, en ce genre, leur étaient inconnues à eux-mêmes, parce que la généralité des lecteurs ne comprenait que l'idiome du pays. Il faut d'ailleurs, pour écrire en latin sur les sciences et sur la philosophie, créer des mots qui n'existent pas dans les auteurs anciens. Ainsi, les savants se sont servis d'une langue tout à la fois morte et factice, tandis que les poètes s'astreignaient aux expressions purement classiques; et l'Italie, où le latin retentissait encore sur les bords du Tibre, a possédé des écrivains tels que Fra-Castor, Politien, Sannazar, qui s'approchaient, dit-on, du style de Virgile et d'Horace; mais si leur réputation dure, leurs ouvrages ne se lisent plus hors du siècle des érudits; et c'est une triste gloire littéraire que celle dont l'imitation doit être la base. Ces poètes latins du moyen âge ont été traduits en italien dans leur propre patrie: tant il est naturel de préférer la langue qui vous rappelle les émotions de votre propre vie, à celle qu'on ne peut se retracer que par l'étude!

La meilleure manière, j'en conviens, pour se passer des traductions, serait de savoir toutes les langues dans lesquelles les ouvrages des grands poètes ont été composés; le grec, le latin, l'italien, le français, l'anglais, l'espagnol, le portugais, l'allemand: mais un tel travail exige beaucoup de temps, beaucoup de secours, et jamais on ne peut se flatter que des connaissances si difficiles à acquérir soient universelles. Or, c'est à l'universel qu'il faut tendre, lorsqu'on veut faire du bien aux hommes. Je dirai plus: lors même qu'on entendrait bien les langues étrangères, on pourrait goûter encore, par une traduction bien faite dans sa propre langue, un plaisir plus familier et plus intime. Ces beautés naturalisées donnent au style national des tournures nouvelles et des expressions plus originales. Les traductions des poètes étrangers peuvent, plus efficacement que tout autre moyen, préserver la littérature d'un pays de ces tournures banales qui sont les signes les plus certains de sa décadence.

Mais, pour tirer de ce travail un véritable avantage, il ne faut pas, comme les Français, donner sa propre couleur à tout ce qu'on traduit; quand même on devrait par là changer en or tout ce que l'on touche, il n'en résulterait pas moins que l'on ne pourrait pas s'en nourrir; on n'y trouverait pas des aliments nouveaux pour sa pensée, et l'on reverrait toujours le même visage avec des parures à peine différentes. Ce reproche, justement mérité par les Français, tient aux entraves de toute espèce imposées, dans leur langue, à l'art d'écrire en vers. La rareté de la rime, l'uniformité de vers, la difficulté des inversions, renferment le poète dans un certain cercle qui ramène nécessairement, si ce n'est les mêmes pensées, au moins des hémistiches semblables, et je ne sais quelle monotonie dans le langage poétique, à laquelle le génie échappe, quand il s'élève très-haut, mais dont il ne peut s'affranchir dans les transitions, dans les développements, enfin, dans tout ce qui prépare et réunit les grands effets.

On trouverait donc difficilement, dans la littérature française, une bonne traduction en vers, excepté celle des *Géorgiques* par l'abbé Delille. Il y a de belles imitations, des conquêtes à jamais confondues avec les richesses nationales; mais on ne saurait citer un ouvrage en vers qui portât d'aucune manière le caractère étranger, et même je ne crois pas qu'un tel essai pût jamais réussir. Si les *Géorgiques* de l'abbé Delille ont été justement admirées, c'est parce que la langue française peut s'assimiler plus facilement à la langue latine qu'à toute autre; elle en dérive, et elle en conserve la pompe et la majesté; mais les langues modernes ont tant de diversités, que la poésie française ne saurait s'y plier avec grâce.

Les Anglais, dont la langue admet les inversions, et dont la versification est soumise à des règles beaucoup moins sévères que celle des Français, auraient pu enrichir leur littérature de traductions exactes et naturelles tout ensemble; mais leurs grands auteurs n'ont point entrepris ce travail; et Pope, le seul qui s'y soit consacré, a fait deux beaux poèmes de l'*Iliade* et de l'*Odyssée;* mais il n'y a point conservé cette antique simplicité qui nous fait sentir le secret de la supériorité d'Homère.

En effet, il n'est pas vraisemblable que le génie d'un homme ait surpassé depuis trois mille ans celui de tous les autres poètes; mais il y avait quelque chose de primitif dans les traditions, dans les moeurs, dans les opinions, dans l'air de cette époque, dont le charme est inépuisable; et c'est ce début du genre humain, cette jeunesse du temps, qui renouvelle dans notre âme, en lisant Homère, une sorte d'émotion pareille à celle que nous éprouvons par les souvenirs de notre propre enfance: cette émotion se confondant avec ses rêves de l'âge d'or, nous fait donner au plus ancien des poètes la préférence sur tous ses successeurs. Si vous ôtez à sa composition la simplicité des premiers jours du monde, ce qu'elle a d'unique disparaît.

En Allemagne, plusieurs savants ont prétendu que les oeuvres d'Homère n'avaient pas été composées par un seul homme, et qu'on devait considérer l'*Iliade*, et même l'*Odyssée*, comme une réunion de chants héroïques, pour célébrer en Grèce la conquête de Troie et le retour des vainqueurs. Il me semble qu'il est facile de combattre cette opinion, et que l'unité de l'*Iliade* surtout ne permet pas de l'adopter. Pourquoi s'en serait-on tenu au récit de la colère d'Achille? Les événements subséquents, la prise de Troie qui les termine, auraient dû naturellement faire partie de la collection des rapsodies qu'on suppose appartenir à divers auteurs. La conception de l'unité d'un événement, la colère d'Achille, ne peut être que le plan formé par un seul homme. Sans vouloir toutefois discuter ici un système, pour et contre lequel on doit être armé d'une érudition effrayante, au moins faut-il avouer que la principale grandeur d'Homère tient à son siècle, puisqu'on a cru que les poètes d'alors, ou du moins un très grand nombre d'entre eux, avaient travaillé à l'*Iliade*. C'est une preuve de plus que ce poème est l'image de la société humaine, à tel degré de la civilisation, et qu'il porte encore plus l'empreinte du temps que celle d'un homme.

Les Allemands ne se sont point bornés à ces recherches savantes sur l'existence d'Homère; ils ont tâché de le faire revivre chez eux, et la traduction de Voss est reconnue pour la plus exacte qui existe dans aucune langue. Il s'est servi du rythme des anciens, et l'on assure que son hexamètre allemand suit presque mot à mot l'hexamètre grec. Une telle traduction sert efficacement à la connaissance précise du poème ancien; mais est-il certain que le charme, pour lequel il ne suffit ni des règles ni des études, soit entièrement transporté dans la langue allemande? Les quantités syllabiques sont conservées; mais l'harmonie des sons ne saurait être la même. La poésie allemande perd de son naturel, en suivant pas à pas les traces du grec, sans pouvoir acquérir la beauté du langage musical qui se chantait sur la lyre.

L'italien est de toutes les langues modernes celle qui se prête le plus à nous rendre toutes les sensations produites par l'Homère grec. Il n'a pas, il est vrai, le même rythme que l'original; l'hexamètre ne peut guère s'introduire dans nos idiomes modernes; les longues et les brèves n'y sont pas assez marquées pour que l'on puisse égaler les anciens à cet égard. Mais les paroles italiennes ont une harmonie qui peut se passer de la symétrie des dactyles et des spondées, et la construction grammaticale en italien se prête à l'imitation parfaite des inversions du grec: les *versi sciolti,* étant dégagés de la rime, ne gênent pas plus la pensée que la prose, tout en conservant la grâce et la mesure du vers.

La traduction d'Homère par Monti est sûrement de toutes celles qui existent en Europe celle qui approche le plus du plaisir que l'original même pourrait causer. Elle a de la pompe et de la simplicité tout ensemble; les usages les plus ordinaires de la vie, les vêtements, les festins sont relevés par la dignité naturelle des expressions; et les plus grandes circonstances sont mises à notre portée par la vérité des tableaux et la facilité du style. Personne, en Italie, ne traduira plus désormais l'*Iliade;* Homère y a pris pour jamais le costume de Monti, et il me semble que, même dans les autres pays de l'Europe, quiconque ne peut s'élever jusqu'à lire Homère dans l'original, aura l'idée du plaisir qu'il peut causer, par la traduction italienne. Traduire un poète, ce n'est pas prendre un compas, et copier les dimensions de l'édifice; c'est animer du même souffle de vie un instrument différent. On demande encore plus une jouissance du même genre que des traits parfaitement semblables.

Il serait fort à désirer, ce me semble, que les Italiens s'occupassent de traduire avec soin diverses poésies nouvelles des Anglais et des Allemands; ils feraient ainsi connaître un genre nouveau à leurs compatriotes, qui s'en tiennent, pour la plupart, aux images tirées de la mythologie ancienne: or, elles commencent à s'épuiser, et le paganisme de la poésie ne subsiste presque plus dans le reste de l'Europe. Il importe aux progrès de la pensée, dans la belle Italie, de regarder souvent au delà des Alpes, non pour emprunter, mais pour connaître; non pour imiter, mais pour s'affranchir de certaines formes convenues qui se maintiennent en littérature comme les phrases officielles dans la société, et qui en bannissent de même toute vérité naturelle.

Si les traductions des poèmes enrichissent les belles-lettres, celles des pièces de théâtre pourraient exercer encore une plus grande influence; car le théâtre est vraiment le pouvoir exécutif de la littérature. A. W. Schlegel a fait une traduction de Shakespeare, qui, réunissant l'exactitude à l'inspiration, est tout à fait nationale en Allemagne. Les pièces anglaises ainsi transmises sont jouées sur le théâtre allemand, et Shakespeare et Schiller y sont devenus compatriotes. Il serait possible en Italie d'obtenir un résultat du même genre; les auteurs dramatiques français se rapprochent autant du goût des Italiens que Shakespeare de celui des Allemands, et peut-être pourrait-on représenter *Athalie* avec succès sur le beau théâtre de Milan, en donnant aux choeurs l'accompagnement de l'admirable musique italienne. On a beau dire que l'on ne va pas au spectacle en Italie pour écouter, mais pour causer, et se réunir dans les loges avec sa société intime; il n'en est pas moins certain que d'entendre tous les jours, pendant cinq heures, plus ou moins, ce qu'on est convenu d'appeler des paroles dans la plupart des opéras italiens, c'est, à la longue, une manière sûre de diminuer les facultés intellectuelles d'une nation. Lorsque Casti faisait des opéras comiques, lorsque Métastase adaptait si bien à la musique des pensées pleines de charme et d'élévation, l'amusement n'y perdait rien, et la raison y gagnait beaucoup. Au milieu de la frivolité habituelle de la société, lorsque chacun cherche à se débarrasser de soi par le secours des autres, si vous pouvez faire arriver quelques idées et quelques sentiments à travers les plaisirs, vous formez l'esprit à quelque chose de sérieux qui peut lui donner enfin une véritable valeur.

La littérature italienne est partagée maintenant entre les érudits qui sassent et ressassent les cendres du passé, pour tâcher d'y retrouver encore quelques paillettes d'or, et les écrivains qui se fient à l'harmonie de leur langue pour faire des accords sans idées, pour mettre ensemble des exclamations, des déclamations, des invocations où il n'y a pas un mot qui parte du coeur et qui y arrive. Ne serait-il donc pas possible qu'une émulation active, celle des succès au théâtre, ramenât par degrés l'originalité d'esprit et la vérité de style, sans lesquelles il n'y a point de littérature, ni peut-être même aucune des qualités qu'il faudrait pour en avoir une?

Le goût du drame sentimental s'est emparé de la scène italienne, et au lieu de cette gaieté piquante qu'on y voyait régner autrefois, au lieu de ces personnages de comédie qui sont classiques dans toute l'Europe, on voit représenter, dès les premières scènes de ces drames, les assassinats les plus insipides, si l'on peut s'exprimer ainsi, dont on puisse donner le misérable spectacle. N'est-ce pas une pauvre éducation pour un nombre très considérable de personnes, que de tels plaisirs si souvent répétés? Le goût des Italiens, dans les beaux-arts, est aussi simple que noble; mais la parole est aussi un des beaux-arts, et il faudrait lui donner le même caractère; elle tient de plus près à tout ce qui constitue l'homme, et l'on se passe plutôt de tableaux et de monuments que des sentiments auxquels ils doivent être consacrés.

Les Italiens sont très enthousiastes de leur langue; de grands hommes l'ont fait valoir, et les distinctions de l'esprit ont été les seules jouissances, et souvent aussi les seules consolations de la nation italienne. Afin que chaque homme capable de penser se sente un motif pour se développer lui-même, il faut que toutes les nations aient un principe actif d'intérêt: les unes sont militaires, les autres politiques. Les Italiens doivent se faire remarquer par la littérature et les beaux-arts; sinon leur pays tomberait dans une sorte d'apathie dont le soleil même pourrait à peine le réveiller.

Claire de Duras

OURIKA[1]

This is to be alone, this, this, is solitude!
Lord Byron.

Introduction

J'étais arrivé depuis peu de mois de Montpellier, et je suivais à Paris la profession de la médecine, lorsque je fus appelé un matin au faubourg Saint-Jacques, pour voir dans un couvent une jeune religieuse malade. L'empereur Napoléon avait permis depuis peu le rétablissement de quelques-uns de ces couvents: celui où je me rendais était destiné à l'éducation de la jeunesse, et appartenait à l'ordre des Ursulines. La révolution avait ruiné une partie de l'édifice; le cloître était à découvert d'un côté par la démolition de l'antique église, dont on ne voyait plus que quelques arceaux. Une religieuse m'introduisit dans ce cloître que nous traversâmes en marchant sur de longues pierres plates qui formaient le pavé de ces galeries: je m'aperçus que c'étaient des tombes, car elles portaient toutes des inscriptions pour la plupart effacées par le temps. Quelques-unes de ces pierres avaient été brisées pendant la révolution: la soeur me le fit remarquer, en me disant qu'on n'avait pas encore eu le temps de les réparer. Je n'avais jamais vu l'intérieur d'un couvent; ce spectacle était tout nouveau pour moi. Du cloître nous passâmes dans le jardin, où la religieuse me dit qu'on avait porté la soeur malade: en effet, je l'aperçus à l'extrémité d'une longue allée de charmille; elle était assise, et son grand voile noir l'enveloppait presque tout entière. Voici le médecin, dit la soeur. Et elle s'éloigna au même moment. Je m'approchai timidement, car mon coeur s'était serré en voyant ces tombes, et je me figurais que j'allais

---

1. This edition is based on the 1824 edition published by Ladvocat, Paris.

contempler une nouvelle victime des cloîtres; les préjugés de ma jeunesse venaient de se réveiller, et mon intérêt s'exaltait pour celle que j'allais visiter, en proportion du genre de malheur que je lui supposais. Elle se tourna vers moi, et je fus étrangement surpris en apercevant une négresse! Mon étonnement s'accrut encore par la politesse de son accueil et le choix des expressions dont elle se servait. Vous venez voir une personne bien malade, me dit-elle: à présent je désire guérir, mais je ne l'ai pas toujours souhaité, et c'est peut-être ce qui m'a fait tant de mal. Je la questionnai sur sa maladie. J'éprouve, me dit-elle, une oppression continuelle, je n'ai plus de sommeil, et la fièvre ne me quitte pas. Son aspect ne confirmait que trop cette triste description de son état: sa maigreur était excessive, ses yeux brillants et fort grands, ses dents d'une blancheur éblouissante, éclairaient seuls sa physionomie; l'âme vivait encore, mais le corps était détruit, et elle portait toutes les marques d'un long et violent chagrin. Touché au-delà de l'expression, je résolus de tout tenter pour la sauver; je commençai à lui parler de la nécessité de calmer son imagination, de se distraire, d'éloigner des sentiments pénibles. Je suis heureuse, me dit-elle, jamais je n'ai éprouvé tant de calme et de bonheur. L'accent de sa voix était sincère, cette douce voix ne pouvait tromper; mais mon étonnement s'accroissait à chaque instant. Vous n'avez pas toujours pensé ainsi, lui dis-je, et vous portez la trace de bien longues souffrances. Il est vrai, dit-elle, j'ai trouvé bien tard le repos de mon coeur, mais à présent je suis heureuse. Eh bien! s'il en est ainsi, repris-je, c'est le passé qu'il faut guérir; espérons que nous en viendrons à bout: mais ce passé, je ne puis le guérir sans le connaître. Hélas! répondit-elle, ce sont des folies! En prononçant ces mots, une larme vint mouiller le bord de sa paupière. Et vous dites que vous êtes heureuse! m'écriai-je. Oui, je le suis, reprit-elle avec fermeté, et je ne changerais pas mon bonheur contre le sort qui m'a fait autrefois tant d'envie. Je n'ai point de secret: mon malheur, c'est l'histoire de toute ma vie. J'ai tant souffert jusqu'au jour où je suis entrée dans cette maison, que peu à peu ma santé s'est ruinée. Je me sentais dépérir avec joie; car je ne voyais dans l'avenir aucune espérance. Cette pensée était bien coupable! vous le voyez, j'en suis punie; et lorsque enfin je souhaite de vivre, peut-être que je ne le pourrai plus. Je la rassurai, je lui donnai des espérances de guérison prochaine; mais en prononçant ces paroles consolantes, en lui promettant la vie, je ne sais quel triste pressentiment m'avertissait qu'il était trop tard et que la mort avait marqué sa victime.

Je revis plusieurs fois cette jeune religieuse; l'intérêt que je montrais parut la toucher. Un jour, elle revint d'elle-même au sujet où je désirais la conduire. Les chagrins que j'ai éprouvés, dit-elle, doivent paraître si étranges, que j'ai toujours senti une grande répugnance à les confier: il n'y a point de juge des peines des autres, et les confidents sont presque toujours des accusateurs. Ne craignez pas cela de moi, lui dis-je; je vois assez le ravage que le chagrin a fait en vous pour croire le vôtre sincère. Vous le trouverez sincère, dit-elle, mais il vous paraîtra déraisonnable. Et en admettant ce que vous dites, repris-je, cela exclut-il la sympathie? Presque toujours, répondit-elle: cependant, si pour me guérir, vous avez besoin de connaître les peines qui ont détruit ma santé, je vous les confierai quand nous nous connaîtrons un peu davantage.

Je rendis mes visites au couvent de plus en plus fréquentes; le traitement que j'indiquai parut produire quelque effet. Enfin, un jour de l'été dernier, la retrouvant seule dans le même berceau, sur le même banc où je l'avais vue la première fois, nous reprîmes la même conversation, et elle me conta ce qui suit.

OURIKA

Je fus rapportée du Sénégal, à l'âge de deux ans, par M. le chevalier de B., qui en était gouverneur. Il eut pitié de moi, un jour qu'il voyait embarquer des esclaves sur un bâtiment négrier qui allait bientôt quitter le port: ma mère était morte, et on m'emportait dans le vaisseau, malgré mes cris. M. de B. m'acheta, et, à son arrivée en France, il me donna à Mme la maréchale de B., sa tante, la personne la plus aimable de son temps, et celle qui sut réunir, aux qualités les plus élevées, la bonté la plus touchante.

Me sauver de l'esclavage, me choisir pour bienfaitrice Mme de B., c'était me donner deux fois la vie: je fus ingrate envers la Providence en n'étant point heureuse; et cependant le bonheur résulte-t-il toujours de ces dons de l'intelligence! Je croirais plutôt le contraire: il faut payer le bienfait de savoir par le désir d'ignorer, et la fable ne nous dit pas si Galatée trouva le bonheur après avoir reçu la vie.

Je ne sus que longtemps après l'histoire des premiers jours de mon enfance. Mes plus anciens souvenirs ne me retracent que le salon de Mme de B.; j'y passais ma vie, aimée d'elle, caressée, gâtée par tous ses amis, accablée de présents, vantée, exaltée comme l'enfant le plus spirituel et le plus aimable.

Le ton de cette société était l'engouement, mais un engouement dont le bon goût savait exclure tout ce qui ressemblait à l'exagération: on louait tout ce qui prêtait à la louange, on excusait tout ce qui prêtait au blâme, et souvent, par une adresse encore plus aimable, on transformait en qualités les défauts mêmes. Le succès donne du courage; on valait près de Mme de B. tout ce qu'on pouvait valoir, et peut-être un peu plus, car elle prêtait quelque chose d'elle à ses amis sans s'en douter elle-même: en la voyant, en l'écoutant, on croyait lui ressembler.

Vêtue à l'orientale, assise aux pieds de Mme de B., j'écoutais, sans la comprendre encore, la conversation des hommes les plus distingués de ce temps-là. Je n'avais rien de la turbulence des enfants; j'étais pensive avant de penser, j'étais heureuse à côté de Mme de B.: aimer, pour moi, c'était être là, c'était l'entendre, lui obéir, la regarder surtout; je ne désirais rien de plus. Je ne pouvais m'étonner de vivre au milieu du luxe, de n'être entourée que des personnes les plus spirituelles et les plus aimables: je ne connaissais pas autre chose; mais, sans le savoir, je prenais un grand dédain pour tout ce qui n'était pas ce monde où je passais ma vie. Le bon goût est à l'esprit ce qu'une oreille juste est aux sons. Encore tout enfant, le manque de goût me blessait; je le sentais avant de pouvoir le définir, et l'habitude eût été dangereuse si j'avais eu un avenir; mais je n'avais pas d'avenir, et je ne m'en doutais pas. J'arrivai jusqu'à l'âge de douze ans sans avoir eu l'idée qu'on pouvait être heureuse autrement que je ne l'étais. Je n'étais pas fâchée d'être une négresse: on me disait que j'étais charmante; d'ailleurs rien ne m'avertissait que ce fût un désavantage; je ne voyais presque pas d'autres enfants; un seul était mon ami, et ma couleur noire ne l'empêchait pas de m'aimer.

Ma bienfaitrice avait deux petits-fils, enfants d'une fille qui était morte jeune. Charles, le cadet, était à peu près de mon âge. Elevé avec moi, il était mon protecteur, mon conseil et mon soutien dans toutes mes petites fautes. A sept ans, il alla au collège; je pleurai en le quittant; ce fut ma première peine. Je pensais souvent à lui, mais je ne le voyais presque plus. Il étudiait, et moi de mon côté, j'apprenais, pour plaire à Mme de B., tout ce qui devait former une éducation parfaite. Elle voulut que j'eusse tous les talents: j'avais de la voix, les maîtres les plus habiles l'exercèrent; j'avais le goût de la peinture, et un peintre célèbre, ami de Mme de B., se chargea de diriger mes efforts; j'appris l'anglais, l'italien, et Mme de B. elle-même s'occupa de mes lectures. Elle guidait mon esprit, formait mon jugement; en causant avec elle, en découvrant tous les trésors de son âme, je sentais la mienne s'élever, et c'était l'admiration qui m'ouvrait les voies de l'intelligence. Hélas! je ne prévoyais pas que ces douces études seraient suivies de jours si amers; je ne pensais qu'à plaire à Mme de B.; un sourire d'approbation sur ses lèvres était tout mon avenir.

Cependant, des lectures multipliées, celle des poètes surtout, commençaient à occuper ma jeune imagination; mais, sans but, sans projet, je promenais au hasard mes pensées errantes, et, avec la confiance de mon jeune âge, je me disais que Mme de B. saurait bien me rendre heureuse: sa tendresse pour moi, la vie que je menais, tout prolongeait mon erreur et autorisait mon aveuglement. Je vais donner un exemple des soins et des préférences dont j'étais l'objet.

Vous aurez peut-être de la peine à croire, en me voyant aujourd'hui, que j'aie été citée pour l'élégance et la beauté de ma taille. Mme de B. vantait souvent ce qu'elle appelait ma grâce, et elle avait voulu que je susse parfaitement danser. Pour faire briller ce talent, ma bienfaitrice donna un bal dont ses petits-fils furent le prétexte, mais dont le véritable motif était de me montrer fort à mon avantage dans un quadrille des quatre parties du monde où je devais représenter l'Afrique. On consulta les voyageurs, on feuilleta les livres de costumes, on lut des ouvrages savants sur la musique africaine, enfin on choisit une *Comba,* danse nationale de mon pays. Mon danseur mit un crêpe sur son visage: hélas! je n'eus pas besoin d'en mettre sur le mien; mais je ne fis pas alors cette réflexion. Tout entière au plaisir du bal, je dansai la *comba,* et j'eus tout le succès qu'on pouvait attendre de la nouveauté de spectacle et du choix des spectateurs, dont la plupart, amis de Mme de B., s'enthousiasmaient pour moi et croyaient lui faire plaisir en se laissant aller à toute la vivacité de ce sentiment. La danse d'ailleurs était piquante; elle se composait d'un mélange d'attitudes et de pas mesurés; on y peignait l'amour, la douleur, le triomphe et le désespoir. Je ne connaissais encore aucun de ces mouvements violents de l'âme; mais je ne sais quel instinct me les faisait deviner; enfin je réussis. On m'applaudit, on m'entoura, on m'accabla d'éloges: ce plaisir fut sans mélange; rien ne troublait alors ma sécurité. Ce fut peu de jours après ce bal qu'une conversation, que j'entendis par hasard, ouvrit mes yeux et finit ma jeunesse.

Il y avait dans le salon de Mme de B. un grand paravent de laque. Ce paravent cachait une porte; mais il s'étendait aussi près d'une des fenêtres, et entre le paravent et la fenêtre, se trouvait une table où je dessinais quelquefois. Un jour, je finissais avec application une miniature; absorbée par mon travail, j'étais restée longtemps immobile, et sans doute madame de B. me croyait sortie, lorsqu'on annonça une de ses amies, la marquise de. . . . C'était une personne d'une raison froide, d'un esprit tranchant, positive jusqu'à la sécheresse; elle portait ce caractère dans l'amitié: les sacrifices ne lui coûtaient rien pour le bien et pour l'avantage de ses amis; mais elle leur faisait payer cher ce grand attachement. Inquisitive et difficile, son exigence égalait son dévouement, et elle était la moins aimable des amies de Mme de B. Je la craignais, quoiqu'elle fût bonne pour moi; mais elle l'était à sa manière: examiner, et même assez sévèrement, était pour elle un signe d'intérêt. Hélas! j'étais si accoutumée à la bienveillance, que la justice me semblait toujours redoutable. Pendant que nous sommes seules, dit Mme de . . . à Mme de B., je veux vous parler d'Ourika: elle devient charmante, son esprit est tout à fait formé, elle causera comme vous, elle est pleine de talents, elle est piquante, naturelle; mais que deviendra-t-elle? et enfin qu'en ferez-vous? Hélas! dit Mme de B., cette pensée m'occupe souvent, et, je vous l'avoue, toujours avec tristesse: je l'aime comme si elle était ma fille; je ferais tout pour la rendre heureuse; et cependant, lorsque je réfléchis à sa position, je la trouve sans remède. Pauvre Ourika! je la vois seule, pour toujours seule dans la vie!

Il me serait impossible de vous peindre l'effet que produisit en moi ce peu de paroles, l'éclair n'est pas plus prompt; je vis tout; je me vis négresse, dépendante, méprisée, sans fortune, sans appui, sans un être de mon espèce à qui unir mon sort, jusqu'ici un jouet, un amusement pour ma bienfaitrice, bientôt rejetée d'un monde où je n'étais pas faite pour être admise. Une affreuse palpitation me saisit, mes yeux s'obscurcirent, le battement de mon coeur m'ôta un instant la faculté d'écouter encore; enfin je me remis assez pour entendre la suite de cette conversation.

Je crains, disait Mme de . . . , que vous ne la rendiez malheureuse. Que voulez-vous qui la satisfasse, maintenant qu'elle a passé sa vie dans l'intimité de votre société? Mais elle y restera, dit Mme de B. Oui, reprit Mme de . . . , tant qu'elle est une enfant: mais elle a quinze ans; à qui la marierez-vous, avec l'esprit qu'elle a et l'éducation que vous lui avez donnée? Qui voudra jamais épouser une négresse? Et si, à force d'argent, vous trouvez quelqu'un qui consente à avoir des enfants nègres, ce sera un homme d'une condition inférieure, et avec qui elle se trouvera malheureuse. Elle ne peut vouloir que de ceux qui ne voudront pas d'elle. Tout cela est vrai, dit Mme de B.; mais heureusement elle ne s'en doute point encore, et elle a pour moi un attachement qui, j'espère, la préservera longtemps de juger sa position. Pour la rendre heureuse, il eût fallu en faire une personne commune: je crois sincèrement que cela était impossible. Eh bien! peut-être sera-t-elle assez distinguée pour se placer au-dessus de son sort, n'ayant pu rester au-dessous. Vous vous faites des chimères, dit Mme de . . . : la philosophie nous place au-dessus des maux de la fortune, mais elle ne peut rien contre les maux qui viennent d'avoir brisé l'ordre de la nature. Ourika n'a pas rempli sa destinée: elle s'est placée dans la société sans sa permission; la société se vengera. Assurément, dit Mme de B., elle est bien innocente de ce crime; mais vous êtes sévère pour cette pauvre enfant. Je lui veux plus de bien que vous, reprit Mme de . . . ; je désire son bonheur, et vous la perdez. Mme de B. répondit avec impatience, et j'allais être la cause d'une querelle entre les deux amies, quand on anneonça une visite: je me glissai derrière le paravent; je m'échappai; je courus dans ma chambre où un déluge de larmes soulagea un instant mon pauvre coeur.

C'était un grand changement dans ma vie, que la perte de ce prestige qui m'avait environnée jusqu'alors! Il y a des illusions qui sont comme la lumière du jour; quand on les perd, tout disparaît avec elles. Dans la confusion des nouvelles idées qui m'assaillaient, je ne retrouvais plus rien de ce qui m'avait occupée jusqu'alors: c'était un abîme avec toutes ses terreurs. Ce mépris dont je me voyais poursuivie; cette société où j'étais déplacée; cet homme qui, à prix d'argent, consentirait peut-être que ses enfants fussent nègres! toutes ces pensées s'élevaient successivement comme des fantômes et s'attachaient sur moi comme des furies: l'isolement surtout; cette conviction que j'étais seule, pour toujours seule dans la vie, Mme de B. l'avait dit et à chaque instant je me répétais, seule! pour toujours seule! La veille encore, que m'importait d'être seule? Je n'en savais rien; je ne le sentais pas; j'avais besoin de ce que j'aimais, je ne songeais pas que ce que j'aimais n'avait pas besoin de moi. Mais à présent mes yeux étaient ouverts, et le malheur avait déjà fait entrer la défiance dans mon âme.

Quand je revins chez Mme de B., tout le monde fut frappé de mon changement; on me questionna: je dis que j'étais malade; on le crut. Mme de B. envoya chercher Barthez, qui m'examina avec soin, me tâta le pouls, et dit brusquement que je n'avais rien. Mme de B. se rassura et essaya de me distraire et de m'amuser. Je n'ose dire combien j'étais ingrate pour ces soins de ma bienfaitrice; mon âme s'était comme resserrée en elle-même. Les bienfaits qui sont doux à recevoir sont ceux dont le coeur s'acquitte: le mien était rempli d'un sentiment trop amer pour se répandre au dehors. Des combinaisons infinies des mêmes pensées occupaient tout mon temps; elles se reproduisaient sous mille formes différentes: mon imagination leur prêtait les couleurs les plus sombres; souvent mes nuits entières se passaient à pleurer. J'épuisais ma pitié sur moi-même; ma figure me faisait horreur, je n'osais plus me regarder dans une glace; lorsque mes yeux se portaient sur mes mains noires, je croyais voir celles d'un singe; je m'exagérais ma laideur, et cette couleur me paraissait comme le signe de ma réprobation; c'est elle qui me séparait de tous les êtres de mon espèce, qui me condamnait à être seule, toujours seule! jamais aimée!

Un homme, à prix d'argent, consentirait peut-être que ses enfants fussent nègres! Tout mon sang se soulevait d'indignation à cette pensée. J'eus un moment l'idée de demander à Mme B. de me renvoyer dans mon pays; mais là encore j'aurais été isolée: qui m'aurait entendue, qui m'aurait comprise? Hélas! je n'appartenais plus à personne; j'étais étrangère à la race humaine tout entière!

Ce n'est que bien longtemps après que je compris la possibilité de me résigner à un tel sort. Mme de B. n'était point dévote; je devais à un prêtre respectable, qui m'avait instruite pour ma première communion, ce que j'avais de sentiments religieux. Ils étaient sincères comme tout mon caractère; mais je ne savais pas que, pour être profitable, la piété a besoin d'être mêlée à toutes les actions de la vie: la mienne avait occupé quelques instants de mes journées, mais elle était demeurée étrangère à tout le reste. Mon confesseur était un saint vieillard, peu soupçonneux; je le voyais deux ou trois fois par an, et, comme je n'imaginais pas que des chagrins fussent des fautes, je ne lui parlais pas de mes peines. Elles altéraient sensiblement ma santé; mais, chose étrange! elles perfectionnaient mon esprit. Un sage d'Orient a dit: «Celui qui n'a pas souffert, que sait-il?» Je vis que je ne savais rien avant mon malheur, mes impressions étaient toutes des sentiments; je ne jugeais pas; j'aimais: les discours, les actions, les personnes plaisaient ou déplaisaient à mon coeur. A présent, mon esprit s'était séparé de ces mouvements involontaires: le chagrin est comme l'éloignement, il fait juger l'ensemble des objets. Depuis que je me sentais étrangère à tout, j'étais devenue plus difficile, et j'examinais, en le critiquant, presque tout ce qui m'avait plu jusqu'alors.

Cette disposition ne pouvait échapper à Mme de B.; je n'ai jamais su si elle en devina la cause. Elle craignait peut-être d'exalter ma peine en me permettant de la confier: mais elle me montrait encore plus de bonté que de coutume; elle me parlait avec un entier abandon, et, pour me distraire de mes chagrins, elle m'occupait de ceux qu'elle avait elle-même. Elle jugeait bien mon coeur; je ne pouvais en effet me rattacher à la vie, que par l'idée d'être nécessaire ou du moins utile à ma bienfaitrice. La pensée qui me poursuivait le plus, c'est que j'étais isolée sur la terre, et que je pouvais mourir sans laisser de regrets dans le coeur de personne. J'étais injuste pour Mme de B.; elle m'aimait, elle me l'avait assez prouvé; mais elle avait des intérêts qui passaient bien avant moi. Je n'enviais pas sa tendresse à ses petits-fils, surtout à Charles; mais j'aurais voulu pouvoir dire comme eux: Ma mère!

Les liens de famille surtout me faisaient faire des retours bien douloureux sur moi-même, moi qui jamais ne devais être la soeur, la femme, la mère de personne! Je me figurais dans ces liens plus de douceur qu'ils n'en ont peut-être, et je négligeais ceux qui m'étaient permis, parce que je ne pouvais atteindre à ceux-là. Je n'avais point d'amie, personne n'avait ma confiance: ce que j'avais pour Mme de B. était plutôt un culte qu'une affection; mais je crois que je sentais pour Charles tout ce qu'on éprouve pour un frère.

Il était toujours au collège, qu'il allait bientôt quitter pour commencer ses voyages. Il partait avec son frère aîné et son gouverneur, et ils devaient visiter l'Allemagne, l'Angleterre et l'Italie; leur absence devait durer deux ans. Charles était charmé de partir; et moi, je ne fus affligée qu'au dernier moment; car j'étais toujours bien aise de ce qui lui faisait plaisir. Je ne lui avais rien dit de toutes les idées qui m'occupaient; je ne le voyais jamais seul, et il m'aurait fallu bien du temps pour lui expliquer ma peine: je suis sûre qu'alors il m'aurait comprise. Mais il avait, avec son air doux et grave, une disposition à la moquerie, qui me rendait timide: il est vrai qu'il ne l'exerçait guère que sur les ridicules de l'affectation; tout ce qui était sincère le désarmait. Enfin je ne lui dis rien. Son départ, d'ailleurs, était une distraction, et je crois que cela me faisait du bien de m'affliger d'autre chose que de ma douleur habituelle.

Ce fut peu de temps après le départ de Charles, que la révolution prit un caractère plus sérieux: je n'entendais parler tout le jour, dans le salon de Mme de B., que des grands intérêts moraux et politiques que cette révolution remua jusque dans leur source; ils se rattachaient à ce qui avait occupé les esprits supérieurs de tous les temps. Rien n'était plus capable d'étendre et de former mes idées, que le spectacle de cette arène où des hommes distingués remettaient chaque jour en question tout ce qu'on avait pu croire jugé jusqu'alors. Ils approfondissaient tous les sujets, remontaient à l'origine de toutes les institutions, mais trop souvent pour tout ébranler et pour tout détruire.

Croiriez-vous que, jeune comme j'étais, étrangère à tous les intérêts de la société, nourrissant à part ma plaie secrète, la révolution apporta un changement dans mes idées, fit naître dans mon coeur quelques espérances, et suspendit un moment mes maux? tant on cherche vite ce qui peut consoler! J'entrevis donc que, dans ce grand désordre, je pourrais trouver ma place; que toutes les fortunes renversées, tous les rangs confondus, tous les préjugés évanouis, amèneraient peut-être un état de choses où je serais moins étrangère; et que si j'avais quelque supériorité d'âme, quelque qualité cachée, on l'apprécierait lorsque ma couleur ne m'isolerait plus au milieu du monde, comme elle avait fait jusqu'alors. Mais il arriva que ces qualités mêmes que je pouvais me trouver, s'opposèrent vite à mon illusion: je ne pus désirer longtemps beaucoup de mal pour un peu de bien personnel. D'un autre côté, j'apercevais les ridicules de ces personnages qui voulaient maîtriser les événements; je jugeais les petitesses de leurs caractères, je devinais leurs vues secrètes; bientôt leur fausse philanthropie cessa de m'abuser, et je renonçai à l'espérance, en voyant qu'il resterait encore assez de mépris pour moi au milieu de tant d'adversités. Cependant je m'intéressais toujours à ces discussions animées; mais elles ne tardèrent pas à perdre ce qui faisait leur plus grand charme. Déjà le temps n'était plus où l'on ne songeait qu'à plaire, et où la première condition pour y réussir était l'oubli des succès de son amour-propre: lorsque la révolution cessa d'être une belle théorie et qu'elle toucha aux intérêts intimes de chacun, les conversations dégénérèrent en disputes, et l'aigreur, l'amertume et les personnalités prirent la place de la raison. Quelquefois, malgré ma tristesse, je m'amusais de toutes ces violentes opinions, qui n'étaient, au fond, presque jamais que des prétentions, des affectations ou des peurs: mais la gaieté qui vient de l'observation des ridicules ne fait pas de bien; il y a trop de malignité dans cette gaieté pour qu'elle puisse réjouir le coeur qui ne se plaît que dans les joies innocentes. On peut avoir cette gaieté moqueuse, sans cesser d'être malheureux; peut-être même le malheur rend-il plus susceptible de l'éprouver, car l'amertume dont l'âme se nourrit fait l'aliment habituel de ce triste plaisir.

L'espoir sitôt détruit que m'avait inspiré la révolution n'avait point changé la situation de mon âme; toujours mécontente de mon sort, mes chagrins n'étaient adoucis que par la confiance et les bontés de Mme de B. Quelquefois, au milieu de ces conversations politiques dont elle ne pouvait réussir à calmer l'aigreur, elle me regardait tristement; ce regard était un baume pour mon coeur; il semblait me dire: Ourika, vous seule m'entendez!

On commençait à parler de la liberté des nègres: il était impossible que cette question ne me touchât pas vivement; c'était une illusion que j'aimais encore à me faire, qu'ailleurs, du moins, j'avais des semblables: comme ils étaient malheureux, je les croyais bons, et je m'intéressais à leur sort. Hélas! je fus promptement détrompée! Les massacres de Saint-Domingue me causèrent une douleur nouvelle et déchirante: jusqu'ici je m'étais affligée d'appartenir à une race proscrite; maintenant j'avais honte d'appartenir à une race de barbares et d'assassins.

Cependant, la révolution faisait des progrès rapides; on s'effrayait en voyant les hommes les plus violents s'emparer de toutes les places. Bientôt il parut que ces hommes étaient décidés à ne rien respecter: les affreuses journées du 20 juin et du 10 août durent préparer à tout. Ce qui restait de la société de Mme de B. se dispersa à cette époque: les uns fuyaient les persécutions dans les pays étrangers; les autres se cachaient ou se retiraient en province. Mme de B. ne fit ni l'un ni l'autre; elle était fixée chez elle par l'occupation constante de son coeur; elle resta avec un souvenir et près d'un tombeau.

Nous vivions depuis quelques mois dans la solitude, lorsque, à la fin de l'année 1792, parut le décret de confiscation des biens des émigrés. Au milieu de ce désastre général, Mme de B. n'aurait pas compté la perte de sa fortune, si elle n'eût appartenu à ses petits-fils; mais, par des arrangements de famille, elle n'en avait que la jouissance. Elle se décida donc à faire revenir Charles, le plus jeune des deux frères, et à envoyer l'aîné, âgé de près de vingt ans, à l'armée de Condé. Ils étaient alors en Italie, et achevaient ce grand voyage, entrepris, deux ans auparavant, dans des circonstances bien différentes. Charles arriva à Paris au commencement de février 1793; peu de temps après la mort du roi.

Ce grand crime avait causé à Mme de B. la plus violente douleur; elle s'y livrait tout entière, et son âme était assez forte pour proportionner l'horreur du forfait à l'immensité du forfait même. Les grandes douleurs, dans la vieillesse, ont quelque chose de frappant: elles ont pour elles l'autorité de la raison. Mme de B. souffrait avec toute l'énergie de son caractère; sa santé en était altérée, mais je n'imaginais pas qu'on pût essayer de la consoler, ou même de la distraire. Je pleurais, je m'unissais à ses sentiments, j'essayais d'élever mon âme pour la rapprocher de la sienne, pour souffrir du moins autant qu'elle et avec elle.

Je ne pensai presque pas à mes peines, tant que dura la Terreur; j'aurais eu honte de me trouver malheureuse en présence de ces grandes infortunes: d'ailleurs, je ne me sentais plus isolée depuis que tout le monde était malheureux. L'opinion est comme une patrie; c'est un bien dont on jouit ensemble; on est frère pour la soutenir et pour la défendre. Je me disais quelquefois, que moi, pauvre négresse, je tenais pourtant à toutes les âmes élevées, par le besoin de la justice que j'éprouvais en commun avec elles: le jour du triomphe de la vertu et de la vérité serait un jour de triomphe pour moi comme pour elles: mais, hélas! ce jour était bien loin.

Aussitôt que Charles fut arrivé, Mme de B. partit pour la campagne. Tous ses amis étaient cachés ou en fuite; sa société se trouvait presque réduite à un vieil abbé que, depuis dix ans, j'entendais tous les jours se moquer de la religion, et qui à présent s'irritait qu'on eût vendu les biens du clergé parce qu'il y perdait vingt mille livres de rente. Cet abbé vint avec nous à Saint-Germain. Sa société était douce, ou plutôt elle était tranquille: car son calme n'avait rien de doux; il venait de la tournure de son esprit, plutôt que de la paix de son coeur.

Mme de B. avait été toute sa vie dans la position de rendre beaucoup de services: liée avec M. de Choiseul, elle avait pu, pendant ce long ministère, être utile à bien des gens. Deux des hommes les plus influents pendant la Terreur avaient des obligations à Mme de B.; ils s'en souvinrent et se montrèrent reconnaissants. Veillant sans cesse sur elle, ils ne permirent pas qu'elle fût atteinte; ils risquèrent plusieurs fois leurs vies pour dérober la sienne aux fureurs révolutionnaires: car on doit remarquer qu'à cette époque funeste les chefs mêmes des partis les plus violents ne pouvaient faire un peu de bien sans danger: il semblait que, sur cette terre désolée, on ne pût régner que par le mal, tant lui seul donnait et ôtait la puissance. Mme de B. n'alla point en prison; elle fut gardée chez elle, sous prétexte de sa mauvaise santé. Charles, l'abbé et moi, nous restâmes auprès d'elle et nous lui donnions tous nos soins.

Rien ne peut peindre l'état d'anxiété et de terreur des journées que nous passâmes alors, lisant chaque soir, dans les journaux, la condamnation et la mort des amis de Mme de B., et tremblant à tout instant que ses protecteurs n'eussent plus le pouvoir de la garantir du même sort. Nous sûmes qu'en effet elle était au moment de périr, lorsque la mort de Robespierre mit un terme à tant d'horreurs. On respira; les gardes quittèrent la maison de Mme de B., et nous restâmes tous quatre dans la même solitude, comme on se retrouve, j'imagine, après une grande calamité à laquelle on a échappé ensemble. On aurait cru que tous les liens s'étaient resserrés par le malheur: j'avais senti que là, du moins, je n'étais pas étrangère.

Si j'ai connu quelques instants doux dans ma vie, depuis la perte des illusions de mon enfance, c'est l'époque qui suivit ces temps désastreux. Mme de B. possédait au suprême degré ce qui fait le charme de la vie intérieure: indulgente et facile, on pouvait tout dire devant elle; elle savait deviner ce que voulait dire ce qu'on avait dit. Jamais une interprétation sévère ou infidèle ne venait glacer la confiance; les pensées passaient pour ce qu'elles valaient; on n'était responsable de rien. Cette qualité eût fait le bonheur des amis de Mme de B., quand bien même elle n'eût possédé que celle-là. Mais combien d'autres grâces n'avait-elle pas encore! Jamais on ne sentait de vide ni d'ennui dans sa conversation; tout lui servait d'aliment: l'intérêt qu'on prend aux petites choses, qui est de la futilité dans les personnes communes, est la source de mille plaisirs avec une personne distinguée; car c'est le propre des esprits supérieurs de faire quelque chose de rien. L'idée la plus ordinaire devenait féconde si elle passait par la bouche de Mme de B.; son esprit et sa raison savaient la revêtir de mille nouvelles couleurs.

Charles avait des rapports de caractère avec Mme de B., et son esprit aussi ressemblait au sien, c'est-à-dire qu'il était ce que celui de Mme de B. avait dû être, juste, ferme, étendu, mais sans modifications; la jeunesse ne les connaît pas: pour elle, tout est bien, ou, tout est mal, tandis que l'écueil de la vieillesse est souvent de trouver, que rien n'est tout à fait bien, et rien tout à fait mal. Charles avait les deux belles passions de son âge, la justice et la vérité. J'ai dit qu'il haïssait jusqu'à l'ombre de l'affectation; il avait le défaut d'en voir quelquefois où il n'y en avait pas. Habituellement contenu, sa confiance était flatteuse; on voyait qu'il la donnait, qu'elle était le fruit de l'estime, et non le penchant de son caractère: tout ce qu'il accordait avait du prix, car presque rien en lui n'était involontaire, et tout cependant était naturel. Il comptait tellement sur moi, qu'il n'avait pas une pensée qu'il ne me dit aussitôt. Le soir, assis autour d'une table, les conversations étaient infinies: notre vieil abbé y tenait sa place; il s'était fait un enchaînement si complet d'idées fausses, et il les soutenait avec tant de bonne foi, qu'il était une source inépuisable d'amusement pour Mme de B., dont l'esprit juste et lumineux faisaient admirablement ressortir les absurdités du pauvre abbé, qui ne se fâchait jamais; elle jetait tout au travers de son *ordre d'idées* de grands traits de bon sens que nous comparions aux grands coups d'épée de Roland ou de Charlemagne.

Mme de B. aimait à marcher; elle se promenait tous les matins dans la forêt de Saint-Germain, donnant le bras à l'abbé; Charles et moi nous la suivions de loin. C'est alors qu'il me parlait de tout ce qui l'occupait, de ses projets, de ses espérances, de ses idées surtout, sur les choses, sur les hommes, sur les événements. Il ne me cachait rien, et il ne se doutait pas qu'il me confiât quelque chose. Depuis si longtemps il comptait sur moi, que mon amitié était pour lui comme sa vie; il en jouissait sans la sentir; il ne me demandait ni intérêt ni attention; il savait bien qu'en me parlant de lui, il me parlait de moi, et que j'étais plus *lui* que lui-même: charme d'une telle confiance, vous pouvez tout remplacer, remplacer le bonheur même!

Je ne pensais jamais à parler à Charles de ce qui m'avait tant fait souffrir! je l'écoutais, et ces conversations avaient sur moi je ne sais quel effet magique, qui amenait l'oubli de mes peines. S'il m'eût questionnée, il m'en eût fait souvenir; alors je lui aurais tout dit: mais il n'imaginait pas que j'avais aussi un secret. On était accoutumé à me voir souffrante; et Mme de B. faisait tant pour mon bonheur qu'elle devait me croire heureuse. J'aurais dû l'être; je me le disais souvent;

je m'accusais d'ingratitude ou de folie; je ne sais si j'aurais osé avouer jusqu'à quel point ce mal sans remède de ma couleur me rendait malheureuse. Il y a quelque chose d'humiliant à ne pas savoir se soumettre à la nécessité: aussi ces douleurs, quand elles maîtrisent l'âme, ont tous les caractères du désespoir. Ce qui m'intimidait aussi avec Charles, c'est cette tournure un peu sévère de ses idées. Un soir, la conversation s'était établie sur la pitié, et on se demandait si les chagrins inspirent plus d'intérêt par leurs résultats ou par leurs causes. Charles s'était prononcé pour la cause; il pensait donc qu'il fallait que toutes les douleurs fussent raisonnables. Mais qui peut dire ce que c'est que la raison? est-elle la même pour tout le monde? tous les coeurs ont-ils tous les mêmes besoins? et le malheur n'est-il pas la privation des besoins du coeur?

Il était rare cependant que nos conversations du soir me ramenassent ainsi à moi-même; je tâchais d'y penser le moins que je pouvais; j'avais ôté de ma chambre tous les miroirs, je portais toujours des gants; mes vêtements cachaient mon cou et mes bras, et j'avais adopté, pour sortir, un grand chapeau avec un voile, que souvent même je gardais dans la maison. Hélas! je me trompais ainsi moi-même: comme les enfants, je fermais les yeux, et je croyais qu'on ne me voyait pas.

Vers la fin de l'année 1795, la Terreur était finie, et l'on commençait à se retrouver; les débris de la société de Mme de B. se réunirent autour d'elle, et je vis avec peine le cercle de ses amis s'augmenter. Ma position était si fausse dans le monde, que plus la société rentrait dans son ordre naturel, plus je m'en sentais dehors. Toutes les fois que je voyais arriver chez Mme de B. des personnes qui n'y étaient pas encore venues, j'éprouvais un nouveau tourment. L'expression de surprise mêlée de dédain que j'observais sur leur physionomie commençait à me troubler; j'étais sûre d'être bientôt l'objet d'un aparté dans l'embrasure de la fenêtre, ou d'une conversation à voix basse: car il fallait bien se faire expliquer comment une négresse était admise dans la société intime de Mme de B. Je souffrais le martyre pendant ces éclaircissements; j'aurais voulu être transportée dans ma patrie barbare, au milieu des sauvages qui l'habitent, moins à craindre pour moi que cette société cruelle qui me rendait responsable du mal qu'elle seule avait fait. J'étais poursuivie, plusieurs jours de suite, par le souvenir de cette physionomie dédaigneuse; je la voyais en rêve, je la voyais à chaque instant; elle se plaçait devant moi comme ma propre image. Hélas! elle était celle des chimères dont je me laissais obséder! Vous ne m'aviez pas encore appris, ô mon Dieu! à conjurer ces fantômes; je ne savais pas qu'il n'y a de repos qu'en vous.

A présent, c'était dans le coeur de Charles que je cherchais un abri; j'étais fière de son amitié, je l'étais encore plus de ses vertus; je l'admirais comme ce que je connaissais de plus parfait sur la terre. J'avais cru autrefois aimer Charles comme un frère; mais depuis que j'étais toujours souffrante, il me semblait que j'étais vieillie, et que ma tendresse pour lui ressemblait plutôt à celle d'une mère. Une mère, en effet, pouvait seule éprouver ce désir passionné de son bonheur, de ses succès; j'aurais volontiers donné ma vie pour lui épargner un moment de peine. Je voyais bien avant lui l'impression qu'il produisait sur les autres; il était assez heureux pour ne s'en pas soucier: c'est tout simple; il n'avait rien à en redouter, rien ne lui avait donné cette inquiétude habituelle que j'éprouvais sur les pensées des autres; tout était harmonie dans son sort, tout était désaccord dans le mien.

Un matin, un ancien ami de Mme de B. vint chez elle; il était chargé d'une proposition de mariage pour Charles: Melle de Thémines était devenue, d'une manière bien cruelle, une riche héritière; elle avait perdu le même jour, sur l'échafaud, sa famille entière; il ne lui restait plus qu'une grande tante, autrefois religieuse, et qui, devenue tutrice de Melle de Thémines, regardait comme un devoir de la marier, et voulait se presser, parce qu'ayant plus de quatre-vingts ans, elle craignait de mourir et de laisser ainsi sa nièce seule et sans appui dans le monde. Melle de Thémines réunissait tous les avantages de la naissance, de la fortune et de l'éducation; elle avait seize ans; elle était belle comme le jour: on ne pouvait hésiter. Mme de B. en parla à Charles, qui d'abord fut un peu effrayé de se marier si jeune: bientôt il désira voir Melle de Thémines; l'entrevue eut lieu, et alors il n'hésita plus. Anaïs de Thémines possédait en effet tout ce qui pouvait plaire à Charles: jolie sans s'en douter, et d'une modestie si tranquille qu'on voyait qu'elle ne devait qu'à la nature cette charmante vertu. Mme de Thémines permit à Charles d'aller chez elle, et bientôt il devint passionnément amoureux. Il me racontait les progrès de ces sentiments: j'étais impatiente de voir cette belle Anaïs, destinée à faire le bonheur de Charles. Elle vint enfin à Saint-Germain; Charles lui avait parlé de moi; je n'eus point à supporter d'elle ce coup d'oeil dédaigneux et scrutateur qui me faisait toujours tant de mal: elle avait l'air d'un ange de bonté. Je lui promis qu'elle serait heureuse avec Charles; je la rassurai sur sa jeunesse, je lui dis qu'à vingt et un ans il avait la raison solide d'un âge bien plus avancé. Je répondis à toutes ses questions: elle m'en fit beaucoup, parce qu'elle savait que je connaissais Charles depuis son enfance; et il m'était si doux d'en dire du bien, que je me lassais pas d'en parler.

Les arrangements d'affaires retardèrent de quelques semaines la conclusion du mariage. Charles continuait à aller chez Mme de Thémines, et souvent il restait à Paris deux ou trois jours de suite: ces absences m'affligeaient, et j'étais mécontente de moi-même, en voyant que je préférais mon bonheur à celui de Charles; ce n'est pas ainsi que j'étais accoutumée à aimer. Les jours où il revenait étaient des jours de fête; il me racontait ce qui l'avait occupé; et s'il avait fait quelques progrès dans le coeur d'Anaïs, je m'en réjouissais avec lui. Un jour pourtant il me parla de la manière dont il voulait vivre avec elle: Je veux obtenir toute sa confiance, me dit-il, et lui donner toute la mienne; je ne lui cacherai rien, elle saura toutes mes pensées, elle connaîtra tous les mouvements secrets de mon coeur; je veux qu'il y ait entre elle et moi une confiance comme la nôtre, Ourika. Comme la nôtre! Ce mot me fit mal; il me rappela que Charles ne savait pas le seul secret de ma vie, et il m'ôta le désir de le lui confier. Peu à peu les absences de Charles devinrent plus longues; il n'était presque plus à Saint-Germain que des instants; il venait à cheval pour mettre moins de temps en chemin, il retournait l'après-dînée à Paris; de sorte que tous les soirs se passaient sans lui. Mme de B. plaisantait souvent de ces longues absences; j'aurais bien voulu faire comme elle!

Un jour, nous nous promenions dans la forêt. Charles avait été absent presque toute la semaine: je l'aperçus tout à coup à l'extrémité de l'allée où nous marchions; il venait à cheval, et très vite. Quand il fut près de l'endroit où nous étions, il sauta à terre et se mit à se promener avec nous: après quelques minutes de conversation générale, il resta en arrière avec moi, et nous recommençâmes à causer comme autrefois; j'en fis la remarque. Comme autrefois! s'écria-t-il; ah! quelle différence! avais-je donc quelque chose à dire dans cetemps-là? Il me semble que je n'ai commencé à vivre que depuis deux mois. Ourika, je ne vous dirai jamais ce que j'éprouve pour elle! Quelquefois je crois sentir que mon âme tout entière va passer dans la sienne. Quand elle me regarde, je ne respire plus; quand elle rougit, je voudrais me prosterner à ses pieds pour l'adorer. Quand je pense que je vais être le protecteur de cet ange, qu'elle me confie sa vie, sa destinée; ah! que je suis glorieux de la mienne! Que je la rendrai heureuse! Je serai pour elle le père, la mère, qu'elle a perdus: mais je serai aussi son mari, son amant! Elle me donnera son premier amour; tout son coeur s'épanchera dans le mien; nous vivrons de la même vie, et je ne veux pas que, dans le cours de nos longues années, elle puisse dire qu'elle ait passé une heure sans être heureuse. Quelles délices, Ourika, de penser qu'elle sera la mère de mes enfants, qu'ils puiseront la vie dans le sein d'Anaïs! Ah! ils seront doux et beaux comme elle! Qu'ai-je fait, ô Dieu! pour mériter tant de bonheur!

Hélas! j'adressais en ce moment au ciel une question toute contraire! Depuis quelques instants, j'écoutais ces paroles passionnées avec un sentiment indéfinissable. Grand Dieu! vous êtes témoin que j'étais heureuse du bonheur de Charles: mais pourquoi avez-vous donné la vie à la pauvre Ourika? pourquoi n'est-elle pas morte sur ce bâtiment négrier d'où elle fut arrachée, ou sur le sein de sa mère? Un peu de sable d'Afrique eût recouvert son corps, et ce fardeau eût été bien léger! Qu'importait au monde qu'Ourika vécût? Pourquoi était-elle condamnée à la vie? C'était donc pour vivre seule, toujours seule, jamais aimée! O mon Dieu, ne le permettez pas! Retirez de la terre la pauvre Ourika! Personne n'a besoin d'elle: n'est-elle pas seule dans la vie? Cette affreuse pensée me saisit avec plus de violence qu'elle n'avait encore fait. Je me sentis fléchir, je tombai sur les genoux, mes yeux se fermèrent, et je crus que j'allais mourir.

En achevant ces paroles, l'oppression de la pauvre religieuse parut s'augmenter; sa voix s'altéra, et quelques larmes coulèrent le long de ses joues flétries. Je voulus l'engager à suspendre son récit; elle s'y refusa. Ce n'est rien, me dit-elle; maintenant le chagrin ne dure pas dans mon coeur: la racine en est coupée. Dieu a eu pitié de moi; il m'a retirée lui-même de cet abîme où je n'étais tombée que faute de le connaître et de l'aimer. N'oubliez donc pas que je suis heureuse: mais, hélas! ajouta-t-elle, je ne l'étais point alors.

Jusqu'à l'époque dont je viens de vous parler, j'avais supporté mes peines; elles avaient altéré ma santé, mais j'avais conservé ma raison et une sorte d'empire sur moi-même: mon chagrin, comme le ver qui dévore le fruit, avait commencé par le coeur; je portais dans mon sein le germe de la destruction, lorsque tout était encore plein de vie au dehors de moi. La conversation me plaisait, la discussion m'animait; j'avais même conservé une sorte de gaieté d'esprit; mais j'avais perdu les joies du coeur. Enfin jusqu'à l'époque dont je viens de vous parler, j'étais plus forte que mes peines; je sentais qu'à présent mes peines seraient plus fortes que moi.

Charles me rapporta dans ses bras jusqu'à la maison; là tous les secours me furent donnés, et je repris connaissance. En ouvrant les yeux, je vis Mme de B. à côté de mon lit; Charles me tenait une main; ils m'avaient soignée eux-mêmes, et je vis sur leurs visages un mélange d'anxiété et de douleur qui pénétra jusqu'au fond de mon âme: je sentis la vie revenir en moi; mes pleurs coulèrent. Mme de B. les essuyait doucement; elle ne me disait rien, elle ne me faisait point de questions: Charles m'en accabla. Je ne sais ce que je lui répondis; je donnai pour cause à mon accident le chaud, la longueur de la promenade: il me crut, et l'amertume rentra dans mon âme en voyant qu'il me croyait: mes larmes se séchèrent; je me dis qu'il était donc bien facile de tromper ceux dont l'intérêt était ailleurs; je retirai ma main qu'il tenait encore, et je cherchai à paraître tranquille. Charles partit, comme de coutume, à cinq heures; j'en fus blessée; j'aurais voulu qu'il fût inquiet de moi: je souffrais tant! Il serait parti de même, je l'y aurais forcé; mais je me serais dit qu'il me devait le bonheur de sa soirée, et cette pensée m'eût consolée. Je me gardai bien de montrer à Charles ce mouvement de mon coeur; les sentiments délicats ont une sorte de pudeur; s'ils ne sont devinés, ils sont incomplets: on dirait qu'on ne peut les éprouver qu'à deux.

A peine Charles fut-il parti, que la fièvre me prit avec une grande violence; elle augmenta les deux jours suivants. Mme de B. me soignait avec sa bonté accoutumée; elle était désespérée de mon état, et de l'impossibilité de me faire transporter à Paris, où le mariage de Charles l'obligeait à se rendre le lendemain. Les médecins dirent à Mme de B. qu'ils répondaient de ma vie si elle me laissait à Saint-Germain; elle s'y résolut, et elle calma un moment mon coeur. Mais, après son départ, l'isolement complet, réel, où je me trouvais pour la première fois de ma vie, me jeta dans un profond désespoir. Je voyais se réaliser cette situation que mon imagination s'était peinte tant de fois; je mourais loin de ce que j'aimais, et mes tristes gémissements ne parvenaient pas même à leurs oreilles: hélas! ils eussent troublé leur joie. Je les voyais s'abandonnant à toute l'ivresse du bonheur, loin d'Ourika mourante. Ourika n'avait qu'eux dans la vie; mais eux n'avaient pas besoin d'Ourika: personne n'avait besoin d'elle! Cet affreux sentiment de l'inutilité de l'existence est celui qui déchire le plus profondément le coeur: il me donna un tel dégoût de la vie, que je souhaitai sincèrement mourir de la maladie dont j'étais attaquée. Je ne parlais pas, je ne donnais presque aucun signe de connaissance, et cette seule pensée était bien distincte en moi: *je voudrais mourir.* Dans d'autres moments, j'étais plus agitée; je me rappelais tous les mots de cette dernière conversation que j'avais eue avec Charles dans la forêt; je le voyais nageant dans cette mer de délices qu'il m'avait dépeinte, tandis que je mourais abandonnée, seule dans la mort comme dans la vie. Cette idée me donnait une irritation plus pénible encore que la douleur. Je me créais des chimères pour satisfaire à ce nouveau sentiment; je me représentais Charles arrivant à Saint-Germain; on lui disait: Elle est morte. Eh bien! le croiriez-vous? je jouissais de sa douleur; elle me vengeait; et de quoi? Grand Dieu! de ce qu'il avait été l'ange protecteur de ma vie? Cet affreux sentiment me fit bientôt horreur; j'entrevis que si la douleur n'était pas une faute, s'y livrer comme je le faisais pouvait être criminel. Mes idées prirent alors un autre cours; j'essayai de me vaincre, de trouver en moi-même une force pour combattre les sentiments qui m'agitaient; mais je ne la cherchais point, cette force, où elle était. Je me fis honte de mon ingratitude. Je mourrai, me disais-je, je veux mourir; mais je ne veux pas laisser les passions haineuses approcher de mon coeur. Ourika est un enfant déshérité; mais l'innocence lui reste: je ne la laisserai pas se flétrir en moi par l'ingratitude. Je passerai sur la terre comme une ombre; mais, dans le tombeau, j'aurai la paix. O mon Dieu! ils sont déjà bien heureux: eh bien! donnez-leur encore la part d'Ourika, et laissez-la mourir comme la feuille tombe en automne. N'ai-je donc pas assez souffert?

Je ne sortis de la maladie qui avait mis ma vie en danger que pour tomber dans un état de langueur où le chagrin avait beaucoup de part. Mme de B. s'établit à Saint-Germain après le mariage de Charles; il y venait souvent accompagné d'Anaïs, jamais sans elle. Je souffrais toujours davantage quand ils étaient là. Je ne sais si l'image du bonheur me rendait plus sensible ma propre infortune, ou si la présence de Charles réveillait le souvenir de notre ancienne amitié; je cherchais quelquefois à le retrouver, et je ne le reconnaissais plus. Il me disait pourtant à peu près tout ce qu'il me disait autrefois: mais son amitié présente ressemblait à son amitié passée comme la fleur artificielle ressemble à la fleur véritable: c'est la même chose, hors la vie et le parfum.

Charles attribuait au dépérissement de ma santé le changement de mon caractère; je crois que Mme de B. jugeait mieux le triste état de mon âme, qu'elle devinait mes tourments secrets, et qu'elle en était vivement affligée: mais le temps n'était plus où je consolais les autres; je n'avais plus pitié que de moi-même.

Anaïs devint grosse, et nous retournâmes à Paris: ma tristesse augmentait chaque jour. Ce bonheur intérieur si paisible, ces liens de famille si doux! cet amour dans l'innocence, toujours aussi tendre, aussi passionné, quel spectacle pour une malheureuse destinée à passer sa triste vie dans l'isolement! à mourir sans avoir été aimée, sans avoir connu d'autres liens que ceux de la dépendance et de la pitié! Les jours, les mois se passaient ainsi; je ne prenais part à aucune conversation, j'avais abandonné tous mes talents; si je supportais quelques lectures, c'étaient celles où je croyais retrouver la peinture imparfaite des chagrins qui me dévoraient. Je m'en faisais un nouveau poison, je m'enivrais de mes larmes; et, seule dans ma chambre pendant des heures entières, je m'abandonnais à ma douleur.

La naissance d'un fils mit le comble au bonheur de Charles; il accourut pour me le dire, et dans les transports de sa joie, je reconnus quelques accents de son ancienne confiance. Qu'ils me firent mal! Hélas! c'était la voix de l'ami que je n'avais plus! et tous les souvenirs du passé venaient, à cette voix, déchirer de nouveau ma plaie.

L'enfant de Charles était beau comme Anaïs; le tableau de cette jeune mère avec son fils touchait tout le monde: moi seule, par un sort bizarre, j'étais condamnée à le voir avec amertume; mon coeur dévorait cette image d'un bonheur que je ne devais jamais connaître, et l'envie, comme le vautour, se nourrissait dans mon sein. Qu'avais-je fait à ceux qui crurent me sauver en m'amenant sur cette terre d'exil? Pourquoi ne me laissait-on pas suivre son sort? Eh bien! je serais la négresse esclave de quelque riche colon; brûlée par le soleil, je cultiverais la terre d'un autre: mais j'aurais mon humble cabane pour me retirer le soir; j'aurais un compagnon de ma vie, et des enfants de ma couleur, qui m'appelleraient: Ma mère! Ils appuieraient sans dégoût leur petite bouche sur mon front; ils reposeraient leur tête sur mon cou, et s'endormiraient dans mes bras! Qu'ai-je fait pour être condamnée à n'éprouver jamais les affections pour lesquelles seules mon coeur est créé! O mon Dieu! ôtez-moi de ce monde; je sens que je ne puis plus supporter la vie.

A genoux dans ma chambre, j'adressais au Créateur cette prière impie, quand j'entendis ouvrir ma porte: c'était l'amie de Mme de B., la marquise de . . . , qui était revenue depuis peu d'Angleterre, où elle avait passé plusieurs années. Je la vis avec effroi arriver près de moi; sa vue me rappelait toujours que, la première, elle m'avait révélé mon sort; qu'elle m'avait ouvert cette mine de douleurs où j'avais tant puisé. Depuis qu'elle était à Paris, je ne la voyais qu'avec un sentiment pénible.

Je viens vous voir et causer avec vous, ma chère Ourika, me dit-elle. Vous savez combien je vous aime depuis votre enfance, et je ne puis voir sans une véritable peine la mélancolie dans laquelle vous vous plongez. Est-il possible, avec l'esprit que vous avez, que vous ne sachiez pas tirer un meilleur parti de votre situation? L'esprit, madame, lui répondis-je, ne sert guère qu'à augmenter les maux véritables; il les fait voir sous tant de formes diverses! Mais, reprit-elle, lorsque les maux sont sans remède, n'est-ce pas une folie de refuser de s'y soumettre, et de lutter ainsi contre la nécessité? Car enfin, nous ne sommes pas les plus forts. Cela est vrai, dis-je, mais il me semble que, dans ce cas, la nécessité est un mal de plus. Vous conviendrez pourtant, Ourika, que la raison conseille alors de se résigner et de se distraire.—Oui, madame, mais, pour se distraire, il faut entrevoir ailleurs l'espérance.—Vous pourriez du moins vous faire des goûts et des occupations pour remplir votre temps.—Ah! madame, les goûts qu'on se fait sont un effort, et ne sont pas un plaisir.—Mais, dit-elle encore, vous êtes remplie de talents.—Pour que les talents soient une ressource, madame, lui répondis-je, il faut se proposer un but; mes talents seraient comme la fleur du poète anglais, qui perdait son parfum dans le désert.—Vous oubliez vos amis qui en jouiraient.—Je n'ai point d'amis, madame, j'ai des protecteurs, et cela est bien différent!— Ourika, dit-elle, vous vous rendez bien malheureuse, et bien inutilement.—Tout est inutile dans ma vie, madame, même ma douleur.—Comment pouvez-vous prononcer un mot si amer? Vous, Ourika, qui vous êtes montrée si dévouée lorsque vous restiez seule à Mme de B. pendant la Terreur!—Hélas! madame, je suis comme ces génies malfaisants qui n'ont de pouvoir que dans les temps de calamités, et que le bonheur fait fuir.—Confiez-moi votre secret, ma chère Ourika; ouvrez-moi votre coeur; personne ne prend à vous plus d'intérêt que moi, et peut-être que je vous ferai du bien.—Je n'ai point de secret, madame, lui répondis-je, ma position et ma couleur sont tout mon mal, vous le savez.—Allons donc, reprit-elle, pouvez-vous nier que vous renfermez au fond de votre âme une grande peine? Il ne faut que vous voir un instant pour en être sûr.—Je persistai à lui dire ce que je lui avais déjà dit; elle s'impatienta, éleva la voix; je vis que l'orage allait éclater. Est-ce là votre bonne foi? dit-elle; cette sincérité pour laquelle on vous vante? Ourika, prenez-y garde; la réserve quelquefois conduit à la fausseté. Eh! que pourrais-je vous confier, madame, lui dis-je, à vous surtout qui, depuis si longtemps avez prévu quel serait le malheur de ma situation? A vous, moins qu'à personne, je n'ai rien de nouveau à dire là-dessus.—C'est ce que vous ne me persuaderez jamais, répliqua-t-elle; mais puisque vous me refusez votre confiance, et que vous assurez que vous n'avez point de secret, eh bien! Ourika, je me chargerai de vous apprendre que vous en avez un. Oui, Ourika, tous vos regrets, toutes vos douleurs ne viennent que d'une passion malheureuse, d'une passion insensée; et si vous n'étiez pas folle d'amour pour Charles, vous prendriez fort bien votre parti d'être négresse. Adieu, Ourika, je m'en vais, et, je vous le déclare, avec bien moins d'intérêt pour vous que je n'en avais apporté en venant ici. Elle sortit en achevant ces paroles. Je demeurai anéantie. Que venait-elle de me révéler! Quelle lumière affreuse avait-elle jetée sur l'abîme de mes douleurs! Grand Dieu! c'était comme la lumière qui pénétra une fois au fond des enfers, et qui fit regretter les ténèbres à ses malheureux habitants. Quoi! j'avais une passion criminelle! C'est elle qui, jusqu'ici, dévorait mon coeur! Ce désir de tenir ma place dans la chaîne des êtres, ce besoin des affections de la nature, cette douleur de l'isolement, c'étaient les regrets d'un amour coupable! Et lorsque je croyais envier l'image du bonheur, c'est le bonheur lui-même qui était l'objet de mes voeux impies! Mais qu'ai-je donc fait pour qu'on puisse me croire atteinte de cette passion sans espoir? Est-il donc impossible d'aimer plus que sa vie avec innocence? Cette mère qui se jeta dans la gueule du lion pour sauver son fils, quel sentiment l'animait? L'humanité seule ne produit-elle pas tous les jours des dévouements sublimes? Pourquoi donc ne pourrais-je aimer ainsi Charles, le compagnon de mon enfance, le protecteur de ma jeunesse? . . . Et cependant, je ne sais quelle voix crie, au fond de moi-même, qu'on a raison et que je suis criminelle. Grand Dieu! je vais donc recevoir aussi le remords dans mon coeur désolé! Il faut qu'Ourika connaisse tous les genres d'amertume, qu'elle épuise toutes les douleurs! Quoi! mes larmes désormais seront coupables! il me sera défendu de penser à lui! quoi! je n'oserai plus souffrir!

Ces affreuses pensées me jetèrent dans un accablement qui ressemblait à la mort. La même nuit, la fièvre me prit, et, en moins de trois jours, on désespéra de ma vie: le médecin déclara que, si l'on voulait me faire recevoir mes sacrements, il n'y avait pas un instant à perdre. On envoya chercher mon confesseur; il était mort depuis peu de jours. Alors Mme de B. fit avertir un prêtre de la paroisse; il vint et m'administra l'extrême-onction, car j'étais hors d'état de recevoir le viatique; je n'avais aucune connaissance, et on attendait ma mort à chaque instant. C'est sans doute alors que Dieu eut pitié de moi; il commença par me conserver la vie: contre toute attente, mes forces se soutinrent. Je luttai ainsi environ quinze jours; ensuite la connaissance me revint. Mme de B. ne me quittait pas, et Charles paraissait avoir retrouvé pour moi son ancienne affection. Le prêtre continuait à venir me voir chaque jour, car il voulait profiter du premier moment pour me confesser: je le désirais moi-même; je ne sais quel mouvement me portait vers Dieu, et me donnait le besoin de me jeter dans ses bras et d'y chercher le repos. Le prêtre reçut l'aveu de mes fautes: il ne fut point effrayé de l'état de mon âme; comme un vieux matelot, il connaissait toutes ces tempêtes. Il commença par me rassurer sur cette passion dont j'étais accusée: Votre coeur est pur, me dit-il: c'est à vous seule que vous avez fait du mal; mais vous n'en êtes pas moins coupable. Dieu vous demandera compte de votre propre bonheur qu'il vous avait confié; qu'en avez vous fait? Ce bonheur était entre vos mains, car il réside dans l'accomplissement de nos devoirs; les avez-vous seulement connus! Dieu est le but de l'homme: quel a été le vôtre? Mais ne perdez pas courage; priez Dieu, Ourika: il est là, il vous tend les bras; il n'y a pour lui ni nègres ni blancs: tous les coeurs sont égaux devant ses yeux, et le vôtre mérite de devenir digne de lui. C'est ainsi que cet homme respectable encourageait la pauvre Ourika. Ces paroles simples portaient dans mon âme je ne sais quelle paix que je n'avais jamais connue; je les méditais sans cesse, et, comme d'une mine féconde, j'en tirais toujours quelque nouvelle réflexion. Je vis qu'en effet je n'avais point connu mes devoirs: Dieu en a prescrit aux personnes isolées comme à celles qui tiennent au monde; s'il les a privées des liens du sang, il leur a donné l'humanité tout entière pour famille. La soeur de la charité, me disais-je, n'est point seule dans la vie, quoiqu'elle ait renoncé à tout; elle s'est créé une famille de choix; elle est la mère de tous les orphelins, la fille de tous les pauvres vieillards, la soeur de tous les malheureux. Des hommes du monde n'ont-ils pas souvent cherché un isolement volontaire? Ils voulaient être seuls avec Dieu; ils renonçaient à tous les plaisirs pour adorer, dans la solitude, la source pure de tout bien et de tout bonheur; ils travaillaient, dans le secret de leur pensée, à rendre leur âme digne de se présenter devant le Seigneur. C'est pour vous, ô mon Dieu! qu'il est doux d'embellir ainsi son coeur, de le parer, comme pour un jour de fête, de toutes les vertus qui vous plaisent. Hélas! qu'avais-je fait? Jouet insensé des mouvements involontaires de mon âme, j'avais couru après les jouissances de la vie, et j'en avais négligé le bonheur. Mais il n'est pas encore trop tard; Dieu, en me jetant sur cette terre étrangère, voulut peut-être me prédestiner à lui; il m'arracha à la barbarie, à l'ignorance; par un miracle de sa bonté, il me déroba aux vices de l'esclavage, et me fit connaître sa loi: cette loi me montre tous mes devoirs; elle m'enseigne ma route: je la suivrai, ô mon Dieu! je ne me servirai plus de vos bienfaits pour vous offenser, je ne vous accuserai plus de mes fautes.

Ce nouveau jour sous lequel j'envisageais ma position fit rentrer le calme dans mon coeur. Je m'étonnais de la paix qui succédait à tant d'orages: on avait ouvert une issue à ce torrent qui dévastait ses rivages, et maintenant il portait ses flots apaisés dans une mer tranquille.

Je me décidai à me faire religieuse. J'en parlai à Mme de B.; elle s'en affligea, mais elle me dit: Je vous ai fait tant de mal en voulant vous faire du bien, que je ne me sens pas le droit de m'opposer à votre résolution. Charles fut plus vif dans sa résistance; il me pria, il me conjura de rester; je lui dis: Laissez-moi aller, Charles, dans le seul lieu où il me soit permis de penser sans cesse à vous . . .

Ici, la jeune religieuse finit brusquement son récit. Je continuai à lui donner des soins: malheureusement ils furent inutiles; elle mourut à la fin d'octobre; elle tomba avec les dernières feuilles de l'automne.

Notes

1. The bibliography of works cited that appears in this volume provides an extensive list of representative examples of this activity. Many specific references to theoretical and linguistic works appear in chapter 1 and to historical works in chapter 2. Others are provided in the essays included in this volume.

2. Christopher Miller, *Blank Darkness* (Chicago: University of Chicago Press, 1985), 14–15.

3. David Brion Davis, *The Problem of Slavery in the Age of Revolution 1770–1823* (Ithaca, N.Y.: Cornell University Press, 1975). We also follow Davis in using the terms "abolitionism" and "antislavery" as largely interchangeable, 21–22.

4. Raymond Williams, *Marxism and Literature* (New York: Oxford University Press, 1977), 114.

5. 1783 is the date when Olympe de Gouges claims in the preface to *L'esclavage des noirs* to have written that work. 1823 is the date of the original edition of Claire de Duras's *Ourika*, although 1824 is typically given as the date of that work's publication: see Lucien Scheler, "Un best-seller sous Louis XVIII: *Ourika* par Mme de Duras," *Bulletin du bibliophile* 1 (1988): 11–28.

6. This definition is based on a number of features highlighted by Terry Eagleton in *Ideology* (London: Verso, 1991), 1–10.

7. Moira Ferguson, *Subject to Others: British Women Writers and Colonial Slavery, 1670–1834* (New York: Routledge, 1992).

8. Ferguson identifies a number of texts written by English women writers before *Oroonoko* in *Subject to Others*, 15–26.

9. Harriet Beecher Stowe, *La case de l'oncle Tom*, trans. Louise Belloc (Paris: Charpentier, 1853), vi. In this instance and elsewhere, the authors of this volume have themselves provided the translations of all literary and critical passages unless otherwise indicated.

10. In reproducing the original texts and elsewhere in this volume, certain archaic linguistic patterns have been modified to facilitate the task of modern readers. In French, for example, archaic spellings with -oi (françoise, connoître, écrivoit, etc.) have been changed to the modern spelling with -ai, and noun and adjective endings in -ans or -ens (savans, parens) have been changed to modern endings in -ants or -ents. In both English and French, other changes bear on the archaic formation of the letter S

and the use of apostrophes and ampersands. In other cases, when certain archaisms such as the capitalization of nouns have been respected to produce specific effects in translation, the decision to do so is identified and explained.

1. TRANSLATION THEORY AND PRACTICE

1. See Henry Louis Gates, "Introduction: 'Race' and the Difference It Makes," in *"Race," Writing, and Difference* (Chicago: University of Chicago Press, 1986), 1–20 for a discussion of that historical turn.

2. Actually translators and translation critics should agree, once and for all, to discard these words since they represent a notion of language that has been discredited. They could be easily replaced by simply saying "foreign text" and "translated text." These expressions, although simple, have at least the merit of suggesting the movement implied in translation without subscribing to the myth of origin and violence implied by the current expression.

3. Here I want to thank my colleague Carol Maier for bringing to my attention the expression of "translated man" which I used as a model for "translated being." Salman Rushdie uses it in *Shame:* "I, too, am a translated man. I have been *borne across.*" Salman Rushdie, *Shame* (New York: Vintage International, 1983), 24.

4. Tejaswini Niranjana, *Siting Translation. History, Post-structuralism and the Colonial Context* (Berkeley: University of California Press, 1992), 49.

5. André Lefevere defines refraction as the "process of rewriting a text with a view to influencing the way the reader reads" and shows that it is an inescapable process. Although his definition may seem too narrow in that it implies that refraction is deliberate, in fact his further discussion makes clear that refraction is for the most part an unconscious process "through which a culture filters potential influences" and "a channel through which the new, both formally and thematically, enters another literature, or is kept out." André Lefevere, "Translations and Other Ways in Which One Literature Refracts Another," *Symposium* 38 (1984): 139–40.

6. Lori Chamberlain, "Gender and the Metaphorics of Translation," *Signs* 13, no. 3 (1988): 454–72.

7. Barbara Godard, "Theorizing Feminist Discourse/Translation," in *Translation, History, and Culture,* ed. Susan Bassnett and André Lefevere (London: Pinter, 1990), 90.

8. Although the metaphorics of gender and translation have been dissected by Lori Chamberlain, practitioners still rely on the same vocabulary of faithfulness and authority. For example Jean Migrenne, the translator of the American feminist poet Marilyn Hacker, used the following description in a public forum, which Anna Livia gives in her review: "Translation is penetration, he said: when he translated Hacker's work he felt as though he were forcing her to expose herself to him, driving his wedge into her work, the poems themselves a child they had made together." Anna Livia, "Lost in Translation," *The Women's Review of Books* 9 (March 1992): 15–16. The kinds of metaphors used by the translator make clear that this "Jean" is a "John" and that his gender identification expresses an opposite attitude to the one I suggest when I wish to retain the metaphor of "reproduction."

9. In his introduction to *Rethinking Translation* (New York: Routledge, 1992), Lawrence Venuti describes the poor status of translation in this country and the relative lack of works that are actually translated into English. He points out especially translation's lack of recognition by the academic world although it is largely dependent on translation for its own work. Venuti rightly sees that it is not only an increased number of translations into American-English that will change the situation, but the attitude of

translators themselves, or at least of translation critics, that needs to change. They need to relinquish casual remarks about translation and turn to rigorous analysis of the work of translation itself. Similarly, the work of reviewing translations needs to be done by professionals who can appraise what a given translator has attempted to do rather than rely on a critical vocabulary composed of one word judgments, like "fluent," "elegant," "rough," or "awkward."

10. See for example Victor Hugo, *Bug Jargal*, in *Oeuvres complètes*, vol. 7 (Paris: Editions Rencontre, 1967), and Prosper Mérimée, *Tamango*, in *Romans et nouvelles*, vol. 1, ed. M. Parturier (Paris: Garnier, 1967), 285–307.

11. Staël uses the adjective Jolof both for the nationality and the language of what is now Senegal, but the current word for one of the native languages of Senegal is Wolof.

12. Gayatri Spivak, "The Politics of Translation" in *Destabilizing Theory*, ed. Michèle Barrett and Anne Phillips (Stanford, Calif.: Stanford University Press, 1992), 186.

13. For an overview of shifts in translation theory in Western Europe, see Susan Bassnett-McGuire, "History of Translation Theory," in *Translation Studies* (London: Methuen, 1980), 39–75.

14. Godard, "Theorizing Feminist Discourse/Translation," 92.

15. Spivak, "The Politics of Translation," 177.

16. Susanne de Lotbinière-Harwood, *Re-belle et infidèle. La traduction comme pratique de réécriture au féminin/The Body Bilingual. Translation as a Rewriting in the Feminine* (Québec: Les Editions du remue-ménage/Women's Press, 1991), 114.

17. See Suzanne Jill Levine, *The Subversive Scribe: Translating Latin American Fiction* (Minneapolis, Minn.: Greywolf Press, 1991).

18. William B. Cohen, *The French Encounter with Africans: White Responses to Blacks, 1530–1880* (Bloomington, Ind.: Indiana University Press, 1980), 132.

19. In *White Over Black*, historian Winthrop D. Jordan gives a summary of the concept of race in scientific terms: "It is now clear that mankind is a single biological species; that races are neither discrete nor stable units but rather that they are plastic, changing, integral parts of a whole which is itself changing. It is clear, furthermore, that races are best studied as products of a process; and, finally, that racial differences involve the relative frequency of genes and characteristics rather than absolute and mutually exclusive distinctions." *White Over Black* (New York: Norton, 1977), 584.

20. Serge Daget, "Les mots esclave, nègre, Noir, et les jugements de valeur sur la traite négrière dans la littérature abolitionniste française de 1770 à 1845," *Revue française d'histoire d'outre-mer* 60 (1973): 511–48.

21. Serge Daget, "Les mots," 524.

22. Ibid., 525.

23. Geneva Smitherman, *Talkin' and Testifyin': The Language of Black America* (Boston: Houghton Mifflin, 1977), 36.

24. Ibid., 40.

25. Smitherman dates the shift from "Negro" to "black" to "the summer of 1966": ibid., 35.

26. See Antonio Gramsci, *Selections from the Prison Notebooks*, ed. and trans. Quentin Hoare, and Geoffrey Nowell Smith (New York: International Publishing, 1971), 12.

27. Although he is not speaking directly about a third world situation, Lawrence Venuti's advocation of what he calls "resistancy," that is a practice which "preserves the linguistic and cultural difference of the foreign text by producing translations which are strange and estranging, which mark the limits of dominant values in the target-language culture and hinder those values from enacting an imperialistic domestication

of a cultural other," implies the same kinds of views as Niranjana. Venuti, *Rethinking Translation*, 13.

28. Interestingly, the West Indies author Patrick Chamoiseau recently made the same point in his novel *Texaco* which recounts a hundred and fifty years of history in Martinique from plantation slavery to modern-day squatters. Patrick Chamoiseau, *Texaco* (Paris: Gallimard, 1992).

29. Jean Bernabé, Patrick Chamoiseau, and Raphaël Confiant, "In Praise of Creoleness," trans. Mohamed B. Taleb Khyar, *Callaloo* 13 (1990): 892.

30. Ibid., 886.

31. For a discussion of the concept of "hybridity," see Homi K. Bhabha, "The Commitment to Theory," *New Formations* 5 (Summer 1988): 5–23.

32. For a very successful and authentic use of code-mixing, see West Indian author Chamoiseau's code-mixing of Creole and French in *Texaco*.

33. For a discussion of examples of withholding translation, see Gayatri Spivak, "Acting Bits/Identity Talk," *Critical Inquiry* 18 (Summer 1992): 770–803.

34. Of course, to say that orality is important in Africa is not to say that it somehow partakes of an African "essence." As Eileen Julien has pointed out, "[t]he dominance of oral language in Africa is obviously a matter of material conditions and not of an 'African nature.'" Including orality, as opposed to privileging writing only, is a way to attend to these specific material conditions. See Eileen Julien, *African Novels and the Question of Orality* (Bloomington, Ind.: Indiana University Press, 1992), 8.

35. Bernabé et al., "In Praise of Creoleness," 895.

36. On the subject of translating into the "other" tongue, Lotbinière-Harwood, a bilingual Québecoise, offers some interesting comments based on her own experience: "Working into a second language, what comes through (stains) from mother tongue colours other tongue." Lotbinière-Harwood, *Re-belle et infidèle*, 150. She views translating from her mother tongue as a "transgression" of accepted translation practices and as being able to work in a "freer" space. She might add that translating into the second language is extremely empowering as one can do what most readers and what the author cannot do.

37. Lotbinière-Harwood, *Re-belle et infidèle*, 126–31.

2. TRANSLATION IN CONTEXT

1. My discussion of the history of translation in France is informed by a number of significant articles on the subject: Stephen Bann, "Théorie et pratique de la traduction au sein du groupe de Coppet," in *Le groupe de Coppet*, ed. Simone Balayé and Jean-Daniel Candaux (Geneva: Slatkine, 1977), 217–33; Jacques G. A. Béreaud, "La traduction en France à l'époque romantique," *Comparative Literature Studies* 8, no. 3 (1971): 224–44; and José Lambert, "La traduction en France à l'époque romantique," *Revue de littérature comparée* 49, no. 3 (1975): 396–412.

2. For a fuller discussion of "les belles infidèles," see Lori Chamberlain, "Gender and the Metaphorics of Translation," *Signs* 13, no. 3 (1988): 455–58.

3. Philip Robinson, "Traduction ou trahison de *Paul et Virginie*? l'exemple de Helen Maria Williams," *Revue d'histoire littéraire de la France* 89, no. 5 (1989): 846, 852–53.

4. Aphra Behn, *Oronoko*, vol. 1, trans. Pierre Antoine de La Place (Amsterdam: Aux dépens de la compagnie, 1745), viii, x.

5. Behn not only adhered to the same concept of translation but used the same sartorial metaphor to express it in "The Essay on Translated Prose" that serves as a

preface to her translation of Fontenelle's *Entretiens sur la pluralité des mondes:* "But as the French do not value a plain suit without a garniture, they are not satisfied with the advantages they have, but confound their own language with needless repetitions and tautologies; and by a certain rhetorical figure, peculiar to themselves, imply twenty lines, to express what an English man would say, with more ease and sense in five; and this is the great misfortune of translating French into English: If one endeavours to make it English Standard, it is no translation. If one follows their flourishes and embroideries, it is worse than French tinsel."

The only reason for which her translation of Fontenelle follows the original quite closely, she claims, is that she possessed neither "health nor leisure" enough to "give you the subject changed, and made my own." Aphra Behn, *Histories, Novels, and Translations* (London: for S. B., 1700), [I] 5–6, [K] 20.

6. Edward D. Seeber, "Oroonoko in France in the XVIIIth Century," *PMLA* 51 (1936): 953–55.

7. Philippe Van Tieghem, *Les influences étrangères sur la littérature française* (Paris: Presses universitaires de France, 1961), 77.

8. Jean-François Saint Lambert, *Ziméo* (1769); Victor Hugo, *Bug-Jargal* (1826); Prosper Mérimée, *Tamango* (1829).

9. Régis Antoine, for example, attributes French literary works about African slaves in the last thirty years of the eighteenth century chiefly to the influence of Saint-Lambert's *Ziméo,* which he singles out as the primary work linking the themes found in Montesquieu to later works about African slaves. He also claims for the character of Ziméo the highly questionable superiority over Oroonoko of being less abstract and more articulate: *Les Ecrivains français et les antilles des premiers pères blancs aux surréalistes noirs* (Paris: Maisonneuve et Larose, 1978), 153.

10. Moira Ferguson, *Subject to Others: British Women Writers and Colonial Slavery, 1670–1834* (London: Routledge, 1992), 27–49.

11. Jürgen von Stackelberg, "Oroonoko et l'abolition de l'esclavage: le rôle du traducteur," *Revue de littérature comparée* 63, no. 2 (1989): 247, 238.

12. William B. Cohen, "Literature and Race: Nineteenth Century French Fiction, Blacks and Africa, 1800–1880," *Race and Class* 16, no. 2 (1974): 181–82.

13. Robinson, "Traduction ou trahison," 844, 851.

14. Léon-François Hoffman, *Le nègre romantique* (Paris: Payot, 1973), 61–62 and Stackelberg, "Oroonoko et l'abolition," 244–45.

15. Aphra Behn, *Oroonoko and Other Prose Narratives* (1696), ed. Montague Summers (New York: Benjamin Blom, 1967), 190; La Place, *Oronoko,* vol. 2:75. Page references to these two editions, indicated as B and LP, appear in the text.

16. Hoffman, *Le nègre romantique,* 62; Laura Brown, "The Romance of Empire: Oroonoko and the Trade in Slaves," in *The New Eighteenth Century: Theory, Politics, English Literature,* ed. Felicity Nussbaum and Laura Brown (London: Methuen, 1987), 61

17. Stackelberg, "Oroonoko et l'abolition," 243, 247–48.

18. Brown, "The Romance of Empire," 48.

19. Ibid., 43, 49–50.

20. Caryl Phillips, *Cambridge* (New York: Alfred A. Knopf, 1991).

21. Stackelberg, "Oroonoko et l'abolition," 247.

22. Brown, "The Romance of Empire," 52, 55.

23. Stackelberg, "Oroonoko et l'abolition," 246.

24. Brown, "The Romance of Empire," 54–55.

25. Ibid., 61.

26. Other important works from this period include *Réflexions sur l'esclavage des*

nègres, which the Marquis de Condorcet published in Switzerland 1781 under the name of Joachim Schwarz, and *L'an 2440,* which Louis-Sébastien Mercier published in England in 1771. I have not found evidence that either work was translated into English.

27. Wylie Sypher, *Guinea's Captive Kings* (New York: Octagon Books, 1969), 99, and Roger Mercier, *L'Afrique noire dans la littérature française* (Dakar: Publication de la section de langues et littératures, 1962), 174.

28. Edward D. Seeber, *Anti-Slavery Opinion in France During the Second Half of the Eighteenth Century* (New York: Greenwood Press, 1969), 161, 197–99.

29. Sypher, *Guinea's Captive Kings,* 99.

30. Seeber, *Anti-Slavery Opinion in France,* 160–61.

31. Olympe de Gouges, *Oeuvres,* introduction by Benoîte Groult (Paris: Mercure de France, 1986), 16, 20. For Toussaint L'Ouverture and dictation see C. L. R. James, *The Black Jacobins* (New York: Vintage Books, 1989), 197–98.

32. Vèvè A. Clark, "Haiti's Tragic Overture: (Mis)Representations of the Haitian Revolution in World Drama (1796–1975)," in *Representing the French Revolution,* ed. James A. W. Heffernan (Hanover, N.H.: University Press of New England, 1992), 237.

33. Clark, "Haiti's Tragic Overture," 241–42.

34. Joan Wallach Scott, "French Feminists and the Rights of 'Man': Olympe de Gouges's Declarations," *History Workshop* 28 (1989): 9.

35. Gouges is among twenty-three individuals whom the translator omits from the list of those identified by Grégoire in his dedication. The name of Claire de Duras's father, Admiral de Kersaint, is also omitted.

36. Léopold Lacour, *Trois femmes de la révolution* (Paris: Plon-Nourrit, 1900), 43, and James, *The Black Jacobins,* 124.

37. Gouges, *Oeuvres,* ed. Groult, 145.

38. Henri Grégoire, *An Enquiry Concerning the Intellectual and Moral Faculties and Literature of Negroes* (1810), trans. D. B. Warden (College Park, Md.: McGrath Publishing, 1967), 145–46. See also Seeber, *Anti-Slavery Opinion in France,* 190.

39. Alfred Berchtold, "Sismondi et le groupe de Coppet face à l'esclavage et au colonialisme," in *Sismondi Européen,* ed. Stellin-Michaud (Geneva: Slatkine, 1973), 173.

40. I am indebted to Simone Balayé for informing me of the existence of Chaumont, whose baptismal certificate lists Juliette Récamier as godmother and Mathieu de Montmorency as godfather, and whose life has apparently remained shrouded in mystery.

41. François-René de Chateaubriand, *Le génie du christianisme* (1802), vol. 2 (Paris: Ernest Flammarion, 1948), 149–50.

42. Seeber, *Anti-Slavery Opinion in France,* 194.

43. Germaine de Staël, "Considérations sur la révolution française," in *Oeuvres Posthumes* (Geneva: Slatkine, 1967), 178.

44. David Turley, *The Culture of English Antislavery, 1780–1860* (London: Routledge, 1991), 49.

45. Grégoire, *Literature of Negroes,* 13–14.

46. Robert Isaac Wilberforce and Samuel Wilberforce, *The Life of William Wilberforce,* vol. 4 (London: John Murray, 1838), 159, 217.

47. Ibid., 213.

48. Robin Furneaux, *William Wilberforce* (London: Hamish Hamilton, 1974), 248–49.

49. David Brion Davis, *The Problem of Slavery in the Age of Revolution 1770–1823* (Ithaca, N.Y.: Cornell University Press, 1975), 52–66.

50. Norman King analyzes Staël's goals in the *Appel* in his response to Berchtold's "Sismondi," 216–17.

51. Davis, *The Problem of Slavery,* 68.

52. Comtesse Jean de Pange, "Madame de Staël et les nègres," *Revue de France* 5 (1934): 434.

53. James, *The Black Jacobins,* 25.

54. Dena Goodman, "Enlightenment Salons: The Convergence of Female and Philosophic Ambitions," *Eighteenth Century Studies* 22, no. 3 (1989): 340–45; Marguerite Glotz and Madeleine Maire, *Salons du XVIIIe Siècle* (Paris: Nouvelles Editions Latines, 1949), 327–29.

55. Turley, *The Culture of English Antislavery,* 2.

56. Berchtold, "Sismondi," 170–72.

57. Hugh Honour, *The Image of the Black in Western Art* IV, vol. 1 (Cambridge, Mass.: Harvard University Press, 1989), 131.

58. Pange, "Mme de Staël et les nègres," 440–41.

59. Berchtold, "Sismondi," 173.

60. Edith Lucas, *La littérature anti-esclavagiste au dix-neuvième siècle* (Paris: Boccard, 1930), 15.

61. These translations appear in volume 17 of her *Oeuvres complètes* published by Treuttel and Würtz in 1821.

62. Simone Balayé, *Madame de Staël: lumières et liberté* (Paris: Klincksieck, 1979), 224–25.

63. Claudine Hermann, "Introduction," in Claire de Duras, *Ourika* (Paris: Editions des Femmes, 1979), 21.

64. G. Pailhès, *La Duchesse de Duras et Chateaubriand* (Paris: Perin, 1910), 389, 405.

65. Servanne Woodward, "Definitions of Humanity for Young Ladies by Mme Le Prince de Beaumont: 'Beauty and the Beast'," *Romance Languages Annual* (Spring 1993).

66. G. Lenôtre, *Paris révolutionnaire, vieilles maisons, vieux papiers* (Paris: Perrin, 1900), 220.

67. Ferguson, *Subject to Others,* 81.

68. M. de Lescure, "Notice," in Claire de Duras, *Ourika* (Paris: Jouaust, 1878), xix.

69. Ferguson, *Subject to Others,* 82.

70. Winthrop D. Jordan, *White over Black* (New York: Norton, 1977), 368, 371, and Davis, *The Problem of Slavery,* 163.

71. Harriet Beecher Stowe, *La case du père Tom,* trans. Emile de La Bédollière (Paris: Gustave Barba, 1853), 1.

72. Helen Papishvily, *All the Happy Endings* (Port Washington, N.Y.: Kennikat Press, 1972), 74.

73. George Sand, "Harriet Beecher Stowe," in *Autour de la table* (Paris: Michel Lévy, Librairie nouvelle, 1876), 320–25.

74. Harriet Beecher Stowe, *La case de l'oncle Tom,* trans. Louise Belloc (Paris: Charpentier, 1853), vi.

75. Elizabeth Ammons, "Heroines in *Uncle Tom's Cabin*," in *Critical Essays on Harriet Beecher Stowe,* ed. Elizabeth Ammons (Boston: G. K. Hall, 1980), 152–65; Jane Tompkins, "Sentimental Power: *Uncle Tom's Cabin* and the Politics of Literary History," *Glyph* 8 (1981): 80–102.

76. For an insightful analysis of the limitations in Stowe's descriptions of slave life, see Angela Davis, *Women, Race and Class* (New York: Random House, 1981), 27–31.

77. Lucas, *La littérature anti-esclavagiste,* 239–42.

78. James Baldwin, *The Price of the Ticket* (New York: St. Martins, 1985), 28.

79. Gustave Flaubert, *Correspondance* (1887–1893), vol. 2 (Paris: Gallimard, 1980), 203–04.

80. Lucas, *La littérature anti-esclavagiste,* 67.

81. Harry Birdoff, *The World's Greatest Hit: Uncle Tom's Cabin* (New York: S. F. Vanni, 1947), 170–72.

82. The editions referred to in the following analysis are: Harriet Beecher Stowe, *Uncle Tom's Cabin* [1852] (New York: New American Library, 1981); *La case de l'oncle Tom*, trans. Louise Belloc (Paris: Charpentier, 1853); and *La case du père Tom*, trans. Emile de La Bédollière (Paris: Gustave Barba, 1853). Page references to these three editions, indicated as S, B, and LB respectively, appear in the text.

83. Lucas, *La littérature anti-esclavagiste*, 75.

84. Birdoff, *The World's Greatest Hit*, 170.

85. Sand, "Harriet Beecher Stowe," 320.

3 . FEMINISM, THEATER, RACE: *L'ESCLAVAGE DES NOIRS*

1. My essay deliberately focuses on Gouges's drama and on her role as a playwright, not on her life. In the last two hundred years, critics have devoted most of their writings on Gouges to the story of her life, but in my opinion, this emphasis on biography has largely contributed to diverting attention from her literary work. Works dealing with her biography are listed in the bibliography.

2. Most literary critics share Rodmell's view that no play produced during the Revolution "can be rated as an incontestably first-rate drama." Graham E. Rodmell, *French Drama of the Revolutionary Years* (New York: Routledge, 1990), 205.

3. Summarizing a common attitude toward French revolutionary theater, Rodmell writes: "The publisher's 'blurb' on the cover of Daniel Hammiche's book *Le Théâtre et la Révolution* accurately defines the impression which is too easily gained by students of French drama: 'The history of the theatre in France seems to drop off to sleep with *Le Mariage de Figaro*, to wake up again with the uproar surrounding *Hernani*. Nothing seems to have happened in between'." Rodmell, *French Drama*, 11.

4. Olympe de Gouges, *Théâtre politique*, ed. Gisela Thiele-Knobloch (Paris: Côté-femmes, 1991), 8. As illustrations of Thiele-Knobloch's assertions, see Marvin Carlson, *The Theatre of the French Revolution* (Ithaca, N.Y.: Cornell University Press, 1966), 55, 89, 148.

5. Thiele-Knobloch in Gouges, *Théâtre politique*, 8.

6. Thiele-Knobloch in Gouges, *Théâtre politique*, 9–10. See also A. Joannides, *La Comédie Française de 1680 à 1900. Dictionnaire général des pièces et des auteurs* (Paris: Plon-Nourrit, 1910).

7. Without completely rejecting Groult's argument, it is important to remember that Gouges's case was far from being exceptional. After all, as Martine Reid reminds us, "dialects, patois, and foreign languages [were] spoken by more than half of the population" (578) at the time of the Revolution. Martine Reid, "Language under Revolutionary Pressure," *A New History of French Literature*, ed. Denis Hollier (Cambridge, Mass.: Harvard University Press, 1989), 572–79.

8. Benoîte Groult writes: "Olympe de Gouges' style has often been called inflated, naive, awkward. Just reading her *Déclaration*, however, we see that sometimes she knew how to combine brilliant formulas and daring thoughts." Olympe de Gouges, *Oeuvres*, ed. Benoîte Groult (Paris: Mercure de France 1986), 41. Thiele-Knobloch comments on this passage: "This also applies to her plays." In Gouges, *Théâtre politique*, 31.

9. Gouges, *Oeuvres*, 20.

10. Augustin-Charles Renouard, *Traité des droits d'auteurs dans la littérature, les sciences et les beaux-arts* (Paris: Renouard, 1838), 315–16.

11. See Rodmell, *French Drama*, 14; Carlson, *The Theatre*, 338.

12. Rodmell, *French Drama*, 8.

13. "[T]he ideological direction of the cultural revolution in theater did not come from the minor stages . . . but from outside the boulevard and even outside the world of theater." Michèle Root-Bernstein, *Boulevard Theater and Revolution in Eighteenth-Century Paris* (Ann Arbor, Mich.: UMI, 1981), 240.

14. Alfred Jepson Bingham, *Marie-Joseph Chénier. Early Political Life and Ideas* (New York: privately printed, 1939), 8.

15. Ibid., 8.

16. Carlson, *The Theatre*, 55.

17. Bingham, *Marie-Joseph Chénier*, 8.

18. Louis Sébastien Mercier, *Du théâtre ou nouvel essai sur l'art dramatique* [1773] (Geneva: Slatkine, 1970), 7.

19. See Claude Manceron in Olivier Blanc, *Olympe de Gouges* (Paris: Syros, 1981), 5.

20. Olympe de Gouges, *L'Esclavage des noirs, ou l'heureux naufrage* (Paris: Duchesnes, 1792), 3.

21. Sarah Maza, "Domestic Melodrama as Political Ideology: The Case of the Comte de Sanois," *The American Historical Review* 94 (December 1989): 1249–64.

22. Codified as a genre by Pixérécourt in the 1790s, melodrama lost much of its overt political content but continued to prosper during the first two decades of the nineteenth century.

23. Mercier, *Du Théâtre*, 261.

24. Joan Wallach Scott, "'A Woman Who Has Only Paradoxes to Offer': Olympe de Gouges Claims Rights for Women," *Rebel Daughters. Women and the French Revolution,* eds. Sara E. Melzer and Leslie Rabine (New York: Oxford University Press, 1992), 104.

25. Ibid., 111.

26. Ibid., 114.

27. "The Trial of a Feminist Revolutionary, Olympe de Gouges," *Women in Revolutionary Paris 1789–1795,* eds. Darline Gay Levy, Harriet Branson Applewhite, and Mary Durham Johnson (Urbana, Ill.: University Press of Illinois, 1979), 257.

28. Simon Schama, *Citizens: a Chronicle of the French Revolution* (New York: Knopf, 1989), 424.

29. Olympe de Gouges, *Les comédiens démasqués, ou Mme de Gouges ruinée par la Comédie française pour se faire jouer* (Paris: Imprimerie de la Comédie-Francaise, 1790), 48.

30. "If negroes are freed, a few will leave [their masters], but in far smaller numbers than the inhabitants of French rural areas have." Olympe de Gouges, "Réflexions sur les hommes nègres," *Oeuvres de Mme de Gouges* 3, (Paris: Cailleau, 1788), 96.

31. "French people, . . . you want neither liberty nor perfect equality." Olympe de Gouges, *Testament politique d'Olympe de Gouges* [S.I. 1793]. (Fonds Rondel. Rf. 18.231. Paris: Bibliothèque de l'Arsenal), 12.

32. William D. Howarth, "The Playwright as Preacher: Didacticism and Melodrama in the French Theater of the Enlightenment," *Forum for Modern Language Studies* 14 (April 1978): 99.

33. On Amis des Noirs, see also Claude Perroud, "La Société française des Amis des Noirs," *La Révolution Française* 69 (1916): 122–47; Valérie Quinney, "Decisions on Slavery, the Slave Trade and Civil rights for Negroes in the Early French Revolution," *The Journal of Negro History* 55 (April 1970): 117–30; Valérie Quinney, "The Problem of Civil Rights for Free Men of Color in the Early French Revolution," *French Historical Studies* 7 (Fall 1972): 544–58; Daniel P. Resnick, "The Société des Amis des Noirs and the Abolition of Slavery," *French Historical Studies* 7 (Fall 1972): 558–69.

34. Welschinger writes: "In 1787, Olympe de Gouges had sent Mirabeau her drama

L'Esclavage des Nègres [*sic*]. Mirabeau answered her on September 12." Henri Welschinger, *Le Théâtre de la révolution* (Paris: Charavay Frères, 1880), 407. Mirabeau's letter is reproduced in Gouges, *Théâtre politique*, 94–95.

35. Resnick, "The Société des Amis des Noirs," 561.

36. Gabriel Debien, *Les colons de Saint-Domingue et la révolution. Essai sur le Club Massiac (Août 1789-Août 1792)* (Paris: Colin, 1953), 111, 119.

37. Resnick, "The Société des Amis des Noirs," 564.

38. Bingham, *Marie-Joseph Chénier*, 13 [my emphasis].

39. Carlson, *The Theatre*, 148.

40. Welschinger, *Le théâtre de la révolution*, 15.

41. For a discussion of *L'esclavage des noirs*'s reception in the press, see Blanc, *Olympe de Gouges*, 73–75.

42. Welschinger, *Le théâtre de la révolution*, 303–4.

43. See Quinney, "Decisions on Slavery," 122.

44. Carlson, *The Theatre*, 88, 154.

45. Debien, "The Société des Amis des Noirs," 128.

46. Carlson, *The Theatre*, 148.

47. " . . . at last, the battle-field is mine, it is a triumph." Gouges, *Les comédiens démasqués*, 45.

48. Blanc writes that "nearly a thousand people" attended the first performance of *L'esclavage*. The source of this figure, however, is not mentioned. Blanc, *Olympe de Gouges*, 73.

49. Gouges, *Les comédiens démasqués*, 45.

50. Welschinger, *Le Théâtre de la révolution*, 297.

51. Gouges, *Les Comédiens démasqués*, 46.

52. See Renouard, *Traité des droits d'auteurs*, 309–13.

53. Quoted in Renouard, *Traité des droits d'auteurs*, 216–17, 220.

54. "My play is now buried under the Comédie's insane rulings, it has become its property." Gouges, *Les comédiens démasqués*, 47.

55. Quoted in Renouard, *Traité des droits d'auteurs*, 311.

56. Gouges, *Les comédiens démasqués*, 46.

57. Debien, *Les colons de Saint-Domingue*, 115.

58. Lucien Leclerc, "La politique et l'influence du Club de l'Hotel Massiac," *Annales historiques de la Révolution française* 14 (1937): 348.

59. Gouges, *Testament Politique*, 11.

4. TRANSLATIONS OF GOUGES

1. My translation of Olympe de Gouges's "Réflexions sur les hommes nègres" is motivated by the desire to expose contemporary readers to the themes and thoughts of an enlightened and observant writer whose reflections are germane to modern society. I attempt to reconstruct the mood and feeling in her piece, rather than to render a literal translation. My aim, then, is to produce a text that affects the reader in the same powerful way that Gouges did in her own time: to incite readers to question current prejudices that stifle human expression, namely to remove biases of race and gender.

In order to modernize Gouges's "Réflexions" and make it more accessible to the late twentieth-century reader, I have substantially modified the syntax with its attendant punctuation, and, to a lesser extent, the lexicon. The following examples should suffice to illustrate my approach. My decision to translate the fairly lengthy, single French sentence, "Revenons à l'effroyable sort des Nègres; quand s'occupera-t-on de le changer, ou du moins de l'adoucir?" with two sentences in English ("Let us go back to the dreadful lot of the Negroes. When will we turn our attention to changing it, or at least to easing it?") strives to emphasize in a separate phrase Gouges's disapprobation of the condition of the blacks. In another instance, however, I have translated the expression "les hommes nègres" with the word "blacks" because I want to point out the optimism in the situation and feel that the term "Negroes," in current parlance, would have too negative a connotation. In general, though, whenever the term "hommes" was used by Gouges in "Réflexions," I translated it either as "people" or "race," which I perceive to be two neutral terms, in order to avoid masculine specific references. In this way, my translation gives voice to Gouges's political struggle for equality among the sexes as well.

Given that my intent as translator was to have a powerful effect upon the reader, I have solved any difficulties in the translation with this in mind. The French expression "un commerce d'hommes" suggests a number of possible solutions in English, "a commerce of men" being one among them. However, I have opted to use the expression "trading people" to shock the reader with the reprehensible situation created by the juxtaposition of two perfectly acceptable notions: trade and people. Sometimes, I have omitted words in my translation for purposes of effect and clarity: "Why do blonds not claim superiority over brunettes who bear a resemblance to Mulattos?" By eliminating the adjective "fade" ("Blonde fade"), I rid the color system that was in place of affective qualifiers and present difference as an objectively observable, rather than a subjectively experienced, phenomenon. Sometimes, I have added words to Gouges's piece for today's reader who would not necessarily understand the theatrical or political context of her day. Gouges's talent for championing human rights needs to be read against her struggle to persist as a dramatist: "This weak sketch would require a poignant group of scenes for it to serve posterity. Painters ambitious enough to paint the tableau would be considered Fathers of the wisest and most worthwhile Humanity, and I am convinced that they would favor the subject of this small Play over its dramatic expression."

2. My decision to respect Gouges's use of capitalization in the Preface and throughout the play should be seen as a decision to respect the author's originality: Gouges's capitalization of substantives has no apparent system inasmuch as the same nouns are not always capitalized, the word "Slave" being a prime example. Furthermore, rendering the inconsistencies in Gouges's use of capitalization points out the unstable practice of punctuation in eighteenth-century English, and adds to the general recreation of that ethos in my translation.

3. An obvious inadvertancy as the character is called Coraline throughout the entire play.

4. Bayard, Pierre du Terrail, Chevalier de (c. 1473–1524), "le Chevalier sans peur et sans reproche," a famous captain known for his brave exploits in the Italian wars.

5. The expression "Jean Lorgne" designates a fool, a simpleton, someone absolutely mindless. This expression can be found in two forms, as one word or two, in Marivaux's Le Télémaque travesti. An allusion in Voltaire's La pucelle d'Orléans also seems to refer to the expression. (I am indebted to Normand Lalonde at the University of Montreal for this information.)

5. ON TRANSLATING OLYMPE DE GOUGES

1. For a discussion of emotional persuasion in France in the eighteenth century, see Sarah Maza, "Domestic Melodrama as Political Ideology: The Case of the Comte de Sanois," The American Historical Review 94 (1989): 1256.

2. Ibid., 1252–53.

3. See Erica Harth, *Cartesian Women: Versions and Subversions of Rational Discourse in the Old Regime* (Ithaca, N.Y.: Cornell University Press, 1992), 214.

4. Maza, "Domestic Melodrama," 1261.

5. For a discussion of the emergence of a concept of "public opinion" that increasingly served as a surrogate for divine-right authority, see Mona Ozouf, "L'Opinion Publique," 419–34 (qtd. in Maza, 1250).

6. Some argue that Gouges's own statements about her lack of culture and literary skill would have been readily dismissed as a mere *"topos* de modestie" in a man, but have been maintained for over two centuries simply because Gouges was a woman. See Gouges, *Théâtre politique*, ed. Gisela Thiele-Knobloch (Paris: Côté-femmes, 1991), 9.

7. For a discussion of *le droit naturel* and Gouges's fight for the rights of women and blacks, see Gouges, *L'esclavage des noirs*, ed. Eléni Varikas (Paris: Côté-Femmes, 1989), 10.

8. There is perhaps another element which can illuminate the ambiguity in Gouges's thoughts on abolitionism. She had a horror of violence, of all violence be it exerted by noblemen, colonists, black insurgents, or revolutionists. Varikas, *L'esclavage des noirs*, 24.

9. Maza, "Domestic melodrama," 1257–58.

10. See Wylie Sypher, *Guinea's Captive Kings* (New York: Octagon Books, 1969), 106. In *L'esclavage des noirs*, in fact, Gouges confuses American Indians and Africans; I have retained these inconsistencies in the translation for reasons of historical interest and accurate representation of Gouges's perceptions regarding people of color.

11. For an enlightening discussion of black semantics see Geneva Smitherman, *Talkin' and Testifyin': The Language of Black America* (Boston: Houghton Mifflin, 1977), 35–43. See also Serge Daget, "Les mots esclave, nègre, Noir, et les jugements de valeur sur la traite négrière dans la littérature abolitionniste française de 1770 à 1845," *Revue française d'histoire d'outre-mer*, 60, no. 221 (1973): "Because *Noir* is neither sullied with prejudices nor already a stereotype, it pleads against alienation and contributes to the foundation of an abolitionist ideology: it thus arises from an innovation" (518).

12. For an intelligent discussion of the use of componential analysis in translation, see Peter Newmark, *A Textbook of Translation* (New York: Prentice Hall, 1988), especially 114–24 (citation in text from 114).

13. See Thomas Holcroft, *A Tale of Mystery* (London: R. Phillips, 1802).

14. One obvious difference between Gouges's and Wollstonecraft's political attitudes can be seen in that "Wollstonecraft makes Marie Antoinette the emblem of what the revolution had to sweep away" (Donald P. Siebert, *Dictionary of Literary Biography* [Detroit: Gale Research, 1991] 104:356); whereas Gouges dedicates *Déclaration des droits de la femme* to the French queen.

15. In the textual introduction to a critical edition of *A Vindication of the Rights of Woman* (Troy, N.Y.: The Whitston Publishing Company, 1982), Ulrich H. Hardt states: "From the authorities [Wollstonecraft] does cite in *Rights of Woman* we must conclude that she was not familiar with the writings of Mary Astell, "Sophia," Olympe de Gouges, or Condorcet, all of whom had fairly recently written about the education of women and women's rights" (7).

16. Siebert, *Dictionary of Literary Biography*, 352.

17. Olympe de Gouges, *The Rights of Woman*, trans. Val Stevenson (London: Pythia Press, 1989).

6. STAËL, TRANSLATION, AND RACE

1. See in particular Simone Balayé, *Corinne* (Paris: Gallimard, 1985) and *Madame de Staël: lumières et liberté* (Paris: Klincksieck, 1979); Madelyn Gutwirth, *Madame de Staël,*

Novelist (Urbana, Ill.: University of Illinois Press, 1978) and "Madame de Staël, Rousseau and the Woman Question," *PMLA* 86 (January 1971): 100–109; Charlotte Hogsett, *The Literary Existence of Germaine de Staël* (Carbondale, Ill.: Southern Illinois University Press, 1987); Avriel Goldberger, ed. and trans., *Corinne* (New Brunswick, N.J.: Rutgers University Press, 1987).

2. Avriel Goldberger, "Germaine De Staël's *Corinne:* Challenges to the Translator in the 1980s," *French Review* 63 (April 1990): 800–809. In this article, Goldberger analyzes previous translations of *Corinne* and describes the strategies she used for her own translation. Although she does not assess Staël's own connection to translation, her own self-consciousness about translating Staël provides useful insights.

3. Pierre Barbéris, "Madame de Staël: du romantisme, de la littérature et de la France nouvelle," *Europe* 693 (1987): 11.

4. For an insightful account of the relations between Germaine Necker and her mother, see Madelyn Gutwirth, *Madame de Staël, Novelist,* chapter 1.

5. For a discussion of *Lettres* in relation to Staël's position as a woman, see Gutwirth's "Madame de Staël, Rousseau and the Woman Question."

6. I am using the term liberal in its nineteenth-century context of one who follows the philosophical and political system based on individual liberties and equality. The liberalism of Staël is opposed to the despotism of Napoleon or the royalist Restoration which followed him.

7. For a description of her efforts to get Pelasge out of jail, see Comtesse Jean de Pange, "Madame de Staël et les nègres," *Revue de France* 5 (Oct. 1934): 425–34.

8. Germaine de Staël, "Mirza," in *Oeuvres complètes* (Geneva: Slatkine, 1967), 72.

9. Henri Coulet, "Révolution et roman selon Madame de Staël," *Revue d'histoire littéraire de France* 87 (1987): 646.

10. Ibid., 65.

11. Barbéris, "Madame de Staël," 15.

12. Ibid., 12.

13. Pierre Macherey, "Un imaginaire cosmopolite: la pensée littéraire de Madame de Staël," in *A quoi pense la littérature* (Paris: Presses Universitaires de France, 1990), 34.

14. For a discussion of this concept, see Pierre Bourdieu, *Distinction. A Social Critique of Taste,* trans. Richard Nice (Cambridge, Mass.: Harvard University Press, 1984).

15. Staël, *Oeuvres complètes,* 1:88.

16. For a discussion of the ways in which translation can enrich a culture, see Albrecht Neubert and Gregory M. Shreve, *Translation as Text* (Kent, Ohio: Kent State University Press, 1992), 3.

17. Coulet, "Révolution," 647.

18. Richard Switzer, "Mme de Staël, Mme de Duras and the Question of Race," *Kentucky Romance Quarterly* 20 (1973): 308.

19. Macherey, *A quoi pense la littérature,* 36.

20. Switzer, "Mme de Staël," 306.

21. Ibid., 304.

22. Jolof refers to an authentic tribe, but it was a "kingdom," of which "Cayor" was a part. Staël has reversed the importance of the two groups.

23. Actually, the Jolofs have no reason not to trade Mirza since the distinction they make is not between friends and enemies, but between kin and non-kin. Since Mirza is an orphan of unclear origin, she may very well be considered non-kin. For a comprehensive study of slavery in Africa, see Patrick Manning, *Slavery and African Life* (London: Cambridge University Press, 1983) and Paul Lovejoy, *Transformations in Slavery* (London: Cambridge University Press, 1990).

24. For a discussion of the notion of "transparency" in translation see chapter 1 of this volume.

25. This is not to say that *Mirza* is completely free of Eurocentrism. After all Mirza gets her "culture" from a French exile, and the workers on Ximeo's plantation are represented as longing for their former games of bows and arrows, a rather patronizing view of what their culture may have entailed. On the other hand, Staël does not represent the topos of "the" African and is careful to distinguish between two West African tribes.

26. Goldberger, "Challenges to the Translator," 808–9.

27. Tejaswini Niranjana, *Siting Translation: History, Post-Structuralism, and the Colonial Context* (Berkeley: University of California Press, 1992), 3.

28. For a discussion of the term "nègre," see chapter 1.

29. For an interesting discussion of the use of the term "nègre" in another context, see James A. Arnold's article on the translation of Aimé Césaire. His discussion shows that a translation may go astray if it does not distance itself from its own ideology. James A. Arnold, "Translating/Editing 'Race' and 'Culture' from Caribbean French," in *Translating Latin America,* ed. William Luis and Julio Rodriguez-Luis (Binghamton, N.Y.: SUNY University Press, 1991), 215–22.

30. Of course, this hope was in complete opposition to the building of the European colonial empire in the sense that what Europe did in the nineteenth century was to attempt to export its values to its colonies and to impose them on other cultures.

7. Translations of Staël

1. Island off the coast of Senegal.

2. Although the term is now perceived to have a negative connotation in general usage, some historians still use it, and Staël herself uses the word "nègre," not the word "noir."

3. The term is used as a synonym for "estate." Plantations run by blacks existed in the American Colonies as well as in Africa.

4. The French text does not use Jolof at all, but the translation does in an effort to restore the voice of the African characters. See chapter 1 for a discussion of this choice.

5. Famous Greek statue representing the ideal of classic male beauty.

6. Part of the Jolof kingdom.

7. That is, against the Napoleonic perversion of the ideals of the French Revolution. (Trans.)

8. Black on White: Translation, Race, Class, and Power

1. Eileen Julien provides an answer to this: "According to Ruth Finnegan and Honorat Aguessy, European awareness of African oral literature began with the publication in 1828 of Le Baron J. F. Roger's retelling of Wolof tales, *Fables sénégalaises recueillies de l'ouolof et imitées en vers français* (Finnegan 27, Aguessy 183)." Quoted in Eileen Julien, *African Novels and the Question of Orality* (Bloomington, Ind.: Indiana University Press, 1992), 11.

9. Duras, Racism, and Class

1. See Claire de Duras, *Olivier,* ed. Denise Virieux (Paris: Corti, 1971), 63.

2. Quoted in G. Pailhès, *La Duchesse de Duras et Chateaubriand* (Paris: Perin, 1910), 266.

3. Quoted in ibid., 364.

4. Letter to Rosalie de Constant, dated January 14, 1824, quoted in ibid., 280.

5. *Eliza Rivers ou la favorite de la nature,* roman de Mme Burnton traduit de l'anglais par Mme S. (i.e., la Comtesse Molé), letter quoted and reference documented in ibid., 280.

6. Letter quoted in Virieux, *Olivier,* 35.

7. Ironically an anonymous *Olivier* was published on January 21, 1826, by the editing house of Urbain Canel. The counterfeit novel's author was in fact the journalist Hyacinthe de Latouche. To make sure that the book be attributed to Duras, and thus benefit from the interest it had created during its reading in her salon, the author of the hoax had it printed on the same paper with the same format as *Ourika.* Duras reacted quickly by publishing a disclaimer in the *Journal des débats* on January 24, and in *Le moniteur universel* on January 25, 1826.

8. I.e., "bouriquet" pronounced almost the same but meaning "ass, donkey." Duras could not escape her authorship and neither could her family.

9. See Roger Mercier, *L'Afrique noire dans la littérature française* (Dakar: Publication de la section de langues et littératures, 1962), 162–65, for a description and an evaluation of his tenure as governor of Senegal.

10. Ibid., 165.

11. Ibid., 513–14.

12. For a summary of the psychological effects of racism, see David O'Connell, "*Ourika:* Black Face, White Mask," *French Review* 47 (1974): 47–56 and Grant Critchfield, *Three Novels of Mme de Duras* (Le Hague: Mouton, 1975), 54–55.

13. Chantal Bertrand-Jennings, "Condition féminine et impuissance sociale: les romans de la Duchesse de Duras," *Romantisme* 18 (1989): 43.

14. For instance, when he describes the religious ceremonies of the king of Podor, "he makes daily about eight to ten ridiculous prayers on a sheepskin." Boufflers, *Correspondance,* 457, quoted in Mercier, *L'Afrique noire,* 165.

15. Joan Scott, "Differences," in *Feminists Theorize the Political,* ed. Judith Butler and Joan C. Scott (New York: Routledge, 1992), 22–40.

11. OURIKA'S THREE VERSIONS: *A COMPARISON*

1. Claire de Duras, *Ourika: A Tale from the French* (Boston: Carter and Hendee, 1829) and *Ourika,* trans. John Fowles (Austin, Tex.: W. T. Taylor Company, 1977). I was not able to obtain the earliest translation, which was published in London in 1824. The original text referred to is the one published by Ladvocat in 1824. I was not able to obtain or consult the 1823 edition referred to earlier.

2. Among the few existing copies of the 1829 translation, I was able to consult the one found at the American Antiquarian Society in Worcester, Massachusetts. Fowles's translation, although recent, was published as a collector's item in a small printing of only 500 copies. Those libraries that hold copies are often unwilling to lend them.

3. Here and elsewhere in this essay, I have underlined the elements for comparison in Duras's 1824 original, in the anonymous 1829 translation, in Fowles's 1977 translation, and in this volume's 1993 translation. These and other passages from the four versions of *Ourika* quoted in this essay are identified within the text according to their date.

Bibliography

Primary Sources

Behn, Aphra. "An Essay on Translated Prose." In *Histories, Novels, and Translations*, vol. 2. London: for S. B., 1700.

———. *Oroonoko and Other Prose Narratives* (1696). Edited by Montague Summers. New York: Benjamin Blom, 1967.

———. *Oronoko*. 2 vols. Translated by Pierre Antoine de La Place. Amsterdam: Aux dépens de la compagnie, 1745.

Chamoiseau, Patrick. *Texaco*. Paris: Gallimard, 1992.

Chateaubriand, François-René de. *Le génie du christianisme* (1802), vol. 2. Paris: Ernest Flammarion, 1948.

Duras, Claire de. *Ourika*. Paris: Ladvocat, 1824.

———. *Ourika: A Tale from the French*. Boston: Carter and Hendee, 1829.

———. *Ourika*. Translated by John Fowles. Austin, Tex.: W. T. Taylor Company, 1977.

Flaubert, Gustave. *Correspondance* (1887–1893), vol. 2. Paris: Gallimard, 1980.

Gouges, Olympe de. (Marie Gouze). *Les comédiens démasqués, ou Mme de Gouges ruinée par la Comédie-Française pour se faire jouer*. Paris: Imprimerie de la Comédie-Française, 1790.

———. *L'esclavage des noirs, ou l'heureux naufrage* (1789). Paris: Duchesne, 1792.

———. *L'esclavage des noirs*. Edited by Eléni Varikas. Paris: Côté-Femmes, 1989.

———. *Oeuvres*. Edited by Benoîte Groult. Paris: Mercure de France, 1986.

———. "Réponse au champion américain ou colon très-aisé à connaître." In *Traite des noirs et esclavage*, vol. 4. Paris: Editions d'histoire sociale, 1968.

———. *Réflexions* sur les hommes nègres. In *Oeuvres de Mme de Gouges*, vol. 3. Paris: Cailleau, 1788.

———. *The Rights of Woman*. Translated by Val Stevenson. London: Pythia Press, 1989.

———. *Testament politique d'Olympe de Gouges*. [S.I., 1793]. Fonds Rondel. Rf. 18.231. Paris: Bibliothèque de l'Arsenal.

———. *Théâtre politique*. Edited by Gisela Thiele-Knobloch. Paris: Côté-femmes, 1991.

———. *Zamor et Mirza*. In *Oeuvres de Mme de Gouges*, vol. 3. Paris: Cailleau, 1788.

Grégoire, Abbé Henri-Bernard. *De la littérature des nègres.* Paris: Maradan, 1808.
———. *An Enquiry concerning the Intellectual and Moral Faculties and Literature of Negroes* (1810). Translated by D. B. Warden. College Park, Md: McGrath Publishing Co., 1967.
Holcraft, Thomas. *A Tale of Mystery.* London: R. Phillips, 1802.
Hugo, Victor. *Bug Jargal* (1826). In *Oeuvres complètes,* vol. 7. Paris: Editions Rencontre, 1967.
Mérimée, Prosper. *Tamango* (1829). In *Romans et nouvelles,* vol. 1, edited by M. Parturier, 285–307. Paris: Garnier, 1967.
Phillips, Caryl. *Cambridge.* New York: Alfred A. Knopf, 1991.
Rushdie, Salman. *Shame.* New York: Vintage International, 1983.
Saint-Lambert, Jean-François. *Ziméo* (1769). *Contes de Saint-Lambert,* 41–74. Paris: Librairie des bibliophiles, 1883.
Sand, George. "Harriet Beecher Stowe" (1852). In *Autour de la table,* 319–27. Paris: Michel Lévy, Librairie nouvelle, 1876.
Staël, Germaine de. "Appel aux souverains réunis à Paris pour en obtenir l'abolition de la traite des nègres" (1814). In *Oeuvres complètes,* vol. 2: 292–93. Geneva: Slatkine, 1967.
Staël, Germaine de. "Considérations sur la révolution française" (1818). In *Oeuvres posthumes,* 55–334. Geneva: Slatkine, 1967.
———. *Corinne.* Edited by Simone Balayé. Paris: Gallimard, 1985.
———. *Corinne, or Italy.* Translated by Avriel H. Goldberger. New Brunswick, N.J.: Rutgers University Press, 1987.
———. "De l'esprit des traductions" (1816). In *Oeuvres complètes,* vol. 2: 294–97. Geneva: Slatkine, 1967.
———. "Mirza" (1795). In *Oeuvres complètes,* vol. 1:72–78. Geneva: Slatkine, 1967.
———. "Préface pour la traduction d'un ouvrage de M. Wiberforce sur la traite des nègres" (1814). In *Oeuvres complètes,* vol. 2:290–91. Geneva: Slatkine, 1967.
Stowe, Harriet Beecher. *Uncle Tom's Cabin* (1852). New York: New American Library, 1981.
———. *La case de l'oncle Tom.* Translated by Louise Belloc. Paris: Charpentier, 1853.
———. *La case du père Tom.* Translated by Emile de La Bédollière. Paris: Gustave Barba, 1853.
Wilberforce, Robert Isaac and Samuel Wilberforce. *The Life of William Wilberforce,* vol 4. London: John Murray, 1838.
Wollstonecraft, Mary. *A Vindication of the Rights of Woman,* introduction by Ulrich H. Hardt. Troy, N.Y.: The Whitston Publishing Company, 1982.

Secondary Sources

Ammons, Elizabeth. "Heroines in *Uncle Tom's Cabin.*" In *Critical Essays on Harriet Beecher Stowe,* edited by Elizabeth Ammons, 152–65. Boston: G. K. Hall, 1980.

Antoine, Régis. *Les écrivains français et les antilles des premiers pères blancs aux surréalistes noirs.* Paris: Maisonneuve et Larose, 1978.

Arnold, James A. "Translating/Editing 'Race' and 'Culture' from Caribbean French." In *Translating Latin America,* edited by William Luis and Julio Rodriguez-Luis, 215–22. Binghamton, N.Y.: SUNY University Press, 1991.

Balayé, Simone. *Madame de Staël: lumières et liberté.* Paris: Klincksieck, 1979.

Baldwin, James. *The Price of the Ticket.* New York: St. Martin's, 1985.

Bann, Stephen. "Théorie et pratique de la traduction au sein du groupe de Coppet." In *Le groupe de Coppet,* edited by Simone Balayé and Jean-Daniel Candaux, 217–33. Geneva: Slatkine, 1977.

Barbéris, Pierre. "Madame de Staël: du romantisme, de la littérature et de la France nouvelle." *Europe* 693, no. 94 (1987): 6–22.

Bassnett-McGuire, Susan. "History of Translation Theory." In *Translation Studies,* 39–75. London: Methuen, 1980.

Béreaud, Jacques G. A. "La traduction en France à l'époque romantique." *Comparative Literature Studies* 8, no. 3 (1971): 224–44.

Bernabé, Jean, Patrick Chamoiseau, and Raphaël Confiant. "In Praise of Creoleness." Translated by Mohamed B. Taleb Khyar. *Callaloo* 13 (1990): 886–909.

Berchtold, Alfred. "Sismondi et le groupe de Coppet face à l'esclavage et au colonialisme." In *Sismondi européen,* edited by Stellin-Michaud, 169–221. Geneva: Slatkine, 1973.

Bertrand-Jennings, Chantal. "Condition féminine et impuissance sociale: les romans de la Duchesse de Duras." *Romantisme* 18, no. 63 (1989): 39–50.

Bhabha, Homi K. "The Commitment to Theory." *New Formations* 5 (Summer 1988): 5–23.

Bingham, Alfred Jepson. *Marie-Joseph Chénier. Early Political Life and Ideas.* New York: privately printed, 1939.

Birdoff, Harry. *The World's Greatest Hit: Uncle Tom's Cabin.* New York: S. F. Vanni, 1947.

Blanc, Olivier. *Une femme de libertés, Olympe de Gouges.* Paris: Syros, 1989.

Bourdieu, Pierre. *Distinction. A Social Critique of Taste.* Translated by Richard Nice. Cambridge, Mass.: Harvard University Press, 1984.

Brown, Laura. "The Romance of Empire: *Oroonoko* and the Trade in Slaves." In *The New Eighteenth Century: Theory, Politics, English Literature,* edited by Felicity Nussbaum and Laura Brown, 41–61. London: Methuen, 1987.

Carlson, Marvin. *The Theatre of the French Revolution.* Ithaca, N.Y.: Cornell University Press, 1966.

Chamberlain, Lori. "Gender and the Metaphorics of Translation." *Signs* 13, no. 3 (1988): 454–72.

Clark, Vèvè A. "Haiti's Tragic Overture: (Mis)Representations of the Haitian Revolution in World Drama (1796–1975)." In *Representing the French Revolution,* edited by James A. W. Heffernan, 237–60. Hanover, N.H.: University Press of New England, 1992.

Cohen, William B. *The French Encounter with Africans: White Responses to Blacks, 1530–1880.* Bloomington, Ind.: Indiana University Press, 1980.

————. "Literature and Race: Nineteenth Century French Fiction, Blacks and Africa, 1800–1880." *Race and Class* 16, no. 2 (1974): 181–205.

Coulet, Henri. "Révolution et roman selon Madame de Staël." *Revue d'histoire littéraire de la France* 87, no. 4 (1987): 638–60.

Critchfield, Grant. *Three Novels of Mme de Duras.* The Hague: Mouton, 1975.

Daget, Serge. "Les mots esclave, nègre, Noir, et les jugements de valeur sur la traite négrière dans la littérature abolitionniste française de 1770 à 1845." *Revue française d'histoire d'outre-mer* 60, no. 221 (1973): 511–48.

Davis, Angela. *Women, Race and Class.* New York: Random House, 1981.

Davis, David Brion. *The Problem of Slavery in the Age of Revolution 1770–1823.* Ithaca, N.Y.: Cornell University Press, 1975.

Debien, Gabriel. *Les colons de Saint-Domingue et la révolution. Essai sur le Club Massiac (Août 1789-Août 1792).* Paris: Colin, 1953.

Eagleton, Terry. *Ideology.* London: Verso, 1991.

Ferguson, Moira. *Subject to Others: British Women Writers and Colonial Slavery, 1670–1834.* London: Routledge, 1992.

Furneaux, Robin. *William Wilberforce.* London: Hamish Hamilton, 1974.

Gates, Henry Louis. "Introduction: 'Race' and the Difference It Makes." In *"Race," Writing, and Difference,* 1–20. Chicago: University of Chicago Press, 1986.

Glotz, Marguerite, and Madeleine Maire. *Salons du XVIIIe siècle.* Paris: Nouvelles Editions Latines, 1949.

Godard, Barbara. "Theorizing Feminist Discourse/Translation." In *Translation, History, and Culture,* edited by Susan Bassnett and André Lefevere, 87–96. London: Pinter, 1990.

Goldberger, Avriel. "Germaine De Staël's *Corinne:* Challenges to the Translator in the 1980s." *French Review* 63 (April 1990): 800–809.

Goodman, Dena. "Enlightenment Salons: The Convergence of Female and Philosophic Ambitions." *Eighteenth Century Studies* 22, no. 3 (1989): 329–50.

Gramsci, Antonio. *Selections from the Prison Notebooks.* Edited and translated by Quentin Hoare and Geoffrey Nowell Smith. New York: International Publishing, 1971.

Gutwirth, Madelyn. *Madame de Staël, Novelist.* (Urbana, Ill.: University of Illinois Press, 1978.

————. "Madame de Staël, Rousseau and the Woman Question." *PMLA* 86 (1971): 100–109.

Harth, Erica. *Cartesian Women: Versions and Subversions of Rational Discourse in the Old Regime.* Ithaca, N.Y.: Cornell University Press, 1992.

Hermann, Claudine. "Introduction." In Claire de Duras, *Ourika.* Paris: Editions des Femmes, 1979.

Hoffmann, Léon-François. *Le nègre romantique.* Paris: Payot, 1973.

Hogsett, Charlotte. *The Literary Existence of Germaine de Staël.* Carbondale, Ill.: Southern Illinois University Press, 1987.

Honour, Hugh. *The Image of the Black in Western Art,* IV. 2 vols. Cambridge, Mass.: Harvard University Press, 1989.

Howarth, William D. "The Playwright as Preacher: Didactism and Melodrama in the French Theater of the Enlightenment." *Forum for Modern Language Studies* 14 (1978): 97–115.

James, C. L. R. *The Black Jacobins* (1938). New York: Vintage Books, 1989.

Joannides, A. *La Comédie-Française de 1680 à 1900. Dictionnaire général des pièces et des auteurs.* Paris: Plon-Nourrit, 1910.

Jordan, Winthrop D. *White over Black.* New York: Norton, 1977.

Julien, Eileen. *African Novels and the Question of Orality.* Bloomington, Ind.: Indiana University Press, 1992.

Lacour, Léopold. *Trois femmes de la révolution.* Paris: Plon-Nourrit, 1900.

Lambert, José. "La traduction en France à l'époque romantique." *Revue de littérature comparée* 49, no. 3 (1975): 396–412.

Leclerc, Lucien. "La politique et l'influence du Club de l'Hôtel Massiac." *Annales historiques de la révolution française* 14 (1937): 342–63.

Lefevere, André. "Translations and Other Ways in Which One Literature Refracts Another." *Symposium* 38 (1984): 127–42.

Lenôtre, G. *Paris révolutionnaire, vieilles maisons, vieux papiers.* Paris: Perrin, 1900.

Lescure, M. de. "Notice." In Claire de Duras, *Ourika.* Paris: Jouaust, 1878.

Levine, Suzanne Jill, *The Subversive Scribe: Translating Latin American Fiction.* Minneapolis, Minn.: Greywolf Press, 1991.

Levy, Darline Gay, Harriet Branson Applewhite, and Mary Durham Johnson. "The Trial of a Feminist Revolutionary, Olympe de Gouges." In *Women in Revolutionary Paris 1789–1795,* 254–59. Urbana, Ill.: University Press of Illinois, 1979.

Livia, Anna. "Lost in Translation." *The Women's Review of Books* 9 (March 1992): 15–16.

Lotbinière-Harwood, Susanne de. *Re-belle et infidèle. La traduction comme pratique de réécriture au féminin/The Body Bilingual. Translation as a Rewriting in the Feminine.* Québec: Les éditions du remue-ménage/Women's Press, 1991.

Lovejoy, Paul. *Transformations in Slavery.* London: Cambridge University Press, 1990.

Lucas, Edith. *La littérature anti-esclavagiste au dix-neuvième siècle: etude sur Madame Beecher Stowe et son influence en France.* Paris: Boccard, 1930.

Macherey, Pierre. "Un imaginaire cosmopolite: la pensée littéraire de Mme de Staël." In *A quoi pense la littérature,* 17–36. Paris: Presses Universitaires de France, 1990.

Manning, Patrick. *Slavery and African Life.* London: Cambridge University Press, 1983.

Maza, Sarah. "Domestic Melodrama as Political Ideology: The Case of the Comte de Sanois." *The American Historical Review* 94 (1989): 1249–64.

Mercier, Louis Sébastien. *Du théâtre ou nouvel essai* sur l'art dramatique (1773). Geneva: Slatkine, 1970.

Mercier, Roger. *L'Afrique noire dans la littérature française*. Dakar: Publication de la section de langues et littératures, 1962.

Miller, Christopher. *Blank Darkness*. Chicago: University of Chicago Press, 1985.

Neubert, Albrecht, and Gregory M. Shreve. *Translation as Text*. Kent, Ohio: Kent State University Press, 1992.

Newmark, Peter. *A Textbook of Translation*. New York: Prentice-Hall, 1988.

Niranjana, Tejaswini. *Siting Translation: History, Post-Structuralism, and the Colonial Context*. Berkeley, Calif.: University of California Press, 1992.

O'Connell, David. "*Ourika*: Black Face, White Mask." *French Review* 47, no. 6 (1974): 47–56.

Papishvily, Helen. *All the Happy Endings* (1956). Port Washington, N.Y.: Kennikat Press, 1972.

Pailhès, G. *La Duchesse de Duras et Chateaubriand*. Paris: Perin, 1910.

Pange, Comtesse Jean de. "Madame de Staël et les nègres." *Revue de France* 5 (1934): 425–43.

Perroud, Claude. "La société française des Amis des Noirs." *La Révolution Française* 69 (1916): 122–47.

Quinney, Valerie. "Decisions on Slavery, the Slave Trade and Civil rights for Negroes in the Early French Revolution." *The Journal of Negro History* 55 (1970): 117–30.

———. "The Problem of Civil Rights for Free Men of Color in the Early French Revolution." *French Historical Studies* (1972): 544–58.

Reid, Martine. "Language under Revolutionary Pressure." In *A New History of French Literature*, edited by Denis Hollier, 572–79. Cambridge, Mass.: Harvard University Press, 1989.

Renouard, Augustin-Charles. *Traité des droits d'auteurs dans la littérature, les sciences et les beaux-arts*. Paris: Renouard, 1838.

Resnick, Daniel P. "The Société des Amis des Noirs and the Abolition of Slavery." *French Historical Studies* (1972): 558–69.

Robinson, Philip. "Traduction ou trahison de *Paul et Virginie*? l'exemple de Helen Maria Williams." *Revue d'histoire littéraire de la France* 89 (1989): 843–55.

Rodmell, Graham E. *French Drama of the Revolutionary Years*. New York: Routledge, 1990.

Root-Bernstein, Michèle. *Boulevard Theater and Revolution in Eighteenth-Century Paris*. Ann Arbor, Mich.: UMI, 1981.

Schama, Simon. *Citizens: A Chronicle of the French Revolution*. New York: Knopf, 1989.

Scheler, Lucien. "Un best-seller sous Louis XVIII: *Ourika* par Mme de Duras." *Bulletin du bibliophile* 1 (1988): 11–28.

Scott, Joan C. "Differencès." In *Feminists Theorize the Political*, edited by Judith Butler and Joan C. Scott, 22–40. New York: Routledge, 1992.

Scott, Joan Wallach. "French Feminists and the Rights of 'Man': Olympe de Gouges's Declarations." *History Workshop* 28 (1989): 1–21.

―――. "'A Woman Who Has Only Paradoxes to Offer': Olympe de Gouges Claims Rights for Women." In *Rebel Daughters: Women and the French Revolution,* edited by Sara E. Melzer and Leslie Rabine, 102–20. New York: Oxford University Press, 1992.

Seeber, Edward D. *Anti-Slavery Opinion in France During the Second Half of the Eighteenth Century* (1937). New York: Greenwood Press, 1969.

―――. "*Oroonoko in France in the XVIIIth Century.*" *PMLA* 51 (1936): 953–59.

Siebert, Donald P. *Dictionary of Literary Biography.* Detroit: Gala Research, 1991.

Smitherman, Geneva. *Talkin' and Testifyin': The Language of Black America.* Boston: Houghton Mifflin, 1977.

Spivak, Gayatri Chakravorty. "Acting Bits/Identity Talk." *Critical Inquiry* 18 (Summer 1992): 770–803.

―――. "The Politics of Translation." In *Destabilizing Theory,* edited by Michèle Barrett and Anne Phillips, 177–99. Stanford, Calif.: Stanford University Press, 1992.

Stackelberg, Jürgen von. "*Oroonoko* et l'abolition de l'esclavage: le rôle du traducteur." *Revue de littérature comparée* 63, no. 2 (1989): 237–48.

Switzer, Richard. "Madame De Staël, Madame De Duras and the Question of Race." *Kentucky Romance Quarterly* 20 (1973): 303–16.

Sypher, Wylie. *Guinea's Captive Kings* (1942). New York: Octagon Books, 1969.

Tompkins, Jane. "Sentimental Power: *Uncle Tom's Cabin* and the Politics of Literary History." *Glyph* 8 (1981): 80–102.

Turley, David. *The Culture of English Antislavery, 1780–1860.* London: Routledge, 1991.

Van Tieghem, Philippe. *Les influences étrangères sur la littérature française.* Paris: Presses universitaires de France, 1961.

Virieux, Denise. "Introduction." In Claire de Duras, *Ourika.* Paris: Corti, 1971.

Vignols, Léon. "Les sources du 'Tamango' de Mérimée et la littérature 'négrière' à l'époque romantique." *Mercure de France* 200, no. 708 (1927): 542–47.

Welschinger, Henri. *Le théâtre de la révolution.* Paris: Charavay frères, 1880.

Williams, Raymond. *Marxism and Literature.* New York: Oxford University Press, 1977.

Woodward, Servanne. "Definitions of Humanity for Young Ladies by Mme Le Prince de Beaumont: 'Beauty and the Beast'." *Romance Languages Annual* (Spring 1993).

Index

Translating Slavery

was composed in 10/12 ITC New Baskerville
by Coghill Book Typesetting Co., Inc., of Richmond, Virginia.
It was printed by sheet-fed offset on
60-pound Glatfelter Natural acid-free stock,
notch case bound with 88' binder's boards
covered in Holliston Roxite Linen cloth,
by Thomson-Shore, Inc., of Dexter, Michigan.
It was designed by Diana Gordy,
and published by
THE KENT STATE UNIVERSITY PRESS
KENT, OHIO 44242